Spaceship Earth d
emergent evolutionary p
beings to dominance on

endangered. Modern technoɪogy and advanced weapons have brought this process close to a point of no return. We are destroying the very environment that supports human beings and the other life forms of the Earth, and we are becoming ever-more capable of destroying all life with our futuristic weapons of mass destruction. Chaos, conflict, and destruction run rampant.

We are forced to consider how to govern the Earth. Do we want tiny banking elites of the super-wealthy to govern? Do we wish giant corporations devoted exclusively to private profit for their investors to govern? Do we want some dominant nation-state to conquer all other nations and impose a totalitarian regime? Do we desire a new era of ever-increasing fascism, hate, and fear? Do we wish to continue with the chaos of our present world disorder rushing blindly toward destruction?

This book considers our present planetary crises from the point of view of the highest and most enduring developments of human civilization – the concept of democracy and the theory of nonviolence. It shows that we have the tools and resources available to us to begin the wise and responsible piloting of our Spaceship. It not only explains the theoretical foundations for a prosperous and peaceful world order but shows the practical steps by which this can be achieved. *The triumph of civilization* will mean that we can rapidly move into a decent future for all human beings and the protection of our planetary habitat that sustains all life on Earth.

Previous Books by Glen T. Martin:

- *From Nietzsche to Wittgenstein – The Problem of Truth and Nihilism in the Modern World* (1989)

- *Millennium Dawn – The Philosophy of Planetary Crisis and Human Liberation* (2005)

- *World Revolution Through World Law – Basic Documents of the Emerging Earth Federation* (2005)

- *Ascent to Freedom – Practical and Philosophical Foundations of Democratic World Law* (2008)

- *Emerging World Law – Key Documents and Decisions of the Global Constituent Assemblies and the Provisional World Parliament* (co-edited with Eugenia Almand, 2009).

ii

Triumph of Civilization

Democracy, Nonviolence, and the Piloting of Spaceship Earth

Glen T. Martin

Institute for Economic Democracy Press
IED
Sun City, Arizona; Radford, Virginia
2010

Published by: the Institute for Economic Democracy Press
Sun City, Arizona; Radford, Virginia, USA
888.533.1020 / www.ied.info / ied@ied.info
In Cooperation with the Institute on World Problems
www.worldproblems.net
Triumph of Civilization -Version 1.0

Library of Congress Cataloging-in-Publication Data

Martin, Glen T., 1944-
    Triumph of civilization : democracy, nonviolence, and the piloting of spaceship earth / Glen T. Martin.
        p. cm.
    Includes bibliographical references and index.
    ISBN 978-1-933567-24-2 (pbk. : alk. paper) –
    ISBN 978-1-933567-25-9 (hardback : alk. paper)
    1. Democracy. 2. Nonviolence. 3. World politics--21st century.
    4. Civilization, Modern--21st century. I. Title.

    JC423.M3635 2009
    321.8--dc22
                                            2009033044

Book cover designed by Bill Kovarik.
This book is printed on acid free paper.

This book is dedicated to all those who have discovered their fundamental humanity buried beneath layers of egoistic and cultural illusions. It is for all those who have discovered the spirit of democracy, which is the political and economic expression of that fundamental humanity.

Foreword

The triumph of civilization means that human beings have begun to realize, after a long and painful history, what it takes to live together – how to survive as well as flourish under the civilized rule of law. This dawning is not entirely the same as a rebirth of the human spirit, or, to put it more explicitly, this is not the same as the redemption of the human spirit through the discovery in our lives of grace, love, and direct awareness of a higher unity. In my view, the rebirth of the spirit will not and cannot happen until civilization has first triumphed – we must establish the minimum requirements for decent, sustainable, civilized living on the Earth before we can expect a fuller illumination for the human spirit. Democracy, with all that this entails, signals the triumph of civilization, and this book is primarily about that. The questions of spirituality and spiritual rebirth, although in the background, will largely have to await a future book.

Similarly, the tragic and self-defeating aspects of human existence, also implicit in this volume, will also have to wait for future consideration. I do not believe that these tragic aspects of our existence are insurmountable. But our present crisis requires that we narrow the focus to what can be done now – to the democratic legacy of planetary civilization that is available to us in this time of our most dire need. In this sense, civilization can indeed triumph at the present time. But even at this level, a certain rebirth is required – a transformation from parochialism to planetary consciousness, a new maturity that takes us to a higher level existence – that sees our gigantic suicidal problems as *our* problem: *our common human problem.* Only then will the rule of law in human affairs prevail.

I am indebted to far too many persons to mention here for help, support, and encouragement during the difficult process of writing this book while at the same time teaching full time at Radford University. Father Roy Bourgeois, Ellen Hodgson Brown, Roger Kotila, Richard Perkins, and Elaine F. Webster all kindly read the manuscript and offered me valuable feedback. Bill Kovarik did a wonderful job with the book cover. Cliff Dumais provided some wonderful technical support, and J.W. Smith, as Director of IED Press, was extremely supportive and helpful as usual. I also want to thank my wife, Phyllis Turk, and my daughter, Rebekah Martin Turk, for their unfailing support and patience. Ultimately, responsibility for the book rests with me. But whether my efforts will be in vain lies with its readers. It is you who need to respond to the ideas, facts, arguments, and challenges offered below. This book, its meaning and promise, is most fundamentally in your hands.

Table of Contents

x

Introduction

Civilization does not merely need reforming. Our problems are not local problems or technical matters that can be solved by piecemeal changes. Our problems as human beings are fundamental and go deep. They cannot be solved on the level on which we are currently living. They can only be addressed through growth to a higher level, through rebirth to a new attitude and a new way of being. We human beings must learn to govern our Spaceship Earth very soon or face the terrible and inevitable consequences. The simple act of awakening to a *planetary perspective*, based on honesty, integrity, and realism, will mean the triumph of civilization.

The quest to become civilized, to move from barbarism to a civilized world order, has all along been based on a faith that things can be better, that the highest dreams and ideals of our global historical heritage have not been illusions. We find within ourselves, as well as within history, rebirths, awakenings, illuminations, or moments of transformative growth. We will see in this book that there are many signs that today we are in the midst of a great, planetary awakening, an awakening that struggles with systemic repressive forces working to disintegrate its immense hope.

The success of this awakening to a new planetary maturity will mean the triumph of civilization. It will not mean a utopia that spells the end to human frailty, conflict, and illusion. But it will mean living with a reasonable degree of peace, justice, sustainability, and prosperity for the majority of persons on our planet. Today our planet is without a pilot, careening toward disaster, and *is already a living disaster* for the majority of its citizens and the other creatures with whom we share our planetary home. We can and must place people and institutions at the helm that will construct a decent world order and restore a future for the Earth.

We must not be seduced by the cheap and easy answers such as the reply: "that is human nature: human beings are inevitably greedy and selfish." That we are not inevitably greedy and selfish, nor irrevocably violent and aggressive, has been clearly shown by a century of anthropology. A fundamental feature of human life is that we are in constant change, constant growth, constantly actualizing certain possibilities within us and minimizing others. The capacity to learn and grow characterizes one fundamental aspect of our universal human nature.

This truth is a great source of hope for us. We are not hard-wired into self-destruction as may appear from the many self-destructive behaviors and self-defeating institutions that we see about us in today's world. We are capable of rebirth, both as individuals and as a species. This means growing rapidly to a new level of existence. It means actualization of some of the higher possibilities within us. We are capable of being reborn out of our childhood of parochial and partial self-identifications into the universality of our deeper selves and the unity of human civilization.

Recent anthropology also illuminates the dozens of ways in which we share a universal, genetically inherited human nature composed of innumerable abilities ranging from language, common patterns of cognition, common responses to social life, common reactions to our environment, common facial and bodily responses to situations, etc. (Brown 1991). Similarly, the sciences of linguistics and cognitive science for the past half century have demonstrated the universal features of the human language instinct and the universal patterns of thought and communication that it engenders (Pinker 1994). We share a universal human nature not hard wired into violence or greed but flexibly wired into creativity, growth, self-awareness and the capacity for universal recognition of one another and our common humanity.

Just as individual human beings are physically born with the potential for a rebirth embracing the true development or fulfillment of their deeper selves, so human civilization can be reborn into the fulfillment of its own higher potential. The possibility of this rebirth that can unite and govern our Spaceship Earth is the theme of this book. The book seeks to identify these possibilities – the ones that can save us from our present suicidal behaviors and institutions – and to show the simplest and most economical way into a redeemed future. Everything is ready, the technology, infrastructure, and communications are sufficient. The triumph of civilization is now up to us.

I recognize that the word "civilization" has, in some respects, an unfortunate imperial history as in "the civilizational heirs of the Roman Empire," or "the civilizing project of the Christian West." However, in our contemporary world of globalized communications and globalized cultural awareness, the word can be correctly used to refer to our planetary civilization, its universal science, its emerging planetary culture, and its common heritage of wisdom derived from every great religion and traditional culture. This book attempts to describe what is common to all of us on this planet, which can form the basis for a truly planetary civilization.

The chapters below do not appeal to strange new doctrines or ideologies, although they do recognize that our current world disorder constitutes a dead-end for humanity and for civilization. They take things that we already know something about – our common humanity, democracy, nonviolence, common sense economics, good education, common abilities like language, or common institutions like nation-states – and show our potential for a rebirth that embraces all these facets of our existence. The triumph of civilization involves the actualization of the highest fruits of our common history, summed up in the concepts of "democracy" and "nonviolence" with all that these imply.

These chapters outline the simple steps necessary for a rebirth of civilization beyond the current suicidal problems of our day. These steps are the foundational elements of human civilization that must be actualized if the human project is to triumph in peace, sustainability, and harmony with our precious Earth. Most fundamentally, learning to govern our Earth requires that we embrace for ourselves and our institutions the *holism* discovered by twentieth-century science, a holism at the heart of both democracy and nonviolence.

I am not talking about an inevitable and primarily *linear progress* toward a transformed world order, but rather about our potential to be reborn on a higher level that I call *planetary maturity*. If we are to overcome the suicidal and self-destructive aspects of civilization, from the commodification of all existence to the national security state to the development of ever-more hideous weapons to our pervasive bigotries, ideologies, and idolatries, we will have to begin living as a species on a new, more mature, more holistic level of existence.

The New Holism of Our Time

Holism comprises the most fundamental understanding of our world order emerging from the twentieth-century revolutions in science. This holism can transform our entire way of thinking and living on the Earth. It can become the basis for a new ethics, a new metaphysics, and a new understanding of human social and political life. Yet these new understandings simply represent the fulfillment of civilizational fundamentals – like democracy – that go back to the ancient world. This paradigm shift in human thinking has not yet taken root in our ethical, social, or institutional life. We remain trapped in the older paradigms predicated on fragmentation and division. Our immense suicidal problems of the twenty-first century stem from this fragmentation.

Universally – in quantum theory, cosmology, ecology, systems theory, social science, and psychology – part and whole have come to be understood as inseparable from one another. The very meaning, structure, and function of the parts have become incomprehensible apart from the wholes within wholes (fields within fields) within which the parts are embedded and in terms of which their nature, evolution, and functioning must be understood. Yet our thinking remains mired in divisions, separations, and fragments that appear incommensurable with one another. The result is collective and personal egoism, war, conflict, economic exploitation, destruction of nature, and destruction of one another.

Science has revealed that at every level distinct entities, individuals, are part of an interrelated matrix of continua, fields that relate the individuals to one another in a multiplicity of ways and distinguish them as distinct individuals embedded within the fields.   In other words, individuals are not only contradictory to one another in the sense that '*a*' and '*not a*' appear as logically mutually exclusive. *They are simultaneously complimentary to one another* as instances of a more encompassing set of universals or fields (Harris 2000a; Martin 2008: Ch. 3).

Holism means that we must enlarge our thinking to encompass the manifold of fields within which we are embedded. No longer is '*a*' simply incommensurable with '*not a.*' A clear view of reality requires that I discern the ways in which '*not a*' is complementary to '*a.*' The Other person is inseparable from the very possibility of my existence, since it is the fields within which we are embedded that make possible the existence of the Other *and* my existence. The Other does contradict me in an irreconcilable manner, but becomes complementary to me as another essential part within a more encompassing whole.

The other person, indeed, remains a center of moral freedom that cannot be reduced to any scientific or behavioristic set of compulsions or bio-chemical reactions. The absolute dignity of the Other derives from this fact, as we shall see below. However, other persons and I interpenetrate and overlap in a vast multiplicity of ways that unify us as human beings within our common moral and civilizational project. Today, we have also realized that our common civilization project includes the precious Earth on which we dwell – its beauty, its ecological integrity, its fragile biosphere, and its proper, holistic governance.

In his book *The Systems View of the World: A Holistic Vision for Our Time,* systems theorist Ervin Lazlo calls this structure of our world "holarchy." The holism of individuals flourishing within the fields that sustain and make possible their individual existence is reflected in a hierarchy of wholes within more encompassing wholes within still greater wholes from the sub-atomic level to the level of the cosmos. He writes:

A holarchically (rather than hierarchically) integrated system is not a passive system, committed to the *status quo.* It is a dynamic and adaptive entity, reflecting in its own functioning the patterns of change over all levels of the system.... The holistic vision of nature is one of harmony and dynamic balance. Progress is triggered from below without determination from above, and is thus both definite and open-ended. To be "with it" one must adapt, and that means moving along. There is freedom in choosing one's path of progress, yet this freedom is bounded by the limits of compatibility with the dynamic structure of the whole in which one finds oneself. (1996: 58)

Human beings are integral parts, not only of the holism of the cosmos and the ecosystem of the Earth, but of one human species and planetary society encompassing the Earth. However, in practice, just as we have not yet harmonized our civilization to the delicately balanced biosphere that sustains all life on our planet, so we have not harmonized our social life to the holism of planetary society. We remain trapped in systems of fragmentation that are destroying the biosphere and continue to destroy planetary society through war, patterns of exploitation, linguistic forms of deceit, organized violence, and perpetual conflict.

Fragmented systems and fragmented patterns of thought go hand in hand. The holistic view of the cosmos and human life emerging from twentieth-century science has not yet been assimilated into a paradigm shift of the ways that we think and organize our political, economic, and cultural lives. Laszlo says that holarchically organized systems are influenced from below, not determined from above. However, the influence is *reciprocal* in any truly holistic system, for in a true whole the parts function as integral elements in the functioning and maintenance of the system as a whole. The principle of wholeness structures the relationships among the parts, not diminishing individuality but rather actualizing a genuine individuality in which the complementary functioning of the parts integrates and maintains the integrity of the whole.

When applied to human life and ethics, thinkers who understand the principle of holism advocate *linking our individual lives with all human beings,* since our humanity, our oneness with all other persons, is inseparable from our uniqueness as individuals. Our ability to link our lives in this way means discovering our own fundamental humanity. As we become ever-more fully human, we begin to realize that nothing and no one separates me from the others. Our fragmented sense of self *that defines itself in opposition to what it is not* begins to give way to a deeper sense of self that lives from the universality of its own humanity. The higher potential of our self is progressively actualized. This process of actualization of what is universal within ourselves is affirmed by many leading psychologists and thinkers.

Psychologist Erich Fromm affirms that this "means a constant striving to develop one's powers of life and reason to a point at which a new harmony with the world is attained; it means striving for humility, to see one's identity with all beings, and to give up the illusion of a separate, indestructible ego" (1962: 156). Psychologist Robert J. Lifton writes "One moves toward becoming what the early Karl Marx called a "species-being," a fully human being. Once established, the species identification itself contributes to centering and grounding. In no way eliminated, prior identifications are, rather, brought into new alignment within a more inclusive sense of self" (1993: 231).

Holism ultimately means that I am part of what philosopher Eric Gutkind called "the human continuum," that my individuality is inseparably linked to that continuum and emerges as a unique expression of it. It means discovering a new love for life and the world and the progressive diminishing of fear and hate. My individual life becomes ever-more meaningful and fulfilled to the extent that it contributes to the whole of humanity in creative, nonviolent, and democratic ways. Gutkind declares: "At bottom I *am* the 'other.' The more complete the 'thou' that I utter, the more fully will the 'I' be sounded in me. He who is opened and dedicated to every 'thou' is deathless" (1937: 46).

Similarly, psychologist and spiritual teacher Richard De Martino affirms that "to the degree to which I can rid myself of this filter and can experience my self as the universal man, that is, to the degree to which repressedness diminishes, I am in touch with the deepest sources within myself, and that means with all of humanity" (1960: 127). Spiritual teacher Jiddu Krishnamurti declares that "if you don't know how your own mind works you cannot actually understand what society is, because your mind is part of society; it is society.... Your mind is humanity, and when you perceive this, you will have immense compassion" (1989: 83-86). For such spiritual teachers, careful attention to the workings of our own consciousness and our common human situation inevitably illuminate for me my identity with all humanity.

Mahatma Gandhi was also a holistic thinker who understood that each unique person is an expression of the whole, an expression of "Truth." His fundamental principle of ethics and nonviolence was *satyagraha*, literally "clinging to Truth." If we respect the uniqueness of each, instead of privileging our own differences that set us apart from the others, then the truth of the whole will begin to emerge. Our unity, our mutual participation within larger wholes, will begin to become clear to all concerned. We shall examine below some fundamental links between democracy, nonviolence, and holism.

Just as the process of spiritual awakening actualizes the holistic relationship already deep within, many philosophers see *human reason* as affirming this same universality and identity. Nineteenth-century philosopher John Stuart Mill asserts that our link with other persons is the basis of the universal principles of ethics: "This firm foundation is that of the social feelings of mankind—the desire to be in unity with our fellow creatures, which is already a powerful principle in human nature, and happily one of those which tend to become stronger, even without express inculcation, from the influences of advancing civilization.... Any condition, therefore, which is essential to a state of society becomes more and more an inseparable part of every person's conception of the state of things which he is born into, and which is the destiny of a human being" (1957: 40).

In the Eighteenth Century, Immanuel Kant affirmed that "rational beings all stand under the law that each of them should treat himself and all others, never merely as a means, but always at the same time as an end in himself.... morality consists in the relation of all action to the making of laws whereby alone a kingdom of ends is possible" (1964: 100-101). The kingdom of ends as a command of morality, for Kant, means that each of us adopts moral law for ourselves with a view to a world in which every person treats every other as a unique and infinitely valuable "end in himself," a world under universal moral laws in which everyone treats everyone else with unreserved respect and dignity. Individual moral reasoning inevitably links us with all others. Morality directly connects us with the holism of humanity. Following Kant, G.W.F. Hegel, developed this holism by embodying it concretely within the whole of society, showing the interrelation of part and whole at every level of society.

Out of the dozens of thinkers affirming holism since the twentieth-century, I will cite just two more. Throughout his long lifetime of philosophical output, John Dewey affirmed the inseparability of the individual and the community, ultimately the human community as a whole, as the matrix for freedom and the development of our individual potential. For Dewey, the concept of democracy itself simply "projects to their logical and practical limit forces inherent in human nature" (1963: 497). The democratic ideal is simply a projection of our common human potential beyond, for example, "the secondary and provisional character of national sovereignty" (1993:120). Dewey's life work articulates the holism of humanity and its common ideal of an ever-greater actualization of our potential for free and open association with one another within the matrix of our planetary community.

Similarly, philosopher Errol E. Harris affirms that "in human self-awareness, the *nisus* to the whole has become conscious of itself, so the self, being apprised of its own desires and their aims, strives to organize them, in order to attain coherent wholeness, in which it can find complete self-satisfaction; that is, to make them mutually compatible, so as to remove the frustration inherent in internal conflict. It is this self-realization that determines the ultimate standard of value" (2000b: 251). The universal drive at the heart of the evolutionary process (its *nisus*), Harris states, operates in us (as it does everywhere) to promote wholeness, holism: the removal of internal and external conflict so that the individual person (or group or nation) and the human species can live at peace within a dynamic and diverse yet ordered whole. Its standard is *reason*, a reason discerning the holistic character of the world process and progressively conforming our lives and institutions in harmony with it. However, its dynamic includes an integration and harmonization of the *whole person*: thoughts, emotions, intuitions, customs, habits, and instincts.

Laszlo argues that because human beings are self-aware, goal-oriented creatures, all of our ends or purposes constitute value-oriented activity. Our highest value involves the fulfillment of our potential as individual human beings, to become what we are capable of being, which is not possible without the matrix of society and civilization of which we are inseparable parts. Holistic values, therefore, seek to actualize self-fulfillment within the empowering framework of the larger social wholes that encompass us and make our self-actualization possible. It follows that fragmented economic, political, and cultural institutions defeat or interfere with this process. All the above cited thinkers conclude that we must link our individual lives with universal humanity. Our individuality and our humanity become inseparable.

What kind of institutions would reflect this holism? The most basic answer is familiar yet strange to us: *democracy*, properly understood. That is my purpose in this book: to elucidate the deeper nature of democracy, and the democratic promise, which is also the promise of my own human potential. In the face of the immense terrors of our time, we need to understand the fragmentation of our thought and our outdated institutions. We must act to discover the holism within ourselves and how it might be reflected in holistic, nonviolent, and sustainable institutions. This book attempts to show in detail how planetary democracy embodies that holism. Planetary Democracy is the only way to effectively govern our Spaceship Earth.

The current, horrific global economic crisis is a consequence of fragmentation, of a lack of holism and democracy in our institutions. The patchwork attempts at solutions by the Obama administration and other national actors worldwide will inevitably result in failure. The current disastrous world order of poverty, misery, war, and violence is likewise a consequence of lack of holism and democracy. Our survival on this planet, along with the future of our children and other precious living creatures, depends on our ability to establish holistic institutions and holistic patterns of thought within the very near future.

We shall see that these insights form the foundation for rapidly moving to authentic planetary democracy, beyond the dogma of "sovereign nation-states," independent of the rest of humanity. If we understand the holism affirmed by every twentieth-century science, and we simultaneously understand the fragmentation of our present modes of thinking and our cultural, political and economic institutions, we will comprehend the absolute imperative to establish planetary democracy as efficiently as possible. It is planetary democracy that provides the holistic framework for each human being to realize his or her potential to the maximum extent possible – by guaranteeing equal rights and equal freedom to everyone with a matrix of common social, political, and economic institutions. Planetary democracy embodies the holism that is necessary in three essential ways: for our survival on this planet, for the progress and fulfillment of the historical human project, and for our personal fulfillment as individuals.

In a manner similar to all natural systems, planetary democracy will function as a "holarchy." Local communities interact democratically and economically, addressing local problems and issues within a federated world order. Larger regional social and political units (for, example, cantons of China, pradesh of India, or states within the United States) also function democratically, dealing with regional problems and issues. Nations "holarchically" include these smaller units and are themselves included within the Earth Federation that addresses planetary problems and issues, again through democratic processes: through protection of the rights of individuals and the federated units within the system and through enforceable laws maximizing the equal freedom of each to develop his or her potential within a framework of the common good of the whole of humanity and our planetary ecosystem.

This describes in a very brief way the coming great transformation: the rebirth of human civilization that will either develop rapidly, signaling the happy survival and flourishing of the human historical project, or will happen not at all because the human project will have ended in major planetary disaster or possible extinction of our species. We will see below a number of ways in which democracy has been *misunderstood* as well as a number of ways that it has been *manipulated* to prevent its genuinely holistic potential from emerging. We also will come to understand that violence diminishes in our world to the extent that democracy is realized. We will see that democracy and nonviolence go hand and hand in any effective form of governance. Their actualization on Earth will mean the triumph of human civilization.

Basic Arguments of this Book

There are at least ten fundamental theses that this book defends and develops. I will list them here in the Introduction in the hopes that the reader understands that these ideas are developed, argued for, and elucidated at some length in the following chapters. As with many fundamental notions, I believe they appear more and more self-evident to those who reflect on them at great length and live with them in thought, action, and spiritual reflection over time. They comprise the necessary features for a rebirth of civilization. All ten are not only compatible with our deeper spiritual intuitions. They are also grounded in reason, and eminently defensible by reason.

However, initially they may appear naïve or unrealistic to those unfamiliar with the arguments and reflections that spell out their meaning and implications. That is the risk I am taking in this Introduction – that the reader will bear with me as these basic contentions are developed in the course of this book, and that the reader will take seriously the opportunities for further thought, reflection, and action provided by the citations, references, and quotations that permeate my arguments. I will not elaborate the arguments at this point, since that is the purpose of the book. However, the explicit statement of them may serve as an aid in understanding the discussions and reflections that follow. On any journey, it can be helpful to have a picture of the goal in mind even if this picture pales before the living reality experienced at the end of the quest.

All ten of these theses point to a growing understanding of ourselves and our human situation on the Earth and within the Cosmos. They serve as both conclusions to the arguments that follow and as premises of our coming planetary civilization. They hang together, I believe, and serve as a fundamental articulation of *the coming great transformation to a holistic, sustainable Earth civilization.* We shall see that the imperative for rebirth is emerging, not only from our moral lives, not only from our continuing spiritual development, and not only from developing human rational potential: it is emerging from virtually all the great scientific breakthroughs of the twentieth and twenty-first centuries. We have but to discern reality clearly and resolve to act on what we know to be true in order to unite our Spaceship Earth.

1. *The concept and ideal of democracy includes and indicates the growing recognition of our common humanity with all that this implies.* It reflects, as stated above, the paradigm shift to holism that has been the fundamental discovery of all the twentieth-century sciences. Democracy serves, therefore, as *a moral ideal,* an ideal of human association and our common social life reflecting the reality of this holism. It is clearly

fundamental to the development of decent political and economic systems, as we shall see, but transcends these as *a moral framework and an ideal envisioning a peaceful and just world order.*

2. *The promise of democracy includes the actualization of the potential of our common humanity, as well as that of our individual lives.* This potential of our common humanity continues to develop and emerge out of the historical process, and out of our immense evolutionary journey since the great primal flaring forth of the Cosmos. As thoughtful, concerned human beings, we are called to enhance and encourage this process of development. Today, we are nearing a stage of *planetary maturity* that will transform our relations with ourselves and our world from fragmentation to holism.

3. *The concept and ideal of democracy includes the locus and range of our fundamental moral or ethical values, including the so-called golden rule and fundamental human rights such as the rights to life, liberty, and security of person.* The process of interaction with others under conditions of liberty develops our moral autonomy and 'moral personality' that reflects our essential dignity as human beings. Reflection on democracy, therefore, simultaneously involves reflection on *what it means to be a human being* and the moral implications of reason, freedom, and the human community.

4. *Genuine democracy implies the substantial actualization of a nonviolent, just, and prosperous world order.* Under a democratic constitution and democratic moral relationships, people respect majority rule, they agree to disagree and respect the rights of minorities, and they look for legitimate means by which to accommodate conflicting opinions in the interest of the common good. The only alternative to these nonviolent "rules of procedure" is the rule of the stronger and therefore the use or threat of violence. *The concept and ideal of democracy is therefore intimately linked with the concept and ideal of nonviolence* as this has been articulated in a large and dynamic contemporary literature.

5. *Violence, war, injustice, and involuntary poverty derive from various forms of fragmentation and from plainly invalid assumptions concerning the incommensurability of peoples, nations, races, groups, individuals, etc.* These horrible manifestations of our *immaturity* exist to the extent that we violate the democratic concept and ideal, which represents holism in human civilization.   They derive as well from *fragmented institutions* that defeat the above three principles of majority-rule, respect for the nonviolent opinions and rights of minorities, and efforts to comprehend or accommodate conflicting opinions through dialogue and debate. We will investigate this problem at some length in the chapters that follow.

6. *The development of our rational potential that is fundamental to the development of a democratic planetary civilization coincides with the development of our spiritual potential for love, compassion, kindness, and solidarity.* Twentieth and twenty-first century psychology has demonstrated the immense as yet unrealized spiritual and rational potential within each of us and within the human species. The concept and ideal of democracy symbolizes the actualization of that potential, both in each of us as moral persons and within humanity in general. Spirituality and rationality are complementary aspects of our fundamental humanity, and actualizing genuine democracy will enable significant growth within each of these dimensions.

7. *The three (traditionally accepted) basic elements of democracy – liberty, equality, and community – are integrally related and necessary to one another.* The elucidation of each of these three concepts brings us back to the others and serves to clarify the meaning of the coming great transformation to a holistic Earth Civilization and planetary democracy. Liberty must be fundamental and absolutely essential. However, neither liberty nor democracy can exist without *substantial economic and political equality,* and neither liberty nor equality can exist without the vibrant matrix of a supporting *community.*

8. *The democratic concept and ideal live at the heart of other fundamental human enterprises such as the educational enterprise (Chapter 3) and the economic enterprise (Chapter 7), and the enterprise to convert the world to institutions and attitudes of nonviolence (Chapters 7-10).* Insofar as these enterprises are honest and authentic, they strive for actualization of the democratic ideal. Since democracy necessarily involves a conception of our potential for moral development, and serves as a moral framework for human life, it bears on all human relationships and enterprises, from education to economics to the institutions of war and violence.

9. *Since democracy involves our common humanity, our most fundamental values, and our highest ideals, it can only be effectively and fully realized as planetary democracy.* To understand the above premises clearly and deeply, I hope to show, is simultaneously to understand the necessity of planetary democracy and why it is important to work for the realization of planetary democracy as an integral component of the coming holistic, sustainable Earth civilization.

10. These basic conclusions (developed in the chapters that follow) live in contrast to a world that is seething in violence and immense suffering. *In the pages below, we will see that the concept and ideal of democracy is not naïve or utopian in the slightest but rather serves as a living demand that we take the next fundamental step in human maturity.* Both Albert Einstein and Carl Jung declared rightly that one

cannot solve a problem from the same level within which the problem arises. The seemingly intractable problems of our time cannot be solved in terms of our present assumptions or institutions. We need a rebirth, the ascent to *planetary maturity,* within a very short time – for time is rapidly running out – as a host of thinkers, scientists, and spiritual leaders have begun to declare.

To see clearly the horror of our present world disorder with its relentless currents sweeping us toward planetary disaster is to also recognize what must be done. There are many signs today that human life is in the midst of a vast *paradigm shift* from fragmentation to a *unity in diversity* that protects us all under a universal community while enlivening our genuine diversity. World transformation is a very real possibility of our time. Vast, rapid changes in human consciousness have taken place several times in human history to date. We must continue to cultivate within ourselves reflective thought, conscience, creativity, and spirituality while simultaneously placing our lives in the service of a transformed world order. Governing Spaceship Earth demands nothing less.

That is the message of this book. Its descriptions and analyses of the violence, domination, exploitation, and horror of our world disorder are all in the service of the *praxis of world transformation: our absolute need to unite our Spaceship Earth.* We must understand clearly the deep perversity of our present world system if we are to transform our world into one in "harmony with nature's laws of healthy growth and development." In our day, philosophical reasoning takes on a supreme importance in the light of the threats to human existence that confront us.

Similarly, the following accounts of human spirituality, of the overcoming of relativism and skepticism, of educational *praxis,* of the relation of democracy with socialism, of the philosophy of nonviolence, and of the liberating ideas embedded within the *Earth Constitution* are all positive aspects of this *praxis.* Within the world in which we find ourselves, both authentic philosophy and spirituality are transformative activities. They both militate for the nonviolent transformation of our world disorder and for the institutional recognition of the integrity of the human person within a social and economic system that protects and enlivens that integrity. Everything is ready as we enter the third millennium. Millions around the globe now consider themselves planetary citizens. The dawn of the third millennium will cast its morning light on a rebirth of human civilization – a holistic, planetary civilization.

Our choice today is absolute. We no longer have the luxury of postponement. We can allow ourselves to be swept to disaster within the currents of history premised on nationalism, war, racism, bigotry, exploitation, or technocracy. Or we can foster a new *Renaissance for the*

Earth, giving birth to our deeper human possibilities and premised on liberty, equality, and community for our entire planet. This Renaissance is right around the corner – easily available if we have but the political will to turn the corner *from institutions premised on fragmentation to institutions of a holistic Earth civilization.* We find ourselves at high noon – a time of absolute decision when the shadows of ambiguity have disappeared.

Planetary democracy constitutes our great human hope. From this new level of existence our seemingly intractable problems of war, hatred, fear, poverty, and environmental destruction become eminently solvable. From the level of *planetary maturity* our immense problems are not so much solved but dissolved. The coming generation will wonder at the horrors of the twentieth century (the world wars, the genocides, the weapons of mass destruction, the extremes of wealth and poverty) because they will have surpassed the causes of these horrors by actualizing our higher human potential for genuine democracy: for this will make possible a deep transformation of our lives across the spectrum of our problems.

However, the process of growth and institutional transformation will not happen automatically. We can choose either to do nothing and be swept toward our pending doom, possible extinction, and coming perdition, or we can choose to embrace the fullness of life, a fullness that is simultaneously democratic, rational, and spiritual. We can be swept to perdition as we duck beneath the storm to preserve our private security and selfish personal interests. Or we can embrace integrity of personhood for all human beings and precious natural environment that we share with the Earth's other living creatures. We can and must choose to realize our higher human possibilities and to create a human and planetary renaissance for the twenty-first century.

The time is now and the choice is faced by each of us. Planetary democracy as the embodiment of planetary maturity constitutes our great human hope. The chapters in this book intend to help clarify the issues we face and deepen our understanding of how to facilitate the *Renaissance of the Twenty-first Century,* a renaissance that must necessarily include effective governance for the Earth. They intend to promote a deeper understanding of planetary democracy and human maturity as well as to activate *transformative praxis* – action giving birth to a new world order and to a more mature, fulfilled human life on our beautiful planet Earth.

PART ONE

PLANETARY AWAKENING AND THE IMPERATIVE FOR GENUINE DEMOCRACY

Chapter One
Democracy and Our Higher
Human Potential

The Immense Hope and Promise
of the Past Fifty Years

"All" – when what is meant is all without exception – is the most radical and, perhaps, also the most revolutionary term in the lexicon of political thought. It may have been used in the past, but it was never previously meant to include every individual member of the human race, not just the members of one's own class, or even one's fellow countrymen, but every human being everywhere on Earth. That we are now for the first time in history beginning to mean all without exception when we say "all" is another indication of the newness of the emerging ideal of the best society, the institutions of which will benefit all men everywhere, by providing them with the conditions they need to lead good human lives.

Mortimer J. Adler

For the demand calls for something that does not yet exist but should exist, should come to fulfillment. A being that experiences a demand is no longer simply bound to the origin. Human life involves more than a mere development of what already is. Through the demand, humanity is directed to what ought to be. And what ought to be does not emerge with the unfolding of what is; if it did, it would be something that is, rather than something that ought to be. This means, however, that the demand that confronts humanity is an unconditional demand. The question "Whither?" is not contained within the question "Whence?" It is something unconditionally new that transcends what is new and what is old within the sphere of mere development.... The breaking of the myth of the origin by the unconditional demand is the root of liberal, democratic, and socialist thought in politics.... The demand that separates from the ambiguous origin is the demand of justice.

Paul Tillich

At the dawn of the third millennium, the fate of mankind and the meaning of the human project hang in the balance. Caught in the powerful currents of the immense river of history, we are being swept headlong toward disaster for both our planet and humanity. It appears as though solutions to our immense problems are nowhere to be found. Nowhere do there appear possibilities that might save us from a nightmarish future. For many people, the traditional ideals of every human religion and culture pointing toward a world of peace, freedom, and justice appear to have disappeared from our spiritual and intellectual horizon.

Some thinkers have asked whether we are "unteachable," for we have not even learned the lessons of the first fifty years of the twentieth century, let alone the lessons of the past fifty years (Harris 2005: 1-8). We have not understood the disastrous dead ends of nationalism, nation-state sovereignty, racism, religious bigotry, global corporate capitalism, or the worship of technology. All six of these idolatrous and dehumanizing phenomena have proved absolute disasters. They have turned masses of human beings into indoctrinated, utterly fragmented collectivities, into psychopathic creatures of mass hatred, into bigoted denizens of some idolatrously held absolute truth, into economic cogs enslaved for the wealth of others, or into robotic machines themselves, compulsively jerking to electronic flashes on computer screens or video monitors.

Where, today, do we find a sense of the immense dignity of our humanity that animated the poets, religious prophets, mystics, philosophers, and creative thinkers of every culture and every century? Where do we find a sense of the higher possibilities of our common human project? How is it that the inner human being (the inner life of reflective thought, conscience, self-awareness, and personal integrity) seems to have disappeared from culture, literature, and the public media?

Many of those interested in "spirituality" in our day live apart in ashrams, monasteries, temples, cloisters, mosques, or small religious enclaves. They cling to their awareness of the sacred value of the inner life and its connections with deeper meaning of our cosmos while ignoring – or despairing over – the immense river of history sweeping our entire planet toward implacable disaster. They live apart, free of the nationalism, nation-statism, racism, religious bigotry, capitalism, or worship of technology that corrupt and pollute the higher meaning of our humanity and portend the end of history. Yet they see no public path beyond the end, no way to the future except a blind clinging to the sacred inner life in the face of the immense chaos of the outer world.

1.1 Transformative Forces

Yet it is less than fifty years since the modern *environmental movement* began in the early 1960s as a mass movement with the near simultaneous publication of Rachel Carson's *Silent Spring* and the transmission of the first photos of the Earth from space by the Apollo space mission. Those photos and that movement have spread worldwide signaling the dawning of a planetary and ecological consciousness among human beings. A host of wonderful books and videos have appeared that continue to contribute to this transformation. Hundreds of university courses in ecology and dozens of complete programs in environmental studies have appeared within this half century.

In that same fifty years, *peace studies courses, programs, and institutions* have appeared in universities worldwide along with advanced degrees in conflict resolution or some other aspect of peace studies. Such systematic study of peace issues has never previously happened in human history. The human species is beginning to realize that peace is not simply a pious ideal but an emerging historical necessity for planet Earth. The history and strategies of war have been studied for centuries, but the systematic study of peace has only recently become part of the immense transformation of human consciousness that is taking place in our day.

Along with the study of peace that has emerged in the last half century, there emerged a worldwide movement focused on *nonviolence* as the moral equivalent of war. Thousands of books, articles, and films have appeared, along with leading figures devoted to the theory and practice of nonviolence such as Leo Tolstoy, Mahatma Gandhi, and Martin Luther King, Jr. All over the planet people have begun to reflect on the promise and power of nonviolence to address problems of conflict and injustice. Few literate adults have not heard of *satyagraha, ahimsa,* or *swaraj.* The days are numbered for the insanity of militarism. The theory and practice of nonviolence itself portends a rebirth of civilization.

Another dimension of the global transformation of consciousness taking place during our lifetimes involves *the emergence into human awareness of "global issues,"* sometimes referred to as "global problems," or "global crises." People are beginning to realize that severe, involuntary poverty confronts us as a global problem and a global crisis, that rampant militarism, weapons sales, and perpetual wars constitute an extremely problematic global phenomena, that climate change, planetary environmental pollution, and resource depletion (such as the worldwide shrinking of agricultural lands or fresh water supplies) indicate planetary crises that impact all of us as well as the future of our children. Many academic programs and courses now study these issues, dozens of websites are devoted to discussing or posting the statistics concerning these issues, and the general population of Earth is rapidly becoming cognizant of them.

As with environmental awareness and the awareness indicated by peace studies and the philosophy of nonviolence, the world is witnessing the expanding awareness of global issues. *These issues are, by definition and in fact, beyond the coping capacity of individual nations.* Awareness of them places an additional pressure upon our consciousness to continue its transformation in the direction of planetary consciousness. People are beginning to understand that these global issues (also studied by environmental programs and peace studies programs) are interrelated and interdependent.

The global problem of poverty, for example, cannot be addressed without addressing militarism, environmental degradation, climate change, or resource depletion. Peace studies can be approached from the point of view of environmental problems. Global issues, the need for peace, and environmental problems become clearly interrelated. Many people are beginning to draw the connection between the economic and political systems within which we operate and these mounting global crises. A transformative, planetary consciousness is being born all around us.

Another development that has become a transformative force in human life, as we have seen, is the discovery of the pervasive *holism* of human life, nature, and the universe. This discovery serves as an implicit critique of our inherited assumptions, institutions, and patterns of thought. As the destructive consequences of our present fragmentation become ever-more manifest, the insight into holism transforms our forms of life across the board.

Our present era does not represent the first time in human history that human consciousness has rapidly transformed itself. It has happened several times before and this process has been described in books like *The Universe Story* by Thomas Berry and Brian Swimme as well as in several of my own books and articles. We are clearly in the midst of gigantic pressures on our thought and consciousness as well as gigantic historical forces (from climate change to weapons of mass destruction) demanding such a transformation.

This potential for rapid change of consciousness, along with our wonderful human rational capacity for thinking, understanding, and growing in wisdom constitutes our great hope. It is vital that we reflect on where we are going and how to guide the transformations taking place all around us into the most productive and positive form possible. The direction we are headed as yet portends disaster, since we have not transformed our institutions and habitual ways of responding to the crises of our age. As philosopher Hans Jonas expresses this:

The imagined fate of future men, let alone that of the planet, which affects neither me nor anyone else still connected with me by the bonds of love or just of coexistence, does not of itself have this influence on our feeling. And yet it "ought" to have it – that is, *we* should allow this influence by purposely making room for it in our disposition. (1984: 28)

Jürgen Habermas characterizes the *lifeworld* within which all persons are embedded as the set of prereflective assumptions involving cultural norms, society, personality, and immediate everyday certainties as resistant to change largely because it has not been "thematized" or brought into reflective awareness. However, it is precisely crisis situations, he asserts, that can break open the variety of "deep-seated background" world views comprising the cultures of Earth and point the way toward the "moral universalism" indicated by the democratic ideal:

The problematizing pressure brought to bear by such crisis situations, whether of a world-historical or a life-historical type, objectively transforms the conditions for thematization, and only thus creates an illuminating distance from what is most familiar and most taken for granted. An example of this is the thrust toward moral universalism that sets in with the prophetic world religions, disrupting naïve familiarity with the substantive ethical life – commanding reverence from those within it – of the clan or tribal association, a thrust, incidentally, that has sparked off so many regressions that it had to be renewed at intervals right up until this century – until the death camps opened their doors. (1998: 243)

We have reached the limit of civilization's ability to afford regressions. The crises that we face portend the extinction of civilization, a growing brutalization and possible planetary destruction. Yet, for that very reason, *they are bringing the prereflective lifeworld to consciousness in people worldwide.* By constructing the institutional foundations of global democracy we will be preventing further regressions – abolishing the death camps, environmental destruction, and nuclear weapons forever from the Earth.

It is vital that we examine the coming great transformation from the point of view of democracy and democracy's relationship with violence and nonviolence. We will see that the transformational pressures we experience today involve our ascent to *planetary awareness* – that we are growing up in our understanding of ourselves, our human situation, and how to live peacefully and sustainably together with one another on our spaceship Earth. This central question remains: *Will we grow to planetary maturity quickly enough to stave off planetary disaster – a maturity that will necessarily involve democratically governing the Earth.*

This question has been posed in one way or another by all the authors I have mentioned above. As Ervin Laszlo puts it: "We could change direction: with a timely transformation we could create a peaceful and sustainable world. Will we create it? Einstein told us that we cannot solve a problem with the same kind of thinking that produced it. Yet, for the present we are trying to do just that. We are fighting terrorism, poverty, criminality, cultural conflict, climate change, environmental degradation, ill health, even obesity and other 'sicknesses of civilization' with the same means and methods that produced the problems in the first place" (2008: 14). Today, there are immense pressures on all of us to change our assumptions, our attitudes, and our institutions.

We shall see that our "means and methods" that continue to reproduce the same problems that we wish to solve include our reliance on outdated, centuries old, economic and political assumptions. Our consciousness has not yet fully become a *planetary consciousness*; we have not yet begun thinking as *citizens of the Earth*; we have not yet attained *planetary maturity*. Our comprehension of democracy (its meaning, implications, and promise for a peaceful and sustainable future) has remained partial and incomplete, preventing further growth toward planetary maturity. A deeper understanding of these issues has become absolutely essential for the process of creating a holistic Earth civilization.

1.2 The Promise of Democracy

The promise of democracy, the ideal of liberty, equality, and community that emerged out of history with its immense possibilities for a peaceful and just world order, appears to have failed us. Democracy within leading nations has become prostituted to a cacophony of rabid racist, nationalist, or bigoted religious voices spewing forth their poisons from thousands of radio and TV stations nationwide and worldwide. The tyranny of the ignorant that Alex de Tocqueville feared appears to have triumphed. Many of these rabid voices call idolatrously for Armageddon, for global war, for a final catharsis to their pathological hatreds and fears hawked in the name of this or that anthropomorphic idol called "God." Others call for a perpetual state of war against unknown enemies by autonomous nation-states while internally fostering a national security collectivism of fear, conformity, mutual distrust, and suspicion.

At the same time gigantic economic forces of global monopoly capitalism have destroyed democracy in country after country, as we shall see in the chapters below, leaving the majority of humanity not only in abject poverty but without any hope of extricating themselves through the peaceful political processes that democracy represents. Entire nations are caught in the net of global economic forces beyond their control and are helpless to respond to the democratic wishes of the majority of their citizens. Not only have irrational emotions appeared to triumph, an irrational and heartless economic system appears to have driven the final nails into the coffin of the once vivid promise of democracy.

Nevertheless, in our day these immense irrational and ignorant forces compete with emerging nonviolent, democratic, rational, and spiritual movements pointing toward a possible salvation of humanity from impending total disaster. A wealth of literature, philosophy, spirituality, and art has appeared pointing to the possibility of a genuine Renaissance for humanity. Many people are beginning to realize, as Erich Fromm put it, that "the physical survival of the human race depends on a radical change in the human heart" and that "a change in the human heart is possible only to the extent that drastic economic and social changes occur that give the human heart the chance for change and the courage and vision to achieve it" (1996: 9-10).

The final verdict is not yet in, but one thing is clear: those concerned with spiritual transformation and reflective human maturity must actively engage with the great issues of our day, joining with those struggling for democracy and human rights, and with those movements concerned with the sustainable, holistic living, the environment, poverty, ending militarism, justice, and peace. People of maturity and spirituality must publicly struggle for the needed economic and social changes, not leaving the fate of the world to the lowest, most immature elements that now dominate economics and politics.

The promise of democracy, as it developed from its ancient beginnings through the Enlightenment of the eighteenth century, involved ending systems of privilege, domination, and exploitation that crushed the spirit of humanity. It posited the *rational potential* of ordinary citizens to act with common sense and tolerance, entering into dialogue about the issues of the day and collectively forming decisions promoting the common good. Such decisions, flawed though they might sometimes be, would nevertheless promote the good more effectively than decisions made by privileged elites. Democracy, therefore, posited a *community of mutual recognition and communication* that made possible those collective decision-making processes that would foster the common welfare.

Democracy also promised processes for decision-making and creative change that are *inherently nonviolent,* since all decision-making by a few at the expense of the many necessarily involves violence in some form, as will become clear below. In a militarized world of high-tech weapons with immense destructive potential, democracy's promise of nonviolent mechanisms for change becomes all the more compelling. Human beings are very close to the realization that a democratic and nonviolent world order is our only option today and our central hope for a transformed future of peace with justice.

The promise of democracy also included recognizing the *unique value* of each person as person – his or her human rights, dignity, and humanity, and the right of each person to follow his or her own path toward developing the potential, the possibilities, the creative value of his or her life. The assumption behind democracy was that free development of the inner potentialities of each person would become manifest in creative service to humanity, forever enriching the quality and dignity – along with the peace, freedom, and justice – of human life on Earth.

Democracy, in other words, emerged in human history not simply as a flawed political system in competition with the even-more flawed systems of monarchy, oligarchy, authoritarianism, apartheid, patriarchy, etc. The intuition behind democracy derives from the higher promise and possibilities of our common humanity. Yet the meaning and implications of the concept of democracy have not yet been widely or fully understood. Throughout this book, we will spell out that meaning and its higher promise and to elucidate the ways in which this promise can be practically realized in human affairs.

The democratic intuition posited the *inherent rational potential* of the majority of persons, the ability of these persons to participate in a community of dialogue and debate that promotes the common good. It posited the inherent dignity of persons – each of whom has a right to the freedom and social conditions that make possible the development of his or her potential. This is not to say that women, slaves, peoples of color, or minorities did not have to fight for generations for their right to be included in the democratic promise. But their right to be included was premised on the inherent *universality* of the democratic promise that was implicit from the beginning: they too are human beings, they too have rationality, dignity, and the rights to develop their potential as individual persons.

Today, the poor, the marginalized, the faceless and nameless hundreds of millions subsisting in third world slums, continue to struggle to have their humanity recognized in the discourse of civilization. The nearly two billion persons living on less than one U.S. dollar per day remain voiceless, invisible, even within their own nations. Uniting the Earth means uniting *all* together through creating social, political and economic institutions that incorporate *every person* within our world community.

Behind the democratic intuition lie these two interdependent poles of individuality and community. Fulfillment of the democratic promise requires not only the conditions of freedom in which individuals can develop their potential as they think best. It also requires the matrix of a community of rights, responsibilities, common assumptions and expectations that make possible decision-making fostering the common welfare within the context of freedom. The challenge of practical democracy involves finding ways to integrate and mutually enhance these poles. Both reflect fundamental aspects of the democratic promise as this intuits the higher potential of our common humanity. This aspect of democracy has been ignored or misunderstood in today's world.

1.3 Rationality and Community

All forms of fragmentation are anathema to the democratic spirit: all ideas that prevent people from forming vibrant, ever-more universal communities or that inhibit the free development of individual potential. The crisis of democracy in our day derives from our nearly universal embrace of fragmented forms of thought and our refusal to include authentic community (as well as equality) as essential features of democracy. We need to understand in what ways democracy is essential to this holistic, planetary civilization and how the democratic promise can facilitate this transformation.

Not all thinkers working at the cutting edge of the emerging planetary consciousness understand the fundamental role of the democratic intuition within this process. They often emphasize a holism influenced by the postmodern critique of Enlightenment rationalism, thereby suggesting that the harmony of intuition supersedes the Enlightenment emphasis on reason. However, Enlightenment rationalism needs to be *enlarged* to encompass the holism revealed by twentieth-century science, not abandoned.

It is unfortunate in this respect, for example, that Ervin Laszlo in his otherwise insightful book entitled *Quantum Shift in the Global Brain: How the New Scientific Reality Can Change Us and Our World* (2008) contrasts what he calls a discredited and now superseded "culture of logos" with the emerging "culture of holos." Of course, we very much need to develop a "culture of holos." However, democracy is precisely the *fulfillment* of the *logos* spirit (the spirit of reason related to an ordered universe) that first activated during the Axial Period in the Ancient world some 2500 years ago. The *culture of logos* elucidates and elaborates our fundamental human rational capacities and their interface with the rationally comprehensible structures of the universe. Einstein correctly stated that he was filled with wonder that the human mind could comprehend the structures of our universe. This comprehension reflects the astonishing relation between the *logos* within us and the *logos* of the universe without.

For the Greeks, *logos* indicated not only the orderly lawfulness of the cosmos but also the rational potential of the human mind to comprehend and live in accord with this order. The fragmentation characterizing modern life that Laszlo seeks to overcome is *not* due to a "culture of logos" as we shall see. The culture of *logos* has been in the process of development for some 2500 years and has yet to bear its full fruit in the form of an ever-fuller realization of our human rational potential. Insightful contemporary elaborations of *logos* focus on the "discursive" aspects of *logos*, as thinkers as diverse as Jean-Paul Sartre and Jürgen Habermas have done.

"Discursive," here, suggests the common rationality embodied in human dialogue and discourse: *logos* as a product of our collective human endeavor to understand ourselves and the world. The "new scientific reality" discerning the pervasive holism of our universe is precisely a fruition of the culture of *logos*. Our present fragmentation arises from *not properly discerning the logos of the universe* as revealed by contemporary science and *not* living according to its holistic and ecological structure. Authentic democracy would embody this holism within a universal community as an expression of the deeper rationality of the human spirit.

Habermas (1979) has shown in great detail the failure of early modern thought to discern the difference between *instrumental* uses of reason and *communicative* reason at the heart of human languages. For much of early modern thought, reason was reduced to a mere *instrument* for seeking wealth or the technological domination of nature. The ends or goals of human life were taken to be subjective and irrational. This misdirection led to the economic and political fragmentations of modern life: not the culture of *logos*, but the abandonment of our deeper human rationality in the service of mere power and domination, reason as an instrument of irrational ends. Democracy, much of spirituality, and most legitimate human values arise, however, from this deeper rationality. The *fulfillment of the culture of logos is precisely the emerging planetary culture of holos.*

It is also unfortunate that a dominant cultural force in our day is relativism: post-modern relativism, philosophical relativism, cultural relativism, social scientific relativism, theoretical relativism, life-world relativism, linguistic relativism, ethical relativism, etc., seemingly without end. Much of this derives from what scientist of languages Steven Pinker calls "the Standard Social Science Model (SSM)" that dominated intellectual life for much of the twentieth century (1994: 421). The central idea behind most of these relativisms is that people can only think, know, or act with *assumptions*, presuppositions, or with a prior framework that conditions their thinking, knowing, and acting.

Even Habermas tends to fall into this trap by assuming that the universal presuppositions of language that he has discovered are inevitably conditioned by people's local upbringing within some culture or other to the point where the universality of the values pointed to by language are seriously truncated. I have criticized these assumptions of Habermas in Chapter Eight of *Ascent to Freedom* and will not repeat them here. All of these relativisms assume what Pinker calls a "pre-scientific, magical model" that looks at human beings as "caused" by either heredity or environment or both (p. 423). They leave out the recursive and transcending effect of self-awareness, self-consciousness, and the infinite possibilities of speaking, writing, and thinking provided by our language instinct (Ch. 13). A creature aware of causality in itself can creatively engage and thereby transcend that causality through a wide variety of strategies.

Self-awareness or self-consciousness gives us this astonishing human characteristic that we see nowhere else in nature: *rational freedom*. Not an absolute magical freedom that ignores heredity or environmental conditioning, but a relative freedom that allows a process of growth in us to ever-more universal levels of species self-identification. Anthropologist Donald E. Brown (1991) identifies dozens of "human universals" that link human beings within a common humanity that far transcends those cultural variations that often loom so large in our thinking. In the following chapters we will examine a number of ways in which our universal common humanity emerges beyond all the factors that divide us from one another on this planet: beyond race, ethnicity, culture, religion, nationality, language, class, and sub-group.

The progress of science, scholarship, and philosophical thought throughout the past century activated an on-going critique of the limitations of each of these fragmenting factors and a simultaneous planetary ascent to our common, universal humanity. This ascent to our common humanity (and the ever-greater levels of recursive freedom that it implies) makes possible a holistic Earth civilization and planetary community at the dawn of the third millennium. The concept of democracy, deeply and correctly understood, can establish *a planetary public mind characterized by unity in diversity* in which the vast range of our diversities (race, ethnicity, etc.) are embraced within a holistic field of unity that simultaneously affirms them while disarming their destructive potential.

The democratic promise emerges from the same intuition at the heart of our common human drive toward spiritual illumination. Authentic spiritual illumination reveals the universality of the spirit at the heart of the cosmos and every human life just as democracy is predicated on the universal dignity and rational freedom of every human being. Both include our immense potential for overcoming the fragmentations of capitalism, racism, nationalism, and religious fanaticism to develop a global community. Today, the movement of world citizens toward global community is already well advanced. The emergence of authentic spirituality will foster this same universality.

Common bonds, understandings, mutual tolerance, and recognition of "human universals" that transcend our differences also live as features that we associate with authentic *community*. The struggle for democracy is endangered in our day not because of the failure of the democratic ideal but because we have never even come close to practical realization of the democratic ideal. The false division between "free" capitalism and a dictated "community" under communism intervened to destroy democracy on both sides. Community and a "new man" cannot be dictated by the state but must be a product of liberty and developing human maturity. *We are capable of community identifications not only on the local or national levels but holistically at a planetary level.* But this requires that we critically examine the ideological slogans and assumptions that appear to divide us.

For example, the linking of democratic liberty with the "economic freedom" of the powerful corporations to exploit the masses of people twists the promise of democracy into a perversion of freedom and a travesty of justice. The lie that a penniless laboring person may enter into a "free contract" with capital or face starvation is not a premise of democracy but a condition of totalitarian domination. The right to economic freedom for all people surely cannot mean the unlimited right of the rich to dominate and exploit the poor. Each side of this ideological divide embraced a partial truth and totalized it as the absolute truth. In doing so, each side produced the nightmare of totalitarianism – communism through an enforced conformity that posed as "community" and capitalism through a system of exploitation and domination that posed as "freedom."

The democratic ideal has never been realized and is becoming discredited in our time because it was always conjoined with profoundly undemocratic incompatibles: with an individualism that abjures genuine community, with the freedom of capital to exploit, with a totalitarian imposition of a communist collectivity, with the attempt by some nation-states to command economic and social life, with the nationalism and exclusivism of sovereign nation-states, with ethnic or racial prejudices, or with the religious identity of certain intolerant religious groups.

In each case the point of democracy – the inner dignity of persons and the free development of their possibilities for self-realization within community – was perverted by something exterior to personhood and destructive of it. Corporate capitalism, as we have known it, creates an immense inequality that makes the self-development of the majority of persons impossible. Nationalism suppresses human interiority with the ideological demand of conformity, patriotism, and acquiescence to the imperial or cultural goals of the nation. A religious identity colonizing governmental systems crushes authentic human spirituality in the name of externally imposed systems of morality and religious conformity.

The authentic insight of democratic socialism into the imperative for a universal human community must be coupled with insight into the need for economically free markets within the proper sphere of such markets and the empowerment of local communities from the ground up. If everything is dominated by the state and a planned economy, liberty is crushed and genuine community cannot develop. However, if everything is dominated by capital under the misconceived privatization of all human economic activities, neither can genuine community develop. The society becomes atomized, fragmented, and predatory, lacking any community bond but operating only in terms of dog-eat-dog competition, exploiters, and exploited.

Democracy requires not only individual liberty but the community of mutual trust, mutual commitment to human rights and liberties, mutual adherence to due process, and mutual insistence on genuine dialogue, communication, and open discourse. Hence, the ideal of *community* deriving from socialism must be conjoined with an appropriate sphere of economic freedom. People as economic actors must be empowered from the bottom up to create networks of sustainable, interdependent economic communities, truly free markets, unlike what passes for "free markets" today (which are really monopoly-controlled markets in the service of the one to two percent of the world's population who control 47% of the global wealth). Truly free markets, we will see in Part Three below, require substantial economic equality.

Authentic democracy maximizes rational freedom to the extent that this is possible within the framework of genuine community. More than this, it involves the interdependent network of the community itself, for only genuine community can empower and sustain freedom. In the process of conjoining freedom and community, freedom is transformed. It no longer operates as unbridled individualism at the expense of others but freely commits itself to the common good of the community in innumerable ways. Everybody benefits, and the promise of democracy is fulfilled. Given our common global problems and crises on this planet, and given our common human nature and condition, it is not difficult to imagine a holistic sense of community embracing all peoples and nations on Earth.

Abraham Maslow's well-known hierarchy of needs tells us something fundamental about the process of developing human beings mature enough to engage in and empower authentic democracy. People must *first* be able to satisfy their basic physical needs, then the need for safety and security, then the need for belonging and love, then the need for self-esteem, and finally the need for self-actualization and/or self-transcendence. Very generally speaking, only the two needs that are satisfied *last* (self-esteem and self-actualization) develop sufficient human maturity and spirituality to empower authentic democracy. However, to actualize our higher human potential for democratic community we must *first* deal effectively and universally with satisfying the most basic human needs – our most basic physical needs and our needs for safety and security. A viable theory of democracy, therefore, requires addressing the entire spectrum of needs simultaneously.

People who are starving or living in constant insecurity do not generally concern themselves with nuances of due process of law or with building democratic communities. The development of human maturity and spirituality strengthens our sense of oneness with the Cosmos, develops love and compassion, affirmation of diversity, and the awareness of interdependence and interrelationships necessary to community. This is one reason why society must ensure that the basic needs of all are met within the security of democratically enforceable law and due process protections. For the development of our human potential that makes possible authentic democracy, generally speaking, only follows upon satisfaction of these needs lower in the hierarchy.

The conception of "liberal democracy" that has dominated in the United States and much of the Western tradition involves an arbitrarily constructed sense of self that poses as independent of the community that nurtures that self and makes possible the mutuality and interactions of human relationships. As political philosopher Benjamin R. Barber expresses this (in his critique of the broad tradition that includes Thomas Hobbes, John Locke, James Madison, John Rawls and Robert Nozik): "Liberalism is a politics of negativity, which enthrones not simply the individual but the individual defined by his perimeters, his parapets, and his entrenched solitude…. Politics understood as reactive negativity and the denial of every commonality other than that of aggregated individuality reduces the role of the will to one of obstinate resistance. Hence, it obstructs common willing – what Rousseau called general willing – where communities essay to disclose common purposes or discover common ground through the political interaction of active wills" (1998: 7-8).

The liberal tradition positing a sovereign individual who finds his political stance merely in resisting the encroachments of other people and government ultimately results in the destruction of democracy. This easily transmutes into the capitalist ethos of private gain at the expense of nature and other persons. It becomes a kind of terrorist attack on society in the mode of resistance against the anonymous system. It flowers into the private life of depoliticized consumers indulging their private pleasures unconcerned with nature, human beings, or future generations. (A recent documentary film entitled "What Would Jesus Buy?" featuring the Reverend Billie and the Stop-Shopping Gospel Choir underlines the horror and emptiness of the depoliticized consumer society within the United States.) The purely liberal tradition is destructive of authentic democracy that requires a vibrant public space undergirded by genuine community to flourish and bring liberty, equality, and fraternity to fruition.

Democracy repudiates both a tyranny of the majority and of the minority. It involves a set of institutions protecting the integrity and autonomy of personal life insofar as this is compatible with the equal freedom of all the rest, within a community supportive of these principles. It is the recognition of the value of the unique human being embedded within a community that empowers him or her that is at stake. External social movements that subvert personal integrity – such as nationalism, totalitarianism, fascism, racism, religious fundamentalism, capitalism, or technocracy – subvert the development of human spiritual integrity and autonomy. They tend toward the antithesis of democracy and cannot be conjoined with democracy in significant ways without destroying its fundamental value.

The artificial, antisocial selfhood of political liberalism misses the true uniqueness and value of each individual person that arises from the universality of our common humanity and cannot be understood apart from that commonality. Personhood and community arise together as social scientist George Herbert Mead and others have shown at length. Human beings are inherently social – their autonomy and uniqueness arising from the communities that nurture them and incomprehensible apart from those communities and from their common humanity which makes this possible. Habermas, we shall see, has also shown at length in what ways these dynamics are rooted in our common ability for language, one of our defining human characteristics and the source of the deep communicative rationality at the heart of the democratic spirit.

1.4 Our Higher Human Potential

It is only when we break the connection of democracy with any and all of these fragmenting phenomena that its ability to enliven our higher human possibilities can be released. *Authentic democratic institutions provide a framework for the actualization of our higher human possibilities, a framework for human reflective thought, communicative rationality, conscience, creativity, and spirituality.* The conditions for our self-realization ultimately require a planetary community.

Writers who speak of our age as one of transformation to a higher level of consciousness do not necessarily emphasize the role of democracy in this transformation. Rather, they often emphasize community, consensus, compassion, holistic conceptions, and ecological sensitivity. Or they may speak of "participatory democracy" based on consensus that is only applicable to tiny, localized communities. Brian Swimme and Thomas Berry (1992) speak of our transition from the present *technozoic* consciousness to an *ecozoic* consciousness. Ervin Laszlo, we have seen, speaks of moving from a *culture of logos* to a *culture of holos.*

When these thinkers ignore or minimize the immense promise of democracy, they may have in mind the liberal distortions of democracy that separate the concept from its necessary rootedness in community. This is unfortunate, since the democratic idea provides precisely the framework necessary for developing community, consensus, compassion, holistic thinking, and ecological sustainability. We will see that these values cannot be realized without creating a democratic community for the Earth. To speak of the need to develop a planetary *culture of holos,* as Laszlo does, without specifying democracy as the essential means for this development, is to omit something crucial to human survival and flourishing.

In *The New Science of Sustainability*, Sally Goerner, Robert Dyck, and Dorothy Lagerroos are right on target by emphasizing that achieving sustainability (a holistic Earth civilization) requires "reweaving democracy," reestablishing community, and "expanding the blessings of liberty, equality, democracy, community, reason, and the rights of all human beings to a fuller, more effective extent." They correctly call this "an Enlightenment project," thereby underlining the connection between the Enlightenment ideal of developing our universal human rational potential and the ecological ideal of "living in harmony with nature's laws of healthy growth and development" (2008: 232-233).

In this sense democracy becomes both ends and means. Social democracy ensuring that the basic physical and safety needs of the community are met provides the conditions for the self-actualization of its members. On the other hand, the development of authentic democracy depends on people with sufficient human maturity and spirituality to institutionalize and augment a framework of mutual tolerance, respect for persons, and community participation. Democracy takes on a meaning far beyond that of a mere political system among others. It becomes the modality through which human maturity and our common human potential alone can be realized. It becomes the fundamental structure of human ethical relationships.

The hermeneutics of this spiral must be faced in many areas of human endeavor as we attempt to realize the higher promise of our humanity that involves the meaning of our existence upon the Earth and within this Cosmos. Those who have had the good fortune and opportunity for self-actualization must assume leadership to create the framework for authentic democracy upon the Earth that can then empower all people to actualize their higher human potential for reflective thought, love, compassion, tolerance, community, and mutual respect. The spirit of democracy, as Mortimer Adler asserts at the head of this chapter, contains the most revolutionary term in our lexicon of political terms: the word "all." The institutions of democracy guarantee this "all." If the legal and community protection of "all" is lacking, then the institutions are not democratic.

Benjamin Barber appears to misunderstand the need to overcome the private egoistic self of liberalism as striking a balance with community on a continuum that ultimately leads to the tyranny of collectivism. "Taking participation seriously," he writes, "does not reverse the priority of individual and community (which would produce some form of totalist collectivism) but strikes a genuine balance between the two" (ibid. p. 10). However, "community" is not an alternative pole that must be balanced with individuality. It is more properly understood as the holistic matrix that makes individuality possible. A threat to individuality might indeed be posed by *collectivism,* which is entirely different from community. Authentic community is what sustains, enhances, and makes possible our personality and freedom.

Collectivism, on the other hand, requires *human immaturity* for its triumph. Collectivism (as in Nazi Germany) depends on fragmented, fearful, and stunted individuals who submerge their moral, creative, ethical, and self-aware possibilities within a sea of emotionalism and puerile collective identifications. Authentic communities nurture and empower individual persons. They are the matrix within which individual potential becomes most fully developed.

The paradox of political liberalism includes the fact that its cultivation of a false individualism in resistance to the state and the encroachment of other private individuals *fails* to provide a vision of human growth that can move people toward planetary maturity and authentic democratic community. It therefore opens the door to consumerist and capitalist private greed at the expense of nature and society as well as the door to Nazi style totalist collectivism. Without an understanding of the dynamics of a progressively developing maturity within an evolving self embedded within a nexus of communities making this realization of our human potential possible, liberalism problematically lays the groundwork for the very tyrannies that it fears: tyranny of the state, tyranny of the majority, or tyranny of the few.

At the same time, democracy is also a *consequence* of our past development with respect to this higher promise. The insights into the universality of our humanity and its potential, into our individual dignity and human rights, and into the deeper meaning of freedom all derive from our two million years of development on this planet (cf. Martin 2008). Out of this immense journey there arose the first reflections on freedom and democracy among the Ancients, then the Renaissance breakthrough beyond medieval metaphysical dogmatisms, then the Enlightenment realization of the universality of human reason and dignity, and today the extension of this trajectory to a sustainable planetary civilization. Democracy is not only a means to human liberation, it is also an end in itself – the social organization of our higher human potential for rational freedom and community, both ends and means to the development of planetary maturity.

The immense potential within our common humanity for rational and spiritual development and transformation means that our lives as well as the deep reality of the Cosmos around us carry within them what philosopher Ernst Bloch termed a "utopian surplus." As he expresses this, "not only the specific existent, but all given existence and being itself, has utopian margins which surround actuality with *real and objective possibility*" (1970: 96). The immense rational and spiritual potential within us manifests "real and objective possibility" that things could be transformed, that they could and should be fundamentally different. And we understand quite precisely what the differences would be.

Most of us have a fairly clear notion of what would constitute a world of freedom, peace, justice, and sustainable prosperity. This is not a vision of utopia in the negative sense presupposing human perfection. We cannot and perhaps should not dream of perfection. But we utterly need what I have called a "practical utopia" (2005a) that actualizes some of our vast potential for mature, rational living. We need what Albert Camus termed "relative Utopia": "Relative Utopia is the only realistic choice; it is our last frail hope of saving our skins" (2002: 65).

Relative utopia does not mean the end of conflict. It means the actualization of our vast human potential in the twenty-first century at least to the point where we have institutionalized the means for the nonviolent resolution of conflicts. As Camus puts it, we are "not so crazy" as to expect the ending of conflict, but we must make the absolute decision to make violent conflict *illegitimate* through structuring our world order to make genuine dialogue possible and expected, that is, through the creation of a democratic order for the Earth.

This point is absolutely essential and addresses a fundamental misconception people have regarding the goal of a world of peace, justice, prosperity, and sustainability. Even in such a world, there will be conflict – lots of it. It might not even be desirable to do away with all conflict. Our goal is simply to institutionalize ways of nonviolently dealing with conflict. Planetary democracy structured to empower freedom, equality, and community, serves as both means and ends for this process.

At this stage of our common spiritual and rational development, we need courts, impartial judges, police as public servants, mediators, conflict resolution programs, voting, referendums, public debates, etc. All of these involve ways of nonviolently dealing with conflict. We must bind our planetary community together in a dynamic of *unity in diversity*: the agreement to disagree and to respect the right of the Other to disagree, to be different, and to think differently within the common commitment to democracy and nonviolence.

As the river of history implacably carries us toward impending disaster, our rabid nationalistic, neoliberal, racist, dogmatic, or technocratic "solutions" will only further inhibit the creative interiority that is needed most. Our weapons of mass destruction remain on alert for wiping out civilization due to some terrible error in calculation, fanatical hubris, or power politics. Our environment moves toward total climate collapse and the inability to sustain higher forms of life. What constitutes our most basic hope and promise within this intolerable situation?

The chapters below further articulate this hope in further detail. We must move our thinking to the planetary level, to the level of all humanity, where the essential problem of democracy and its solution soon becomes very clear. For only on the planetary level can we go beyond our fragmented modes of thinking and living. The promise of democracy is inherently a universal one, and, therefore, a transformative one – it is the promise of liberty, equality, and community for *all* human beings. Human maturity embraces this universality and builds it into community thought and institutions. This is more than a new "culture of holos." It necessarily requires the *institutional embodiment of holism* within our economic and political institutions. It requires, in other words, genuine political and economic democracy – the key for effectively governing our Spaceship Earth.

When the freedom, equality, and prosperity of *all* has been institutionalized on the Earth, the differences between nations, races, religions, and persons become precious cultural differences that lose their power to destroy. They lose their power to colonize the democratic idea and subvert it by turning diversity into collectivized "isms" of imposed sameness. Nationalisms, exacerbated by the system of autonomous, sovereign nation-states, lose their absolute character. Their diversity then becomes essential and beautiful as long as it is encompassed within the unity of universal democracy respecting the dignity and autonomy of each person on Earth.

1.5 Holistic Spirituality

The higher potential of our humanity is actualized through development of reflective thought, communicative rationality, conscience, creativity, and the spiritualities of love, compassion, kindness, and solidarity. All of these are forms of spirituality, as I am using the word here. Although rationality should be distinguished as having a demonstrable grounding in the presuppositions of communicative language, it ultimately derives, like all else, from the mysterious depths of the universe intuited by spirituality.

Authentic spirituality may or may not associate itself with a particular religion but it never imposes itself dogmatically on others, demanding an exterior conformity. It involves the actualization of our higher human potentialities, takes many forms, and has taken many names throughout human history. Even the ethical dimension, genuine ethical action, we shall see, requires authentic interiority, and hence the activation of ethical conscience itself involves a form of genuine spirituality.

Spirituality constitutes a significant dimension of our potential. The history of every culture, every religion, and every century is replete with testimonies to the immense possibilities within us, possibilities for mindfulness, meditative thinking, deep rationality, God-centered submission, love, compassion, creative awareness, mystical union, encounter with *suchness*, beatitude, inner illumination, ecstatic inspiration, or eschatological vision. Democracy alone provides the framework and moral ideal that can make possible spiritual actualization in great numbers of people.

Some forms of spirituality have been named and described in the chapters below. They should not be taken as exhaustive. The richness of our inner lives may well be practically unlimited. I have discussed some of these possibilities in Chapters 5 and 6 of *Millennium Dawn* and Chapters 2 and 3 of *Ascent to Freedom*. People attracted to forms of spirituality or to philosophy as the love of wisdom need not withdraw from the world-historical struggle for a decent, democratic world order. Their spirituality and wisdom become essential if we are to create a decent future for ourselves and the other living creatures on this planet. They become vital spokespersons for planetary maturity.

Authentic spirituality is holistic and overcomes the fragmentation imposed by limited identifications and puerile emotions. In his book

Ecological Ethics and the Human Soul, Francisco J. Benzoni contrasts the fragmentation generated by fear with the holism consequent upon love:

> We are at a time in history when the fundamental choice is between fear and love. Fear threatens us – fear of the unknown, fear of terrorists, fear of economic and environmental collapse, fear of meaninglessness as modern life is fragmented and the sacred canopy is shredded, fear of running out of fossil fuel. Fear causes us to hunker down, to protect what is "ours," to lash out at the Other, to seek solace in rationalizations that bolster the importance of the self in the face of any perceived onslaught. Above all, fear refuses vulnerability. Love is open, love reaches out and embraces, love takes chances and so makes us vulnerable. Love embraces freedom and is confident in the final goodness of creation. Fear cannot risk and so is willing to trade freedom for security. Love risks and is never willing to make this trade, for such a trade is to forfeit that which makes life worth living and that which is the basis of human dignity, our very capacity to express ourselves creatively. (2007: 181)

Even though authentic universal democracy alone can provide the necessary framework for the actualization of the human potential within each of us on this planet, many forms of spirituality include realizations that confirm and empower the movement toward authentic democracy. The experience of the *agape* of Jesus described here, for example, includes a direct realization of the sacred value of each person as person and their right to be treated as such, which is a fundamental idea of democracy. It also includes the willingness to reach out and embrace others as part of the same human community, the holistic sharing of respect, caring, and vulnerability that we will see as fundamental to genuine democratic communities.

The evolution of self-consciousness in human beings over the past fifty thousand years or so constitutes an immense accomplishment of the evolutionary process. It has also included tremendous dangers for humanity and for life on Earth because self-consciousness initially alienates and estranges us from nature and one another. We feel alone and lost, cut off, from a world submerged in the primal oneness of nature that operates out of instinct and one-dimensional forms of awareness. We envy the innocence and simplicity of the lower animals and often seek to escape our own growing self-awareness.

However, the great teachers and visionaries among us have, at least since the Axial Period in human history some twenty-five hundred years ago, universally affirmed the need *to move forward to find ourselves once more at home in the world* through developing our reason and our love into a deep affirmation of *unity in diversity.* Reason and love operate in different ways, perhaps even in different dimensions of our being. Yet they share the common feature of *binding together*.

Reason sees patterns, similarities, universals, even the whole. Love affirms the Other and emphasizes relationship, community, mutual respect, and solidarity. Both affirm the equality of all and the matrix of internal relationships that make us what we are. Reason emphasizes justice, and love emphasizes forgiveness! Both are necessary. Both must exist in a healthy balance within the complex conflicts and difficulties of human life.

Take, for example, the ethical principle of the categorical imperative, explicated by Immanuel Kant as deriving solely from human reason. To "treat every person as an end in themselves" is to recognize the dignity and intrinsic human rights that are basic principles of democracy with its standards of justice (*recht*). Kant argues that the impartial love taught by Jesus conforms fully to the categorical imperative taught by reason. We will examine both these options in the chapters below.

Spiritual realization, like ethical awareness, empowers our insight into what *should be*, as the quotation from Paul Tillich at the head of this chapter indicates. It awakens us to the way *all* people should be treated. It also empowers us to nonviolently work for a transformed world, to resist with our bodies and minds all that dehumanizes and destroys human life and our precious animal companions on our planet. Love overcomes fear and empowers, as a consequence, real transformative action. The power of what should be at the living center of our lives points toward the triumph of civilization.

Yet spiritual realization, like reason, has another positive aspect – it reveals jingoism, fear, hatred, bigotry, idolatry, exploitation, domination, and dehumanization for what they are, whether these immaturities arise from organized religions or some other source. It exposes the violence and horror of our world disorder ever-more clearly so that we no longer settle down in a botched and fractured world as if this were the only realistic possibility. It shows us that the model of transformative growth toward genuine self-realization constitutes our real human hope, a hope that can be actualized fairly rapidly if we are willing to create the universal democratic institutions that make it possible.

In this sense spirituality is revolutionary spirituality, just as authentic democracy is *transformative democracy*. The term "transformative" is used in relation to "democracy" in order to indicate the world-changing character of authentic human growth with its political and social implications. The realization of sanctity, personal integrity, or the grace of God within ourselves lays the foundation for a *praxis* of world transformation in history. If we begin to experience Christian *agape*, which extends love to all, or Buddhist compassion (*karuna*) that is oneness with the suffering of all others, or Islamic understanding of the personal responsibility placed on each for a life of submission, charity, and peace (*islam*), or the Hindu life of non-attachment and devotion (*bhakti*), then our actions will address the world's tremendous need for transformation.

This rebirth cannot be limited by nation-states, racial divisions, religious parochialism, economic self-interests, isolated individualism, or technological domination. It can only mean universal democracy respecting the integrity of each person and his or her life-potential, a condition that is inseparable from the development of a universal human community. Within today's inhuman world conditions, both authentic spirituality and democracy are appropriately termed "transformative." To the representatives of the repressive status quo with their fractured forms of privilege and compulsive parochialism, both authentic democracy and genuine spirituality appear "radical," dangerous. Let us, therefore, examine the concept of democracy in greater detail.

Chapter Two

Planetary Maturity and Global Democracy

The Final Option for Spaceship Earth

"Democracy" is not a simple concept. At the simplest level, a society is democratic insofar as its population can make meaningful decisions over matters that concern them. It has long been understood that democratic forms have very limited substance when decisions over the fundamental aspects of life are in the hands of unaccountable concentrations of private power, and society is dominated by "business for private profit through private control of banking, land, industry, reinforced by command of the press, press agents and others means of publicity and propaganda."

I am not quoting the Workers Party, but rather John Dewey, perhaps the most prominent and respected Western social philosopher of the 20th century, whose major concern was democratic theory....

What reasonable people should hope for, I think, is a world system of a very different kind. Alternative visions are crucial at this moment in history.

Noam Chomsky

For Democracy signifies, on one side, that every individual is to share in the duties and rights belonging to control of social affairs, and, on the other side, that social arrangements are to eliminate those external arrangements of status, birth, wealth, sex, etc., which restrict the opportunity of each individual for full development of himself.... As an ideal of social life in its political phase it is much wider than any form of government, although it includes government in its scope. As an ideal, it expresses the need for progress beyond anything yet attained; for nowhere in the world are there institutions which in fact operate equally to secure the development of each individual, and assure to all individuals a share in both the values they contribute and those they receive.

John Dewey

In the early twenty-first century the tradition of democracy appears to be in shambles. Wars continue to ravage human life in many places in the world. Human rights are massively violated around the globe not only through war but through torture, political murder, terrorism, repression, human trafficking, poverty, and lack of opportunity for billions of persons. Fifty percent of the world's nations are dictatorships of one sort or another. Within so called democracies, political participation by citizens is at an all time low. It appears that the trend toward democratic governance of the Earth has failed.

Politicians are thought by the citizens to be corrupt and beholden to big business and the rich for their expensive campaign costs. The threat of terrorism progressively destroys liberty and security within traditional democratic states while foreign wars convert formerly transparent institutions into the closed bastions of the national security state. Global crises, such as global warming and impending climate collapse, threaten to overwhelm the governance institutions of the world with climatic disasters and chaos utterly beyond their organizational or planning capacities.

Has the Enlightenment affirmation of liberty, equality, and fraternity failed in its promises to the world of peace, prosperity, and freedom for humankind? Were those promises ever legitimate in the first place? Has democracy become nothing more than the freedom to consume endless environmentally destructive goods by manipulated and passive spectators of a political process engineered by the mass media and oligarchic managers of state? What is authentic democracy and what is its deeper promise? How is democracy related, if at all, to human life and the future of human beings living on spaceship Earth?

2.1 Early-modern Atomism, Liberal Democracy, and the New Holism

Twentieth-century scholarship liberated us from the traditional one-dimensional perspectives that identified our various religions and cultural traditions as embodying an absolute a-historical truth. We owe a great deal to those scholars who showed the cultural and historical rootedness of the various world religions and who critically analyzed traditional metaphysical world views in ways that revealed their cultural, ideological, and historical rootedness. We are liberated today to investigate the deeper meaning of our religious traditions, our cultural traditions, and our traditional metaphysical world views. We are liberated to see our human situation more clearly – from a multi-dimensional and historically developmental perspective – than were any of the thinkers or cultures of the past. Our position is an enviable one because we see our human situation more deeply and more clearly. We can, therefore, act with more understanding than our predecessors.

However, there has been a cost. We have lost the unquestioned certainties that characterized the lives of our ancestors in their closed cultural and religious worlds. Our world has been turned upside down by what I termed in *Millennium Dawn* "the Copernican revolution in religion." At the very least, our world has been severed from its secure foundations and placed into the orbit of relativism and multiculturalism. Our traditional religious and cultural foundations no longer tie us together in a seemingly "natural" way.

We are left wondering how to act and what to do. We look for a meaningful framework from which to derive reasons to act. In lieu of this, many in the first world lapse into endless consumerism and myopic attention to family and private, everyday concerns of household, children, or workplace. We do not comfortably face the big questions of human life on this planet and the immense problems confronting those who are concerned with the fate of the Earth or future generations.

Many do not find the intellectual revolutions of the twentieth century liberating, as freeing us from historically bound ideological frameworks and providing the possibility of building a new world on real insight into the truths of our human situation. Even thoughtful and educated people are often lost in patterns of deconstruction, deracination, and delegitimation. We face a world where the desperate few confronted with the perception of massive injustice and inequalities sometimes resort to violence and terrorism and the desperate bureaucrats of nation-states resort to militarism, war, and other forms of state sponsored terror. As Benjamin R. Barber (1995) puts it, our world today involves a clash of "Jihad versus McWorld" (various forms of fundamentalism and war versus mindless, unsustainable consumerism), and neither option rings true or meaningful. Where do we go from here?

Today, we are rapidly becoming aware that the fate of the world hangs in the balance in the early twenty-first century. If ever used, weapons of mass destruction, thousands of which remain on hair trigger alert, could wipe out the existence of human life on Earth. Global militarism continues to foment war, destruction, and human misery. Global climate collapse continues unabated. The global population continues to soar to ever-more unsustainable levels. Basic planetary resources, such as ocean fisheries, arable land, and fresh water, are disappearing at alarming rates. Planetary poverty, disease, and misery continue to grow and today engulf the lives of more than fifty percent of the world's population. And the global institutions that we have in place, such as the United Nations, are wholly inadequate to deal with any of these crises, let alone the interdependent nexus of their totality.

At the very juncture when we need to act to secure a future for our planet and future generations we are paralyzed in the face of the seeming rootlessness and relativism of all our traditional religious and metaphysical ideas. We are lost in a cacophony of competing voices, none of which appear compelling and none of which appear to address our situation adequately. Traditional ideas of liberal democracy continue to permeate the intellectual horizon and continue to carry enough prestige to serve as ideological justifications by dictators, multinational corporations, and warring nations alike. Yet populations are failing to participate in whatever political processes are open to them, and there appears to be a general loss of faith in the possibilities for democracy to deal with our most fundamental issues.

It is becoming clear to many persons that present-day so-called democracies are really oligarchies run by the rich and powerful largely in their own interests. Lawyers for multinational corporate drug companies or weapons manufacturers write legislation and present it to the U.S. Congress for rubber stamp approval. Congress gives away the entire electro-magnetic spectrum, belonging to the people of the U.S., to huge private media corporations at nominal costs. Politicians openly support the same private medical corporations and insurance companies that contribute huge sums to their political campaigns.

The Pentagon war machine targets the people of the U.S. with huge quantities of propaganda for its wars and immense budget. The Bill of Rights in the U.S. Constitution is gutted to make room for "homeland security." These facts are not isolated phenomena. They are part and parcel of a system that what been institutionalized in the U.S., Great Britain, and many other countries. In significant measure, they are consequences of the failure of the system of liberal democracy that has dominated the intellectual horizon for the past two centuries.

During the twentieth century, democracy also came under attack by a number of theoreticians who tended to see the masses of people as incapable of governing themselves through democratic processes and who formulated various theories of social engineering or management of populations by ruling elites. *We shall see that such theoreticians misunderstand not only democracy, but human history, and the human situation in general.* These included Nazi legal theoretician Carl Schmitt, Joseph Schumpeter, Friedrich von Hayek, Leo Strauss (the darling of today's conservatives), and theoretician of international "political realism," Hans Morgenthau.

In his book *Politics Among Nations* (1948), Morgenthau correctly saw that relations among sovereign nation-states amounted to little more than power politics, each state pursuing its own self-interest through political maneuvering (and ultimately war) in which neither morality, nor human welfare, nor international law had any more than instrumental value in the service of naked power interests. Most of the above theorists advocated the ruling national elite manipulating and lying to their populations in the service of the brutal power struggle of imperial nation-states.

If this is an accurate description of the relationships among sovereign nations, then the obvious question becomes what of democracy *within* nations? Can leaders who are amoral political "realists" in their foreign policies really protect and promote democracy within their nations, since democracy is (in all its versions) founded on moral concepts of *universal* human rights, dignity, equality, and freedom? Is democracy possible *within* nations when the condition *between* nations remains the antithesis of democracy that is in essence a state of *de facto* war? Can democracy survive when leaders systematically manipulate and lie to their own populations in the service of their Machiavellian foreign policies?

The above named critics of democracy not only challenged the coherence and legitimacy of democracy within nations, but they all tended to see human relationships (most clearly exemplified in the relations between nations) as a Hobbsian condition of the war of all against all. Politics, even within nations, reduces to the drive for power among competing parties, ideologies, and leaders. As Machiavelli had claimed in *The Prince*, the rulers may appeal to moral principles to garner support from the people, but ultimately these principles are merely instrumental in the process of consolidating and maintaining their power over the people.

Nevertheless, most people today continue to sense something extremely fundamental and important in the idea of democracy but remain unclear how we might solve our immense planetary crises in the light of this idea or how we might bring civilized order within the chaos of competing sovereign nation-states. And, of course, democracy itself has seen several competing theoretical formulations. The dominant group of formulations, most influential within the United States and therefore widely known throughout the world, were termed "liberal democracy," and were framed in terms of a *social contract* between citizens and a government they placed in power over themselves.

In its social contract and "consent of the governed" formulations, liberal democracy largely involves a negative set of concepts, wholly inadequate to our present need. It takes its stand on the rights and liberties of an artificially conceived, individual "person" who must perpetually defend his or her liberty and autonomy against the encroachments of government or other persons similarly conceived. Government becomes an umpire for adjucating the competing interests of the self-promoting monadic persons under its jurisdiction, a regulator providing a level playing field for the competition of individual or corporate interests, and, ultimately, a danger capable of encroaching upon the liberties of these individuals and their corporate enterprises.

Individuals and corporations have rights that government must protect, and ultimately the Earth and its resources must be privatized: for the only thing truly real about the world, on this view, are competing *private* interests. The notions of the public good, the common good, the civic welfare of the whole, or the welfare of future generations are mere abstractions having little or no claim upon the fundamental nature of the social contract that makes government the servant and regulator of competing private interests, which alone are real and tangible.

In *The Post-Corporate World. Life After Capitalism,* David C. Korten singles out the fundamental economic premises in John Locke's *Two Treatises on Government,* widely regarded as a founding document of liberal democratic theory. Regarding the right to unlimited accumulation of private wealth by the monadic, autonomously conceived persons to whom a liberal government is responsible, Locke's assumptions include these ideas: "the accumulated capital of the wealthy is invested in productive activity that increases useful output and thereby the total wealth of the society. Natural capital remains abundant relative to need so that one person's increased use of land and other resources does not deprive another of like opportunity. The benefits of increased useful output are widely shared." Korten continues:

> Unfortunately, as we have seen in previous chapters, none of these assumptions currently hold up. The capital being accumulated by the rich is primarily financial and it is used to finance speculative and extractive investments that destroy living capital and future productive capacity Natural wealth has become scarce relative to need, and its monopolization by the wealthy is actively displacing the poor and depriving them of a means of living. Finally, the benefits of economic growth are going primarily to the top 1 percent of the world population, while 80 percent suffer stagnation or absolute decline. (1999: 169)

It should be clear that the economic system here described is not a product of democracy and is fundamentally incompatible with democracy. Locke promoted this system as deriving from the fundamental *a priori* rights of "life, liberty, and property" that have become the basis for liberal democracy's defense against government regulation and encroachment. However, as Korten and others have pointed out, the "natural right" to unlimited accumulation of private property not only destroys political democracy but the very basis of life for the majority. According to Locke, the right of private property is a "natural right" prior to a person's social relationships. It is a primary function of democratic government, he says, to protect this right.

Such theories of liberal democracy are a product of the same movement that can be termed a "loss of traditional metaphysical foundations." Despite Locke's appeal to God's natural law as identical with the laws of reason (reason as conceived by him), such theories tended to abjure broad religious or metaphysically based conceptions of society and human life (given by earlier thinkers such as Thomas Aquinas, Nicholas of Cusa, or Baruch Spinoza) in favor of the priority of the individual freedoms, rights, and liberties. Much of traditional western thought (from Plato through Spinoza) had involved a *static holism* that placed the individual within the community that encompassed him or her. (Today's holism, by contrast, involves a dynamic, *evolutionary holism*. Both, however, emphasize the primary role of community.)

By abjuring this foundationalism, Locke and other early-modern thinkers generated a false concept of the human self as an isolated atom *prior to its social relationships*, resulting in the social theory behind liberal democracy. The roots of modern Western philosophy from René Descartes to Thomas Hobbes, John Locke, David Hume, and John Stuart Mill largely followed a host of early scientific assumptions about the mechanistic and atomistic structure of a universe understood as a collection of "bodies in motion" (cf. Harris 2000a). They projected the mechanism and atomism of early-modern science onto human affairs. Locke's concept of a human person was derived from this atomistic model. Today's social and natural sciences have made it clear that the atomistic model misconceives our human reality and that the universe is holistic through and through.

These thinkers repudiated the metaphysical theories of the medieval period and attempted to proceed in a strictly scientific and rational manner. The capitalist philosophy of Locke, Adam Smith, and others gave atomistic human beings an unlimited right to accumulate private wealth in competition with others and posited the function of democratic government to protect this competition and right to private accumulation. The obligation of government to promote the "common good" was strictly secondary in Locke's philosophy. Where it appears, the "common good" is often understood as universally protecting the *a priori* rights of autonomous individuals.

Today's heirs of such philosophies have not yet come upon the insight crucial to ecology and many other twentieth-century sciences that human life and the universe emerge as a series of interrelated wholes within wholes that are not reducible to their component parts and not reducible to a philosophy of atomism. The dominant trend in contemporary psychology, social theory, and philosophy recognizes this holistic structure of human life and the natural world. The mechanistic philosophy of capitalism (economics as reducible to competing human or corporate atoms operating on the basis of rational self-interest), like the liberal philosophy of *a priori* rights that must be protected from society and government is not only incompatible with genuine democracy but represents a hidden form of early-modern atomistic metaphysics.

We have discussed the fact that our universe is characterized by a holism differentiated into a multiplicity of interrelated parts and subsystems that emerged from every contemporary science (Martin 2008: Ch. 3). The insight that this same dynamic of a holism of interrelated parts also should characterize human life on Earth has been slower in coming. The fragmentation that we insist on maintaining within both our thinking and our dominant economic and political institutions may well be the source of the ever-growing destruction occurring all around us as we are swept toward disaster on this planet. Philosopher of science Errol E. Harris sums up the understanding of contemporary science as follows:

> We must notice that this priority of structure to individuation is not just an empirical discovery but is essential to any and every principle of individuation. What distinguishes and defines individuals is their relations to one another; and every relation of whatever sort presupposes a background system appropriate to it. The relations between points in space (or events in space-time) presuppose the metrical field in which they are determined, and the relations of number presuppose the system of natural numbers. Family relations presuppose both a biological system and a social system. It is true that such systems are constituted by relations, but not by relations which pre-exist or could survive independent of the system. The moral of all this is that relations between distinguishable individuals are incurably 'internal'. The attempt to externalize them by separating the individuals, by whatever method whether physically or in theory, destroys the terms. The proper understanding of the nature of relatedness is thus crucial to the conception of whole and part. (1965: 456)

In morality, social theory, and philosophy of democracy it is crucial to realize that our relations with one another cannot be correctly conceived as "external relations." Individuals are not autonomous realities separate from the holistic matrix within which they are embedded. In any holistic matrix (e.g. human beings have evolved on this planet as a single species of *homo sapiens* within a single encompassing biosystem) the relations between individuals are "internal" because our very individuality arises from the holistic reality itself, from the community, and not the reverse.

We find ourselves born into a social world temporally structured between past, present, and future. Our possibilities for future action derive from the past social actions of generations now gone. The social and historical matrix, created from the past, into which we are born, structures future possibilities. As social philosopher Charles M. Sherover asserts:

No individual starts in a vacuum, lives in a vacuum, evaluates in a vacuum. Every social response is a response to a socially presented problem, question, or issue. No matter how idiosyncratic, therefore, a human being's living activity may be, it is inherently socially bound.... We are each born and remain *members* of the historically developing society to which we continue to belong, no matter how conformist or deliberately disengaged we become.... Whatever else a relevant public philosophy may proclaim, it must, if it is to have relevance, acknowledge at the outset the social matrix out of which individuality develops and in which it is always rooted. (1989: 24-25)

Today, we understand that we are born not only into the culture and history of a particular nation or ethnic grouping but into a *planetary culture with a planetary history.* Our individuality is not only necessarily a social product; today it encompasses our awareness of ourselves a members of the human species historically developing from a parochial and childlike past toward ever-greater cognizance of our common human social matrix and common future as revealed by science.

Our institutions and our freedoms will fail us insofar as they are predicated on assumptions that contradict the scientific realities of our situation. We are failing democratically, environmentally, economically, and spiritually, not necessarily because of a lack of good intentions or intelligence but because our most basic assumptions (including our assumptions about democracy) do not sufficiently mesh with reality. All forms of atomism and the fragmentation they imply must be replaced with the *unity in diversity* that science has shown to be operative across the board, from the universe as a whole to its most microscopic aspects.

A viable theory of democracy must similarly overcome the atomistic idea of *negative liberty* in which individuals oppose society and the state in the name of private freedoms. It must found democracy on the realities of interdependence and levels of community that include and embrace the self and root the self in our common human experience. Negative liberty means the atomistic self must defend its freedoms *against* government and other persons. Government itself must be premised on the understanding that good government is an expression of its communities and not an alien power set against them. *Positive liberty* understands that freedom arises from the matrix of democratic community and is inseparable from the healthy functioning of that community.

Just this positive liberty is reflected in the relationship of love as *agape,* discussed above. Love recognizes the mutual interdependence of our selves in the processes of successful living and fulfillment of our respective individual potentials. It understands that the self-realization of each of us is intimately connected with the common flourishing of all of us. Love recognizes that there is no true freedom without a community in which the majority recognize the interdependence and mutuality of all. Each individual flourishes, and their fulfillment in life is maximized when they are involved with relationships of kindness, gentleness, equality, and mutual support with all the others. In contrast to the negative liberty of a competitive society of self-interested individuals, positive liberty arises from a cooperative society in which the common good provides the matrix for the maximum fulfillment of each individual.

2.2 Positive Freedom and Planetary Democracy

Anyone who has traveled widely in the world knows that human beings everywhere share a common consciousness. Despite tremendous variety in customs, languages, religions, and traditions, people everywhere understand one another on many levels. They are structured the same, function the same, have the same basic needs and wants, and in many ways think the same. Precisely because it is so pervasive, people often live unaware of this common consciousness or sameness.

Every person comes from the social unit of a family and has grown up as part of a larger series of communities from the neighborhood to the town to the region to the nation. Everyone's selfhood has emerged through these interactions and is a resultant of interaction between the person's individual biological and personal characteristics and the environing communities. Every normal person speaks a language or languages. Every person is aware of themselves as a human being who lives as a resident and citizen of the Earth.

Over the past several centuries philosophers have developed a profound alternative tradition to the negative freedom of philosophical liberalism, a tradition that understands freedom as a positive quality of human life that arises out of, and cannot be detached from, it roots in the communities in which people participate. This alternative tradition runs through such thinkers as Baruch Spinoza, Jean-Jacques Rousseau, Immanuel Kant, G. W. F. Hegel, T.H. Green, Bernard Bosanquet, Ernest Barker, Errol E. Harris, and Jürgen Habermas. Habermas has demonstrated through his analysis of language (perhaps our most fundamental social and communal capacity) the empirical fact of the self arising from the matrix of community and the universal procedural principles of justice, equality, and reciprocity that are necessarily presupposed by every user of language (1998b).

Nevertheless, by showing that the basic procedures of democracy are integral to the presuppositions of the very possibility of language and human communication (and hence scientifically grounding democratic theory) Habermas is not adding substantially to the conception of democratic liberty developed by the other thinkers mentioned here. The presuppositions making language possible – the equal right to speak, the equal right of ideas to be considered, the equality of participants in the act of speaking, etc., were already understood as the heart of democracy within this tradition. Ernest Barker (1874-1960), for example, writes concerning democracy:

> Men naturally concentrate their attention on these matters of regulation and the problems which they involve – problems such as proportional representation, the right of dissolution, the right of referendum, and whatever else can be made a matter of formal legal right. But when constitutional law has done its utmost, it leaves a sphere which needs control, and yet cannot be controlled by legal rule. Discussion, by its very nature and in its own essence, transcends the scope of legal control. What it cannot transcend is the rules of its own inner logic and its own inward ethics – or rather it can only transcend them at the cost of annihilating itself. Discussion which refuses any control becomes a civil war; and civil war is the end of discussion. (1967: 72)

We are bound together on planet Earth in a community of discussion, debate, and collective decision-making. Just as language itself contains its "own inner logic and its own inward ethics," so genuine democracy has long been understood to embody these requirements. Our individual freedoms arise from communities that internalize and support these fundamental and universal human ethical conditions. The only alternative to discussion and cooperative decision-making is some form of coercion or strategic manipulation, necessarily involving violence or the threat of violence.

Liberty arises from the common consciousness and supporting matrix of a community. If other persons are not in mutual support and do not make the kind of assumptions that support one another's liberties: if others resist or mistrust or limit relationships to impersonal "contracts," rigorous "security" measures, or atomistic economic interests, then liberty becomes seriously impeded. It becomes a perpetual fight to do what one wishes over and against the community, the government, the neighbors, or the law. Unless the community empowers my freedom through its internal relationships and basic assumptions, I am trapped in relationships of social and legal coercion against which I must struggle.

On the other hand, relations of mutual trust and understanding open up dimensions of liberty far beyond anything possible through the struggle of an individual over and against the community. Just as the essentially social nature of the self makes of the Lockean self (that assumes *a priori* rights and autonomy before giving its "consent" to civil society) a profound falsification of reality, so the negative idea that freedom can only be won through limiting government, resisting community, and distrusting neighbors is a profound falsification of freedom.

Positive freedom emerges within the context of a "general will" or mutually understood common good that affirms a diversity of individuals and their freedom precisely because these are rooted in the unity of the community supporting common assumptions about the rights and freedoms of each. Philosopher Alan Gewirth (1996) calls this the "community of rights." The French revolutionary slogan "liberty, equality, and fraternity" had it correct, since there is no liberty without both substantial equality and community. The liberal tradition takes only the first of these seriously, treating the second as merely an equality of rights for atomized individuals to be let alone by the state or other persons irrespective of vast economic inequalities, and largely discounting the third.

The very *concept of government* changes with this understanding of positive freedom. Rather than a necessary evil that must be limited in every way possible under the premise advocated by such thinkers as John Stuart Mill and Henry David Thoreau asserting "that government is best which governs least," positive concepts of democracy and community understand that government can really function as the empowering foundation of liberty, equality, and fraternity. *Government of the people, by the people, and for the people* is not only possible but necessary if we are to have authentic democracy. Government must arise from the people through the public space of dialogue and debate and a commitment to the common good.

Barker argues that "discussion" is the very essence of democracy. For when genuine political discussion takes place within society, individual points of view are modified, enhanced, and transformed of a common good transcending the multiplicity of conflicting individual goods:

> So far as the society exists by dynamic process, it exists for and by the mutual interchange of conceptions and convictions about the good to be attained in human life and the methods of its attainment. It thus exists for and by a system of social discussion, under which each is free to give and receive, and all can freely join in determining the content or substance of social thought—the good to be sought, and the way of life in which it issues. Now such discussion is also, as we have seen, the essence of democracy. (1967: 19)

Similarly, Errol E. Harris observes that there is a "general will" or deeper "common good of the social whole" that arises when the community is understood as the matrix and womb of democracy rather than its nemesis. Human rights, as well as the possibility of a genuine common good, arise from within communities that form the matrix and sustainer of our individualities:

> Many thinkers who oppose civil society to the state continue the tradition of individualistic theories, which see law and regulation as a limitation on freedom rather than the means of its realization through the protection of legitimate rights.... It is from this mutual recognition alone that rights and duties derive, and it is only from this that one can decide what rights ought to be recognized, which (in any particular society) may not be. Apart from mutual recognition of persons there can be no prior "natural" rights attaching to individuals as such, as if they could exist independently of society and mutual recognition.... The democratic state, according to the thinkers we have been reviewing, is one in which the whole community participates, through its civil and administrative institutions, in a process of intercommunication, commerce and discussion, which generates a general will that, because it represents the common good of the social whole, is supreme and thus exercises sovereign authority invested in the institutions of government. (2008: 32)

As we will see further below, Jürgen Habermas has also elucidated the dynamics of democracy as a communicative community, showing that the laws by which people are governed must be legitimated by people recognizing in these laws the results of their own communicative activity. Government thereby becomes the ultimate expression of the community rather than an antithesis to civil society and a threat to individual liberty. It becomes the institutionalization of a communicatively constructed common good within the framework of liberty, equality, and fraternity.

Under the Lockean conception of liberal democracy, a conception largely institutionalized today in the United States and promoted worldwide through U.S. imperial policies, the individual right to unlimited accumulation of private property remains axiomatic, functioning within a conceptual framework in which government merely protects the competitive pursuits of private interests. Here the notion of the common good has little meaning beyond the idea of a common, conflictive pursuit of personalized goods. Immense concentrations of wealth give extraordinary political power to a tiny elite, undermining democracy at every turn. The second foundation of positive freedom, therefore, requires reasonable economic equality.

Karl Marx was fundamentally correct that political democracy cannot exist in any real way without economic democracy. A truly common good can only emerge when political democracy is supplemented by what Marx termed "substantive" or complete democracy. Economic democracy today must be understood, not as enforced collectivization (as the propaganda system would have us believe), but as the economic empowerment of individuals from the grass roots up in ways that supply the basic necessities of all persons while reducing vast accumulations of private wealth (equals power) that inevitably undermine and corrupt political democracy. Economic democracy does not abolish free markets, as we shall see. It simply prevents markets from being monopolized by the rich and powerful.

This conception of positive freedom emerging from genuine community does not involve a return to the religious or metaphysical foundationalisms of the past. It is rooted in the empirical realities of our situation much more firmly than the fragmented and negative conceptions of philosophical liberalism that derive from incorrect early-modern scientific assumptions. Many thinkers today are developing this alternative conception of freedom with its profound social and economic implications. These thinkers include economists such as David C. Korten and Herman E. Daly, progressive writers such as William Greider and Naomi Klein, and philosophers such as Jürgen Habermas, Benjamin R. Barber, Enrique Dussel, and Errol E. Harris.

At this juncture of planetary crises threatening the very future of human beings on this planet, the conversion to positive freedom takes on much more than theoretical significance. Early modern philosophies of atomism and consequent fragmentation have been overthrown across the board. We will only survive and prosper on this planet if the institutional and theoretical systems by which we conceptualize and organize our lives flourish in fundamental harmony with the scientific realities of our situation. We have moved beyond earlier metaphysical foundations for our human community, and we have moved beyond the atomism of early-modern thought. The new foundation involves the pervasive holism of our human situation as revealed by contemporary science.

Nevertheless, with the notable exceptions of Harris and Barker, most of the above mentioned thinkers do not see their way clear to embracing *planetary democracy*. They correctly understand that economics and government must be community oriented, rooted in localities, and organized in such a way as to allow moral and practical values of community members (winnowed through rational dialogue and debate) to articulate a common good that becomes the framework for action. Commodity and exchange relationships, the pure profit-motive, and government as a militarized security-system enforcing merely contractual relationships must be transformed into a framework in which people and nature come first, in which economics and government serve the common good and not the private interests of the few. Korten, for example, expresses this as follows:

To survive on a living spaceship we must create a system of economic relationships that mimics the balance and cooperative efficiency of a healthy biological community. It must distribute rights equitably and link power to the consequences of its use. In short, we must commit ourselves to establish an economic, as well as political, democracy. A substantial body of proven experience suggests that such systems can be built around smaller enterprises functioning as self-directing members of larger networks in ways that are efficient, flexible, and innovative, and thereby secure the freedom and livelihood of the individual while nurturing mindful responsibility. (1999: 181)

This might serve as a brief description of meaningful positive freedom (which must include economic as well as political democracy) and what must happen on a planetary scale if we are to create a decent future for generations to come. However, like many of the other thinkers mentioned, Korten retains the liberal suspicion of government as a threat to liberty and does not deeply see the truth, emphasized by philosophers such as Hegel, Barker, and Harris, that the social matrix as a whole includes family, social organizations, and government as aspects of the same fundamental human community.

A radical distinction between government and civil society becomes less necessary within this framework (however true it remains that *vigilance* on the part of citizens is the price of freedom). Korten realizes that the positive conception of democracy that he affirms must be planetary in scope. However, even in the face of the above enumerated planetary crises, he can only manage the weak and very unlikely suggestion that the current undemocratic domination of global trade and finances by the World Trade Organization and IMF be replaced with "an international agreement regulating international corporations and finance" (ibid. p. 191).

Korten's suggestion that sovereign militarized nation-states in historic competition with one another negotiate treaties for "an international agreement regulating international corporations and finance" becomes simply bizarre in the face of the global realities that threaten human existence on Earth. A similar criticism should be made of Barber's idea that citizens be consulted by "referenda" that replace representative national government as we know it with these new, cumbersome procedures. He calls this "strong democracy" and provides a compelling picture of what participatory governance would be like. However, rather than transforming government as we know it into authentic democracy and enlarging it to its proper global dimensions, he appears to reduce government to a truncated form that would be utterly incapable of dealing with the global crises that threaten humanity.

A similar lacuna appears in *The New Science of Sustainability –
Building a Foundation for Great Change* by Goerner, Dyck, Lagerroos
(2008), mentioned above. This excellent book delves deeply into the
contrast between the older "world hypothesis" deriving from early
modern science, liberal theories of democracy, and monopoly capitalism
and the new science of sustainable economics, ecology, civilization, and
community-oriented democracy. These authors see democracy as people
empowered through cooperative, supportive social structures, vibrant
communities, and horizontal economic relationships providing sustainable
incomes for the majority. They critically examine neoliberal economics
and its subversion of democracy through promotion of elite wealth and
power at the expense of nature and the majority of persons.

Their book takes it stand on the need for "great change" through
transforming all the failed assumptions of the traditional hierarchical
concepts of modernity regarding democracy, economics, evolution, the
structure of the universe, etc. The authors recognize the great
transformation that contemporary science has effected: providing the
insight that interdependency, unities, dynamic communities, and wholes
sustain nature and the universe rather than the mechanistic, atomistic, and
competitive relationships assumed by the early-modern hypothesis.
However, amazingly, for all their claims that they are transforming the
false set of modern assumptions, these authors *never* mention the
sovereign nation-state.

They never recognize this institution as a foundational modern
assumption creating fragmentation and war and wreaking havoc in our
world. Their book includes an extensive analysis of capitalist economics
and proposes economic democracy, but it omits the insight, expressed by
social scientist Christopher Chase-Dunn, that "the state and the interstate
system are not separate from capitalism, but rather are the main
institutional supports of capitalist production relations" (1998: 61). Their
book fails, therefore, to adequately lay the foundations for a sustainable
civilization because they make their numerous arguments for great change
without recognizing a central impediment to that change in sovereign
nationhood.

Their analysis of democracy similarly fails on this account. They see
the need for economic democracy, a "committed, collaborative
community," "restoring civil society and civilizing mores" and "linking
governance systems at multiple levels" (pp. 229-243), but they never
follow through on the grounds of their own planetary perspective to the
conclusion that "great change" requires planetary democratic government
replacing the destructive system of autonomous sovereign nation-states
that defeats planetary democracy, peace, and civilized human
relationships on every side.

"Governance" cannot be linked at multiple levels, as they claim, if sovereign nations remain incommensurable with one another, each a law unto itself with no common law for them all. In line with these same uncriticized premises, the analysis of these authors focuses on the United States, as if creating holistic democracy in the U.S. will somehow solve our planetary crises and create a sustainable future for the Earth. The foundations they lay for sustainability appear seriously incomplete since they quietly accept a major impediment to sustainability inherited from false early-modern premises.

Goerner, Dyck, and Lagerroos promote the proper insight regarding our unity on the Earth, as when they quote R. Buckminster Fuller: "We are not going to be able to operate our Spaceship Earth successfully nor for much longer unless we see it as a whole spaceship and our fate as common. It has to be everybody or nobody" (p. 230). However, they do not follow through on this insight to the conclusion that we must unite together in one democratic world order, that it *cannot* be "everybody" unless everybody is protected equally by a set of democratically legislated enforceable laws. There is absolutely no way to include everybody unless *everybody* is united under a single constitution providing the framework for genuine planetary democracy. Their vision remains fragmented by incommensurables.

But positive freedom opens up new possibilities that are closed to negative freedom that is always in struggle with its perceived threats of government and community. By uniting as a global community under a democratic constitution, our positive freedom to deal with our planetary future would be immeasurably enhanced. Sherover describes this process enhanced by positive freedom:

> These positive freedoms or prescriptive rights are, be it noted, future oriented; they open up an area of futurity for exploration and development by individual members who may wish to do so, in the belief that such individual activity contributes to the common good of all.... The specific positive freedoms or prescriptive rights that characterize the members of a particular society are their specified authorization to plan on a future opening before them; these positive freedoms or specified rights open up the vistas, as protected opportunities, their members, as a socially constituted body, authorize or encourage each other to pursue. (1989:79-80)

Our global situation today requires the vision to create a constitutionally mandated planetary community of positive freedom in which human beings are empowered to deal with the global crises that threaten our existence and future generations on this planet. Under our fragmented contemporary political and economic institutions, our freedom as human beings to create a sustainable future of peace, justice, and prosperity is severely restricted. Despite the best efforts of thousands of concerned world citizens, little progress is made due to the security, economic self-interest, and warlike measures of militarized nation-states with their immense restrictions and practices that inhibit the actualization of a planetary common good.

The "common good of all" needs to be the product of a global positive freedom that is only possible under a democratic *Earth Constitution*. As Sherover suggests, the creation of government alone will not suffice. However, government as the mainspring of positive freedom that empowers and enhances the creative possibilities of the world's citizens remains the *necessary* prerequisite for a truly transformed world order. Unless we *plan the future together* with the rest of the human community, there is little hope for actualizing a future beyond our present suicidal trajectories.

Although Ernest Barker primarily restricts his discussion of democracy to the nation-state, he does recognize the inherent universality of the concept of a democratic constitution as an "organization" that encompasses all men: "Ultimately, all other organizations of men must come to the bar of the organization of all men, if that can ever come to pass. We can imagine a high measure of general liberty under a system of national societies and national States. We can imagine a perfect liberty only in a world society and a world State" (1967: 28).

Hence, with the exceptions we have noted of Harris and Barker, most of today's thinkers concerning world problems mentioned remain trapped in the mythology of "sovereign nation-states" that history shows clearly as a major source of the global crises of war, poverty, exploitation, and chaos that we face today. As world citizen Harold Bidmead puts it, "The enemies of a peaceful international order are the worshippers of the false god of national sovereignty, the idol with feet of clay" (2005:123). My *Ascent to Freedom* (2008) trances the history of this mythology in some detail. Democracy must indeed be "strong democracy" empowered from the grass roots level, but democracy must be simultaneously *global democracy*, something that is only possible if sovereign *nation-states* federate as interdependent regions within a system of binding world law legislated by a genuine world parliament. This act, and this act alone, can open up a future for humanity.

The system of sovereign nations recognizing no effective law above themselves must be transformed into an Earth Federation legislating laws binding on all individuals and capable of ascertaining, implementing, and encouraging action for the common good of human beings and the Earth that sustains us. Twenty-first-century realities show that the system of sovereign nation-states has lost its *raison d'être* and no nation can any longer claim full democratic legitimacy. In *21st Century Democratic Renaissance* Harris writes:

At the present time, the two fundamental principles justifying national sovereignty – the rule of law and the pursuit of the common good of its subjects, have become undermined, so that national sovereignty, as such, has become obsolete. Democracy, the sovereignty of the people, can no longer be claimed by separate national groups, because, as such, they can no longer maintain these two fundamental conditions.... It is thus clear that under the currently existing world conditions the traditional conception of democracy, whether in the form envisaged by the individualistic thinkers of the seventeenth to nineteenth centuries or that entertained by later idealistic philosophers, cannot be realized. What they conceived as the necessary condition of the exercise of sovereign power in the state – its service of the common good – has become unsustainable within the national state.... In the world today the only form of democracy that could aspire to the ideals of the traditional philosophical conception would have to be global, one that could legislate to implement global measures to deal with global problems (as sovereign nation-states cannot) and could maintain the Rule of Law worldwide (which the exercise of sovereign rights by independent nations prevents).... Were such a democratically constituted World Government to be established it would not automatically solve the problems so urgently crying our for resolution, but it is the indispensible precondition of any effectual remedy to global crises, if only because sovereign nations are bound by their very nature and definition to generate the conditions that exacerbate current crises. (2008: 134-135 & 138)

It would not be prohibitively difficult to activate a global grass-roots-oriented system of participatory democracy generating an authentic general will toward the common good. There are already dozens of groups meeting and organizing in such a fashion to dialogue concerning global problems: from United Nations conferences on the environment to the World Social Forum to Oxfam to Greenpeace to Amnesty International to the Provisional World Parliament. And the computer technology exists that could activate real global democracy. *The only legitimate sovereignty of the people is that of all the people of Earth, for all persons on Earth have the same universal rights, dignity, and equality and the same universal responsibility for the future of the Earth and their children.* There is no other route to generate a democratically articulated common good of the Earth than through the universal participation of the people of Earth.

The world community is now the only legitimate locus of sovereignty and the appropriate source of strong democracy. As long ago as 1946, Emery Reves stated that "as the world is organized today, sovereignty does not reside in the community, but is exercised in an absolute form by groups of individuals we call nations. This is in total contradiction to the original democratic conception of sovereignty" (pp. 132-133). The original democratic idea is that sovereignty resides in the community of the whole, Reves says, and the twentieth-century has realized that all humankind constitutes that community. The community of the whole then delegates its authority to the world, national, and local levels:

> Only if the people, in whom rests all sovereign power, delegate parts of their sovereignty to institutions created for and capable of dealing with specific problems, can we say that we have a democratic form of government. Only through such separation of sovereignties, through the organization of independent institutions, deriving their authority from the sovereignty of the community, can we have a social order in which men live in peace with each other, endowed with equal rights and equal obligations before law. Only in a world order based on such separation of sovereignties can individual freedom be real. (pp. 139-140)

Sovereignty, as the legitimate authority for planetary democracy, only derives from the community of all the people living upon the Earth. Nations can no longer be sovereign because, at least since the nineteenth century, the Earth has been understood as the planetary home of all humankind. Sovereign nation-states today exacerbate our planetary crises and destroy human freedom, which can only arise through a planetary community structured as a democratic federation dealing with problems at the local, national, and planetary levels. Neither can there be a common good for the planet arising from the general will of humanity without an Earth Federation under a genuine world constitution.

Jerry Tetalman and Byron Belitsos (2005) affirm this same truth today. They call national sovereignty "the profound political problem of our time" (p. 22). They argue that "if sovereignty has its source in the people, and if the world has progressively moved in the direction of increasing democracy in recognition of this fact, then this concept must have an even greater destiny than we see today" (p. 10). Sovereignty lies with the people of Earth, with the human community as a whole. They conclude that *"competitive nationalism is the greatest barrier to redefining our community as all humanity"* (p. 15).

The sovereign people of Earth properly delegate some of their authority to governments: to local government to deal with local problems, to regional or national government to deal with regional or national problems, and to world government to deal with global problems. In the absence of the latter not only is positive freedom impossible, but community and democracy disintegrate as well. By abjuring the holism of our situation, we exacerbate our present fragmentation at every level.

To think that there might be a democratic participatory formulation of a general will to a planetary common good simultaneously among some 193 sovereign nation-states is simply naïve utopianism of the worst kind. The strong democracy necessary to our present planetary situation is inhibited by the system of sovereign nation-states with their militarism, secrecy, nationalism, and competitive economics. In point of fact, the absolute sovereignty of nation-states has been steadily mitigated as the world has become more interdependent and as international law has evolved that recognizes universal principles applying to all states and persons, as within the new International Criminal Court (ICC).

However, this slow evolutionary processs is entirely inadequate to deal with the nexus of interdependent global crises. The Earth will be practically uninhabitable by the time the U.N. evolutionary process has evolved into something approximating strong democracy. On the other hand, strong democracy can be activated with relative ease if these *impediments to democracy* are removed and the *unity in diversity* of the peoples of Earth is institutionalized under a coherent *Constitution for the Federation of Earth.*

2.3 Democracy and Human Evolution

Reves' 1946 insight that the only legitimate community for the locus of sovereignty is that of the Earth occurred only yesterday. Few thinkers today adopt a long enough historic view of democracy to situate it within the framework of emergent human evolution. If democracy is associated with fundamental ideas of universal human rights, equality, freedom, and dignity, one would think that a broad historic view would be necessary, since democracy involves a set of moral principles universal to all human beings that have slowly emerged into clarity over the past 2500 years. What is there about human development on Earth that has given us this awareness of these universal features of human existence that must be institutionalized in systems that we call democratic? Why is it that current-day forms known as "democratic" fail to do this?

The literal meaning of the word "democracy" (i.e., "rule of the people," formulated within the dynamics of ancient Greek city-states) does not capture the full meaning of the phenomenon of democracy as this has emerged in human history. In our day, there is a vague intuition concerning the significance of democracy worldwide but hardly any deep comprehension of the true meaning of democracy as this is emerging in human affairs. Human beings have been on Earth between one and two million years, having evolved over previous millions of years from pre-human creatures (hominids), – and, ultimately over 4.6 billion years out of the evolutionary processes that define the development of life on Earth.

Some contemporary physicists posit the "Anthropic Principle" linking human evolution to the evolutionary matrix of the universe itself over perhaps twelve billion years since the Big Bang (cf. Harris 1991).

Not only have ever-more-complex biological and ecological systems emerged out of this process (systems interrelated as a series of wholes within ever-greater wholes to make up the ecology of nature and the dynamics of the evolving universe) but so have the values we associate with democracy. If human beings have the universal rights and dignity associated with the democratic imperative, then *values* have emerged out of this process as well. A creature has evolved out of the cosmic process bearing *intrinsic* dignity, innately valuable simply in virtue of being a human being. The universe is therefore clearly characterized by *emergent levels of being and value.*

And human beings themselves, in their *one to two million year history*, have been characterized by emergent levels of consciousness (reflecting being and value) from the primal oneness in which we were an unconscious part of nature, to the age of magic in which our symbolic and imaginative capacities began to develop, to the age of mythology during which we responded to the universe with an intimate, living I-Thou relationship, to the age of philosophy and science that began during the Axial Period in human history within the first millennium BCE (cf. Swimme and Berry 1992; Martin 2005a: Ch. 1).

Philosophical reflection concerning democracy, human values, justice, and the proper way to organize society began during this Axial Period, sometimes identified as the period between 800 and 200 BCE. Human beings had now evolved to the level of self-awareness and reasoning ability that made possible both philosophical thought and the scientific endeavor to understand the structures of the natural world. The Axial Period in the West witnessed the philosophical activity of Socrates, Plato, Aristotle, and the Stoic philosophers, all of whom reflected on the intrinsic values associated with human life and the best ways to create human society to preserve and enhance these values. Even though Plato and Aristotle associated the word "democracy" with the rule of the mob, both thinkers represent the emergence of awareness of the intrinsic value of human beings since both recognized value as something objective and inherent in our situation and attempted to formulate the best societies for preserving and enhancing this value.

The Stoics explicitly understood that the intrinsic dignity of human life was universal to all persons on Earth. Marcus Aurelius (121-180 CE) compared the universe to a city shared by all human beings whose rational souls made them essentially the same. A century earlier, Cicero had stated that "there is only one justice, which constitutes the bond among humans, and which was established by one law, which is right reason in commands and prohibitions" (2006:120-121). If democracy includes recognition of the universal dignity of human beings and the attempt to embody this in institutions that recognize this dignity, then the first systematic theorists of democracy were Plato, Aristotle, and the Stoic thinkers.

In Medieval philosophy, the sense of intrinsic value and dignity of human beings was primarily expressed in Biblical terms as persons made in the image of God and living as children of God. From St. Augustine and onwards through Erigena, St. Anslem, St. Thomas Aquinas, Duns Scotus, and Nicholas of Cusa, this common theme persists. These thinkers developed sophisticated metaphysical philosophies to articulate the nature of God and God's relationship to human beings and the world. The idea of intrinsic value linking human beings and God (of which we first became conscious during the Axial Period) here generates tremendous philosophical creativity and insight. Some of the basic values behind democracy were being elaborated even within this medieval theocratic social framework.

St. Thomas Aquinas (1225-1274), for example, saw the natural law (innate to God's creation) as reflecting the common good of humanity institutionalized in positive laws that were to be judged by their degree of justice, fairness, truth, and universality. He argued that any law made by a ruler not meeting these standards was no genuine law and need not be obeyed. Laws that violate justice (and hence the intrinsic dignity of persons) are not laws at all because what has emerged in human life is precisely consciousness of the reality of this intrinsic value. Aquinas formulated this awareness within the framework of medieval Church-dominated society, but the awareness nevertheless remains foundational for democracy.

Nevertheless, the foundational understanding of democracy that there is a universal reciprocity and common dignity among human beings was historically inhibited by medieval political and ecclesiastical forces, delaying its full emergence until first the Enlightenment and then the scientific paradigm-shift of the twentieth century. This foundational understanding constitutes our basic human ethical relationship (expressed, for example, in the universality of the golden rule, cf. Hick 1989: 313-314) that we have seen echoed in the democratic ethic of liberty, equality, and community. Despite the development outlined above from the ancient to medieval thinkers, the Roman Church derived its immense political and social power at least in part from clinging to the *imperium* of Roman class society and system of emperor worship transmuted into the Biblical God as king and emperor sitting at the top of a hierarchical world order beginning with the Pope and descending through the ranks to the lowest commoners and slaves.

When Christianity triumphed in the fourth century, it was able to draw on the overtly anthropomorphic characterization of God in the Old Testament that closely resembled the absolute power of the deified Roman Emperor. Morality, in this anthropomorphic and politically inspired perversion, became whatever God willed, and whatever God's representatives on Earth willed, since the earthly order was considered divinely ordained and mandated by this absolute potentate. The struggles during the middle ages and within the emerging early modern nation-states regarding the power of the Church, the aristocracy, and the absolute sovereignty of the king derived from this childlike, very anthropomorphic reading of the Bible and its clear political implications for those wanting to retain a political hierarchy of domination within society (cf. Rivage-Seoul 2007).

In many ways, the teachings of Jesus, insofar as we are able to discern them in the Gospels, powerfully reflect the democratic intuition of universal human equality and dignity and the simple reciprocal relationship of *agape*: "that you love one another; even as I have loved you" (John 13: 34). The temporal power of the Church (and the Roman and Medieval and early modern ruling classes that used Christianity to justify their hierarchical power and arbitrary authority) had to subvert the democratic spirit of Jesus' teaching through emphasizing the autocratic, arbitrary warrior god depicted in much of the Old Testament. In the sixteenth century political philosophy of Jean Bodin (1992), for example, the king was the embodiment of the nation, was divinely ordained, and his absolute power of making laws was justly reflected in the people's moral obligation to obey those laws.

Nevertheless, by the time of Renaissance thinkers like Johannes Althusius (1557-1638), the abstract notion of "the people" (the king or emperor were ultimately said to represent the people) begins to crystallize into the concept of the sovereignty of the people understood as an authority residing in the common humanity of people that granted or delegated specific powers to those who ruled in government and to whom those in authority were responsible. Sovereignty does not reside with the king or "optimates," Althusius affirms, but with the entire body of commonwealth of the realm. This idea of the sovereignty of the people becomes extremely important for recognizing that the intrinsic value that resides in the people both individually and collectively is the source and justification for the authority of government.

Democracy means just this: that no government is legitimate that does not (1) represent and institutionalize the intrinsic value of persons through its protection of human rights, equality, dignity, and freedom, (2) provide adequate mechanisms for assessing and encouraging the "general will" of this community, and (3) attempt to represent the common good of the community. Out of the Renaissance, we have seen, there also emerged an exaggerated individualism that tended to inhibit the reciprocity and community of the democratic spirit. Nevertheless, the development of the central understanding of democracy as an essential interfacing of liberty, equality, and community continued throughout the modern period.

This excessive individualism nevertheless underlined a central purpose of the democratic framework: to make possible the maximum development of the potential of each member of the community. The over-all *telos* of the emerging democratic idea was to combine this possibility *with the actualization of the potential of the human community itself.* It is not only individuals whose life-possibilities must be maximized, the human community itself actualizes the potential of our common humanity within history. The meaning of democracy includes both. The integrity of the community and the integrity of persons are interrelated and interdependent concepts.

In the seventeenth century Spinoza affirmed, like Althusius, that sovereignty belongs to the community as a whole and that the purpose of government is to institutionalize freedom through fostering the mutual cooperation of persons in the light of reason. Spinoza recognizes that freedom is a function of social organization and cooperation, not an *a priori* inherent characteristic of atomistic individuals who stand apart from society and withhold their "consent" from what does not suit their individual rights and interests. In the eighteenth century Jean-Jacques Rousseau uses the conception of the social contract (as does Locke), but in a way that goes far beyond the idea that government involves the consent of free individuals to serve their limited purposes of protecting their individualistic liberty and property.

For Rousseau, persons give up all their rights in the contract to the community and immediately receive them all back with a new and more profound dimension added. That profound dimension means that each is "as free as before" but now has the force of the entire community to protect and empower that freedom. People go from being mere private individuals to *citizens* protected and empowered by the common will and matrix of the community. The concept of freedom, therefore, makes a quantum leap in Rousseau's social contract from being a characteristic of isolated individuals to being a secure framework institutionalized within the entire community.

Later in the eighteenth century, Immanuel Kant states that he received his political inspiration from Rousseau. He went on to develop this new and more adequate conception the social contract into a full blown moral and theoretical framework for human life under "republican government." Kant understands that living under republican government (and the *moral community* thus constituted) is an absolute moral obligation for human beings. (This is expressed in the "categorical imperative" that we universalize our situation to one of equality under the law: see Chapter Eight below.) According to Kant, without the rule of laws legislated for the public good under the sovereignty of the people in order to establish freedom with its concomitant moral dimension, human beings are nothing more than savages or barbarians.

In his thought, the intrinsic dignity and value of human beings *complements* the absolute moral imperative to live under a government that institutionalizes and protects this intrinsic value. Political institutions are not a mere secondary set of external obligations tacked onto the ethical core of life. They are the public expression of the absolute commands of morality that arise from the free, rational capacity of human beings to legislate moral laws for themselves. The political community assumes its full significance in Kant's thought, becoming the matrix of the political freedom that mirrors our personal moral freedom. The foundation stone for strong, planetary democracy has been laid.

Upon this foundation, Hegel developed our understanding of society as an *integrated totality*, including civil society, family, business, government, and all other social relationships. Political institutions are an integral part of this whole, which is defined by moral relationships at every level. Today, we are in a position to understand this whole as necessarily involving global society and every person living on spaceship Earth. Following Hegel, Marx understood that we cannot idealize away the immense suffering of the majority who are victims of distorted, class-dominated totalities. We must critically examine this integrated totality of exploitation and domination and *transform* it into a democratic system.

Kant's 1795 essay *Perpetual Peace* also shows the rational impossibility and immorality of the system of sovereign nation-states, which is intrinsically a war system and destructive of civilized human values because it places nations outside the moral imperative to live under republican government protecting the freedom and dignity of each person as citizens and institutionalizing means for realizing the common good. Nations, Kant correctly reasoned, as sovereign, place themselves beyond and above the rule of enforceable republican law. The world order, therefore, remains a "savage and barbaric" one that defeats on every side rational, legally-constituted, empowered freedom. It remains our absolute moral obligation to strive for living under such legally-constituted freedom. Kant correctly reasons, therefore, that there can be no civilized living on the Earth unless the nations are federated under a single constitution that embodies the moral imperative of freedom and the rule of law for all humankind.

This understanding that the matrix of the community itself is the source of freedom for each individual, emphasized by Kant and Hegel, was further developed by Karl Marx, T. H. Green, Bernard Bosanquet, Ernest Baker, Benjamin Barber, Errol E. Harris, Jürgen Habermas and others into the realization that the community must be organized to develop more than the individual potentiality of each of its members. Government must also constitute the framework by which these individual potentialities mesh into a synergy directed toward the common good through the full participation of all the members of the community. Society as a whole has a potential that must be developed concomitantly with individual potential. Today, society as a whole can only be understood as human civilization upon the Earth.

This tradition serves as a fundamental critique of the "thin" and truncated forms of democracy that today face disintegration under the pressure of global crises for which they are entirely inadequate. Today, it is clear that, with the internet, computers, cell phones, and global satellite communications, such participation could be evoked everywhere on Earth with relative ease, making it possible for the first time in history to assess the will of the people of Earth concerning a global common good. Today, there are no institutions whatsoever for assessing and actualizing the common good of the people of Earth.

Even without institutions in place for assessing and implementing the general will of the citizens of Earth, we have a sense of what that general will would be like. Both within the thin democracies of Europe and North America and worldwide, few people desire global warming, environmental pollution, depletion of vital resources, massive poverty for 60% of the Earth, rampant preventable diseases, perpetual wars around the globe, or the threat of nuclear holocaust. Yet all these horrors continue to exist. The people of the U.S. (and worldwide) overwhelmingly opposed the U.S invasion of Iraq in 2003. It happened nevertheless. Thin democracies, like the liberal democratic theory at their root, are no real democracies. There are clearly immense forces in the world operating to defeat democracy and implement the will of the few at the expense of the majority and future generations.

In the twentieth century, Habermas understood that these insights derive, at the very least, from *our common ability to use language*: that the moral imperatives for equality, common participation, and equal rights to speak all inhere in the fundamental assumptions that make language possible (1998b; cf. Martin 2008 and Chapter Three below). Since all human beings share the capacity for language as one of our most defining and central characteristics, and since the presuppositions of the very possibility of language include equality, reciprocity, the right to speak, and procedural standards of justice, skeptics of the idea that there is an intrinsic human equality and worth have their answer.

The fundamental moral principles undergirding strong democracy inhere in our human situation as presuppositions for the very possibility of language, which all persons share. The imperative for organizing human life according to the principles of strong democracy becomes publicly verifiable and planetary in scope. The concept of democracy has evolved to the point where we understand that the nexus of liberty, equality, and community expresses values intrinsic to the human project itself. Individual liberty asserted over and against the equality of all and the community of the whole, destroys democracy and inhibits the actualization of our common human potential for a planetary community of peace with justice.

In the twentieth century, the basic concepts of democracy include government of the people, universal human rights and dignity, substantial economic equity, community as the root of liberty, the necessity of due process legal protections, and the societal ability to learn from experience and change accordingly (and, therefore, an evolving and maturing conception of what constitutes the common good). These concepts have spread throughout the world. *Democracy emerges as a holistic moral and institutional framework that embraces all people.* The intellectual and cultural foundations for human maturity have been laid. All we must do is understand their implications and make the decision to move from our parochial, partial, and adolescent forms of self-identification and their institutional embodiments to the planetary level.

Human thought has been maturing and expanding since its birth as a self-conscious process during the Axial Period. Today, it encompasses not only our planetary dimensions but the universe itself going back to its primal flaring forth some twelve billion years ago. We have outgrown the limited, historically bound perspectives that characterized every culture through at least the eighteenth or nineteenth centuries. As I described at length in *Millennium Dawn,* the twentieth century set us free to grow toward intellectual and spiritual maturity. Twentieth-century scholarship demonstrated clearly the culturally and historically bound nature of all traditional scriptures with their historically limited conceptions of truth.

This evolutionary process has culminated in the immense self-conscious awareness of human beings as creatures of reason, freedom, and purpose. Yet all around us there remain those who would reduce all of this to mechanistic bio-chemical responses, denying the fruits of this immense ascent. Hans Jonas responds that it is our moral obligation to recognize what is highest in ourselves and to shape the future in these terms:

> Reality, or nature, is one and testifies to itself in what it *allows* to come forth from it. What reality is must therefore be gathered from its testimony, and naturally from that which tells the most – from the most

manifest, not the most hidden; the most developed, not the least developed; the fullest and not the poorest – hence from the "highest" that is accessible to us. (1984: 69-70)

Democracy is not the simply the manifestation of another historically particular cultural framework (such as European enlightenment values). It arises from our developing rational and spiritual potential as an expression of our universal humanity and the foundation of our emerging holistic Earth civilization. The realization of positive freedom on a planetary level forms a *necessary condition* for the realization of our higher human potential for peace, justice, and sustainable prosperity. We must judge the "reality" of our world in terms of what is highest within it, from "the fullest and not the poorest."

We have reached the point in history where a true planetary maturity is possible for the first time, since the truths of unity, interdependency, and universality have now been scientifically grounded across the intellectual spectrum. This new human maturity will mean the triumph of civilization. We are now ready for, and capable of, action, since time is very short in the face of the planetary crises emerging in the past half century. We are under the imperative to create a world order commensurate with our new understanding of human life and the universe. This new holistic order must include effective government for Spaceship Earth. Only a planetary democracy under a single *Earth Constitution* can satisfy this imperative.

2.4 The Moral Imperative for Planetary Democracy

Human beings have lived within a *war-system* of one form or another throughout recorded history. We have become accustomed to believing that war is an inevitable and natural aspect of human affairs. At the same time, we have been historically struggling to become more fully human, more fully civilized, and to create systems of governance for ourselves that promote peace, justice, equality, and freedom. These systems of governance have largely centered around the idea of democracy, that, we have seen, was born in the ancient world and was slowly elaborated over the centuries.

In a well-known essay, first published in 1940, Margaret Mead argues that anthropological evidence clearly shows that "Warfare Is Only an Invention – Not a Biological Necessity." The question we need to ask, she insists, is how to replace warfare as an acceptable social institution:

> Propaganda against warfare, documentation of its terrible cost in human suffering and social waste, these prepare the ground by teaching people to feel that warfare is a defective social institution. There is further needed a

belief that social invention is possible and the invention of new methods which will render warfare as out of date as the tractor is making the plow, or the motor car the horse and buggy. A form of behavior becomes out of date only when something else takes its place, and, in order to invent forms of behavior which will make war obsolete, it is a first requirement to believe that an invention is possible. (2000: 22)

Mead apparently does not recognize that a form of social behavior at the heart of human civilization has already been invented that decisively replaces warfare – if that invention is extended and developed into its proper meaning and form. By developing the institutions and habits of democratic governance, people convert from arbitrary power relations involving the threat or use of violence to nonviolent methods of social change and organization. Differences and conflicts are settled through dialogue, education, courtroom procedures, mediators, fear of legal entanglements, social and moral pressure to obey the law, public debates, referendums, or elections.

Alternative visions of social change express themselves through political parties, nongovernmental organizations, or movements that nonviolently vie for recognition by an electorate or their fellow citizens in general. When the majority make decisions through a referendum or an election, the minority, the losing parties in a democracy, nonviolently accede to the results. Minorities acquiesce in the rule of the majority for its term of office and continue to dialogue and debate the issues to convince people of the direction that social change, or the next election, should take. Minority rights and freedoms remain protected even when their party or leaders are not in office. Critics of government policies or injustices with protected civil liberties join the discourse concerning the common good and the way into a better future.

Government officials, including police, are themselves governed by the rule of democratically legislated laws and are accountable to those laws. The possible use of force by the police is carefully regulated by law to protect the functioning of the democratic system itself. Minorities and nonviolent dissidents remain free to advocate change. The elected government voluntarily gives up power when its term is up or when it is voted out of power. Effective democratic government must indeed possess a monopoly on the legitimate use of force. However, we will see that this monopoly of legitimate force is precisely the opposite of war, for it is governed, regulated, and controlled by the principle of non-violence at the heart of the democratic idea.

Properly designed and understood democracy is the premier *peace system* for the Earth. Our task involves articulation of this "proper meaning and form," demonstrating its role as the triumph of human civilization and its function as the substitute for war and destruction. We will see that war is historically a social product of systems of privilege, dictatorship, and domination that continue to persist even within today's so-called democratic systems.

Non-democratic totalitarian regimes of any sort institutionalize the threat of arbitrary violence against any who challenge the system, protest the status quo, or who advocate an alternative future for the society. Totalitarian regimes are immoral and illegitimate for this very reason. They violate the fundamental moral dimension of human life in which every person has intrinsic value as a human being and an inherent human right to life, liberty, security of person, and political participation. Totalitarian regimes, in effect, constitute the threat of war, or outright war, against their own populations or against "enemy" populations, even if this is only done through the arbitrary detention, disappearance, or torture of a few dissidents as is the case with today's "war on terror."

The process of "manufacturing consent" within today's so-called democracies similarly violates the moral dimension of human life. The oligarchies of the rich and powerful who run these "democracies" behind the scenes depend on their control of the mass-media and other means of communication to propagandize populations into accepting vast economic inequality within a world of violence, potential war, and repression directed toward maintaining the dominance of these elites and protecting their financial interests. The capacity to use force on the part of government through police and military no longer serves to protect the equality and liberty of all but becomes the threat of violence against those who would challenge the system of inequality and injustice. Even nonviolent protesters experience the brutal wrath of the police along with arbitrary arrest and detention, as seen, for example, at the recent G-20 protests in Pittsburg, Pennsylavania.

War itself is immoral insofar as it involves the suspension of civilized democratic processes of decision-making and resorts to deciding conflict issues through violence and destruction. Arbitrary arrest, imprisonment, or torture, constitute war in one of its many clandestine and corrupt forms, as do so-called covert actions. In war, the decisions regarding the course of future events are left to the victors. Power relations replace democratic relations and the protection of the intrinsic dignity of persons with their rights to life, liberty, and security of person is sacrificed at the terrible alter of institutionalized and systematic violence directed at subduing and destroying a perceived enemy, whether that enemy be individuals, groups, or entire nations. "Just war theory," so called, is primarily a cover-up for this profoundly immoral set of relationships. (Chapter Eight will explore these issues at some length.)

In his famous 1946 essay, "Neither Victims nor Executioners," Albert Camus argues that our world has come to the point where a fundamental choice faces humankind, for "a crisis which tears the whole world apart must be met on a world scale.... Either we accept the consequences of being murderers ourselves, or the accomplices of murderers," or we choose to repudiate murder and violence through establishing "international democracy.... A world parliament...which will enact legislation which will exercise authority over national governments" (2002: 73 & 67). We must choose between the present system of violence with its fear and silence and the "universal intercommunication" of human beings – either continuation of the global system of war or affirmation of a system of peace based on truly free dialogue and debate.

Democracy, Camus understands, represents the institutional embodiment of a *peace system*. Peace does not mean a world of saints where people do not have violent emotions, hatreds, fears, conflicts, or selfish motives. Peace means the *institutionalization of procedures and social processes* minimizing the possibility of turning to the use or threat of violence to get one's way, or to get the way of one's party, group, religious ideology, or nation. It means, in Camus' terms, a civilization based on dialogue (*civilization du dialogue*) – the institutionalization of which is planetary democracy.

Democratic processes constitute, therefore, the central alternative to violence and war. The world does not need first and foremost to evolve spiritually toward an inner peace that will someday translate into outer peace. It needs first and foremost to *institutionalize* a peace system in the form of genuine democracy. Sherover describes this procedural aspect of democracy:

> The primary bond holding a particular group together is its center of a common concern and shared evaluative outlook concerning it. That shared interpretative outlook includes as the core of its elements, as the cement that binds its members together, its own implicitly understood way to make whatever decisions it is joined to make. When these ways are flouted, members feel betrayed. An interpretive community holds together primarily by the ways it proceeds to resolve disagreements within its common bond by accommodating those who disagree....
>
> What binds a group together is a twofold commitment: to face the future together in terms of its unifying concerns *and also* to an acceptable procedure to decide how to do so. The import of procedure is precisely that it defines the freedom of its members, individually within it and together in future-referring prescriptive terms. (1989: 82-83)

In the face of our numerous interrelated global crises, we lack both a mechanism for unifying our concerns globally and an acceptable procedure by which to act on these concerns as we move into the future. We lack any framework for unifying our planet and the democratic procedures to nonviolently act on our concerns. Today's super-wealthy banking elite that today controls the world's money supply forms an undemocratic oligarchy in tandem with gigantic multinational corporations devoted exclusively to accumulation of private profit for their investors. This oligarchy controls 47% of the world's wealth and power for themselves (with the help of massive institutionalized violence – see Chapters Four through Six below).

They have no interest in unifying the world democratically or facing a common future in a relation of equality to the rest of humanity and giving up their lives of unimaginable luxury and power. This ruling oligarchy promotes today's global "governance" that manipulates the nation-states in its own interests through recruiting the powerful imperial nations to protect their planetary system of domination and exploitation. The people of the world, desperate at global chaos, violence, and destruction, descend ever-more easily into hate, fear, fascism, and violence. Nation-states, responding to both these forces, arm themselves to the teeth, making peace increasingly fragile and unlikely.

The U.N. clearly represents a major failure in this respect since it functions primarily as an ideological posturing society in which each nation promotes its self-interest within a profoundly undemocratic procedural framework. It, too, has been colonized by the world's ruling oligarchy. A peace system on Earth means precisely democratic procedures for decision making protected by an *Earth Constitution* that articulates both unifying goals and a common future (ending war, securing human rights, creating universal prosperity, protecting the planetary environment and future generations, respecting the legitimate internal affairs of nations, etc.). It also means the procedures for addressing these goals through "resolving disagreements within its common bond by accommodating those who disagree." In other words: peace can only be secured by establishing the Earth as a *holistic system of unity in diversity* under a democratic world parliament.

The present fragmented system of sovereign nation-states evolved during the early modern era out of the earlier feudal system. By the seventeenth century serious thinkers were already recognizing *the nation-state system as a war system.* Beyond the borders of sovereign nation-states there is no rule of enforceable law, no democratic procedures for resolving differences, no unifying vision of common concerns, no institutionalized framework in which conflicts can be adjucated by enforceable mediation or judicial decisions, no processes of election or dialogue allowing for nonviolent transitions of power or other forms of social change. There is only *power politics*: the strategic and deceitful use of language called diplomacy, the implicit threat of violence, or the overt use of violence to serve national interests, which are generally the interests of the ruling oligarchies of wealth and power.

In the seventeenth century, Spinoza recognized that states will wage war according to their perceived national interests as they see fit, since there is no higher authority that can arbitrate or mitigate the resort to violence. Similarly, British philosopher Thomas Hobbes declared that outside of their borders states confront one another "as gladiators." Both Spinoza and Hobbes referred to human relationships outside the rule of enforceable law as "the state of nature" (a condition in which there is no enforceable law and no effective government) which Hobbes declared to be a "war of all against all."

In the relation between sovereign nations, therefore, there exists a condition of war, even when no active fighting is taking place. In the absence of any governmental authority above the nations that can institutionalize peaceful processes of change and decision-making, all that is left is violence or the threat of violence (always implicit within the "diplomacy" conducted by militarized nation-states). This condition violates the most fundamental of ethical principles, we have seen, and is inherently immoral. In his *Philosophy of Right* (1821), Hegel declares "if no agreement can be reached between particular wills, conflict between states can only be settled by war" (#334). In *Perpetual Peace* (1795), Kant also describes the relation between sovereign nations as the immoral condition of war.

During the entire modern period, nations have found themselves in this condition (i.e. in a world of other sovereign nations recognizing no law above themselves) and have accordingly developed military capabilities to prepare for defense and for the possibility of war. Citizens have acquiesced in this process believing that they could successfully create nonviolent institutionalized processes of social change and conflict resolution *within* their nations (through constitutionally republican or democratic states) while needing to prepare for violent conflict in their nation's external affairs. Kant stresses correctly that this is a tragic and immoral course of action to take.

If one finds oneself in a situation of *defacto war* a (where there are no democratic institutions in place protecting processes of nonviolent change), then *the central moral obligation dictates that we escape that condition* as rapidly as possible. To remain in that condition is to live in an immoral relationship (of *defacto* war) to all other persons in all other countries beyond one's own. To be a government or citizen of such a nation is to exist in an *immoral* relationship with all other nations and their citizens.

We have seen that democracy institutionalizes moral relationships between persons by removing arbitrary power relationships. Beyond the nation-state nothing even remotely resembling democracy exists. Clearly the U.N. has no similarity to real, democratic government, nor does the World Bank, IMF, World Trade Organization, the global banking system, or the powerful system of multinational corporations.

The central moral obligation placed upon human beings under the system of sovereign nation-states, therefore, is not to prepare for possible war and self-defense but to leave the condition of actual and *defacto* war as rapidly as possible. *Our central moral obligation is to create democratic world government so that all human relationships are brought under a morally justifiable peace system and that our relation with all other persons on the planet becomes the moral one in which their life, liberty, and security of person is institutionally protected equally with our own.*

We must choose either the way of murder, or being accessories to murder, or the way of dialogue – authentic democracy. The only fully moral relationship with other persons (any and all other persons) necessarily involves a democratic framework. Under the present world system, no such relationship is available with the majority of other persons on the planet and we are thrown back to the condition of war: the threat or use of violence, fear, and enforced silence to solve conflicts or create social change.

2.5 Maturity and Democracy

The development of the self-consciousness necessary for objective reasoning, philosophical reflection, and scientific investigation became possible for human beings for the first time during the Axial Period of human history during the first millennium BCE. This was only yesterday on the scale of human development. Since the time of Plato, Aristotle and the Stoics our brief 2500 year period of reflection has led us through several phases that moved from the initiation of the world's major religions within ancient slave societies to metaphysical articulations of the relation of God and the world during the medieval era, and to the Renaissance with its elaboration of modern individualism, progressive scientific discovery, and democratic political theory.

The changes have been so rapid and the institutions by which we organize our common life so historically bound and haphazard in nature that we have been caught by surprise, so to speak. Planetary crises that threaten our future on Earth have come upon us unawares. Both individually and collectively, these crises arise from our lack of planetary perspective and maturity. Many people remain trapped to some extent in medieval modes of religious thought, giving rise to dogmatisms and symbologies that impede the development of democracy on the Earth.

Others continue to think in the early modern categories that inform the philosophy of global capitalism: the perfect mathematical formulas by which atomized human units maximizing their rational self-interest in a market of free competition theoretically generate a maximized common prosperity and productivity. Still others are philosophically caught in the centuries old set of assumptions behind the system of sovereign nation-states that today, like religious dogmatism and capitalism, seriously impede our transformation to planetary maturity.

The same is true of democracy. The somewhat haphazard, trial and error democracies that arose out of the French and American revolutions in the eighteenth century and the many constitutional democracies that followed, dotting the globe, have been the subject of attack and criticism from a wide range of critics, from Alex de Tocqueville to Leo Strauss. We will examine some of these criticisms below. The important point here is that *democracy serves as an ethical and regulative ideal of human maturity,* and its institutionalization is premised on the moral obligation of human beings to relate to one another as free and equal citizens under common, impartially enforced and democratically legislated laws, to leave the condition of *defacto* war in which peace is dependent on the whims, emotions, inclinations, or perceived self-interests of persons or nation-state actors, and *establish* a morally and institutionally grounded system of peace.

As we will see in Chapter Three, contemporary educators, psychologists, and scholars of spirituality have arrived at an amazing theoretical consensus – what appears most significant about human beings involves our *potential* for moral, psychological, and spiritual growth, not some fixed, hard-wired aggressive human nature. We are not trapped within some genetically determined "violent" human nature or fixed as a "unit of rational self-interest" or forever discontented by a "struggle with irrational libidinal urges" as some modern philosophers, economists, and psychologists have assumed. Our conceptual, imaginative, and moral potential is immense and may be practically unlimited according to many contemporary thinkers.

Chapter Six of *Millennium* Dawn and Chapter Two of *Ascent to Freedom* described at some length the significant consensus within contemporary psychology concerning levels of human maturity and the *nisus* for wholeness, integration, and self-realization that characterizes normal human development. These results need not be repeated here. We know a great deal about what constitutes human maturity. Abraham Maslow's well-known "hierarchy of needs," we have seen, tells us a great deal about the process of self-realization, growth, and integration into ever-greater wholes that takes place in mature people once their more basic needs for food and security have been met. If we wish to take the next step in human maturity, we must organize our institutions on this planet to make this possible.

We possess a potential to become mature, loving, world-embracing, creative, and tolerant persons who daily continue to learn and grow ever more in the direction of wholeness and spiritual openness throughout life. Persons approximate *planetary maturity* who have reached a level that embraces the whole of human and natural life on Earth with their love and affirmation. Planetary maturity reflects a certain level of integration that is within the capacity of nearly every human being. Peace and justice will only fully arrive on our planet when we as a species have attained a reasonable level of planetary maturity. However, to date, *we have severely limited our growth as a species by clinging to centuries-old institutions that inhibit the development of democratic and peaceful relationships.*

We are bound and limited today, not because our potential for transformation is limited but because the institutions through which we organize our lives strangle that potential by structurally imposing regimes of fear, selfishness, pettiness, incommensurability, and immaturity. The development of planetary maturity, while happening all around us as an inevitable result of the human evolutionary upsurge, remains truncated for most because of these outdated, centuries-old institutions that are no longer adequate to our planetary crises and globalized situation. Democracy cannot flourish, thereby further developing our planetary maturity, under these conditions.

Planetary maturity first and foremost characterizes persons who experience human existence from a global and holistic perspective. We are a single species, everywhere nearly identical with one another, that has colonized the Earth to the point where we must become its stewards, lovers, and protectors. Nations, races, ethnicities, cultures, and religions are all secondary to this fundamental reality. Our thinking about how to protect the marvelous diversity of nations, races, ethnicities, cultures and religions must originate from this basic truth. Without this gigantic unity, human life becomes a Hobbesian imperialist struggle where all these multiplicities compete with one another and the stronger assimilate, dominate, destroy, or digest the weaker. Such a relationship, we have seen, is deeply immoral, and our central obligation is to exit it as rapidly as possible and institute authentic democracy in its place.

If we begin from the oneness of humanity living on spaceship Earth with the responsibility to protect and nurture our planetary home, then the first conceptual error that must be jettisoned involves the assumption of the *incommensurability* of these multiplicities. Nations cannot be understood as sovereign territorial power centers standing guard over absolute borders in a warlike posture of defense and mutually hostile security against one another. This kind of fragmented thinking will destroy our future on this planet, a future that must inevitably include the oneness of humanity governing our spaceship home. The diversity of nations can only be preserved in a valuable, moral, and non-lethal form if they are joined in a unity that de-absolutizes that diversity and protects each equally under the rule of democratic law.

Exactly the same principle applies to the other diversities mentioned. Races, ethnicities, cultures and religions can and must be preserved in their wonderful diversity and beautiful multiplicity. But this cannot be done through any "clash of civilizations" or struggle for ascendency and dominance of any segment of these diversities, a situation which is inevitable under our current global institutions. The rule of law coupled with a community spirit of mutual respect remains our only option.

Thinking in terms of incommensurables follows this same basic pattern: "since the United States is a sovereign nation we must protect its borders and territory from all other people on the Earth" (or) "since Christianity is the Truth then Islam must be a false religion" (or) "the white race and the black race are incompatible and should be living in separate but equal conditions." Such thinking not only falsifies reality (structured according to the principle of *unity in diversity*) but lays the groundwork for an unpacified world order – a continuation of the immoral struggle of imperialism, lust for domination, and mutual destruction of cultures, religions, and nations that has characterized nearly every grouping for the past several millennia.

We can only live in peace, freedom, and prosperity on this planet if we take our stand on the immense truth of human unity informed by diversity, and on the right of *every* human being to be nonviolently diverse. This is the first principle of planetary maturity. Our primary home is the Earth, not this nation, religion, culture, ethnicity, or race. This does not at all mean that we must be unfaithful to the religious, national, or cultural roots that nurtured us and formed our selves within their matrix. Just the opposite. To be really true to my roots means that my roots must contribute to the rich diversity of human life through being preserved and protected through the only truthful means that can effectively preserve them: the gigantic unity of our common human project on the Earth in the form of effective planetary democracy.

The immense wealth of twentieth-century scholarship in nearly all these areas of diversity (religions, cultures, races, ethnicities, etc.) has challenged across the board the traditionally assumed incommensurability of these diversities. Scholarship is even beginning to challenge the assumed incommensurability of the nation-states, as I summarized in my *Ascent to Freedom*, although the mythology and dogmatisms of the nation-state have proved so powerful that a planetary perspective in this regard lags somewhat behind the insight into the relativity of these other diversities. Relativism within the unity of the development of our species and the overcoming of the error of incommensurability does not mean giving up one's religion or one's patriotism. It means bringing religion or patriotism to a higher and more encompassing level where they properly belong and where their destructive and demonic features have been overcome with love, respect, and toleration through embracing a more encompassing holism.

Unity is not a secondary feature added onto the diversity. We are not trying to build the higher unity of the religions or the nations by adding together the multiplicity of religions or nations. *The unity is inseparable from the diversity at the most fundamental level.* What we as a civilization have not yet understood fully and refuse to see is the *truth of unity.* The diverse multiplicities of the world, from creatures to ecosystems to social systems to nation-states, emerge from a structure of *unity in diversity* that encompasses and empowers them.

Religious fundamentalism, so wide-spread today, especially in Christianity, Judaism, Islam, and Hinduism, involves an immature and even demonic response to the results of twentieth-century scholarship and the evolutionary demands of human maturity. Rather than moving to a higher and deeper religious level of existence in response to the historical and cultural relativity that scholarship has revealed, rather than discerning the more profound and encompassing truth at the heart of each of these religions, fundamentalists have rejected the development of human intellectual and psychological maturity altogether. They live today in a schizophrenic dual world – using all the results of science and scholarship that encompass our lives in our transformed technological world, on the one hand, and denying any validity to that scholarship and science in the service of their idolatrously worshipped image of God, on the other. Such cognitive dissidence cannot endure, although it may cause immense harm while it persists, as it is doing today in the United States, Israel, India, Iran, and elsewhere.

Planetary maturity, then, is not merely the personal maturity to which each of us as individuals can aspire. It involves the species consciousness that each of us assimilates to one degree or another. (Karl Marx used the phrase "species being.") Our species consciousness involves our awareness of ourselves as one species inhabiting the Earth and our understanding of the progressive developments of science and the multi-faceted planetary cultural developments that reveal our deeper unities across the board. It beckons us to begin living on a more profound and deeper level of existence – a level right in front of our faces if we would but choose to recognize and embrace it.

Christian philosopher and scientist Pierre Teilhard de Chardin (1959) termed this growing species awareness the *noösphere*. In the emergent evolutionary process, he argued, the physical earth (the geosphere) was encompassed by an enveloping field of life (the biosphere), and, during the evolution of human life out of the biosphere, another dimension of reality emerged, encircling and encompassing the biosphere, the reality of mind (*noösphere*). The inherent goal of these developments, he argued, based on his studies of human evolution, involves a profound unity, the *unity in diversity* of all the peoples and religions of Earth. Teilhard calls this emergent unity the Omega point or the Christ of universal love and affirmation – all individuals and things caught up together in the bond of loving unity that preserves and enhances their distinct individuality. The inner spiritual dimension of the world and the outer physical dimension now become integrated together in an era of fulfillment – the kingdom of God on Earth.

Such planetary consciousness (here derived from the study of evolution) has long been a characteristic of mystics, sages, and the most advanced thinkers. It was not until the scientific revolutions of the twentieth century that it became established by empirical and experimental means. (The works of Errol E. Harris have demonstrated the latter at length in terms of the evolutionary developments of science and reason.) The wisest people throughout the ages have understood the deeper unities, whereas the majority have nearly always been trapped in partial perspectives, within the illusions of incommensurable diversities that gave priority to the cultural, religious, ethnic, racial, or national fragment within which they happen to have been born and raised. By contrast, twentieth-century Indian sage Sri Aurobindo expresses planetary wisdom in the following way:

> The oneness that is secretly at the foundation of all things, the evolving spirit of nature is moved to realize consciously at the top, the evolution moves through diversity, from a simple to a complex oneness. Unity the race moves towards and must one day realize.... The truest order is that which is founded on the greatest possible liberty; for liberty is at once the condition of vigorous variation and the condition of self-finding. Nature secures variation by division into groups and insists on liberty by the force of individuality in the members of the group. Therefore the unity of the human race to be entirely sound and in consonance with the deepest laws of life must be founded on free groupings, and the grouping again must be the natural association of free individuals. (1962: 490-491)

> At the same time, while diversity is essential for power and fruitfulness of life, unity is necessary for its order, arrangement, and stability. Unity we must create, but not necessarily uniformity. If man could realize a perfect spiritual unity, no sort of uniformity would be necessary; for the utmost play of diversity would be securely possible on that foundation. If again he could realize a secure, clear, and firmly held unity in the principle, a rich, even an unlimited diversity in its application might be possible without any fear of disorder, confusion or strife. (1962: 401)

The perennial intuition of the world's sages of the oneness at the foundation of all things includes as its complement the insight that oneness works through diversity and, in the case of human beings, liberty. If our groupings are to be "free groupings," we must freely choose our national, religious, cultural, or ethnic allegiances: freely affirm, for example, the religion into which we happen to have been born. Unity comprises the *necessary* (and inevitable) component of reality with regard to "order, arrangement, and stability." Without unity there is only the fratricide of fanatically held visions of incommensurability. However, to the extent that true unity is realized, uniformity is not necessary, for true unity gives maximum play to liberty and diversity without ever compromising that unity.

Here we have the foundational insights of both planetary maturity and planetary democracy. Democracy means institutions designed to ensure fundamental respect for individuals with regard to their dignity and rights as human beings. But it also means an encompassing unity in which all are equal and these principles are universally applied within the framework of a supporting community. The concrete procedures by which people participate in the polity and by which decisions take place are of secondary concern to these founding principles.

There may be a variety of ways that diverse cultures or nations may wish to institutionalize the *unity in diversity* of planetary democracy within their specific conditions. But there cannot be any significant democracy on the local level (in nations or communities) if the conditions of incommensurability remain (this is *our* nation or community or religion whose territory or "truth" we defend against the encroachments of all others). Witness the immense suffering that Zionism and exclusivist Judaism have visited upon the Palestinians and on the world. Witness the immense suffering that "God bless America" has wrought upon the world.

For the very act of exclusion of "the others" (those who are not us) is arbitrary and undemocratic in the extreme. Democratic communities must indeed decide whose voice or vote will be counted from the local to the planetary level (e.g., should children, retarded persons, prison inmates, or mental patients have a vote?). However, this decision must be made on rational and practical grounds, not on the basis of irrational incommensurables. Ultimately, democracy can only be planetary democracy, in which all local levels are empowered through democratic participation in the unity of a whole from which no one is excluded on the basis of incommensurability. May God bless the entire Earth and its creatures.

We are all one human family, all one interdependent and highly social species, living on one spaceship Earth, all with the same universal human rights and dignity. If these rights are violated anywhere on the planet, then I and my community are compromised, and I cannot pretend to be living under democracy. If my community excludes anyone on Earth because "in that other country the government does not recognize these basic rights," then my community cannot be a democracy premised on *universal* rights and dignity. Democracy is meaningless if it remains a mere "ideal" and not institutionalized in ways that make universality effective and real. Either there is planetary maturity and planetary democracy or there is no real democracy.

All forms of incommensurability, all absolute fragmentations (whether religious, nation-state, racial, or any other) destroy the fundamental principle of democracy. You cannot have democracy for the few (whether it involves one nation or one elite group), for then it is not democracy but some new form of elitism or segmented privilege. Democracy can only mean liberty, equality, and community for *all* persons on Earth – for human rights and human dignity are universal and demand universal institutional embodiment.

Those who reject planetary democracy embodied in a civilian, non-military Earth Federation in favor of a plethora of tiny, egalitarian communities living peacefully on the Earth are in truth enemies of democracy. For what they affirm is both a practical and theoretical impossibility. Both Noam Chomsky and Howard Zinn appear to fall into this group advocating a naïve syndicalism without any universal rule of law.

One cannot bury one's head in the sand on some local beach and pretend that the dignity and freedom of those on some distant shore will take care of itself. Chomsky and Zinn should know better. We are a planetary community and responsible for one another as citizens of Spaceship Earth. As Chomsky himself insists, "we are responsible for the likely consequences of our actions." The likely consequences of our focusing on local communities to the exclusion of our common human responsibility is nothing short of planetary disaster.

Planetary maturity involves the deep consciousness in action of this *unity in diversity*. Planetary democracy is the *institutionalization* of this *unity in diversity* in effective, practical procedures for governing ourselves. Uniting the Earth under a single *Earth Constitution* will foster planetary maturity among the inhabitants of Earth in an immense and natural way. Claiming that we must wait until the majority of people on Earth *evolve* into planetary maturity is a dangerous fallacy. The institutions now structuring our world system foster precisely the opposite of planetary maturity.

As Errol E. Harris says above, sovereign states are *impediments* to solving our planetary problems. Capitalism fosters greed, egoism, the commodification of existence, lack of compassion for people and nature, and the lust for power and domination. The system of sovereign nation-states fosters absolute fragmentation of the world into artificially defined, militarized territories that treats these political units as incommensurable with one another. It structures our relationships with all other peoples on the planet into the immoral relation of *defacto* war. By contrast, planetary democracy and reasonable global equity form the foundation stones for our next step in actualizing planetary maturity.

This maturity can be defined as the ever-deeper realization of the unity of our humanity and our human situation in relationship to the multiplicity of ways that we are interdependent, including our interdependence regarding the possibilities within us for truth, justice, freedom, equality, and dignity. Society as a collective endeavor becomes a foundational reality of human life, prior to the largely illusory individuality that today makes successful or exceptional individuals believe they have accomplished something entirely beyond or independent of what society has made possible for them. We stand not only on the shoulders of giants; we stand on the shoulders of the millions who made those giants possible.

And society today is planetary society, for multiplicity of cultures and ways of living in the world all share the fundamental human dynamics. Communication today extends worldwide and instantaneously. We all live as inherently social animals (as Aristotle declared), and because of this sameness we are all part of one planetary society (as the Stoics affirmed) in spite of the marvelous and welcome diversity of cultures, languages, and traditions at the regional level.

Planetary democracy is the institutionalization of this understanding that fosters the fulfillment of our common life and the realization of our highest human potential as this emerges from our common life. The institutional structures by which we operate today and that we call "democracy" are far from the collective realization of our human potential that lives at the heart of the democratic ideal and the democratic thrust of human history. By and large, today's structures appear not only as weakly democratic but as fundamentally undemocratic. Whatever gestures we have made toward political democracy are defeated by monopoly capitalism and the system of sovereign nation-states. We must transform all the forces that now hinder planetary maturity and planetary democracy: unfettered capitalism, nation-state sovereignty, consumerism, colonized public spaces, lack of unified global planning and coordination, religious fundamentalism, militarism, and immature thinking in terms of incommensurable diversities.

The only effective path to rapidly transform each of these forces proceeds through global government under an *Earth Constitution*. We are at the end of the line and time has run out. We do not have another 50 years to "evolve" the unworkable U.N. Charter into a democratic *Earth Constitution*. The only way for human beings to actualize their potential for authentic democracy is through *founding* a decent world order on a unifying document that embodies planetary democracy from the very beginning.

The *Constitution for the Federation of Earth* is the best possible candidate for such a new beginning for democracy and our human project. It is widely available, translated into twenty-three languages, ready to be actualized, and can easily replace the U.N. Charter while leaving all the valuable agencies of the U.N. intact. Planetary maturity (our human and species maturity) includes democratic maturity. How this is possible was shown at length in my *Ascent to Freedom* and in the chapters below. If we are to create a decent future for our children and future generations, then these two forces must rapidly coalesce as one unified civilization of *unity in diversity* upon the Earth.

The following chapter explores the roles of education, reason, and fundamental forms of spirituality for the realization of planetary maturity and global democracy. It relates these themes to the most fundamental philosophical questions concerning what it means to be a human being (or as Kant put these questions: what can we know, how must we act, and what may we hope?) while at the same time elucidating the profound contributions many thinkers have made to understanding the dynamics of human transformation toward a liberated, mature world order.

The three chapters comprising Part Two (Chapters Four through Six) go deeply into our current world disorder of immense violence and injustice and show the dynamics of a global conversion to nonviolence and justice. They attempt to show that this conversion is both fundamental and practically realizable, for both the technical resources and human capacity exist in abundance for actualizing the *Renaissance of the Twenty-first Century*. All that is lacking is clear thinking about our human situation in conjunction with the political will to make planetary democracy a reality. Part Three (Chapters Seven through Ten, "Dawning of a Democratic Earth Civilization") examines in some detail how we can institutionalize both nonviolence and justice in human affairs. It provides a road map for acting here and now to create a decent world order for today and tomorrow.

Chapter Three

Education and Values
for a Democratic World Order

*Laying the Foundations for
a New Planetary Ethic*

Certainly freedom is the central theme of the history of modern political philosophy.... Those who were concerned to prevent and resist despotism insisted on the natural rights of the individual as an unchallengeable limit to the powers of the ruler. But, in the end, philosophers came to see that actual freedom was attainable only in a well-organized society regulated by law enforced by a government which ruled by popular consent.... In such a community freedom is not simply license, it is not just the right to be left alone – to be unrestricted in pursuing one's personal aims. It is the security of life in a society of interacting and co-operating citizens, the mutual intercourse of whom generates a tradition of common thought and will aiming at a common good.

Errol E. Harris

Life is really very beautiful, it is not this ugly thing that we have made of it; and you can appreciate its richness, its depth, its extraordinary loveliness only when you revolt against everything – against organized religion, against tradition, against the present rotten society – so that you as a human being find out for yourself what is true.

Jiddu Krishnamurti

W hat is a human being? What does it mean to be rational? To be free? To be moral? To have dignity, integrity, or the capacity for excellence as a human being? What kind of social, economic, and educational order is necessary for human beings who are rational, free, and moral? Is it possible, as Krishnamurti says, to find in ourselves what is true? Can we be reborn from a fragmented false consciousness to a truer, more holistic consciousness? These questions involve the entire meaning of our human project on planet Earth.

These questions ask about a creature that has emerged out of the cosmic process itself, perhaps twelve billion years in the making, a creature that has emerged out of the "immense journey" of life on this planet, perhaps four billion years in process, a creature who is about two million years old on this planet, who, only yesterday, emerged into self-awareness and developed the ability to ask these questions. They are questions concerning which contemporary science has much to say.

Human beings have the capacity, attested by mystics of every century and religion, to live with a direct awareness of the fullness of existence prior to language, ideologies, or conceptual frameworks. Persons at their highest levels of development, discussed below, often mention moments of such awareness engendering a creative, responsive relationship to all of life. Such persons also often assert the emergence of universal values in their lives. These facts indicate a developmental potential that may well exist within all human beings.

Our developmental potential is not vitiated by the immense variation of human practices, customs, and beliefs among thousands of cultures worldwide. We have seen that anthropologists have begun to discern clearly the substantial number of "human universals" that characterize every person on Earth and define our responses, habits, instincts, and cognitive abilities as uniquely human and common to all of us (D. Brown 1991). As Steven Pinker, professor of psycho-linguistics at Harvard University, expresses this: "Just as there is a universal design to the computations of grammar, there is a universal design to the rest of the human mind – an assumption that is not just a hopeful wish for human unity and brotherhood, but an actual discovery about the human species that is well motivated by evolutionary biology and genetics" (1994: 425-426).

Education involves, at its deepest level, an implicit conception of what it means to be human, or at least an intimation that this is a central question to be asked and that we have universal human abilities that need to be actualized. Education intuits the centrality of such questions to understanding what we need to know about our place in the family, the society, the planet, and the cosmos. It addresses our highest human potentialities. Buried within our humanity, within our potential as human beings, lies a general image of what it means to be human, a broad, ideal image traditionally shared by nearly all cultures and religions.

This image most often connects us with the very foundations of the universe, to Mother-nature, to the One behind duality, or to God. It refers to us as "children of God," as bearers of "Buddha-nature," the "*logos*" common to all persons, or as outward reflections of an inner "Atman" that is both universal and sacred. It is an image that intimates the "utopian surplus" that lives within our vast rational and spiritual potential. Twentieth-century science and scholarship have discovered an empirical grounding for this perennial image (cf. Martin 2005: Chs. 4-5). It is the goal of education to evoke this image and to actualize our deeper human potential.

3.1 Philosophical and Social-Scientific Understanding of Human Development

Social-scientific studies and philosophical works by such thinkers as John Dewey, Jean-Paul Sartre, Lawrence Kohlberg, Jürgen Habermas, Erich Fromm, Paulo Freire, and others have borne out the idea that there are a series of developmental stages through which persons have the capacity to grow. These stages include not only intellectual development but development in understanding universal moral principles. This trajectory of moral and intellectual development presents us with a conception of human maturity that includes a broad image (capable of a wide diversity of embodiments) of rational, free, moral persons acting as responsible citizens within rational, free, just societies, and living at peace with all other persons with whom we share this planet.

According to Sartre, the capacity to develop toward a transformed future reflects the existential structure of our personal growth as well as our historically developing human project. At the heart of human temporality lies the image of a redeemed future characterized by ever-greater freedom and "unification" of the human enterprise (1996: 96). The very structure of human action involves actualizing our possibilities, and, therefore, that future exists as a "real and permanent" feature of our present actuality:

> For us man is characterized above all by his going beyond a situation, and by what he succeeds in making of what he has been made – even if he never

recognizes himself in his objectification. This going beyond we find at the very root of the human.... Now this surpassing is conceivable only as the relation of the existent to its possible. Furthermore, to say what man "is" is also to say what he can be – and vice versa.... It is by transcending the given toward the field of possibles and by realizing one possibility from among all the others that the individual objectifies himself and contributes to making history.... Therefore we must conceive of possibility as doubly determined. On the one side, it is at the very heart of the particular action, the presence of the future as *that which is lacking* and that which, by its very absence, reveals reality. On the other hand, it is the real and permanent future which the collectivity forever maintains and transforms. (1989: 206-207)

Aristotle, as early as the fourth century BCE, had already identified the temporal structure of human life (and the universe) as the process of actualizing potentiality. For human beings, this meant actualizing a potential lying within each of us for the development of our *specifically human rational qualities.* Proper human development moved towards *phronesis* (or intellectual and moral excellence) that could be actualized by most human beings within a broad range of specific forms of virtue.

Immanuel Kant, in the 18th century, added to this the idea that rational autonomy is linked to an inherent human dignity that is immeasurable (beyond all price) precisely because each person is a free, moral agent emerging from the matrix of the mysterious and unknowable ultimate reality that encompasses our lives (1964). These three concepts together, the existential structure of human life directed towards ever-greater freedom and unification (emphasized by Sartre), the development of our human rational and spiritual potentialities toward ever-greater excellence, and the recognition that each person has intrinsic dignity inherent in his or her moral freedom, form the basis for understanding the connection between education and values.

In *Millennium Dawn,* I linked this ontogenetic development of which each person is capable with the idea of phylogenetic stages through which our species has been growing toward human maturity for at least the past 50,000 years (Chs. 1 & 6). Education and values are linked through the stages of intellectual and moral growth common to all human beings, and this growth can easily become a planetary phenomenon developing the rational and moral level of our entire human species. Education cannot and should not teach "moral rules" but should foster creative thinking about values and ethical principles in relation to the universal problems faced by all human beings, from specific ethical dilemmas to global issues of resource depletion, environmental destruction, war, and systematic violence. It should make possible our highest development as human beings and as a species, a development that includes intellectual and moral maturity, on the one hand, and a direct awareness of the depths of the living moment on the other.

It is only through the development of *planetary maturity* among human beings, we have seen, that a new world of peace and justice can be born. Education, as Plato pointed out in the *Meno*, cannot teach values in the same way that we teach ordinary facts. However, its primary aim should be to foster human intellectual and moral development. John Dewey writes:

> Every one grants that the primary aim of education is the training of the powers of intelligence and will – that the object to be attained is a certain quality of character.... To say this is simply to proclaim that the problem of education is essentially an ethical and psychological problem. The problem can be solved only as we know the true nature and destination of man as a rational being, and the rational methods by which the perfection of his nature may be realized.... A knowledge of the structure and functions of the human being can alone elevate the school from the position of a mere workshop, a more or less cumbrous, uncertain, and even baneful institution, to that of a vital, certain, and effective instrument in the greatest of all constructions – the building of a free and powerful character. (1964: 197-198)

And philosopher Alfred North Whitehead insists that education must develop the powers of creativity and the imagination that emerge with human intellectual maturity:

> The justification for a university is that it preserves the connection between knowledge and the zest of life, by uniting the young and the old in the imaginative consideration of learning. The university imports information, but it imparts it imaginatively. At least, this is the function which it should perform for society. A university which fails in this respect has no reason for existence. (1957: 93)

Psychologist Lawrence Kohlberg and others have studied the cognitive levels through which children move as they develop. At each stage there is a direct correlation between the cognitive capacity of the child and the way the child experiences and processes moral ideas. The process does not automatically extend into adulthood. Many adults are frozen short of their full potential for cognitive and moral development. Powerful institutions (considered further below) prevent their growth toward planetary maturity. Kohlberg summarizes these stages of development:

> At each higher stage...the conception of justice is reorganized. At Stage 1, justice is punishing the bad in terms of "an eye for an eye and a tooth for a

tooth." At Stage 2, it is exchanging favors and goods in an equal manner. At Stages 3 and 4, it is treating people as they desire in terms of the conventional rules. At Stage 5, it is recognized that all rules and laws flow from justice, from a social contract between the governors and the governed designed to protect the equal rights of all. At Stage 6, personally chosen moral principles are also principles of justice, the principles any member of society would choose for that society if he did not know what his position was to be in the society and in which he might be the least advantaged. Principles chosen from this point of view are, first, the maximum liberty compatible with the like liberty of others and, second, no inequalities of goods and respect which are not to the benefit of all, including the least advantaged. (1977: 57)

Kohlberg, Habermas, and others debate the features of a "highest stage" of human moral and intellectual development that they often refer to as "Stage 7," a stage that, according to Kohlberg, "culminates in a synthetic, nondualistic sense of participation, and identity with, a cosmic order" (1984: 249). At the highest stages of development persons begin to become aware of the deep connections between our immense developmental journey out of the womb of the cosmos and the deepest meanings of being human. This phylogenetic trajectory points to a goal that can become a living experience of fully aware persons who encounter the holism implicit in our human situation. Their experience suggests the possibility of a global transformation of human life on planet Earth, as internationalist thinker Richard Falk suggests: "the rediscovery of normative and spiritual ground upon which to find meaning in human existence" (1992: 7).

However, such a highest stage of human development (often termed Stage 7) is not necessary for the emergence of universal values in socially responsible world citizens. The development of universal principles of justice reasoning (Stage 6) in a majority of the Earth's population, principles easily within the potential of every normal human being, would be sufficient to transform our brutal world order and solve most of the apparently suicidal global problems that currently portend a very bleak future for humanity. They imply a democratic world order with universal peace and prosperity that I will describe below. Kohlberg describes the structure of Stage 6 justice reasoning as follows:

The tradition of moral philosophy to which we appeal is the liberal or rational tradition, in particular the "formalistic" or "deontological" tradition running from Immanuel Kant to John Rawls. Central to this tradition is the claim that an adequate morality is *principled*, i.e., that it makes judgments in terms of *universal* principles applicable to all mankind. *Principles* are to be distinguished from *rules*. Conventional morality is grounded on rules, primarily "thou shalt nots" such as are represented by the Ten

Commandments, prescriptions of kinds of actions. Principles are, rather, universal guides to making a moral decision.   An example is Kant's "categorical imperative," formulated two ways. The first is the maxim of respect for the human personality, "Act always toward the other as an end, not as a means." The second is the maximum of universalization, "Choose only as you would be willing to have everyone choose in your situation." Principles like that of Kant's state the formal conditions of a moral choice or action. (1984: 57)

Another way of expressing the values inherent in our humanity, arising as Stages 5 and 6 values, is through the discourse of human rights. Lists of "inalienable human rights" embodied in various documents from the U.S. Declaration of Independence to the U.N. Universal Declaration of Human Rights to Articles 12 and 13 of the *Constitution for the Federation of Earth* express the dignity understood to inhere in each of us simply in virtue of our being human. They express Kant's principle that each person is to be treated as an "end," never merely as a means.

Each person is understood to have duties owed to them by all others, inviolable protections such as the right to life, liberty, and security of person, simply in virtue of being human. Human rights are universal values that are recognized in connection with our common humanity. They are articulated, defended, and described most fully by mature persons who have developmentally realized the depth and significance of being human. They are principles directly derived from the "universal design" of the human mind. Nevertheless, Canadian peace researcher Hanna Newcombe writes concerning Kolhberg's stages that "it has been found that many adults in North America remain at stages 3 or 4 throughout life. This can have appalling consequences for their receptivity to new ideas, new styles of life, new world institutions" (1983: 300).

In a philosophically developed account of human rights, American philosopher Alan Gewirth argues that human rights are identical with the most fundamental of our moral principles:

Human rights are of supreme importance, and are central to all other moral considerations, because they are rights of every human being to the necessary conditions of human action, i.e., those conditions that must be fulfilled if human action is to be possible either at all or with general chances of success in achieving the purposes for which humans act. Because they are such rights, they must be respected by every human being, and the primary justification of governments is that they serve to secure these rights. Thus the Subjects as well as the respondents of human rights are all human beings: the Objects of the rights are the aforesaid necessary conditions of human action and of successful action in general; and the Justifying Basis of the rights is the moral principle which establishes that all

humans are equally entitled to have these necessary conditions, to fulfill the
general needs of human agency. (1982: 3)

As necessary conditions for human action (which presuppose the
possibility of rational moral action that Kant had identified as the source
of our human dignity), human rights are inalienable, Gewirth argues.
They are necessary for our functioning as full human beings. They fall
into two broad categories: the rights of freedom and the rights of well-
being: "These necessary conditions of his action and successful action are
freedom and well-being, where freedom consists in controlling one's
behavior by one's unforced choice while having knowledge of relevant
circumstances, and well-being consists in having the other general
abilities and conditions required for agency" (ibid. p. 47).

I will discuss below the kind of democratic world order necessary to
ensure both the rights of freedom (political rights) and the rights to well
being (economic and social rights). In education, it is important to show
that the entire concept of human rights flows from universal rational
principles as Gewirth attempts to do. Human rights are not a cultural bias
of certain cultures as sometimes claimed. How to itemize a listing of such
rights is certainly a topic of debate, and may well have some cultural
implications, but the idea of universal human rights is itself based on
moral principles as these are ever more clearly understood in the course of
human cognitive and moral development.

The implications for law and government with respect to the values
implicit in the human potential for planetary maturity are not difficult to
discern. They have been articulated in various ways by many political
thinkers from John Locke to Jean-Jacques Rousseau to Immanuel Kant to
John Rawls. Gewirth articulates these implications in the following way:

> Governments are justified insofar as they recognize and help to secure the
> human rights justified in the direct applications, especially the basic rights.
> Because freedom is a basic human right, such governments must use certain
> democratic procedures and guarantee certain freedoms as well as certain
> components of well being.... It is in the context of these indirect
> applications that there emerges the connection between the necessary
> conditions of action and the political and civil rights, including not only the
> rights...to a fair trial, emigration, and nationality, but also the rights to the
> various civil liberties and political participation. All these human rights are
> either species of the generic right to freedom or components of the rights
> that must be guaranteed by governments that fulfill the justificatory
> requirements of the PGC [Principle of Generic Consistency]. (Ibid. p. 9)

Implicit in human moral and cognitive development are the
principles of democracy understood as social arrangements that guarantee

freedoms and democratic procedures equally for all and provide the conditions for sufficient well-being in the citizens. These arrangements are logically necessary to ensure that our human capacity for free action is not diminished or destroyed. The Principle of Generic Consistency, "act in accord with the generic rights of your recipients as well as of yourself," is similar to Kant's categorical imperative to treat every person as an end in themselves, never merely as a means. Treating people as ends in themselves, such as acting in accord with their generic rights to freedom and well-being, implies democratic principles on both personal and governmental levels. Authentic education that develops the cognitive and moral potential of students, therefore, is also education for freedom, democracy, and human rights.

A related central value that emerges out of the higher stages of human maturity is universality in the sense of *holism*, an orientation to the whole human community and/or a sense of relatedness to the cosmos itself. The ability to act autonomously on self-affirmed universal principles is simultaneously the ability to enter with others into cooperative action as a community of equals. Social conformity and the fear of violating the values of a culture, nation, or community belong to a lower level of moral maturity. Autonomous persons, as Habermas points out, are capable of entering into a real discourse with others directed to a goal of mutual understanding in which all participants are changed by the experience (1979: Ch. 2).

Communicative action (and its procedural requirements) is entirely different from the fear of violating social norms or community values and requires sufficient moral maturity and independence. Such a procedural framework – equal rights to speak, to frequency of speech, to disagree with any assertion, etc. (1998a: Ch. 1) – is an essential foundation of democracy and makes possible cooperative action and a community of equals: "Naturally," Habermas writes, "this flow of communication requires sensitivity, breaking down barriers, dependency – in short, a cognitive style marked as field-dependent" (1979: 93-94). The capacity for community, respect for differences, and mutual appreciation of diversity grows with moral autonomy and independence.

Reflecting on "peace among men as well as between men and their Other," philosopher Theodore Adorno affirms that "reconciliation" among human beings requires "neither the undistinguished unity of subject and object nor their antithetical hostility." Persons who are authentic subjects do not submerge their identity into others (as in fascism), nor do they oppose their identity in confrontation with others and the community (as in capitalism and political liberalism). Again, we discern the dynamic of respect for differences within the framework of mutual solidarity as fundamental to human development. Adorno concludes that "peace is the state of distinctness without domination with the distinct participating in each other" (1995: 499-500). With all these thinkers, we find the lineaments for genuine democracy articulated in terms our potential for reconciliation and peace among human beings: individuality and community require one another.

For psychoanalyst and philosopher Erich Fromm, the process of living itself produces a new relatedness to the world and to other human beings. This is one way of characterizing planetary maturity. It involves a creative aliveness and relatedness to all of life as well as with all other human beings. It is this potential in all of us that is impeded and destroyed by present day institutions. These are the values behind an education directed toward real human growth:

> Living is a process of continuous birth. The tragedy in the life of most of us is that we die before we are fully born. Being born, however, does not only mean to be free *from* the womb, the lap, the hand, etc., but also to be free *to* be active and creative. Just as the infant must breathe once the umbilical cord is cut, so man must be active and creative at every moment of birth. To the extent that man is fully born, he finds a new kind of rootedness; that life in his creative relatedness to the world, and in the ensuing experience of solidarity with all man and with all nature. From being *passively* rooted in nature and in the womb, man becomes one again – but this time actively and creatively with all life. (1981: 7)

This creative and engaged response to life includes, Fromm asserts, an "experience of solidarity" with human beings and with nature. A "fully born" human being experiences a deep community with other human beings and with nature. This solidarity can be articulated in terms of the principle of *unity in diversity*.

3.2 Education, Holism, and the Principle of *Unity in Diversity*

It is not only in social theory (such as those of Gewirth, Habermas, Adorno, or Fromm) that the twentieth century has seen the principle of interrelation and interdependency linking whole and parts. We have seen that the entire gamut of scientific breakthroughs in both the life-sciences and physical sciences has understood that the fundamental principle of the universe we live in involves holism: the parts cannot be understood apart from their interdependence with wholes, whether these be ecosystems, human communities, micro-particle systems, or astro-physical systems.

Human beings are all one species with a nearly identical potential for developing through the states of moral maturity to where universality and particularity coincide. Moral principles are valid if they can be universally applied within this particular situation and with respect to these particular human beings who must be treated as ends in themselves. The principle of *unity in diversity*, therefore, becomes a fundamental value for planetary maturity. We have seen psychologist Robert J. Lifton refer to human growth as "evolution of the self" (1993: 231).

Holism is also at the heart of environmental biology in the realization that organisms cannot be separated from their environment from the micro level to the planetary level. Biology now understands that our planet is an encompassing ecosystem that will not support human life if we continue its destruction. In physics, similar principles hold from the micro to the macro levels. Physicist Fritjof Capra writes that "modern physics shows us once again – this time at the macroscopic level – that material objects are not distinct entities, but are inseparably linked to their environment; that their properties can only be understood in terms of their interaction with the rest of the world" (1975: 209).

We have also seen that philosopher of science Errol E. Harris has shown the implications of these principles at length in many of his books. In *Apocalypse and Paradigm: Science and Everyday Thinking*, he describes the scientific process by which the fragmented "Newtonian Paradigm" has been replaced by the twentieth-century Holistic Paradigm. The implications of a holistic paradigm in which *unity in diversity* is understood as the fundamental principle of life and the universe are immense. Explanation becomes "teleological" in the sense that parts can only be understood in terms of the wholes of which they are a part. Similarly, human growth and development can be understood in terms of the realization of universality: Marx's "species-being" (the whole of our species), now understood to be a central goal of individual and evolutionary development. Planetary maturity includes phylogenetic as well as ontogenetic dimensions. Harris writes:

> If the implications of this scientific revolution and the new paradigm it introduces are taken seriously, holism should be the dominating concept in all our thinking. In considering the diverse problems and crises that have arisen out of practices inspired by the Newtonian paradigm, it is now essential to think globally. Atomism, individualism, separatism, and reductionism have become obsolete, are no longer tolerable, and must be given up.... In short, explanation must be teleological, for the proper import of teleology is the domination and direction of the part by the whole. Further, the parts discovered are to be treated as provisional wholes in their own right, participant in and contributory to more complex and more highly integrated wholes. Such holistic thinking would make an incisive and far-reaching difference to both theory and practice in every field of human interest and activity. (2000a: 90)

The implications of the pervasive holism of our universe bears on every domain of thought, including morality, social theory, and education. Human development must be understood in terms of the *telos* implicit in our humanity. In addition, human beings must come together in a political, social, and economic unity that does not exclude their diversity and particularity but enhances it as a necessary factor in planetary maturity. The intellectual and moral growth of the individual human being leads toward a moral universality that by its very nature respects human individuality. Authentic education fosters this development. Harris elaborates:

> Morality is an outcome of the development of self-consciousness – the essence of human reason, which has now transpired as the principle of organization that has been at work throughout the scale of natural forms, raised to the level of self-consciousness. As such, reason is the source and agency of order and unification. When it manifests itself in the life of human beings as social order, morality arises as a necessary aspect of social conduct....
>
> This is the basis and source of moral obligation, the social equivalent of which in principle translates into political obligation. Its ultimate aim is a coherence and wholeness of life, the implications of which, when fully unfolded under conditions prevailing today in which common interests include the preservation of the planetary ecology and the maintenance of world peace, disclose the demand for a universal community of mankind and a concomitant universality of moral principle. Relativity to the group and its culture proves to be merely provisional and finds its proper fulfillment only in the universal standard of common to all human beings. (Ibid. pp. 101-102)

Political obligation is now an obligation to all other human beings, not merely to a country or a state in which I happen to have been born. For Harris (2005), institutions must be created that mirror this universality of political obligation in democratic world government. We have seen the inseparability of moral development from the development of political institutions (democracy) that reflect the freedom, universality, and dignity implicit in our humanity and progressively explicit in the morally mature human being. The universality of thought and action in the morally mature person must be mirrored in the universality of democratic institutions that encompass humanity in its species-being.

Education must educate for wholeness, for a living awareness of the principle of *unity in diversity*, not through any form of didacticism but through encouraging the processes that lead to authentic growth. Not only are these value principles inherent in the *telos* of human beings developing phylogenetically on this planet over the past two million years. At this point in the early twenty-first century, they are necessary to the very survival of the human race. Harris concludes:

> If human and other living beings are to survive the coming century, it is essential that we should learn to think holistically. The twentieth-century scientific paradigm must become intrinsic to the millennial outlook, and the millennial objective ought to be the initiation of unified global organization. The unity of humanity should be the watchword of the new epoch, inspiring all our thinking and action. It is essential to stress the unity of the whole in and through difference. In all local action, the global perspective has to be kept firmly in mind. (Ibid. p. 132)

What are the impediments to the realization of this vision and potential within us for planetary maturity? Why has humankind thus far remained mired in fragmentation and fractured existence? The broad answer given by Harris is that the twentieth-century scientific paradigm has not yet informed human thinking and acting, which remains mired in the fragmented Newtonian paradigm. The Newtonian paradigm understood the universe and human life in terms of the fundamental metaphor of the machine rather than using the organic metaphor that became fundamental with twentieth-century biology. People become locked into fragmented patterns of thought that have been held in place by fragmented institutions. The result is the impending disaster underlined by Harris.

In *Education, Modernity, and Fractured Meaning: Toward a Process Theory of Teaching and Learning*, Donald W. Oliver and Kathleen Waldron Gershman agree that humankind remains locked into self-destructive metaphors:

> Our guess is that once our imaginative energies become locked into a narrow range of metaphors, that is to say, as modern people have come to focus on the machine, qualities of reality which would normally extend beyond the convenience of the single dominant metaphor are inappropriately perceived and understood. Hunger on a worldwide basis, for example, is construed as economic scarcity (we have too small an economic machine) rather than as the result of human greed, exploitation, or thoughtlessness. Paranoid fears between alien peoples are seen as problems to be solved literally with machines – organized armies, weapons of mass destruction – or through conversations between technically trained diplomats and negotiators. (1989: 19)

The paradigms or metaphors that dominate our thinking have immense destructive consequences. Nevertheless, as Oliver and Gershman understand, there is much more to the fractured nature of modernity than this fixation on a narrow range of metaphors, true as this may be. For the problem of fragmentation (and education complicit in fragmentation) has been going on for much longer than the modern era since the Renaissance. Education historically has nearly always been in the service of special interests and conducted by educators themselves products of fragmented institutions. And phylogenetically, human beings have been in a long process of growing toward this holism that frees us from former partial perspectives.

3.3 The Fragmented Modern World and Historical Forces that Impede Human Development

Oliver and Gershman are very much to the mark in their prescription for how we might frame an educational philosophy that goes deeper than perpetuating the dominant metaphors of this or that historical era. They recognize that fragmentation must be overcome and that the machine metaphor is not only one that applies to human problems like economic scarcity or fears between people but is a metaphor that informs people's entire view of the cosmos. We need to free ourselves from the outdated Newtonian paradigm and embrace the holism uncovered by twentieth-century science, and we need to foster the development of planetary maturity in all the world's citizens.

This holism simultaneously connects us to cosmic processes from which we have emerged and to which we are intimately related. Just as Harris refers us to the Cosmic Anthropic Principle that connects the emergence of human life with the fundamental physical parameters of the early universe (2000a: 111-112) so Oliver and Gershman connect us with our past that has emerged out of the cosmic process:

> We argue here for a reconsideration of this piecemeal way of viewing modern educational change, seeing it not within the limited framework of our progressive functionalist ideology, not simply as part of a machine that is to be analyzed, improved and made more efficient, but rather within the broader framework that emerges when we consider the full evolutionary potential of the human species. This requires us to take seriously the first million years of human history – as best as can be reconstructed – as we take the last five thousand years of 'civilized man' or the last four hundred years of 'scientific-technological man.' We would then see the human record as considerably more than an evolutionary climb from savagery to barbarism to feudalism to the modern industrial state. We might then discover human cultures and systems of belief which suggest creative and positive ways by which the unbalanced and fragmented qualities of modernity can be reconsidered. (1989: 30)

Holism has roots both in our distant past and many of its traditions as well as in the emerging scientific present. Indeed, the account of planetary maturity sketched above resonates with the teachings of a number of philosophical and religious teachers throughout Western and Eastern history. Many great teachers have reached Stage 7 awareness of the cosmic holism out of which human life emerges and to which we are related. On the other hand, concrete human beings and their societies have rarely approximated this image in their educational or social practices. Human history can be understood as a long struggle toward human liberation, toward becoming, so to speak, what we are, or what we are meant to be.

We have yet to even begin to significantly realize our potential as human beings living on this planet. Our educational, social, and economic institutions have often worked against the development of our full human potential. The values they have sought to inculcate are not rationally developed universal values but narrow, partial, and parochial values that seek control rather than liberation. They have not been holistic values but fragmented and fractured values.

Primitive societies evolved into class societies several thousand years ago. These class societies used law, religion, military forces, and propaganda to exploit and dominate both their own lower classes and other societies through conquest, spheres of hegemony (requiring payment of tribute), or through direct colonial or neo-colonial rule. Jean-Jacques Rousseau begins his account of the development of the social contract by stating "Man is born free, but everywhere he is in chains." The situation is similar today under the global domination of the neoliberal agenda promoted by the imperial governments of the world and sponsored by big capital and multinational corporations (Korten 1995).

Today, education is not available for hundreds of millions of people whose human potential is being strangled and sacrificed. Where education is available, it is most often used in the service of a dominant class, power interests, or the owners of capital. Rarely is the goal the development of freedom, rational autonomy, moral integrity, or independence. Very often it is in the service of economics, training people to be cogs in an economic machine that they are not expected to critically examine or investigate deeply. Very often education is in the service of the forces of domination that give themselves false ideological names: domination is called "freedom," capitalist economic exploitation is called "democracy," the propaganda system is called "a free press," going to war is called "peace keeping," holding official enemies accountable for misdeeds in mock trials is called "seeking justice," and the department of war is called "the Department of Defense" (Chomsky 1996: 86-91).

What would education have to be like if it were put in the service the real development of our human potential as Karl Marx, for example, insisted it should be? (1990: 739). How can education be connected with the values of human liberation? If on its deepest level education is connected with an understanding of what it means to be human, then the values of freedom, reason, and moral integrity must live at the heart of our educational project. Education should address and evoke the "utopian surplus," the immense potential, within us. How can this process be directed to this realization of our highest human potential?

We have seen that perhaps the two most pervasive global institutions that today promote and perpetuate our fragmented world order are global monopoly capitalism and the system of so-called sovereign nation-states. Although there has been extensive analysis and commentary on each of these institutions and the havoc they have wrought throughout the modern era since the Renaissance, few have pointed out their substantial interdependencies and interconnections. It only makes sense that the capitalist ruling class within each country would use its influence over governmental power not only to frame laws that allow its exploitation of the workers and environment but to influence foreign policy in such a way as to maximize their profits in trade and imperial relations with foreign countries.

Even the official "legal" separation between private capital and government in our day makes little substantive difference. The heads of corporations become key government officials and advisors while generals or former high government administrators retire to lucrative jobs within major corporations. The history of this intimate relationship between political power and capital is traced by Terry Boswell and Christopher Chase-Dunn in *The Spiral of Capitalism and Socialism: Toward Global Democracy* (2000).

A key concept behind the entire modern system can be termed "plunder by trade." This concept is developed and traced historically by J.W. Smith in *Economic Democracy: The Political Struggle of the Twenty-First Century* (2003). The essential feature of the global imperial system has not been Adam Smith "free trade" or "fair competition." It has involved framing the rules and conditions of trade to favor the imperial nations at the expense of their victims. "Plunder by trade" has enriched the powerful nations at the expense of the rest of humankind, aided by military invasion or other forms of outright manipulation and domination (Blum 2000).

Both of these most fundamental institutions of the modern world teach and promote fragmentation of our world in thought as well as in practice. Capitalism teaches a doctrine of global competition that, over the past five centuries, has resulted in a world in which, by 1994, the wealthiest 20 percent of the world's population had 78 times the income of the poorest 20 percent. Today, the 225 richest people in the world have a net worth of more than $1.3 trillion. This is equal to the annual incomes of the poorest 2.5 billion people (Nelson 2008).

The world, as Oliver and Gershman point out above, is locked into a conceptual strait jacket promoted endlessly by the capitalist media (who frame the agenda and perspective of the majority of media in the world). This perspective says that the problem of the immense poverty in the world after five centuries of capitalism is not due to exploitation, theft, and systemic greed but to insufficient growth in the capitalist system. The absurdity of this idea in the face of the realities of today's world is there for all to see who care to open their eyes. But as long as the mass media *control the frame through which the "facts" are interpreted,* "seeing" itself will require the development of a critical consciousness (cf. Chomsky 1989; Martin 2005a: Ch. 3).

Just as mature people develop universal values that concern themselves for the welfare of all others as "ends in themselves" so mature educational institutions promote reflection on economic values in the light of the goodness and necessity of human flourishing. Such reflection would result in a profound modification of capitalism in the direction of economic democracy and an economics of universal prosperity rather than one of scarcity with absolute winners and losers. However, big capital has immense influence over the politicians who structure educational institutions and over the food, services, books, films, and materials that are used in classrooms worldwide. This influence keeps the propaganda of corporate capitalism drumming into the minds of each new generation, perpetuating the fragmentation of a world full of starving, desperate, and marginalized people. It treats a human-created institution (capitalism) as if it were a natural law mirroring some Darwinian struggle for survival in ways that are entirely out of place for mature human beings.

Similarly, the drum beat of today's education focuses on the so-called "sovereign" nation-state as if this were not an historical creation (formalized at the European Treaty of Westphalia in 1648) but another "natural" pattern of human political organization. The world consequently remains divided into approximately 193 autonomous units by and large recognizing no significant law above themselves. These nations all believe that "security" is a necessary and fundamental objective since (in a fragmented world) no state can fully trust other states and must be ready to defend itself in case of attack. The result is an educational fiasco where children are taught nationalism and parochialism rather than being encouraged to grow in their thinking and acting into mature adults.

In both cases, deeply intertwined with one another, the educational process twists away from its true meaning as the actualizer of human potential into the perpetuator of human immaturity and fragmentation. Instead, education induces people to acquiesce in the distorted ideological world full of contradictions and absurdities. As Herbert Marcuse explains:

> Under these circumstances, the spoken phrase is an expression of the individual who speaks it, *and* of those who make him speak as he does, *and* of whatever tension or contradiction may interrelate them. In speaking their own language, people also speak the language of their masters, benefactors, advertisers. Thus they do not express *themselves*, their own knowledge, feelings, and aspirations, but also something other than themselves. Describing "by themselves" the political situation, either in their home town or in the international scene, they...describe what "their" media of mass communication tell them – and this merges with what they really think and feel.... What they mean cannot be taken at face value – not because they lie, but because the universe of thought and practice in which they live is a universe of manipulated contradictions. (1964: 193-194)

Both the holism discovered by twentieth-century science and the *unity in diversity* recognized by intellectually and morally mature human beings live in direct contradiction with educational practices the world over as these exist today. Instead of actualizing our higher human potential, most education forces us into "a universe of manipulated contradictions." The true meaning of education, as it has emerged in thinkers throughout history and as it has been articulated in numerous social-scientific studies throughout the twentieth century, has yet to be realized in any significant way in educational practices worldwide.

3.4 Education for Critical Consciousness

A proper term for the system of education that is institutionalized on behalf of the nation-states and global capitalism is "brainwashing." For both globalized capitalism and the sovereign nation-state systems are so bad, so destructive of the human welfare, the environment, and the possibility of human fulfillment on this planet that they would not continue to exist if it were not for massive worldwide brainwashing of new generations to accept this madness as "natural," as inevitable laws of nature (cf. Martin 2005a: Chs. 8-9). This is why authentic education must develop *critical consciousness* along the lines often referred to as "critical social theory," the tradition (deriving from Marx and others) understanding that *every class society generates a set of ideological self-justifications to cover up an exploitative and ugly reality.* I would add to this the fact that every nation-state does the same thing to cover up its inability to govern democratically.

It is not that there is a "conspiracy" going on in any highly defined sense of this word. Rather, the ruling classes of all nations work together to perpetuate the system. Many in the ruling classes are themselves brainwashed by their elite educations at Harvard, Yale, Princeton, or Oxford. Many have been arrested in their intellectual and moral development by a system of systematic greed and domination that has no use for anything approximating planetary maturity. Still others of the elite intuitively understand that their wealth and power are predicated upon maintaining a high level of *immaturity* in the general population. Many of those in government understand that their immense undemocratic powers come to them from the "national-security" and military systems intrinsic to the fragmented system of so-called "sovereign" nation-states. The industrial-educational-military complex dominates life in a variety of subtle yet pervasive ways.

A critically developed consciousness has the intellectual maturity to discern the framework hidden behind any presentation of "facts." It is sophisticated enough to know that there is no such thing as a bare fact, that all facts are interpreted within a framework of assumptions that are usually never mentioned in the presentation. Facts are framed, slanted, emphasized, deemphasized, suppressed, distorted, interpreted, or selected according to some unspoken agenda. Just as intellectual maturity understands this and remains alert to the propaganda function of most presentations of "facts" so moral maturity understands that one cannot treat people as ends in themselves unless one is fully aware of situations and their implications. A person cannot live morally if he or she accepts a skewed ideological picture of the world, of causes and effects, and of the consequences of his or her actions.

We have seen that human maturity implies democracy. However, democracy cannot flourish unless citizens have developed sufficient critical consciousness to understand the manipulation of people and ideas that takes place from powerful corporate interests or non-democratic political forces. Regardless of the rhetoric heard everywhere today, education does not promote mature citizens who take their political responsibility seriously as the central actors within a democracy. Education is largely controlled by hidden structural forces reinforcing the twisted logics of capitalism and the nation-state system (Giroux 1983).

Everywhere in today's world, education is directed toward creating nationalistic sympathies, fearful participants in military and other non-democratic institutions, and passive consumers of corporate-generated, ecologically harmful trash. Education today is largely directed toward fitting people to become cogs in an economic machine that they are not supposed to examine too closely, and it is directed toward brainwashing them in the service of global capitalism and the nationalism of the nation-state system. The last thing education wants us to ask is: "What does it mean to be a human being?" and "What are the political-social-economic conditions necessary for a fulfilled and fulfilling human life in community with others?" For asking these questions calls into doubt the fragmented premises of our entire world order.

Simply framing these questions pulls us in the direction of human maturity. Indian born spiritual philosopher Jiddu Krishnamurti raises the issue in this way:

> I wonder if we have ever asked ourselves what education means. Why do we go to school, why do we learn various subjects, why do we pass examinations and compete with each other for better grades? What does this so-called education mean, and what is it all about? This is really a very important question, not only for the students, but also for the parents, for the teachers, and for everyone who loves this earth. Why do we go through the struggle to be educated? Is it merely in order to pass some examinations and get a job? Or is the function of education to prepare us while we are young to understand the whole process of life? Having a job and earning one's livelihood is necessary – but is that all? Are we being educated only for that? Surely, life is not merely a job, an occupation; life is something extraordinarily wide and profound, it is a great mystery, a vast realm in which we function as human beings. (1964: 9)

People often fail to realize that today's education does not simply direct students into learning what is necessary for employment but develops the "social character" necessary to accept absurd forms of employment without question, forms of employment directed to the destruction of people and things (the military), or that destroy the environment, or that exploit the poor in the service of the rich. It is this "social character" that then willingly and naturally perpetuates the fragmented thinking and institutions that are threatening the very future of humankind.

There is a vicious circle: perverse institutions brainwash new generations into absurd patterns of thinking (a pathological social character), then the majority of citizens demand more of these same institutions since these fit perfectly with the world view embedded in their social character. Fromm writes:

> The starting point for these reflections is the statement that the character structure of the average individual and the socio-economic structure of society of which he or she is a part are interdependent. I call the blending of the individual psychical sphere and the socioeconomic structure *social character*.... The socioeconomic structure of a society molds the social

character of its members so that they *wish* to do what they *have* to do. Simultaneously, the social character influences the socioeconomic structure of society, acting either as cement to give further stability to the social structure or, under special circumstances, as dynamite that tends to break up the social structure. (1996: 133-134)

Fromm calls the social character inculcated by contemporary society a "Having" mode of existence, whereas humankind's fulfillment and maturity lie in a "Being" mode of existence. The mode of Being is a condition of mature self-awareness very much in accord with what Krishnamurti is suggesting in the above quotation. Contemporary education inculcates a social character that compulsively strives for possessions, ambition, ego-gratification, and domination over others by individuals who assume they stand apart from life as something to be manipulated and molded in the service of insatiable desires. (Or, concomitantly, it inculcates servility, conformity, and adaptation to perverse social conditions.) People immaturely believe the meaning of life lies in *having* rather than *being*. They become brainwashed in the service of commercial, economic, and power interests destructive of democracy and mature human freedom.

Brazilian-born philosopher of education Paulo Freire agrees. In *Pedagogy of the Oppressed*, he asserts that "the oppressor classes" are themselves dehumanized by their dehumanization of others (treating them as a means rather than as ends in themselves). Their consciousness involves a "to have" model of being human: "The oppressor consciousness tends to transform everything surrounding it into an object of its domination. The Earth, property, production, the creations of men, men themselves, time – everything is reduced to the status of objects at its disposal." This is the very negation, he says, "of their ontological vocation to be more fully human" (1974: 43-44). In *Education for Critical Consciousness*, Freire places education into the larger historical context related to a fulfilled and mature mode of human existence:

Men play a crucial role in the fulfillment and in the superseding of epochs. Whether or not men can perceive the epochal themes and above all, how they act upon the reality within which these themes are generated will largely determine their humanization or dehumanization, their affirmation as Subjects or their reduction as objects. For only as men grasp the themes can they intervene in reality instead of remaining mere onlookers. And only by developing a permanently critical attitude can men overcome a posture of adjustment in order to become integrated with the spirit of the time....

But unfortunately, what happens to a greater or lesser degree in the various "worlds" into which the world is divided is that the ordinary person is crushed, diminished, converted into a spectator, maneuvered by myths which powerful social forces have created. These myths turn against him; they destroy and annihilate him. Tragically frightened, men fear authentic relationships and even doubt the possibility of their existence. On the other hand, fearing solitude, they gather in groups lacking in any critical and loving ties which might transform them into a cooperating unity, into a true community....

Perhaps the greatest tragedy of modern man is his domination by the force of these myths and his manipulation by organized advertising, ideological or otherwise. Gradually, without even realizing the loss, he relinquishes his capacity for choice; he is expelled from the orbit of decisions. Ordinary men do not perceive the tasks of the time; the latter are interpreted by an "elite" and presented in the forms of recipes, of prescriptions. And when men try to save themselves by following the prescriptions, they drown in leveling anonymity, without hope and without faith, domesticated and adjusted. (1990: 5-6)

The development of a critical consciousness at once activates our creative relationship to life, as Erich Fromm asserts above, and allows us not to be submerged in our culture and its ideology, as Paulo Freire asserts. Developing a critical consciousness means becoming aware of the contradictions inherent in all class societies that necessarily spew forth an ideology that justifies the domination of the few "for the greater good of all" while simultaneously exploiting the majority and suppressing their life-potential as human beings. Developing a critical consciousness also lives at the heart of our common *telos* to become ever "more fully human." A human being lacking critical consciousness reflects a failure of education, no matter how high he or she may have scored on examinations.

We are creatures emerging out of a nature twelve billion years in process, with our own two-million-year history, who need to educate ourselves in the light of this immense evolutionary journey. As Krishnamurti exclaims, life is very beautiful as we realize the immense potential for living within us, as we realize and begin to experience what it means to be a human being. Life is not this ugly thing we have made of it. The "having" mode of existence fostered by capitalism and the nation-state system strangles our higher human possibilities.

Critical consciousness sees deeper than everyday experience into what philosopher of education, Henry A. Giroux, terms the "structural determinants" that condition and inform everyday existence. A critical consciousness sees that human creativity can make history and that our possibilities are truly liberating, since neither capitalism nor the nation-state are inevitable natural phenomena. Giroux writes:

Radical pedagogy needs an anthropological grounding but one that recognizes the force of structural determinants that do not show up in the most immediate experiences of teachers and students. The ideological and the concrete cannot be reduced to a mere shadow of the institutional workings of capital, but must be seen as starting points by which to analyze their particular relationship to institutions such as schools, family, and work so that these relationships can be viewed critically and transformed when possible.... The conditions for a new mode of pedagogy as well as a more humane society begin when we as educators can reveal how the self-constituting nature of individuals and classes is not something that can be subsumed within the rationality that legitimizes the existing society. For at the heart of praxis is that first moment when the human subject truly believes that he or she can begin to make history. (1981: 31-32)

Human beings who are encouraged to ask real questions in the process of developing their own intellectual and moral autonomy will tend to develop a critical consciousness. Such a consciousness includes awareness of the way "facts" are manipulated and framed to support the dominant order. It is "disobedient," as Fromm asserts, to the extent that it is willing to question power and authority in the service of truth and genuine understanding. It is "dialectical," as Freire asserts, in that it sees more deeply into the processes of history and the possibility of progressive and liberating social change. It is aware that the fullness of life is distorted and diminished by "structural determinants" of capitalism and the nation-state system that block our common "ontological vocation to be more fully human."

3.5 Education for a Democratic World Order

Reflection concerning the nature and requirements of democracy becomes fundamental to a liberating education. So-called "civic education" in many countries assumes that the participants are living in a "democracy" and simply studies the formal mechanisms by which this is supposed to work. Such education never develops a critical consciousness that discerns why this does not work and why there is no genuine democracy.

However, we have seen that the nature of democracy remains a theoretical and existential problem for human beings. Democracy is not something we know about, whose implementation we have solved, except in the propaganda of profoundly undemocratic societies that want the population to believe they live in a democracy. Democracy remains implicit in human intellectual and moral development as a future form of cooperative living that still needs to be more fully worked out on planet Earth. A critical consciousness does not hide from the immense problems involved in creating and maintaining a democratic world order.

So-called "civic education" does not recognize that treating every person as an end in themselves means institutionalizing this in the form of universal human rights, universal freedoms, and an economic system predicated on universal prosperity rather than immense wealth for the few and denial of the right to live with well being for the immense majority. Human beings must realize their potential for planetary maturity and become active participants in the community of humankind rather than passive victims of the system of haves and have-nots. They must realize their potential for "being" rather than having. As Fromm emphatically asserts: *"To achieve a society based on being, all people must actively participate in their economic function and as citizens. Hence, our liberation from the having mode of existence is possible only through the full realization of industrial and political participatory democracy"* (1996: 181).

By distinguishing "industrial" from "political" democracy, Fromm is indicating that formal political democracy alone cannot give genuine life, liberty, or security of person as long as we live under the economic totalitarianism of big capital manipulating and exploiting us in the service of private profit. We have seen Alan Gewirth define human rights in terms of the necessary conditions for meaningful human action. These necessary conditions fall into two broad categories of "freedom" and "well being." Just as people cannot meaningfully act without guaranteed rights to speech, press, assembly, and protection against governmental interference, so they cannot act without sufficient well-being in the form of food, clothing, housing, tools of communication, transportation, etc. An economic order premised on universal prosperity must replace the present order of exploitation and scarcity for the majority if there is ever to be democracy or respect for human rights on this planet.

For human beings to realize their intellectual and moral potential, that is, for planetary maturity to be possible among human beings, there must be some form of "socialism" in the sense of a society that is concerned with making possible the "good life" for the vast majority of its citizens. (This theme is developed in greater detail in Chapter Seven below.) Such socialism or "economic democracy" must be realized within the context of political freedom and cannot be engineered by any totalitarian form of government. Here we have another issue confronting intellectually and morally mature human beings and another educational issue that can contribute to their growth. How do we combine economic and political democracy on Earth to create a world in which our higher human potential can be realized for the great majority of persons?

American philosopher Michael Luntley, in his book *The Meaning of Socialism*, reflects on the conditions for moral maturity and the realization of the good life for human beings:

> Socialism is not a moral theory which offers a particular version of the good life, instead it is a theory about how the good life is possible. It is, in short,

a theory about the conditions necessary for creating a society in which our lives are shaped by moral values – we defer to the authority of the good – rather than a society in which our moral traditions have been erased by forces inimical to the moral life. And part of this theory about the conditions necessary for the good life provides the leading critical aspect of socialism. That part is the claim that it is capitalism which has been largely responsible for the destruction of the conditions necessary for the good life. (1990: 15)

"Forces inimical to the moral life" are the forces of capitalism that *alienate* people from building true communities, *commodify* all things by turning them into mere monetary values, and *destroy liberty* by colonizing communications, media, and the range of free discussion in the service of the interests of the wealthy. Socialism, as Luntley understands it, begins with respect for persons within a framework of community that fosters equality of voice and personal dignity, thereby making possible "a society in which our lives are shaped by moral values."

Human beings, treated as ends in themselves and not exploited as a means to someone else's enrichment, have their rights to "well being" respected. Society and government must be democratic in the sense of representing the common good of all the citizens and not controlled by oligarchic forces of big capital that manipulate the laws in the service of their own interests. This alone makes morality possible. Education for human development implies the values linked to some form of social democracy.

Similarly, British thinker Terry Eagleton describes the features of the capitalist system that make it inimical to morality and human well being:

Capitalist modernity, so it appeared, had landed us with an economic system which was almost purely instrumental. It was a way of life dedicated to power, profit, and the business of material survival, rather than to fostering the values of human sharing and solidarity. The political realm was more of management and manipulation than of the communal shaping of a common life. Reason itself had been debased to a mere self-interested calculation. As for morality, this too, had become an increasingly private affair, more relevant to the bedroom than the boardroom. (2007: 22)

Capitalism not only abjures moral reasoning (since reasoning for it is merely "self-interested calculation"), it creates an environment in which the democratic values of "sharing and solidarity" are discouraged. Business considerations are purely instrumental: how can we maximize "power and profit," and morality is now considered merely personal and subjective, not something objectively applicable to business considerations in relation to the common good.

In *Reflections on Government* (1967), British philosopher Ernest Barker argues that the moral foundations of democracy lie in the free development of the human "moral personality," which is only possible within the context of democracy based on genuine discussion: the free interchange of ideas and conceptions of the good (p. 16). Great concentrations of wealth inevitably destroy this foundation: "in this way the process of discussion is perverted. It is not controlled by the weight of argument: it is directed by the power of wealth. That power is able to influence every organ of democracy" (p. 110).

Just as capitalism is inimical to human moral development, so is the autonomous nation-state. In a world of so-called "sovereign" nation-states, each recognizing no significant law above themselves, there is an explicit contradiction with their demands that we citizens obey their laws. Citizens must obey the law, but nations do not even have to recognize the rule of law above themselves in world affairs, since they are "sovereign" (cf. Martin 2005b: Ch. 1). Citizens are to obey the law, except when their military commanders order them to kill or destroy citizens in other countries. Citizens must obey the law, but "intelligence services" of their respective countries simultaneously lie, manipulate, assassinate, blackmail, torture, and coerce in the interests of their "sovereign" nation outside of any democratically legislated or enforceable world law.

As we have seen, under the system of nation-states democracy *within* nations is also nearly impossible. Gigantic forces steal sovereignty from the people and place decision-making in the hands of military necessities, security forces, and economic elites. Globalized weaponry, communications, economics, and environmental interdependency mean that no nation is any longer in control of its own fate. The perpetual need for "security" and the threat of war mean that immense resources must be relegated to a non-democratic military system. Global economic conditions force nations into externally determined "structural adjustment" programs or other economic measures outside the control of the people. Even the most powerful nations are subject to global economic downturns or depressions beyond their control. In some countries, gigantic multinational corporations operate with impunity outside the regulation of both the host government and the local population. Environmental breakdown threatens the well-being of all nations (cf. Daly 1996; Seth 2004).

Global problems such as overpopulation, resource depletion, climate change, environmental pollution, destruction of the ozone layer, militarism and wars, terrorism and insecurity, and human rights violations flourish unchecked and impact the destinies of nation-states. Many forms of international crime are committed by nations, corporations, or private groups (such as the drug trade, the weapons trade, piracy, human trafficking, sex-slavery, money laundering, and terrorism). These flourish within the anarchic, lawless international system that makes democracy within particular nations a sham and a lie.

The people of Australia cannot operate a democracy in that country when their physical well-being is destroyed by cancer-causing solar radiation due to the destruction of the ozone layer above their country. Democracy at the very least requires the protection of life, liberty, and security of person, the three most fundamental rights specified in Article 3 of the U.N. Universal Declaration of Human Rights. The peoples of Latin America cannot operate democracies within their countries when the World Bank and IMF, based in Washington, DC, dictate economic policy to their central banks. Global conditions steal the decision-making power of local peoples and reveal the only viable democracy as world federalized democracy.

The ontogenetic development of individuals leading to universal principles implying the equality and freedom of democracy is mirrored by the phylogenetic development of human beings on the Earth. Planetary maturity implies democratic world government. Only democratic world law (dealing with global problems and ensuring global equality among nations and people) can activate and empower democracy at the local level. Our immediate moral obligation involves making this a reality.

The dogma of the "sovereign" nation-state forbids the realization of the planetary maturity of democratic world law that applies equally to all persons. So-called "international law" under the United Nations system primarily regulates nation-states, not persons, and is only enforceable by the bizarre methods of punishing entire populations for the crimes of the few. It is only "enforceable" through economic sanctions that starve entire populations or by military actions that attack entire nations as if they were individuals who could be held morally responsible through the carnage of war. The mythology of "sovereign" nation-states currently fracturing our world order must be replaced by a federation of limited political entities whose job is local administration according to the framework supplied by a democratic *Constitution for the Federation of Earth*.

Planetary democracy is a fundamental value that emerges with human intellectual and moral development. Like all genuine values, it is inherently universal and understands that every human being is an end in him or her self, with inherent dignity and inalienable rights, and part of a universal planetary community that has yet to fully emerge. Under today's globalized world order, with its immense planetary problems intractable at the local level, democracy can no longer function within nation-states. It can only function in any meaningful way as non-military democratic world government that creates universal economic prosperity and federates the nations under world law. Both are embodied within the *Constitution for the Federation of Earth*.

Education must be education for creativity, for exploration, for genuine questioning and examination. It must promote the development of our highest human possibilities. Education cannot teach values in the same way that it teaches facts, but it can encourage the examination of real, fundamental questions. Curricula can be designed at various educational levels for examining questions like "What is democracy and how can authentic democracy be organized and activated?" "What is sustainable living within the framework of a finite, delicately balanced planetary ecosystem?" "What is world peace and how can this be institutionalized and protected?" "How can we design an economics of prosperity for all people on Earth?" "How can human rights and human dignity be protected worldwide?"

Perhaps the most fundamental issue of all (that must form the basis of all genuine education in relation to values) revolves around the immense question: "What does it mean to be a human being?" "Life is really very beautiful," Krishnamurti asserts, "it is not this ugly thing that we have made of it; and you can appreciate its richness, its depth, its extraordinary loveliness only when you revolt against everything – against organized religion, against tradition, against the present rotten society – so that you as a human being find out for yourself what is true."

Education must keep this question in the forefront of our inquiries. Does this ugly thing that we have made of the world, this present rotten society, really reflect our deeper nature and potential as human beings? Understanding what is true about ourselves and our holistic universe (as revealed by both science, self-awareness, and spiritual teachers of all traditions) will determine the deeper premises of the coming holistic Earth civilization. Education must activate genuine revolt and inquiry, while at the same time activating the yearning to actualize our higher human rational and spiritual potential. The "utopian surplus" living within us all needs to emerge. We can and must think, act, and live beautiful democratic lives.

PART TWO

IMPERIAL DOMINATION AND SYSTEMIC WORLD DISORDER

Chapter Four

The Deep Violence of Today's World System

Religion and the Global Transformation from Deep Violence to Deep Nonviolence

The world consists of Center and Periphery nations; and each nation, in turn, has its centers and periphery. Hence, our concern is with the mechanism underlying this discrepancy, particularly between the center in the Center, and the periphery in the Periphery. In other words, how to conceive of, how to explain, and how to counteract inequality as one of the major forms of structural violence. Any theory of liberation from structural violence presupposes theoretically and practically adequate ideas of the dominance system against which liberation is directed; and the special type of dominance system to be discussed here is imperialism.

Johan Galtung

Our present system of national sovereignty is in absolute contradiction to the original democratic conception of sovereignty, which meant – and still means – sovereignty of the community....

The inescapable economic and technical realities of our age make it imperative to re-examine and reinterpret the notion of sovereignty and to create sovereign institutions based on the community, according to the original democratic conception. Sovereignty of the people must stand above the nations so that under it each nation may be equal, just as each individual is equal under the law in a civilized state.

The question is not one of "surrendering" national sovereignty. The problem is not negative and does not involve giving up something we already have. The problem is positive – creating something we lack, something we have never had, but that we imperatively need.

The creation of institutions with universal sovereign power is merely another phase of the same process in the development of human history – the extension of law and order into another field of human association which heretofore has remained unregulated and in anarchy.

Emery Reeves

On one important level, the basic analysis used in this book involves "systems analysis." A fundamental aspect of the paradigm shift in our understanding of the world bequeathed by twentieth-century science is the rise of a systems view of the world (Laszlo 1996). I am sensitive to the criticism that systems analyses tend to leave out human action and human agency and have included these through my reflections on psychology and spirituality. Nevertheless, throughout the scientific spectrum, from physics information theory to biology to sociology and psychology, the realization became clear that the world can be comprehended in terms of wholes, fields, and dynamic systems rather than atomistically in terms of the reduction of wholes to their component parts. Properties show up at the level of whole systems that cannot be derived from a summing up of the parts.

The development of the science of ecology has made this strikingly clear. Only in the past half-century have we come to realize that organisms are *incomprehensible* apart from the ecosystems that encompass and sustain them, and that the biosphere of our planet as a whole is an ecosystem comprehending all life on Earth, the maintenance and protection of which is absolutely necessary for the survival of that life. Human beings also organize themselves into systems comprehensible as wholes manifesting characteristic properties. One can investigate a cultural system, an economic system, a political system, or a social system in terms of the dynamics of its functioning, its structures of renewal and maintenance, and its consequences.

In this chapter, we examine more deeply our modern world system in its two fundamentally interrelated aspects: its political organization (the system of sovereign nation-states) and its economic organization (the system of globalized capitalism). In doing so I will cite a number of other thinkers who have undertaken a systems analysis of this world system, but the focus here, I believe, is fairly unique in that one key variable used in the analysis involves the concept of violence as opposed to nonviolence. *If democracy can be understood as a form of human association that minimizes violence in human relationships, then the degree of violence appearing in our world system is indicative of the degree to which that system is antidemocratic.* Indeed, it will become clear that not only is the modern world economic and political system antidemocratic but it is actively destructive of democracy with all that democracy implies for human freedom, equality, community, and well-being.

The social systems within which we live substantially influence our behavior, and we have seen that such systems are a major source of injustice, war, exploitation, and violence in the world. This is why Thomas Carlyle's "great man theory of history" can be fundamentally misleading. The deep institutions like monopoly capitalism and the sovereign nation-state system are not likely to be fundamentally altered by single individuals. Unless there are a matrix of historical circumstances and a mass movement for structural change behind great leaders, the systems will prevail nearly every time.

That is also why the tremendous excitement of the world at the inauguration of Barack Obama as the 44th President of the United States may well be misguided. The systemic features determining Obama's limited options are so deep and pervasive that they are unlikely to change. The most promising option for a holistic Earth civilization remains the ratification of a *founding document* such as the *Earth Constitution* by a significant group of leaders acting together or by direct ratification by a substantial number of the people of Earth. Structural change would then be mandated by the founding constitutional principles working with a newly formed World Parliament, not by the initiative of single individuals from within the former world system. The system itself resists significant change.

It is important, however, to remind ourselves of the reciprocal and dynamic interrelation between the systems within which we live and the possibilities of both human spirituality and communicative rationality. Social systems have a tremendous influence over which of our human possibilities flourish. Perhaps the most fundamental dividing point is fragmentation versus holism. Fragmented systems tend to cultivate hate, egoism, fear, or mercilessness. Holistic systems tend to cultivate kindness, compassion, and human solidarity. If we understand this reciprocal relationship, we will also understand the need for transforming our world system if we are to actualize our higher rational and spiritual potentialities.

This chapter considers four main topics. First, very briefly, in what ways nonviolence is the essence of both spirituality and religion; second, the dynamics of deep structural violence that characterizes our world disorder; third, the massive overt military violence that is necessary to keep the structural violence in place and operating for the benefit of the few at the expense of the many. Finally, the chapter discusses the *value nihilism* behind the production of weapons of mass destruction.

Ultimately, this value-nihilism manifests the same value-nihilism behind institutional violence and the military violence necessary to keep this "rotten" world system in place. We begin with the questions of spirituality and religion in relation to nonviolence precisely because our fundamental need is to address the question of authentic sources of value for our time. In the background remains our fundamental problem of the twenty-first century: how we can create a democratic, nonviolent world order based on the insight that democracy (with its inherent nonviolence in dealing with human affairs) involves a manifestation of authentic value and a higher level of human development.

4.1 Spirituality and Nonviolence

The existential breakthrough beyond language to the *mysterium magnum* of existence can lead to a spiritual development that awakens ever more deeply to the unsayable depths of the universe. This journey leads to a progressive (or sometimes immediate) reduction of domination by the empirical ego that *defines itself over and against what is not itself.* This awakened spirituality grows ever more deeply toward what some have termed a larger self or the "true self." Mystics of all traditions have testified to this holism (see Fox 1978; Franck 1988), but so has much of contemporary psychology.

Psychologist Robert J. Lifton, we have seen, writes of "the evolution of the self toward its own species.... One moves toward becoming...a fully human being...within a more inclusive sense of self." Psychologist Robert Ornstein speaks of our undertaking "conscious evolution" to evoke this deeper self (1991: 279), and psychologist Gardner Murphy suggests that our real human potential is precisely this capacity for real transformation (1975: 300). Contemporary Zen-Buddhism (Abe 1985) and some twentieth-century Western philosophers fundamentally agree (e.g. Bugbee 1961; Heidegger 1971a; Jacobson 1983).

Psychoanalyst Erich Fromm insists that we must address our deepest problems not only with the critical intellect (as in "systems analysis" or "critical social theory," important as these are), but with *the whole person*, with the concrete fullness of our emotional, spiritual, and lived physical lives. He affirms that the mess we have made of our world involves the fact that we have not begun living fully. We have "yet to be *fully born*, to develop one's awareness, one's reason, one's capacity to love, to such a point that one transcends one's own egocentric involvement, and arrives at a new harmony, at a new oneness with the world" (1960: 87). We have within us this immense potential to free ourselves from our egoistic and parochial obsessions and live from a deeper, more holistic, more life-affirming level.

It may be that spirituality intuits the "depths of being" not ordinarily available to our self-conscious subjectivity. These depths of being appear consonant with the highest truths that inform our subjectivity. Our higher purposes – to achieve the good, to love, to act from universal principles, to protect nature and future generations – resonate with the cosmic purposes intuited by spirituality. Hans Jonas writes:

As subjectivity is in some sense a surface phenomenon of nature – the visible tip of a much larger iceberg – it speaks for the silent interior beneath. Or: The fruit betrays something of the root and the stem out of which it grew. Because subjectivity displays efficacious purpose, indeed wholly lives in it, we must concede to the silent interior which finds language only through it, that is, to matter, that it harbors purpose or its analogue within itself in nonsubjective form. (1984: 71)

The most fundamental roots of the philosophy of nonviolence derive not only from our common rational and communicative social nature but also from this realization of a selfhood (the "silent interior" of nature that is also the silent interior of our selves) that is ultimately deeper than language, deeper than the empirical ego, and more basic than either for both ethics and human relationships. Through intuiting this silent interior we can discern our own higher human purposes for achieving the good and acting from universal principles. It may be this larger selfhood that ultimately makes possible, whether we realize it or not, compassion for the other and reverence for the personhood of others.

Chapter One described "human spirituality" as the root of compassion, kindness, and solidarity. This deeper selfhood, we have also seen, makes possible the *agape* taught by Jesus. As Christian philosopher Charles Hartshorne puts it, only on this basis is it possible to love one's neighbor as oneself (in Jacobson 1983: 99). That is, only on the basis of living from a deeper sense of self in which we realize our *spiritual unity* with other persons.

In his Introduction to *Gandhi on Nonviolence*, Christian thinker and spiritual teacher Thomas Merton writes:

Gandhi's dedicated struggle for Indian freedom and his insistence on nonviolent means in the struggle – both resulted from his new understanding of India and of himself after his contract with a *universally valid* spiritual tradition which he saw to be common to both East and West....

In rediscovering India and his own "right mind".... he was identifying himself...with the starving masses and in particular with the outcaste "untouchables.... But the message of the Indian spirit, of Indian wisdom, was not for India alone. It was for the entire world. Hence Gandhi's message was valid for India and for himself in so far as he represented *the awakening of a new world*....

In Gandhi's mind, nonviolence was not simply a political tactic which was supremely useful and efficacious in liberating his people from foreign rule, in order that India might then concentrate on realizing its own national identity. On the contrary, the spirit of nonviolence sprang from *an inner realization of spiritual unity in himself.* The whole Gandhian concept of nonviolent action and *satyagraha* is incomprehensible if it is thought to be a means of achieving unity rather than as *the fruit of inner unity already achieved*....

The spiritual life of one person is simply the life of all manifesting itself in him. While it is very necessary to emphasize the truth that as the person deepens his own thought in silence he enters into a deeper understanding of and communion with the spirit of his entire people (or his Church), it is also important to remember that as he becomes engaged in the crucial struggles of his people, in seeking justice and truth together with his brother, he tends to liberate the truth in himself by seeking true liberty for all....

The liberation of India was to Gandhi a *religious* duty because for him the liberation of India was only a step to the liberation of all mankind from the tyranny of violence in others, but chiefly in themselves. So Gandhi could say, "When the practice of *ahimsa* becomes universal, God will reign on earth as He does in heaven." (1964: 4-7)

The awakening experienced by Gandhi was essentially identical to that experienced by Martin Luther King, Jr. and many others throughout the ages and across cultures. For Gandhi, "a new world" was dawning, a world that springs from a process in which all human beings participate, a process of growing toward planetary maturity. This maturing of the self involves discovering, as it did with Gandhi, a *"universally valid* spiritual tradition which he saw to be common to both East and West." The causes of violence in ourselves diminish to the extent that we realize our holistic, universal self and no longer compulsively cling to what Freire calls "the oppressor consciousness" that possesses not only things in the world but supremely itself – its ego-consciousness of self-interest, superiority, and domination.

To be able to experience compassion for others involves not only recognizing their personhood, their invaluable Otherness as persons, it involves forgiving their guilt and their evil just as we can find forgiveness for our own guilt. In so far as ego-consciousness is suspended or diminished, we become ever-more capable of seeing the ambiguity and confusion of our own lives with their tendency to objectify the Other in categories that dehumanize the Other and make us capable of negating their personhood. This appears to be the meaning of Jesus' teaching in John 8: 2-11:

And early in the morning He came again into the Temple, and all the people came unto Him; and He sat down, and taught them.

And the scribes and Pharisees brought unto Him a woman taken in adultery; and when they had set her in the midst, They said unto Him, "Master, this woman was taken in adultery, in the very act. Now Moses in the Law commanded us, that such should be stoned: but what sayest Thou?"

This they said, tempting Him, that they might have to accuse Him. But Jesus stooped down, and with His finger wrote on the ground, as though He heard them not. So when they continued asking Him, He lifted up Himself, and said unto them, "He that is without sin among you, let him first cast a stone at her." And again He stooped down, and wrote on the ground.

And they which heard it, being convicted by their own conscience, went out one by one, beginning at the eldest, even unto the last: and Jesus was left alone, and the woman standing in the midst.

When Jesus had lifted up Himself, and saw none but the woman, He said unto her, "Woman, where are those thine accusers? Hath no man condemned thee?" She said, "No man, Lord."

And Jesus said unto her, Neither do I condemn thee: go, and sin no more." (King James Version)

To do violence to a real or imagined enemy is to assume both that there is an irredeemable evil in that enemy that must be eliminated through their elimination and that one's self remains "good" in some fundamental way that allows us to judge their evilness and exterminate it. Such black and white thinking implies an inherent totalitarianism. Any who doubt the worthiness of the enemy to be exterminated or marginalized are by that token suspicious, not "either with us or with the enemy" as George W. Bush expressed this in his declaration of perpetual war against "terrorism" by means of counter-terrorism. These assumptions may not be fully conscious, but nevertheless have implicitly turned those against whom violence is to be used into something less than human: "gooks" in Vietnam, "ragheads" in Iraq, "blacks" in South Africa, "Communists" in Pinochet's Chile, "terrorists" as conceived by the Pentagon of 2009. Fragmented thinking, like fragmented systems, spawns violence and destruction.

Those who discern at all the dynamics of their own inner lives and the complexity (and guilt) of their own spiritual growth understand both the hate, fear, and evil that leads others to violence and the redeemability of all persons whose lives can be transformed through forgiveness, personal growth, and increased self-awareness. Nonviolence as a technique of struggle includes this dimension for it insists that the "enemy" not be eliminated through violence but always remain open to the possibility of transformation and redemption, for the so-called enemy and oneself are intrinsically and holistically linked within a single field. *This very same dynamic applies to democracy.*

This is precisely why democracy asserts the innocence of the accused until proven guilty in a court of law within a social framework in which suspects are arrested with a minimum of violence, have their rights protected pending trial, and are only punished on a rationally determined scale in which punishment fits the crime after reasonable proof of guilt. Any violence beyond the minimum force necessary to the orderly conduct of a democratic society is inherently destructive of democracy, as this and subsequent chapters will make clear.

We have seen that democracy at its core also involves the institutionalization of nonviolent methods of social, political, and economic change. For this to happen, mechanisms of dialogue, information dissemination, and decision-making must be in place that allow persons to enter into a discourse capable of changing minds while engaging in processes of mutual learning and collective, rationally-motivated action. Democracy provides the framework for social as well as personal growth and development, since growth cannot normally take place without both freedom and the matrix of a supporting community.

Hence, democracy requires that citizens understand in basic ways their own fallibility, guilt, ignorance, and partiality so that authentic dialogue becomes possible leading to collective development and decision-making concerning courses of action (or leaders who implement courses of action). Intolerance, the assumption that one possesses absolute truth, or the egoistic assumption of some form of superiority over others, or the assumption that one is without guilt, lead only to totalitarianism. Democracy as a moral ideal and the spiritual development behind nonviolence derive from one and the same source. Political philosopher Hannah Arendt writes:

> Nonviolence has a different logic. It recognizes that sin is an everyday occurrence which is in the very nature of actions' constant establishment of new relationships within a web of relations, and it needs forgiving, dismissing, in order to make it possible for life to go on by constantly releasing men from what they have done unknowingly. Only through this constant mutual release from what they do can men remain free agents, only by their constant willingness to change their minds and start again can they be trusted with so great a power as that to begin something new. (In Merton 1964: 14)

4.2 Religion and Nonviolence

Nonviolence and universality radiate from the heart of authentic religion and from all the great world religions. Religion flows from a diversity of sources, all of which have emerged with the maturation process of human beings since the Axial Period in human history during the first millennium BCE. All sources of authentic religion point toward nonviolence, just as they point toward planetary maturity (Martin 2005a). By "authentic religion" I do not mean religion as an escape or postponement as some authors have described it. And I do not mean by religion the arrogant and ignorant assumption that because God's grace has already forgiven my sins, I have the right to destroy the enemies of God whose sins have not yet been forgiven.

I mean religion as involving mature spiritual awakening or realization. Here I will mention four fundamental sources of authentic religion. My purpose is not to give an exhaustive account of the huge and complex phenomenon of religion that would take us far beyond the scope of this book. My purpose is to suggest some fundamental themes that can illuminate the relationship between authentic religion and nonviolence. My assumption is that authentic religion arises from some form of spiritual realization, understanding, or openness to the deeper sources of our being (God, Allah, Atman, Tao, Buddha nature, the One, etc.)

First, spiritual awakening points forward to planetary maturity and world unity. All thought and language arise from the deep silence that permeates the universe, as thinkers as diverse as fourteenth century Christian thinker Meister Eckhart (1980), the thirteenth century Islamic thinker Jelaluddin Rumi (1995), and twentieth century philosopher Max Picard (1952) have explained. A growing openness to this silence leads to a direct awareness of the oneness of others with myself, a central root of nonviolence. In much of Buddhism and Hinduism, this transforming compassion is extended to all sentient beings. Both the way of life directed toward *moksa* or *nirvana* must be nonviolent and the way of life consequent upon *moksa* or *nirvana* remains nonviolent. Means and ends are inseparable.

Second, to briefly draw upon the philosophy of religion articulated by Christian theologian Paul Tillich (1987), the prophetic openness to the word of God is a consequence of a participation in the infinite *Power of Being* characterized as *agape*, the transforming love consequent upon the experience of grace, the saving power that grasps us when we participate with authentic ultimate concern in relation to God, the infinite ground of our being. The result is a love that rejects no human being and ultimately rejects the idea of violence against any human being. To be established in the love of God, Jesus proclaims in Matthew 22: 34-40, also establishes us in the love of our neighbor as ourselves.

In response to the question "And who is my neighbor?" Jesus tells the story of the good Samaritan (Luke 10:25-37). The Samaritans were looked down upon by Jesus' Jewish audience, yet the essence of obeying God's commandment to love is embodied in the Samaritan who exemplified the simple life of *agape*, loving others as oneself. "When you have done it unto one of the least of these my brethren you have done it unto me" expresses the source of authentic religion insofar as we participate with love and openness in the ground of our own being (Matt. 25: 40).

Third, authentic religion fulfills itself in nonviolence as a result of the historical process of development of religious consciousness and understanding. As human beings grow historically toward *planetary maturity*, they understand the structure of the universe and "the real" from which nonviolence flows ever more fully. For example, the structure of consciousness, of our minds, reflecting as this does, the fundamental organizing principle of the universe, points to human apperception as conscious *unity in diversity*. Science in the twentieth century has discovered the human mind as a reflection of the absolute oneness or unity of the universe that constitutes an evolving whole diversifying itself in ever greater forms of complexification and organization (cf. Harris 1992: Ch. 1).

Similarly, since Kant, many have understood that the synthetic unity of human apperception constitutes a single organizational principle that comprehends the multiplicity of the universe within an all-embracing unity (ibid). Once again, we see that the *Other* cannot be alienated from us as a fragment over and against our own being. Our very ability to relate to and know the *Other* requires the all-embracing unity characteristic of both the universe and human consciousness. The other person, nation, race, or religion cannot be separated from me as a fragment contradicting my own being. The very possibility of my encounter with the *Other* presupposes this all-embracing unity. To really respect their otherness as Other, as a unique freedom different from my own, I must embrace the *Other* and myself within the larger unity of nonviolence.

Fourth, this *unity in diversity* of human awareness may be a basic source of our sense of our universal humanity, the sense that we are human beings first in ways that cannot be separated from our respective individual identities. This awareness functions as a ground for the concept of universal human rights. It involves our "species being," our fundamental oneness as human beings expressed, for example, in the moral principle fundamental to all religions: do unto others as you would have them do unto you (cf. Miranda 1986). The recognition of the humanity of the *Other*, as philosopher Leonard Nelson (1956) has pointed out, is also an immediate recognition of the other's rights vis-à-vis myself. Once again, I am not free to do violence against my neighbor. This principle, as expressed in the words of philosopher Emmanuel Levinas, involves the recognition of the "infinity in the face of the other" and includes an immediate claim upon me that says "thou shall not kill" (1985: 89).

Each of the great world religions and many of the minor world religions such as the Baha'i religion, the Oomoto religion, or Unitarian Universalism proclaim the universality of God, Allah, Brahman, Tao, or Dharmakaya. Their origins often involve the famous "scandal of particularity" (cf. H. Smith 1991: 308). They originated under particular circumstances within a particular culture but the deeper message is one of a universal sacred principle available to all human beings and recognizing the sanctity of all human beings (and potentially all life). As contemporary Islamic thinker Rashid Shaz expresses this: "Islam…is neither eastern nor western but only bears 'the colour of God' calling people to attain a God-centered identity" (2008: 63).

This message is most simply formulated by all authentic religions as some form of the golden rule (cf. John Hick's discussion of this in *An Interpretation of Religion*, Chs. 17 & 18). The consequence of the golden rule is nonviolence, just as the consequence of Immanuel Kant's categorical imperative is nonviolence: always treat every person as an end in themselves never merely as a means (1964). If persons are treated as ends in themselves, they cannot be legitimately killed in any form of military or violent conflict (see Chapter 8 below where I will also consider the question of self-defense).

What all these sources of authentic religion have in common is the inseparability of myself from the other within a diversity embraced by a unity that cannot be dissolved but makes possible affirmation and recognition of that diversity. The alternative to this, and a root cause of violence, is fragmentation – the human mind, misidentifying itself in terms of its egoistic isolation and out of touch with its epistemic or metaphysical roots, objectifying and alienating the *Other* as an opposite, as a contradiction to its being, as evil, or as enemy. This fragmentation is philosophically, scientifically, and religiously false, and ultimately denies its own being that cannot be affirmed apart from its *unity in diversity* with the being of the *Other*. In Part Three below, I will return to practical ways that we can promote the *unity in diversity* of humankind.

4.3 The Violent Structure of Today's World System

If the source of nonviolence flows from our primal *unity in diversity* as human beings, then violence involves everything that structurally, economically, socially, politically, or personally denies this principle. Violence is what violates the personhood of other human beings, whether using them without their consent, manipulating them, coercing them, or harming them physically, economically, socially, culturally, or personally. (For the sake of simplicity here, I am leaving aside the very important question of violence against animals and nature in general.) The heart of all the great religions is the respect for the diversity of each person as an end in his or her self and a concomitant affirmation of the unity of all persons that makes this respect possible. From this principle, I have derived the following description of the deep violence of today's world disorder in terms of both extent and significance.

Theoretical analyses of the inherent violence of today's world system are not lacking and will be further examined in Chapters Five and Six. However, within imperial societies such analyses are often buried under endless forms of ideological self justification to the point where awareness of what should be obvious to everyone is obscured through collective illusions. Mexican thinker José Miranda describes "that mechanism of violence which we call the market, whether the consumer market, the wage market, or both" (1974: 12). North American Sociologists Terry Boswell and Christopher Chase-Dunn affirm that "at all points of exchange in production, capitalists have institutionalized *coercive power* as employers, bosses, lenders, and landlords" (2000: 21), and world systems theorist Johann Galtung (quoted at the head of this chapter) describes our world order as one of "structural violence" (1971: 43).

The three central categories of violence outlined below appear in order of their pervasiveness and significance: *first*, structural violence (primarily poverty and deprivation) and the process of creating ever more structural violence; *second*, the imperial violence of nation-states or oppressive governments that extends and maintains this structural violence; *third*, the nihilistic violence imbedded in weapons of mass destruction, such as nuclear weapons, and in research in devising ever-more horrific ways of destroying human beings and their life-support systems. In Chapter Five, I will examine the issues of religious, revolutionary, and rebellious violence that often react to the first three forms of violence, usually with religious, ethnic, or sectarian identities that inspire yet more violence.

First, the central form of violence on our planet today involves the dynamic of structural violence that manifests itself in the impoverishment of the vast majority. This structural violence is an historical consequence of the system of the private accumulation of wealth that has been imposed upon the world for the past several centuries. Today:

Half the world — more than three billion people — live on less than two dollars a day. Nearly a billion people entered the twenty-first century unable to read a book or sign their names. Less than one per cent of what the world spends each year on weapons can put every child on Earth into school. The poorer the country, the more likely it is that debt repayments are being extracted directly from people who neither contracted the loans nor received any of the money.

The developing world now spends $13 on debt repayment for every $1 it receives in grants. Approximately 790 million people in the developing world are still chronically undernourished. 30,000 children die each day due to poverty. 2.2 million children die each year because they have not been immunized. Some 1.1 billion people in developing countries have inadequate access to water, and 2.6 billion lack basic sanitation. The slice of the economic pie taken by the richest 1% of the world's people is the same size as that available to the poorest 57% of humankind. The Gross Domestic Product of the poorest 48 nations (i.e. twenty-five percent of the world's countries) is less than the wealth of the world's three richest people combined.

(http://www.globalissues.org.)

The international system of property rights and trade rules imposed upon the world from within the system of nation-states makes involuntary poverty clearly a form of violence. If people do not choose to live in these conditions of horrible suffering and deprivation, it is because there is a system in place that *prevents* them from altering their condition for the better. The system of property rights today dominates worldwide. Giant corporations own the resources in poor countries and exploit these for private profit, not for the benefit of the host countries. Giant banking consortiums loan money (their private concentrations of wealth) through the World Bank and IMF to poor countries and subsequent generations are permanently saddled with unsustainable debt. These property rights (both intellectual and material) are kept in place by law, and by the police and military both within and without poor countries. Structural violence is enforced by the threat of overt violence.

Any system of "exploitation" will be a system of structural violence (Galtung 1971). In general, we mean by "exploitation" a situation in which the exploited persons have something taken from them that they would not voluntarily give, for example, the surplus value of their labor that is robbed from them through paying them very low or starvation wages. "In reality," Miranda writes, "the accumulation of capital in a few hands, could not and cannot be achieved without...institutional violence," a violence aided by "ideologies, education, and communications media," which comprise "the violence of deception" (1974: 12 & 14).

The *second* form of violence after structural violence, therefore, involves the imperial violence of nation-states, and their neocolonial representatives within poor countries (rulers, police, and military), working to intimidate, enforce, and control the populations subjected to structural violence. Neither exploitation nor structural violence could take place were it not for the threat of overt violence used to enforce the system of property rights, trade rules, and other legal instruments by which this violence is organized and protected. Neither could it exist, as Miranda points out, without "the violence of deception" both in education and the mass media.

This system of sovereign nation-states was first formally recognized in the 1648 Treaty of Westphalia (cf. Philpott 2001). These early imperial centers proceeded to divide the world among themselves, appropriating for themselves the cheap slave labor and resources of the majority of humankind who were organized as colonies of these imperial centers of capital. The imperial powers controlled this system conceptually with their ideologies of sovereign nation-states, notions of religious and civilizational superiority, and claimed imperial rights of domination over their colonies. The imperial nations also adopted the ideology of Adam Smith: "free trade" as a cover for their nationalistic competition to control the global wealth-producing process in their own interests (J.W. Smith 2006: Chs. 1-4). They affirmed the ideology of unlimited capital expansion (at the expense of nature and the poor) as the only possible route to development and prosperity but attempted to channel this process of expansion (in ways that were anything but "free trade") to the ruling classes of their respective nation-states.

This system of exploitation and domination in the name of both ruling classes and imperial nations was firmly rejected by Mahatma Gandhi. Gandhi often spoke of "the organized violence of economic exploitation" (Jesudasan 1984: 120). A world order in which these conditions of political domination and economic exploitation prevail is inherently violent for Gandhi. "Economics that hurt the moral well-being of an individual or nation are immoral and, therefore, sinful," he wrote. "Thus, the economics that permit one country to prey upon another are immoral" (ibid). "True economics," he said, "stands for social justice, it promotes the good of all equally including the weakest, and is indispensable for decent life" (ibid). Gandhi placed nonviolence in an historical perspective in which human beings, in real time, came to understand their *unity in diversity* and simultaneously to repudiate the dominant economic system and imperial nation-state system as *both* inherently violent.

With decolonization, we have seen, the system did not change its fundamental character. Just as the colonies had been kept weak and impoverished by the sovereign overseers, after decolonization the newly "free" nations became subject to manipulation, overthrow, destabilization, or invasion by one or the other of their former colonial masters. They also became subject to financial control by the World Bank, IMF, and other gigantic private banking consortiums (cf. E. Brown 2007). Hundreds of millions of poor now live in these countries as in prison camps, unable to leave and utterly unable to improve their own condition – controlled economically, politically, and militarily from abroad.

The structural violence of enforced poverty and misery is not an accident. It is a direct consequence of the imperial conquest and exploitation of the world by the European nations and their imperial heir, the United States, from the time of Columbus to the present. Today, despite decolonization, that system of exploitation continues in the global economic system protected by the military might and political power of the imperial nations, under the leadership of the United States. The United States globally enforces this system of structural violence and death with its military, economic, and political might in the service, as throughout its history, not of its people but of its ruling class and their powerful transnational corporations (Parenti 1995).

Naomi Klein's book *The Shock Doctrine: The Rise of Disaster Capitalism* (2007) documents this principle at length with regard to the U.S. role in the horrific dictatorships and disaster economics (disaster for the poor, unparalleled success for multinational corporations and the rich) in Chile, Argentina, Brazil, Uruguay, Bolivia, Poland, Russia, South Africa, Iraq, and elsewhere. The book documents extensively the relationship between neoliberal capitalist economics and torture in dozens of countries where the neoliberal economic "shock doctrine" has been imposed upon already suffering and desperate peoples. The book chronicles the shock doctrine as fundamental to economic ideology within the United States and England as well as the ways that the neoliberal elite and corporate oligarchy continue to solidify their control over people and resources worldwide.

In *Empire with Imperialism: The Globalizing Dynamics of Neo-liberal Capitalism* (2005), James Petras and Henry Veltmeyer present a detailed analysis and careful factual and statistical description of the dynamics of the world imperial system today. Under the undisputed leadership of the United States, they show the inseparable relationship between the global economic system and its military, police, and terroristic enforcement by imperial forces and their agents in the periphery of empire. As with unimaginable concentrations of wealth, massive poverty in today's world is not an accident but very much a consequence of this imperial system and its globalized capitalist economics. It is inherently a system of violence and domination.

If I have poor women utterly dependent upon me as their employer or slave owner and I demand sex from them, I am guilty of violence against them even if I never use overt violence. Exactly the same principle operates if I force structural adjustment upon poor nations or impose globalized trade rules upon them about which they have no choice. Globalization in the service of the world's powerful corporations and economies is a rape of the poorest 80% of humanity. It is a dynamic of violence, pure and simple. GATT and WTO trade rules are coercive rules that demand of poor countries that they open their economies to foreign economic investment under the threat of economic retaliation and punishment (Mander and Goldsmith 1996).

Part of the mechanism by which this is done also includes what I call "spiritual violence" (cf. Martin 2005a: Ch. 3). Spiritual violence involves the violence of lies and deception in order to foster my self-interest at the expense of others. We saw above that authentic religion in all its forms affirms love of other human beings as oneself. We saw that this is essentially the same as Kant's categorical imperative that requires treating others as ends in themselves and never merely as a means. Lies and deception in the service of domination and economic self-interest violate the personhood of others and are therefore a form of violence. The distortions and lies of the corporate owned mass media have become indispensible agents for the maintenance of the global system of structural violence (Calidcott 1992: Ch. 8; Edwards 1996; Chomsky and Hermann 2002).

There are many examples of this that could be given from the ideological arsenal of the globalizers. For example, the concept of "free trade" itself is such a lie. There is nothing free about this trade. It is coerced from the very beginning and forced upon the majority of humankind. It is structured for the advantage of the ruling classes of the world at the expense of everyone else and the environment. If human beings are ever to find real freedom for themselves, it will have to include real democratic freedom for all, including sufficient economic prosperity to allow the freedom from disease, suffering, and early death (cf. Chang 2008; Martin 2005b: Ch. 4).

The spiritual violence of lies and deception forms a key element through which this dynamic of structural violence continues in today's world. Vandana Shiva describes the development of the concept of the "production boundary" that defines productivity according to WTO rules in today's globalized economy (1997b). The production boundary is an arbitrary definition created to define growth and trade between nations. It was decided that if people consume what they produce, then they are not producing. Only what is produced and traded on the global market is defined as production and entered into the economic calculations that measure economic growth. This decision, while obviously entirely stipulative, is far from arbitrary. Its intent is very clear.

With this definition, the hard productive work to survive and live contributed by most of humanity simply disappears: all the subsistence farming and production that goes on throughout the third world, all the work of women inside the home, all the care-giving and sharing that defines and honors the humanity of the poor majority who often work together for survival is counted at nothing (Shiva 1997b). In other words, what makes us human, our cooperation and hard work to give care to one another within our families, communities, and nations, is counted as zero in the institutionalized violence that is globalized trade organized and defined by the WTO. It all simply disappears with intellectual lies and ideological distortions such as this concept of the production boundary. Not only do such lies constitute a vicious spiritual violence against our humanity, their institutional consequences in the form of suffering, death, and disease are immeasurable.

When the poor are hurt by globalized trade policies or by structural adjustment programs, they sometimes rebel. Their rebellion may take the form of trying to democratically elect or create programs that counter these imposed economic policies (often futile since they are not in control of their own societies), or they may take the form of guerrilla warfare in an attempt to take control of their societies from the imperial forces of domination, or they may engage in acts of social or political violence, which the dominators call "terrorism." Such rebellion is an obvious and expected consequence of economic globalization. This expected consequence of the system of planetary exploitation has led the imperial powers to redefine the role of governments to adapt to the new neocolonial imperial system. Governments no longer protect their people and act for the defense of their people and the common good. In fact, this power is being taken away from them, since under WTO rules corporations now have the right to sue governments that restrict their economic exploitation within host nations.

Governments are today being redefined as security forces for multinational investors. Their responsibility is no longer to consider their citizens' basic needs, nor to provide essential services or utilities, nor to foster the common good. All these functions are now placed in the hands of multinational corporate investors whose sole motivation is private accumulation of wealth for themselves. Rather, these governments are now to be solely concerned with their police and enforcement functions on behalf of foreign investors primarily residing outside the country.

Their military and police are being trained by first-world imperial military forces to put down internal rebellion and subversion and to protect foreign economic assets within the host nations. As political analyst Michael Parenti puts this: "Since World War II, the U.S. government has given over $200 billion in military aid to train, equip, and subsidize more than 2.3 million troops and internal security forces in some eighty countries, the purpose being not to defend them from outside invasions but to protect ruling oligarchs and multinational corporate investors from the dangers of anticapitalist insurgency" (1995: 37). The 2008 election of Barack Obama will not change this system significantly precisely because it is *institutionalized* down to the very roots of the current world order.

The imposition and protection of this global system of exploitation and death goes far beyond mere training and funding for police repression of the poor worldwide. Every empire in history has used massive systematic terror inflicted on dominated peoples to appropriate their land, labor, and resources. The U.S.-led global empire of today is no different. The proper definition of the overwhelming quantity of violence to which the poor of the world have been subjected should be termed "state terrorism." Compared to state terror, the private terror of weak and marginalized groups forms a drop in the bucket. Unlike what we hear from mass media propaganda, private terror is not a major problem in the world. *The major world problem is global structural violence protected and enhanced by massive nation-state violence.* Parenti writes:

> U.S. leaders profess a dedication to democracy. Yet over the past five decades, democratically elected reformist governments in Guatemala, Guyana, the Dominican Republic, Brazil, Chile, Uruguay, Syria, Indonesia (under Sukarno), Greece, Argentina, Bolivia, Haiti, and numerous other nations were overthrown by pro-capitalist militaries that were funded and aided by the U.S. national security state.
>
> The U.S. national security state has participated in covert actions or proxy mercenary wars against revolutionary governments in Cuba, Angola, Mozambique, Ethiopia, Portugal, Nicaragua, Cambodia, East Timor, Western Sahara, and elsewhere, usually with dreadful devastation and loss of life for the indigenous populations. Hostile actions also have been directed against reformist governments in Egypt, Lebanon, Peru, Iran, Syria, Zaire, Jamaica, South Yemen, the Fiji Islands, and elsewhere.
>
> Since World War II, U.S. forces have directly invaded or launched aerial attacks against Vietnam, the Dominican Republic, North Korea, Laos, Cambodia, Lebanon, Grenada, Panama, Libya, Iraq, and Somalia, sowing varying degrees of death and destruction. (Ibid. p. 38)

In Vietnam alone, the U.S. genocidally wiped out the civilian population through massive saturation bombing of their villages and cities, causing the deaths of three to four million persons. Private terrorism is a blip on the screen compared to the massive state terrorism of our world disorder led by the United States. This is not an accident. Vietnam was not a "tragic mistake" as the propaganda system would have us believe. It was part of the dynamic of global imperial domination in the service of capital exploitation of the cheap labor and resources of the entire world.

Nowhere on Earth is safe from attack if the people of some small nation want to take their economic destiny into their own hands. The U.S. invasion of the tiny island of Granada under President Reagan was not about nutmeg (the island's chief export), as President Reagan himself proclaimed. The economy of that country had zero significance for the U.S. economy. But the invasion was a message to every

Caribbean and Latin American nation that if you try to control your own resources in the interest of your own people, this is the kind of terror you are inviting upon yourselves (ibid.).

The invasion of Iraq and the utter devastation of their society and destruction of hundreds of thousands of Iraqi lives was not only about oil. It was also about geopolitical control of the Middle East, indicated by the building of four gigantic, permanent U.S. military bases on Iraqi soil. There is no intention of ever relinquishing control of Iraq, but maintaining control under some form of puppet government. Even the Democrats in the U.S. Congress, most of whom are representatives of the U.S. ruling class, know this very well.

Yet there was still another purpose to the terrorist destruction of the Iraqi society and its people: the military "shock and awe" devastation of that country in a matter of days was intended as a world demonstration of the U.S. capacity for state terror. It was intended to send a message to the entire world that if you oppose the empire of the United States, you will be subjected to your own total destruction through a similar "shock and awe" inflicted by the superpower. This is the very definition of terrorism: the use of violence for political or social purposes (cf. Blum 2000: 32). Every imperial nation in history has used massive violence to achieve its political and social goals. The United States may well hold the record in this regard: while the ideological lies formulated by the U.S. mass media leave the majority of its population clueless.

4.4 Weapons of Mass Destruction and the Violence of Nihilism

The *third* form of violence in today's world involves the development, production, and deployment of weapons of mass destruction, primarily nuclear weapons, and the diabolic research that continues in the service of developing ever-more hideous forms of destruction. Nuclear weapons have no coherent military use and have been declared illegal by the World Court in 1996 and repeatedly in sessions of the Provisional World Parliament from 1982 to the present (the latter can be found at www.worldproblems.net). The utter nihilistic violence indicated by the very existence of weapons of total destruction underlies the intrinsic violence of our world disorder.

Since none of these weapons have any legitimate military value (assuming for the moment that there *can* be legitimate military action), and since they are intended for nihilistic destruction of entire cities and populations (here incarnated in a human-made machine form) these doomsday weapons are violence pure and simple: nihilistic, absurd, and absolutely criminal violence. Informed studies of these weapons and the entire nuclear industry can be found in *Nuclear Madness* (1994) by Helen

Caldicott and *The Criminality of Nuclear Deterrence* (2002) by Francis A. Boyle. These weapons could not exist at all if there were even the slightest respect for human beings, life on planet Earth, or for God.

They exist because there is no such respect, as evidenced in the structural violence imposed upon the Earth's majority by the few who also develop these hideous weapons. Like the hatred of life and human beings evidenced in the system of structural violence and state terrorism in the service of structural violence, these nuclear weapons evidence the ultimate demonic hatred of God's creation and human life. Whether they are used or not is irrelevant to this point. The deep violence of today's world disorder is a violence permeated by the nihilistic criminality of all the nuclear-weapons-possessing nation-states and their weapons-directed research and production.

But this value-nihilism reflects merely the final result of the negation of our humanity by the imperative of capital accumulation. When all human values are negated – love, kindness, cooperation, sharing, the value of people as ends in themselves – by an economic system that turns people and nature into commodities whose labor and resources are exploited in the service of capital expansion, and by the military might of nation-states who place themselves in the service of capital accumulation by their respective ruling classes – then all values eventually appear to be relative and the result reflects pure nihilism on the part of the ruling classes. As political economist Istvan Meszaros expresses this:

> From capital's uncritical self-expansionary vantage point there can be no difference between destruction and consumption. One is as good as the other for the required purpose. This is so because the commercial transaction in the capital relation – even of the most destructive kind, embodied in the ware of the military/industrial complex and the use to which it is put in its inhuman wars – successfully completes the cycle of capital's enlarged self-reproduction, so as to be able to open a new cycle. This is the only thing that really matters to capital, no matter how unsustainable might be the consequences. (2007: 26)

The inhuman construction of weapons of mass destruction, like the endless manufacture of bombs and others weapons and their use in wars for control of the wealth-producing process, like the massive use of "private military contractors" in Iraq, Afghanistan, and elsewhere, count, in the twisted economic calculations of capitalism, as economic health, as contributing to an expanding GNP. The result includes value-nihilism with its concomitant systems of violence and death. The massive production of weapons of war by the dominant imperial systems of the world is necessary to enforce its dominance over the system of structural violence suffocating humanity.

However, nuclear weapons deserve their own category, since they are *vehicles of indiscriminate mass destruction* and cannot even be used with the selective violence necessary to enforce exploitation upon oppressed populations. Spiritually speaking, they reveal that the dominant world system as a whole is premised on the hatred of life. This system is most fundamentally a system of destruction, violence, and death. It is the ultimate denial of the holism of our universe, our planetary biosystem, human civilization, morality, and human spirituality.

Human beings have not yet discovered the deep love and respect for life that flows from spiritual, psychological, and intellectual health and well-being. They remain fragmented and pathologically committed as much to death as they are to life. Only the founding of a holistic world system, originating from entirely different (holistic) premises and the ascent to planetary maturity, can make possible a decent future for our children and our fellow living creatures on this planet.

Chapter Five

Religious and Revolutionary Violence

Understandable Reactions to a Horrific World System

That is why I say there are pestilences and there are victims; nor more than that. If, by making that statement, I, too, become a carrier of the plague-germ, at least I don't do it willfully. I try, in short to be an innocent murderer. You see, I've no great ambitions. I grant that there should be a third category: that of the true healers. But it's a fact one doesn't come across many of them, and anyhow it must be a hard vocation. That is why I decided to take, in every predicament, the victim's side, so as to reduce the damage done.

Albert Camus

The reader may well object that a compassionate society is a utopian dream which has never existed anywhere on Earth. The author would, of course, agree, with the qualification that some individuals and some small groups have been highly compassionate. However, the instant recognition of the utopian character of a compassionate society is a sure sign of how far we are from actualizing such a society, which seems to be required if human existence is going to continue on this Earth very much longer.

William Eckhardt

Our world includes many people passionately committed to peace with justice who maintain that violence is a necessary last resort against the horrific suffering and dehumanization imposed worldwide by the dominant imperial and capitalist economic systems. They often see the Gandhian techniques of nonviolent resistance as hopelessly inadequate against the savage and inhuman brutality of the "shock and awe" imperial dominators who destroy homes, buildings, workplaces, water-systems, and people's lives from the air without ever seeing their victims face to face – without compassion, remorse, or feeling, as the Israelis are doing to the Palestinians of the Gaza strip as I write these words, and as in a dozen other wars raging around the world – in most of which the great powers have a hand.

The devastation wrought in Vietnam from the air that destroyed the lives, villages, and sustaining environment of some three or four million Vietnamese people – ninety percent of them civilians: old people, women and children – is also a case in point. And on the ground in Vietnam, torture was rampant and widespread among the dominators (Goff 2004). Today, unmanned Predator drones kill civilians indiscriminately in Afghanistan, Pakistan and elsewhere, raining missiles from the air, in their soulless hunt for those opposing the U.S. invasion and destruction of their countries.

5.1 Rebellious Violence and the Response of "Counter-Insurgency" Warfare

Stan Goff's book, *Full Spectrum Disorder: The Military in the New American Century,* is valuable in understanding the widespread use of torture by American troops as well as the obsession with "full spectrum dominance" that has little or nothing to do with the defense of the United States and everything to do with the imperial imposition of the capitalist nightmare on the majority of poor but resource rich countries of the world. Global capitalism thrives on poverty, unemployment, and on the system of very poor, weak nations who are heavily dependent upon the imperial centers of capital for their survival. This opens up the "world market" to extremely cheap labor and the exploitation of cheap natural resources with very little responsibility for preserving people's lives or protecting the environment.

Writers in struggle against the dominant world disorder who accept revolutionary violence as a necessary means within the struggle (e.g., Mao Tse-Tung, Kwame Nkrumah, Ho Chi Minh, or Ché Guevara) often wrote treatises about guerrilla warfare, sometimes claiming that this was the only legitimate form of violence because it could not succeed without the widespread support of the people. Their justification for the revolutionary violence includes their defense of the starving and repressed poor against terrible exploitation, poverty, misery, and on-going repression. Their arguments were often seriously compelling and made the case that justice could not be attained without such violence. Even so-called "democratic" processes in third-world countries were demonstrably and routinely manipulated and subverted by the imperial centers and the mass-media, thereby preventing peaceful change. All this was and is, for the most part, sadly true.

The revolutionary band sailing from Mexico in a single cabin cruiser that landed in eastern Cuba in the late 1950s, for example, would have been easily crushed by the military might of the U.S.-supported dictator Fulgencio Batista but for the fact that the people of Cuba sheltered, supplied, gave logistical information to, and aided the guerrillas to recruit additional revolutionary fighters and ultimately triumph. The propaganda system of the big capitalist media often characterizes such revolutionary actions as if they were introducing violence (or "terrorism") into a society, rather than attempting to solve problems peacefully (as the U.S. and the capitalist system presumably advocate).

However, in the light of our discussion above of the three central kinds of violence permeating our world disorder, it should be clear that such revolutionary forms of violence almost inevitably constitute *a response* to a horrific system of structural violence and the military and police system designed to protect that structural violence, to normalize it, and stabilize it. Revolutionary violence most often does not initiate violence but forms a defense and a reaction against devastating systems of structural and repressive violence. Meanwhile, the imperial propaganda systems (multinational corporate news media), primarily targeting the populations of the imperial centers, speak of protecting "a stable investment climate," "free trade," "promoting democracy," or training foreign military in "protecting human rights," never of protecting systems of structural violence. (The most basic "human right" to be protected by this foreign military training is, of course, the right of private property for foreign investors and their private accumulation of wealth.)

Analyses such as that in Vandana Shiva's book *Protect or Plunder? Understanding Intellectual Property Rights,* J.W. Smith's book *Economic Democracy: The Political Struggle of the 21st Century,* or Ha-Joon Chang's book *Bad Samaritans: The Myth of Free Trade and the Secret History of Capitalism* reveal that the orderly "free trade" promoted by the imperial centers is anything but free trade but simply a cover for the plunder of the Earth's riches and the poor by those who already control the wealth and power of the planet. Detailed histories such as that by Greg Grandin in *Empire's Workshop – Latin America, the United States, and the Rise of the New Imperialism* or Noam Chomsky's *What Uncle Sam*

Really Wants show the manipulation of the political processes of Latin America in order to keep the system of domination and plunder by trade in place. When the manipulation fails, there is "counter-insurgency" warfare and repression.

A fundamental component of U.S foreign policy involves the training of military personnel from dozens of countries around the world in "counter-insurgency warfare." This training does not involve ways to defend countries from other countries but rather methods of repression of the people within the military's own country who attempt to make changes in the status quo. In practice, the results of this training have involved the use of paramilitary death squads that target social workers, union organizers, community activists, teachers, or religious workers advocating change. The School of the Americas (SOA) in Fort Benning, GA, (today called the Western Hemispheric Institute for Security Cooperation, WHISC) has produced a list of graduates that could function as a who's who of dictators, torturers, and murderers for Latin America (Hodge and Cooper 2004).

This counter-insurgency warfare doctrine has been developed systematically by the United States since the early 1960s and taught, we have seen, to the militaries of dozens of countries around the world. It has a very special character. The counter-insurgency analysts in the Pentagon have studied the writings about guerilla warfare by revolutionary leaders and have understood that the support of the people is crucial to the success of any guerrilla revolutionary struggle. Therefore "counter-revolutionary" doctrine *targets the people* as well as the revolutionaries themselves. Anyone promoting progressive change becomes a "subversive."

This normally must be done in indirect and plausibly deniable ways, since the populations in the imperial centers must believe that their military fights "terrorists" or "violent rebels," not the majority of citizens in foreign countries who are not involved with violent resistance. Nevertheless, Pentagon planners (many of whom understand that they work for the imperial capitalist system of corporations and the rich largely centered in the United States) understand very well that poor people live in misery and are likely to tacitly or actively support both nonviolent methods of taking control of their resources in order to get out of poverty (democracy and "socialism") or violent methods of resistance (guerilla warfare). In either case, they must be stopped, and the dual key to stopping a vast majority of people who are discontented is a combination of instilling hopelessness and instilling terror.

In some cases their foreign military trainees in El Salvador or Guatemala (graduates of the infamous School of the Americas) have gone overboard with this policy and simply wiped out entire villages in areas where guerillas are suspected of operating. It is not that this policy is repugnant to the Pentagon (in Vietnam, Laos, and Cambodia they did this on a scale unimaginable in El Salvador or Guatemala) but that this policy is in danger of becoming known for what it is by the population of the imperial center: genocide. Even though the U.S. exempted itself from the international Genocide Convention when it finally ratified that convention in 1988, 40 years after it was agreed upon by most of the world's nations, the accusation of genocide involves negative images that the public relations wing of the Pentagon tries to avoid (Johnson 2004: Ch. 10).

In actual practice, the preferred method of creating the feeling of hopelessness in populations and paralyzing their capacity for action is anonymous terror inculcated through death squads and clandestine torture centers. In most nations (even dictatorships) indiscriminate killing or torture by the military and police is officially against the law or bad publicity for government. However, if military or police remove indentifying markings from their clothing and undertake raids that disappear human rights workers, union leaders, liberation educators, honest journalists, progressive intellectuals, or church workers among the poor, the government can claim that it either does not know who is responsible or that its political enemies (usually the left-wing guerrillas or "terrorists") are involved.

Naomi Klein's book *The Shock Doctrine* makes clear that these policies are not simply a reaction to the threat of violence from those who wish to defend the poor through guerrilla warfare. The Pentagon and CIA doctrine of "counter-insurgency warfare" is a misnomer. For its central purpose is not counter-insurgency but shocking and terrifying civilian populations into accepting the imposition of economic policies that impoverish the majority while enriching the multinational corporations and the elite few.

Klein points out that the Argentine revolutionary group, the Montoneros, and the Uruguayan revolutionary group, the Tupamaros, already had been completely dismantled before the bulk of the terror was unleashed on the populations of these countries during the 1970s and 80s (2007: 97). The "war on terror," Klein demonstrates, is merely a cover story for the real attempt to dismantle the will of the people, the "solidarity" of ordinary people with one another and the poor. Its goal is both to instill hopelessness and terror so that people will refuse to support guerrilla insurgencies and to inculcate the regime of pure selfishness and greed required by neoliberal economics being imposed from the United States using the ideological work of Milton Friedman and University of Chicago School of Economics (pp. 111-114).

The economists know what their friends the dictators in third-world countries also understand deeply: that the masses of people in any poor society are likely to be sympathetic to projects like land reform,

nationalization of key industries, public education, public health care or
other "socialist" ideas that are anathema to neoliberal capitalism.
Populations must be terrorized into the feelings of hopelessness or
paralyzing fear for themselves or their loved ones. If the world is to be
effectively converted to the "pure" capitalism of neoliberal doctrine, then
terror must be instituted on populations simultaneously with the economic
shock of people's having their entire economies undercut and transformed
into systems of pure exploitation ("free markets") with no holds barred.

We have seen in previous chapters that the emergent evolutionary
upsurge moving human beings to ever-higher levels of existence involves
the continual development of *agape,* compassion, socialist solidarity,
communicative rationality, and democratic community. None of these
developing human capacities can support the amoral and inhuman
workings of capitalism. Like any system of oligarchic power and rule that
is inherently undemocratic, today's economic system is also inherently
violent. Hence, in countries where the "pure" capitalist experiment is to
be implemented, people have to not only be terrorized into not interfering,
but their activists, leaders, and spokespersons must have their
personalities and deepest values erased through torture and remade in the
ruthless, selfish image of human nature coming out of the University of
Chicago, the Pentagon, and Washington, DC.

When the U.S. helped Chilean General Pinochet (trained in "counter-
insurgency" warfare at the U.S. Army School of the Americas) overthrow
the democratically elected government of Chile in 1973, it supported
mass repression by the military of the people of Chile (with weapons,
military training, and political support for the new dictatorship). But this
raised tremendous publicity problems with the international press. Still
the problem remained: how do you impose horrific economic conditions
on unwilling populations? Klein continues:

> The newly declassified documents from Brazil show that when Argentina's
> generals were preparing their 1976 coup, they wanted "to avoid suffering an
> international campaign like the one that has been unleashed against Chile."
> To achieve that goal, less sensational repression tactics were needed – lower
> profile ones capable of spreading terror but not so visible to the prying
> international press. In Chile, Pinochet soon settled on disappearances.
> Rather than openly killing or even arresting their prey, soldiers would
> snatch them, take them to clandestine camps, torture and often kill them,
> then deny any knowledge....
>
> By the mid-seventies, disappearances had become the primary
> enforcement tool of the Chicago School juntas throughout the Southern
> Cone.... Disappearances, officially denied, were very public spectacles
> enlisting the silent complicity of entire neighborhoods. When someone was
> targeted to be eliminated, a fleet of military vehicles showed up at that

person's home or workplace and cordoned off the block, often with a helicopter buzzing overhead. In broad daylight and in full view of the neighbors, police or soldiers battered down the door and dragged out the victim, who often shouted his or her name before disappearing into a waiting Ford Falcon, in the hope that news of the event would reach the family....

The public character of terror did not stop with the initial capture. Once in custody, prisoners in Argentina were taken to one of the more than three hundred torture camps across the country. Many of them were located in densely populated residential areas; one of the most notorious was in a former athletic club on a busy street in Buenos Aires, another in a schoolhouse in central Bahia Blanca and yet another in a wing of a working hospital. At these torture centers, military vehicles sped in and out at odd hours, screams could be heard through the badly insulated walls and strange, body-shaped parcels were spotted being carried in and out, all silently registered by the nearby residents. (pp. 89-91)

The purpose of torture is rarely to elicit information. Before the Bush administration, the official Pentagon doctrine was that the U.S. did not torture because it was an extremely poor method of eliciting "righteous" information, since torture victims will say anything to make it stop. This may be true, but the Pentagon never mentioned that the widespread use torture and the public terror that it clandestinely spreads may well be *the most effective method of controlling unwilling populations.* In this the Pentagon and CIA are world leaders and experts. The U.S.-supported and CIA advised military regime in El Salvador would often throw the mutilated bodies of torture victims in the garbage dump or on a public roadway to be discovered by relatives searching for their disappeared loved ones. Similar officially denied but very public practices occurred in all these nations under assault by the multinational capitalist regime emanating from the United States along with generous police and military support from the imperial center.

That these were not isolated country by country instances of repression but part of a coordinated, continent-wide plan (called "Operation Condor") in which the CIA and U.S. military were heavily involved is evidenced by the amount of collaboration and U.S.-supported coordination among the oppressors. Klein continues:

Since those wanted by the various juntas often took refuge in neighboring countries, the regional governments collaborated with each other in the notorious Operation Condor. Under Condor, the intelligence agencies of the Southern Cone shared information about "subversives" – aided by a state-of-the-art computer system provided by Washington – and then gave each other's agents safe passage to carry out cross-border kidnappings and torture, a system eerily resembling the CIA's "extraordinary rendition" network today. The juntas also exchanged information about the most effective means each had found to extract information from their prisoners....

There were countless opportunities for such exchanges in this period, many of them running through the United States and involving the CIA. A 1975 U.S. Senate investigation into U.S. intervention in Chile found that the CIA had provided training to Pinochet's military in methods for "controlling subversion." And U.S. training of Brazilian and Uruguayan police in interrogation techniques has been heavily documented. According to court testimony quoted in the country's truth commission report, *Brazil, Never Again,* published in 1985, military officers attended formal "torture classes" at army police units where they watched slides depicting various excruciating methods. During these sessions, prisoners were brought in for "practical demonstrations" –brutally tortured while as many as a hundred army sergeants looked on and learned. The report states that "one of the first people to introduce this practice into Brazil was Dan Mitrione, an American police officer." (pp. 91-92)

James Petras agrees that the targets of the architects of U.S. empire include the masses of people themselves. While not focusing on the strategy of torture and disappearances (calculated to instill terror in subject populations), he confirms that the rationale behind the genocidal massacres of whole populations derives from their popular resistance to empire:

The ascendancy of the US to the position of dominant imperialist power was directly related to tri-continental genocides or multiple genocides in Asia—the US-Korean (1950-53) and the US-Indochinese (1961-1975); in Africa—the proxy genocides in Angola, Mozambique, Congo/Zaire (1961-1990s); and in Central America (1979-1990) and the Middle East (Iraq 1991-2006). For methodological reasons we have excluded the state-directed military extermination via the atomic bombing of Japanese cities (Hiroshima/Nagasaki) and the US-directed proxy extermination campaign in Indonesia in 1966 resulting in the killing of over 1.5 million unarmed trade unionists and communist party members or affiliates and family members... The death count resulting from the extermination campaigns of 'late US imperialism' is comparable to their Japanese and German predecessors; four million each in Indo-China and Korea, uncounted millions in the genocide of Southern Africa, nearly 500,000 in the proxy genocides of Central America (300,000 Mayans in Guatemala, 75,000 in El Salvador, 50,000 in Nicaragua and 10,000 each in Honduras and Panama, the latter inflicted by a direct military invasion) and over one million in Iraq, and growing. The total war strategies employed by US imperialism lead directly to genocide-scale killing fields because the distinction between civilian and military targets are obliterated. Particularly because the resistance to US Empire is built on deeply held and widely based beliefs of the resisting masses, imperialist conquest deliberately seeks to decimate the huge reservoir of resistance supporters, recruits and suppliers of food and intelligence. (2007: 81)

The conclusion to be drawn from this history, and from many sources examining the present world situation (such as the 911 Truth Movement) is that the "war on terror" is a fraud. Not only are poor and repressed populations slow to turn to violent revolution in an attempt to solve their problems (they are much more likely to try to turn to democracy, which is why the imperial center attempts to defeat effective democracy everywhere it can), but terrorism by private, marginalized groups is miniscule in comparison with the massive terror of nation-states and their imperial supporters. However, whatever private terror exists serves as a convenient propaganda excuse for the repression, torture, murder, and genocidal extermination of human beings the world over in the service protecting the interests of the world's economic oligarchy.

Today's global economic collapse, which should expose this criminal economic system for all to see, will not likely be sufficient to awaken the people of Earth to the deception that has been forced upon them. The planetary ruling class (the 10% of the Earth's population who control 85% of its wealth) remain in control of the mass media, most governments, the dominant cultural institutions, global banking, and most of the military systems of the planet. Barack Obama leads the way in bailing out the criminal class whose greed has thrown our planet into an economic dead zone. *The people of Earth have yet to understand that democracy means a world system that serves the vast majority, and that effective democracy appears nowhere within today's world system.*

The propaganda would also have us believe that extremist Islamic groups actively promote terrorism worldwide, and that we are struggling in a "clash of civilizations" between democratic views and draconian Medieval Islamic laws and their modern fanatics. Such simplistic ideas serve very well the purposes of those attempting to impose the system of domination and exploitation by corporations and the rich on the rest of the world. The idea that there exists a war to be fought against an implacable and fanatical enemy (formerly "Communists," today Islamic terrorists) is crucial to continuing the violent methods essential if monopoly capitalist economics is going to triumph worldwide. Let us examine these ideas of religiously motivated violence in more detail.

5.2 Religiously Motivated Violence

In theologian Paul Tillich's analysis of our existential human condition, all people are religious (1987: Ch. 2). That is, all people attempt to deal with the anxieties of finitude, guilt, and pending death by grasping for a meaning in life though "ultimate concern" or "faith" in something larger than themselves (1957: Ch. 1). For Tillich, this grasp of a religiously inspired world-view (the ultimate concern of our lives) defines our very identity as persons. Tillich's analysis is useful for our purposes because it allows us to contrast the nonviolence of authentic religion with idolatry of all forms: the worship of power, the nation-state, wealth, one's ethnic group, or one's religious sect. In Tillich's analysis, to invest faith in something finite and limited is to court the disaster of idolatry, for the finite will always fail (ibid. Ch. 3).

All forms of religious fundamentalism fall prey to this. Similarily, faith in the nation, wealth, or power also attempts to escape the courage and transcendence of authentic faith through the substitution of some worldly, finite institution in which one can invest one's life. The dominators of the world clearly do this, manifesting a hatred of human beings and life that borders on the demonic. Only authentic faith, for Tillich, can affirm life in a healthy and holistic manner, since idolatry raises some aspect of the finite to absolute value thereby devaluing and doing violence to whatever is not that finite thing: for example, "my nation right or wrong," "wealth and power are the only things that really matter in life," or "the global capitalist system must be preserved at all costs."

The infinite God, as the object of authentic religion, transcends the opposition between subject and object found on the finite level and hence encompasses all beings in God's embrace or love. Love manifests the *power of Being* to sustain and redeem, the power to integrate and unite what is separated (1987: Ch. 16). Faith in a finite idol such as wealth, power, or nation places one in opposition (deep existential opposition) to those of different idolatries, clinging to different finite gods. It also places one in deep opposition to the loving *power of Being* (the God beyond the gods of idolatry). Hence, its demonic quality. This is what is happening all around us today, not only in what is called religious political violence but also in the idolatrous violence of economic imperialism and globalization. Neo-liberal globalizers, Chicago school economists, and religious fundamentalists have something deeply in common: they worship false gods.

When people feel insecure and threatened, or when they feel damaged or violated, they often regress to ever-more virulent forms of idolatry. They bond together in group solidarities to defend their identity, their culture, their lives, and their life-meanings. Religious sectarian identities (Shiite versus Sunni), national identities (Iraqi, Iranian, British, or American), religious resistance identities (Al-Qaeda), ethnic or cultural identities (Tamil versus Sinhalese), or fundamentalist group identities (Israeli Zionists or the Taliban) are all instances of this phenomenon.

Christian groupings show the same range of solidarities and idolatrous identities, often worshipping the false gods of earthly power and wealth (cf. Dussel, *Ethics and Community* and Rivage-Seoul, *The Emperor's God: Misunderstandings of Christianity*). When the present writer was a guest of Libya in April, 2006, at the twentieth anniversary of the U.S. bombing of Libya in 1986, one Libyan official recited in his speech the atrocities committed by the U.S. and Israel against the Palestinians, the Afghans, the Iraqis, the Libyans and others and then shouted at the audience: "This is war! This is total war for our very survival!"

He did not represent the dominant point of view in Libya, nor at that conference. Nevertheless, his point is easily understandable. Threatened and violated people instinctively stand together against their violators and cling ever-more tenaciously to their collective identities, in this case their identity as Arabs, as Libyans, and as Moslems. During the 1980s, the CIA callously used this instinctive tendency to arm and religiously motivate the Taliban in Afghanistan to fight with terrorist and guerrilla tactics against the Soviet army that had invaded their country. The strategy, of course, invited *blowback*, as all such evil and violent strategies do. Once the Soviets had been driven out of Afghanistan, the Taliban turned its attention to the other "Great Satan" of the world.

Political theorist Terry Eagleton reflects on the terrorist destruction of the World Trade Center in 2001:

> It is true that some of the debate took its cue from there – an ominous fact, since intellectual debate is not at its finest when it springs from grief, hatred, hysteria, humiliation, and the urge for vengeance, along with some deep-seated racist fears and fantasies. 9/11, however, was not really about religion.... Radical Islam generally understands exceedingly little about its own religious faith, and there is good evidence, as we have seen, to suggest that its actions are for the most part politically driven.... The much-trumpeted Death of History, meaning that capitalism is now the only game in town, reflects the arrogance of the West's project of global domination; and it is that aggressive project which has triggered a backlash in the form of radical Islam, thus disproving the thesis that history is over. (2009: 141-142)

The economic, cultural, and military assault on the world after the fall of the Soviet Union variously known as neoliberalism, economic globalization, or neo-conservatism engendered the intensified backlash loosely termed Islamic radicalism. People resist the giving up their wealth, resources, cultures, and dignity to the imperative of capital accumulation and its brutal CIA-Pentagon-driven wars of enforcement. This phenomenon, Eagleton says, is for the most part *politically* driven.

Those called "terrorists" are often weak, oppressed, and angry groups who construct improvised bombs and attempt to set these off clandestinely or suicidally. A terrorist, therefore, is someone with a bomb but not an air force with which to deliver it. Those who have tens of thousands of more destructive bombs and sophisticated aircraft to deliver them (such as the Israelis currently slaughtering the helpless population of Gaza) are not labeled terrorists. The latter activity is innocuously called "self-defense." Israeli "Self-defense Forces" ideologically mirror the U.S. war machine's self-description as the "Department of Defense." Again, we see that lies are integral to the deep violence of our world order. James Petras describes the increase in Islamic religious violence as follows:

> In the midst of the chaos, violence, dislocation, pillage, and occupation of a country, a whole people are adversely affected. As they reach out to respond, to protest, to survive, they seek protest movements and institutions that have some resources, a modicum of power. In the past there were powerful nationalist, socialist, and communist parties, dynamic trade unions and peasant movements. In a few countries these are still active and a force to be reckoned with. In many regions, however, they have been decimated by US client regimes, local secular or "religious" dictators, and by the disintegration of the Communist parties. Under harsh conditions requiring clandestine activity and mass support, many secular activists have joined politically-oriented religious movements, which embrace anti-colonial, anti-imperialist, and social welfare programs. The catalyst for secular "conversion" to Muslim-inspired movements is politics, not religion. (2006: 150-151)

Middle East political analyst and economist Samir Amin presents a related view of politics in Islamic countries:

> The image of bearded men bowed low and groups of veiled women give rise to hasty conclusions about the intensity of religious adherence among individuals. Western "culturalist" friends who call for respect for diversity of beliefs rarely find out about the procedures implemented by the authorities to present an image that is convenient for them.... In this larger region, political traditions have been strongly marked by the radical currents of modernity: the ideas of the Enlightenment, the French Revolution, the Russian Revolution, and the communism of the Third International were present in the minds of everyone and were much more important than the parliamentarianism of Westminster, for example. (2007: 6)

In 1986, the nations of the world through the U.N. General Assembly attempted to come together cooperatively to fight terrorism. They wanted to develop "measures to prevent international terrorism, to study the underlying political and economic causes of terrorism, to convene a conference to define terrorism and to differentiate it from the struggle of people for national liberation." The vote in the General Assembly was

153 for this effort (nearly unanimous), and 2 against it (the U.S. and Israel) (Blum, 2000: 197). Naturally, it was vetoed by the U.S. in the Security Council and did not happen.

The reasons the U.S. is against real measures to prevent international terrorism and differentiate it from the struggle of people for national liberation are threefold and quite obvious to impartial observers. *First*, with the fall of the illusory threat of Communism, the U.S. needed a new implacable universal enemy as an ideological cover for its wars of imperial domination. *Second*, to distinguish terrorism from authentic struggles for liberation would expose the U.S. global support for the violence of domination and exploitation, and much of what is now called terrorism would be seen as legitimate resistance to the violence of its neo-colonial economic empire.

Third, official (yet clandestine) state sponsored terrorism, or semi-official terrorism fostered by lawless networks within imperial intelligence and military organizations, accounts for a large part of what is mistakenly identified as Islamic, ethnic, or national-liberation terrorist activity. For a variety of strategic and tactical reasons, imperial states routinely carry out *false-flag terrorist operations* and attribute these atrocities to enemy groups. This gives the deceptive appearance that private terrorism pervades our world requiring a virulent military response to the pervasive danger, including surrendering civil liberties in the name of ever-increasing "security" measures. It keeps fearful populations willing to hand over their wealth and freedom to the financial and political elites promising to protect them. Terrorism expert and scholar Webster Griffin Tarpley describes this reality:

> We must stress again that international terrorism should never be seen as a spontaneous sociological phenomenon arising directly out of oppression and misery. International terrorism and national liberation struggles are always mediated through a level of clandestine organization in which the efforts of intelligence agencies come decisively into play. Many international terrorist groups are false-flag operations from the very beginning. Others assume false-flag status as the result of coordinated arrests, assassinations, and takeovers by intelligence agencies. Even where there is an authentic national liberation organization, intelligence agencies will create false-flag operations under their own control to mimic it, perpetrating atrocities in its name in an effort to isolate and discredit it. Here again, deception and dissembling are the rule. (2008: 385)

Much of this clandestine state-sponsored terrorism involves a fundamentalist religious motivation, or at least the influence of apocalyptic and Manichaean ideas idolatrously attributing goodness to "us" and absolute evil to "them." *The Project for a New American*

Century document (www.newamericancentury.org), written by the core of political neocons until recently in control of the Executive Branch of the United States government, exhibits influence of such ideas as well as a pseudo-religious idolatry of their nation-state and its destiny. Their ideas are bolstered by a vast network of fundamentalist Christian ideologues who remain in the U.S. military and intelligence services. Tarpley states that:

> Although the neocons are an obvious focus of danger in the American society of today, they by no means represent the only threat. We must also pay attention to those self-styled religious factions which cultivate notions of the approaching end of the world and the return of the Messiah. These are the groups which propagate notions of the end of historical time through the apocalypse, and embellish this with the imminence of Armageddon, the mythical last battle before the end of the world.... The modern irrationalists who camouflage themselves as Christians have left traditional Christianity behind, and have reduced the content of their religion to the cynical support of such figures as Bush and Ariel Sharon, both regarded, perhaps accurately, as harbingers of the apocalypse.... The various fellowships and chaplaincies of evangelical-Pentecostal stamp in the US military, which are often under the influence of British or Israeli intelligence agencies, therefore represent a grave threat to US national security. Is the US officer corps reliable? Under present conditions of pervasive penetration by the apocalypse-Armageddon network, their reliability is open to grave doubt. (2008: 373)

This immense network of state-sponsored terror organizations involving CIA, FBI, M-6, Mossad, and other imperial intelligence or military organizations has promoted hundreds of billions of dollars in security and military businesses in the service of what Naomi Klein calls "disaster capitalism" (2008: Ch. 14). An immense economic incentive has developed to promote disaster, terror, and violence on a planetary scale. Capitalism has always institutionalized violence through its systems of exploitation and domination. However, in its more recent manifestations, an ever-growing number of capitalists find active promotion of violence and terror as their most lucrative strategy. "Security" may well be the most lucrative of all businesses, and its exorbitant profits require that people feel insecure, terrified, and threatened.

It should be clear that the historical development of human civilization is threatened at today's crucial juncture in world history by a massive, adolescent rebellion against the development of mature reason and planetary democratic values. This rebellion includes not only the immense fanatical forces of terrorist violence forced upon the world primarily through the idolatrous networks within the world's superpower nation-states. It also includes the fanatical worship of capital and the capitalist system of institutionalized greed, exploitation, and domination of the majority of the world's population by a tiny minority.

Commenting on the last Bush presidency, Tarpley underlines the immaturity of the ruling oligarchy in the United States: "Many have noted the primitive and childish quality of the Bush/neocon analysis, with its mindless parroting about good guys and bad guys. Bush's oratory also shares another key feature of the infantile mind – egocentrism, or the tendency to see large and distant events as having been caused by one's own petty actions.... What egocentrism represents in the stunted individual, ethnocentrism accomplishes for the sick society" (2008: 357).

The rebellion against growth toward maturity is not a mass psychological phenomenon independent of the institutions that embed and shape human consciousness. Fragmented institutions condition people toward immature and fragmented world views. By contrast, *the most fundamental unity pervading our human situation involves our common humanity*. Mature rational thought begins with this and logically progresses to the common protection and promotion of that humanity under the universal rule of democratically legislated laws. Such holistic institutions would then promote a holistic sense of *unity in diversity* within human consciousness.

Religiously motivated violence (if one means by this the violence consequent on irrational fundamentalism and its rebellion against democracy and human maturity) becomes a key factor in comprehending the entire planetary system of violence. Mature, civilized values of human freedom within the due process rule of democratically legislated laws become downplayed as unworkable in a world of immediate violence and danger. Few recognize the root of this immaturity as the institutionalized fragmentation and balkanization of human beings on this planet within the system of economic and national competition for power, resources, wealth, and hegemony.

Our broadest category of violence defined above, violence stemming from fragmentation of the human community and the idolatry of finite forces, therefore, illuminates not only what is today often called religious violence but the three previous forms of violence discussed as well. If Tillich's analysis has cogency, then not only is religious violence a form of idolatry but the dogmas of capital accumulation, manifest destiny of the superior nation, and imperial expansionism as the right of hegemonic nations also involve forms of idolatry. Similarly, philosopher Enrique Dussel in his book *Ethics and Community* (1988) defines the contemporary hegemony of empire in service of the dogma of capital accumulation as a supreme idolatry, demonic in quality, violating the integrity of persons and attempting, like the devil himself, to replace God with its own glory and eternity.

Nevertheless, it should be clear that an analysis of violence in terms of the dynamics of idolatrous religion is inadequate unless it is supplemented by a *systems analysis* and a *class analysis* (ibid., cf. Miranda 1986). The system of capitalism, the system of class exploitation, and the system of nation-states are integral to the immense deep-violence of today's world disorder. All three of these involve institutionalized and intentional fragmentation of the human community and the consequent violence that this fragmentation entails.

From the point of view of authentic religion as Tillich conceives it, one could say that these phenomena are not only idolatrous but the ultimate godlessness of base violence, exploitation, and dehumanization of the majority of humankind by the few. Religiously inspired terrorist and guerrilla violence often involve reactions to the exploitation and domination of this seemingly godless world disorder. But the system is not godless in the sense of an atheistic denial of the divine, for apocalyptic and Manichaean ideas penetrate to its very roots. The system itself includes immense idolatrous and fanatical religious elements. It is not so much a godless world disorder as a perverted order of pagan idolatry and insidious violence masquerading under the name of Christianity. Dostoyevsky's *Grand Inquisitor* has triumphed yet again, no longer in sixteenth century Spain, but in the twenty-first century United States of America.

5.3 A Nonviolent Political and Economic Order for Earth

A nonviolent order for the Earth cannot be premised on the system of sovereign nation-states. A nonviolent order for the Earth must be one based on the movement within historical time to ever-fuller awareness and understanding of our human situation. There are approximately 193 sovereign nation-states at present, all competing with one another economically, politically, and militarily. Even regional forms of cooperation exist within a framework of the primary self-interest of the nations involved. In this anarchic condition, the big fish will dominate and devour the little fish. In this system, there is an overwhelming temptation to idolatrously worship one's nation and promote its economic and military ascendency over other nations. The vast majority of these nations today are heavily militarized. Violence is intrinsic to this system.

Similarly, we have also seen that violence is intrinsic to the globalized economic system of monopoly capitalism. You cannot create gigantic institutions like multinational corporations whose sole motive is profit for their investors and expect any form of justice, wide prosperity, environmental integrity, or democratic governance to be the result. The system also inevitably opens itself to the temptation to idolatrously worshiping wealth and power. Democracy and human maturity can only be realized under some form of planetary democratic socialism.

A truly nonviolent order for the Earth can only be brought about through nonmilitary democratic world government under a system such as that articulated in the *Constitution for the Federation of Earth.* The *Constitution for the Federation of Earth* establishes the *unity in diversity* that we have seen as fundamental to both reason and authentic spirituality. It does not establish religion, but the political and economic unity of humankind to the point where both authentic spirituality and communicative rationality can begin to flourish unimpeded.

This general idea was also affirmed by Mahatma Gandhi, who envisioned a world federation premised on socialist equality and freedom for all people. "The structure of a world federation," Gandhi wrote, "can be raised only on a foundation of nonviolence, and violence will have to be given up totally in world affairs" (1987: 460). "If there were no greed," he said, "there would be no occasion for armaments. The principle of nonviolence necessitates complete abstention from exploitation in any form" (1958: 112). "I would not like to live in this world," Gandhi stated, "if it is not to be one world" (1958: 112).

Today, we have seen, the system of imperial nation-states promoting and violently protecting the system of global monopoly capitalism activates in their victims worldwide a hardening of identities as forms of resistance to the anxiety and threat of violation and destruction. People cling to fundamentalist religious identities for the very survival of who they believe they are as Moslems, Jews, Christians, Hindus, Kurds, Palestinians, Iranians, Tamils, Serbs, or Bosnians. This leads people to falsely assume their cultures or religions are incommensurable with one another. The establishment of political and economic *unity in diversity* on Earth will go a long way to relax this instinctive process of hardening identities and promote the universality in uniqueness that is the dual glory of every human being. But this principle cannot be realized on Earth unless it is institutionalized in a planetary political and economic form.

As early as 1946, Albert Camus understood that the destructive power of modern weapons and the unworkable system of nation-states means that we have been "forced into fraternity":

> We know today that there are no more islands, that frontiers are just lines on a map. We know that in a steadily accelerating world, where the Atlantic is crossed in less than a day and Moscow speaks to Washington in a few minutes, we are forced into fraternity.... The only way of extricating ourselves is to create a world parliament through elections in which all peoples will participate, which will enact legislation which will exercise authority over national governments. (2002: 65-67)

The *Earth Constitution* establishes itself firmly on the principle of *unity in diversity*. All persons are united under the unity of one Earth Federation that represents not only their individual interests but the common interests, goals, and needs of all people. It articulates a set of common goals, rights, responsibilities, and communicative processes for the people of Earth. In other words, it initiates planetary fraternity, a global community. It would not be starting from scratch, since today's millions of world citizens from every country on Earth would immediately breathe life into such a Federation.

The only way to institutionalize nonviolence is through authentic democracy that embraces all in a unity (of rights and responsibilities) while providing procedures for decision-making for social and political change that abjure violence. Gandhi advocated the same thing as a democratic socialist who understood that there can be no democracy, when, as he put it, "the few ride on the backs of the millions" (1958: 115). Neither sovereign nation-states nor global monopoly capitalism can give us authentic democracy, for both ultimately defeat the liberty, equality, and community of all people who live upon the Earth.

Democratic world government draws upon the crucial distinction between all forms of militarism and civilian police (developed further in Chapter Eight below). Under the *Earth Constitution* all militaries and weapons of war worldwide would be legally abolished and destroyed. All enforcement of the law would be done by civilian police whose charge is not the destruction of a designated enemy, as in the military, but the apprehension and arrest of *individuals* suspected of violating the law (assuming their innocence until proven guilty), using the minimum of force necessary and with utmost care not to harm innocent bystanders.

The theory and practice of nonviolence is not in the final analysis simply an *ad hoc* technique for dealing with violence outside of the civilized relationships fostered by law under the democratic state. Rather *nonviolence is a manifestation of a planetary maturity that must permeate the political, legal, due process, and economic relationships of every state*. It must be understood historically as the growth of human beings into civilizational adulthood. This growth is simultaneously rational, spiritual, economic, social, and political. Spiritual growth toward nonviolence is meaningless if it ignores economic, political, and social growth.

Government can and should be converted to conscious nonviolence. Police can be trained in substantially nonviolent techniques of apprehension and arrest, and the weapons they are allowed to use can be similarly non-lethal and non-injurious. Courts can operate on the principle of restoring unity with the whole rather than fragmentation and violent punishment. Government can abolish all forms of militarism and war-making capacity. Under the *Earth Constitution*, the Earth Federation makes conflict resolution for groups, nations, and individuals worldwide a fundamental initiative of its global government. It also promotes the sustainable and equitable use of resources essential to conflict reduction.

There can be no peace without unity, and there is no unity for the world without nonmilitary democratic government. The violence of our world has its deepest roots in fragmentation: egoistic fragmentation, class fragmentation, political fragmentation, religious fragmentation, nation-state fragmentation, and economic fragmentation. The creation of political and economic unity will allow people to relax their hardened religious and cultural identities and open themselves to the influx of the spiritual and communicative dimensions of life that live at the real heart of religion as well as nonviolence. Here lie the living roots for the triumph of civilization.

The epistemic structure of a human being, as Kant demonstrated, involves a spontaneous synthesis of apperception, in which a unique individual person confronts the universe as an integrated totality of mutually related parts (cf. Harris 1992: Ch. 1). In other words, each of us encounters the world through a structure of *unity in diversity*. Following Kant, Hegel revealed the dynamic of unity in diversity operating at every level within the totality of society. Twentieth-century science has revealed the dynamic evolutionary upsurge of *unity in diversity* for the entire cosmos. From the initial conditions of the Big Bang, from the micro to the macro levels, the universe is a differentiated unity specifying itself in ever-higher levels of complexification up to human self-consciousness and the construction of integrated systems of human knowledge (ibid.). The historical development of science confirms that at every level the universe is a dynamic confluence of *unity in diversity*. *Holism* reflects our most fundamental epistemic and metaphysical reality.

Yet human history on planet Earth has mirrored neither the structure of human intelligence as *unity in diversity* nor the structure of the evolving cosmos that is a series of ascending levels of *unity in diversity*. Human beings have remained mired in fragmentation (primarily today the fragmentation of global capitalism and the system of sovereign nation-states) and massive planetary violence has been the consequence of this failure. If we ascend to the maturity of a democratic Earth federation, we will rapidly overcome the fragmentation of today's world disorder that is the central root of violence. Both reason and authentic spirituality point us to the nonviolence of a democratic Earth Federation.

The overcoming of fragmentation in economic, social, religious, and political life does not result in some faceless domination of a "superstate" where diversity is sacrificed to a totalitarian unity so feared by those in today's first world who deny their complicity in the present global system of totalitarian domination. The result, rather, is a federation in which people participate in government on many levels, from local to regional to national to world levels. There is no peace without the ascent to democratic world government, which will necessarily mean the overcoming of fragmentation with its concomitant violence.

This ascent will not automatically fully restore the maturity of authentic religion, spirituality, or communicative rationality to humanity. For this restoration requires the free opening by human beings to the sources of grace, love, spiritual illumination, oneness, and common intelligence that flow from communicative rationality as well as the foundations of the universe. But it will provide the necessary conditions for the ascendancy of an authentic spiritual and intellectual life for humanity. The historical ascent to a nonviolent world order inevitably includes a complete conversion of our world system to nonviolence, as Gandhi pointed out. With the ascent to a nonviolent world order, religiously motivated violence will disappear of its own accord, since it is, most fundamentally, a result of the fragmentation of our contemporary world disorder.

Chapter Six

Violent Economics

Understanding Our World System as a Key to Global Peace and Prosperity

Distribution and scale involve relationships with the poor, the future, and other species that are fundamentally social in nature rather than individual. Homo economicus as the self-contained atom of methodological individualism, or as the pure social being of collectivist theory, are both severe abstractions. Our concrete experience is that of "persons in community." We are individual persons, but our very individual identity is defined by the quality of our social relations. Our relations are not just external, they are also internal, that is, the nature of the related entities (ourselves in this case) changes when relations among them changes. We are related not only by a nexus of individual willingnesses to pay for different things, but also by relations of trusteeship for the poor, the future, and other species. The attempt to abstract from these concrete relations of trusteeship and reduce everything to a question of individual willingness to pay is a distortion of our concrete experience as persons in community, an example of A.N. Whitehead's "fallacy of misplaced concreteness."

Herman E. Daly

The novelty of our century, the changes whose completion will set it so utterly apart from the past, are not, however, exhaustively comprised within the limits of the despiritualization of the world and its subjection to a regime of advanced technique. Even those who lack clear knowledge of the subject are becoming decisively aware that they are living in an epoch when the world is undergoing a change so vast as to be hardly comparable to any of the great changes of past millenniums. The mental situation of our day is pregnant with immense dangers and immense possibilities; and it is one which, if we are inadequate to the tasks which await us, will herald the failure of mankind.

Karl Jaspers

B uilding on Chapters Four and Five, this chapter further develops the analysis of the global system as one of structural violence imposed by a tiny ruling elite on the world. Today, this elite includes the two percent of the world's population that controls forty-seven percent of its wealth. This chapter further describes the dynamics of the world economy under the World Trade Organization, IMF, World Bank, global capitalism, and the system of sovereign nation-states. As Chapter Four revealed, this entire system is one of institutionalized violence in which the imperial nations, in the service of the private accumulation of wealth of their ruling classes, use massive state terrorism to crush opposition to the system anywhere in the world.

I pointed out above that a perceptive, detailed account of this system can be found in *Empire with Imperialism: The Globalizing Dynamics of Neo-liberal Capitalism* by James Petras and Henry Veltmeyer (2005) and in a number of other works on this subject in the bibliography. Unless we understand our present world system deeply, we will not manage to transform it correctly. The founding of a *holistic Earth civilization* requires a concomitant deep understanding of the multiple *failures* of our present world disorder.

6.1 Economics and the Triumph of Civilization

If there is any significant truth to this account of the violence of our world disorder, then one thing should also be clear. Most of the economic theories by which this system has been described, including both classical and contemporary economics, have been academic or elite-sponsored ideological efforts to justify this system and cover up its true nature in the eyes of both the imperial and the victim populations. Few mainstream economists, either historically or today, describe the world as we have in Chapter Four. This is not an accident.

Intellectuals and academics of all historical ages have placed themselves in the service of power and *imperium*. By and large, advanced education and the academic profession have only been available to an elite within our modern world order, right to our own day, an elite who then train the each new generation of academics within the framework of ruling class ideologies. Our task in this book is to think economics from the point of view of the ethical, spiritual, ecological and practical heart of human life, in other words, to think economics by taking the side of its victims: who are the majority of human beings and living creatures on this planet.

To think economics from the heart of our common life in this way is to think economics *realistically*. Realism means to interact with the world as it really exists, not imposing an ideological fantasy in the service of our careers, a ruling class, or a particular set of interests. We cannot expect economics to successfully promote human flourishing if it violates the reality of our human and ecological situation. The violence, massive poverty, and ecological destruction of today's world described above shows precisely that the dominant economic ideology has failed the world and is leading us headlong toward total disaster. The triumph of civilization can only be founded on the most powerful honesty, integrity, and realism.

Internationally recognized environmental biologist John Cairns, Jr., described our situation regarding climate change in the summer of 2008. Under the heading "Red Alert – Climate Change: This is the Last Chance," Cairns wrote:

> World-class climate scientist James Hansen has warned Congress that the planet has long passed the "dangerous level" for atmospheric greenhouse gases. Twenty years ago, he warned Congress about the consequences of "business as usual," and his predictions have been validated by the Intergovernmental Panel on Climate Change (IPCC), the national Academy of Sciences, and individual climate scientists.... The Arctic ice melted 100 years ahead of IPCC predictions. Hansen affirms that a frank assessment of scientific data provides a certainty on climate change exceeding 99 percent.
>
> Mark Lynas' book, *Six Degrees,* provides examples of what will happen for each degree of Celsius temperature increase up to 6 degrees (10.6 degrees Fahrenheit) – for example, a climate that is only a degree or so warmer than today could melt enough Greenland ice to drown coastal cities around the planet.
>
> Politicians have set dates, such as 2025 and 2050, for reducing greenhouse gases, but Mother Nature neither bargains nor forgets transgressions. Violate her universal laws and penalties are usually severe and immediate, including starvation, disease, and death. Each day of delay in conforming to Mother Nature's laws forecloses options for providing a quality life for posterity and drives more species that exist as fellow passengers on Spaceship Earth to extinction.
> (http://www.johncairns.net/Commentaries/VT%20Research%20Intro.pdf)

It is surely clear that vast institutional and human impediments have prevented the governmental, corporate, and financial institutions of the world from acting effectively on these deadly environmental facts whose scientific framework "exceeds 99 percent" certainty. Fundamental change must occur that includes both transformation of our ego-centered consciousness to our deeper universal self and transformation of the dominant governmental, corporate, and financial institutions that dominate our planet with their violence while structurally blocking the human population from ascending to a higher level of maturity. The environmental and human consequences of the present world system with its corresponding fragmented and immature selfhood were reviewed in Chapter Four. The ascent to planetary democracy is simultaneously the ascent to both economic democracy and human maturity.

The compulsive self-interest and greed that capitalist theory assumes for human nature may exist as one aspect of our human reality. However, this comprises what is *lowest* in us and what the larger human reality of moral and spiritual imperatives instructs us to transcend. Current economic arrangements *institutionalize* this lowest aspect of our nature. In *An Interpretation of Religion* (2004), John Hick describes the great human awakening that took place in the Axial Period of human history during the first millennium BCE. In that era many human beings achieved a level of self-awareness that allowed them to critically assess the human situation and their own lives and to posit a better state of affairs.

The newly born world religions (later to include Christianity and Islam), Hick says, provided contexts for *"the transformation of human existence from self-centeredness to Reality-centeredness"* (p. 14, emphasis added). This imperative continues to this day. Human beings are tasked to transcend their compulsive self-centeredness (on which economics today is based) and ascend to community, freedom, mutual respect, morally grounded relationships, and cooperative forms of economic well-being, all of which imply relatedness toward deeper and more fundamental realities than our subjective forms of personal greed. Only a conversion to "Reality-centeredness" will allow us to transform the pervasive violence of our world against the majority of human beings and our planetary environment.

We have seen that the most fundamental questions that bear on issues of political and economic organization are the following: What does it mean to be a human being? What is the meaning and purpose of human life? What are the ethical and spiritual dimensions of our lives that illuminate for us meaning and purpose? How are we related to the natural world that sustains us and from which we are in many ways inseparable? How are we related to one another, to the cosmos, and to the ground of Being or God? How can we create liberty, equality, and community on Earth that promote sustainable flourishing for the vast majority of people?

These questions cannot be answered in any simple, factual, or fundamentalist manner. They are addressed only through existential and civilizational *rebirth*, through a conversion to *reality-centeredness*. We must see our human situation clearly and respond from the depths of our fundamental humanity. Whether civilization will triumph depends on whether we can transcend propaganda, ideology, and egoistic interests and establish human life on simple honesty, integrity, and realism. From these alone will emerge an authentic planetary social, political, and economic order.

We saw in Chapter Four that a core insight of the major world religions is the imperative for a transformation of our political and economic systems from violence to nonviolence. A nonviolent economics is a sustainable economics, one that does not steal what is rightfully theirs from the poor, from future generations, or from the Earth's other living species. A nonviolent economics does not pit nation against nation in a brutal struggle for hegemony, control of markets, or resources.

It is ideology pure and simple to think of human beings as "atoms of rational self-interest" and build a capitalist economic system around this simplistic false premise. Each normal person may well include elements of this kind of self-interest and this kind of merely instrumental rationality. But each normal person also feels the demands of communicative rationality, compassion, and moral imperatives to treat others as ends in themselves. Most feel the obligation not exploit or dehumanize others as means to our own self-interest. Each normal person also feels the demand to integrate his or her self toward wholeness and the similar demand to live in harmony with other persons and the environment, not destroying the ability of future generations to flourish on the Earth. Economics cannot succeed without including these *realities* of our human situation.

In the quotation at the head of this chapter, economist Herman E. Daly rightly identifies our situation as "persons in community." Our community today is the community of planet Earth, and he rightly identifies our moral obligations as members of this community as obligations to the poor, to future generations, and to the Earth's other living species. If we are to fulfill our concrete obligations as members of the Earth community we must create sustainable, equitable, and just economic democracy upon the Earth. Economic democracy means both sustainable economics and democratic economics. Neither has existed so far in history to any significant degree.

We saw in Chapter Two that the concept of transformative democracy reveals a truth at the very heart of human existence – the equality and dignity of all human beings and the imperative that our thoughts, words, and deeds direct itself to the realization of this truth within history. These truths and this imperative have been in practice denied by nearly all political and economic systems in history to date. Many have paid lip service to these truths, from the funeral speech of Pericles as this was rendered by Thucydides in the Fifth Century BCE to the noble words of U.S. President George W. Bush that the people of Iraq deserve the democracy and freedom that the U.S. invasion of their country will bring to them.

The truths behind the concepts of democracy, freedom, human rights, and human dignity have indeed become more apparent as history moved forward from Athenian democracy to Stoic thought and the Roman Republic, to free, late-Medieval city-states, to Renaissance humanism to emergent modern democratic theory, to twentieth-century theories of democratic world law (cf. Martin 2008). The distortions of Thucydides may have been less apparent than the lies of George W. Bush. However, to any thinking person, economics has never historically led to anything resembling respect for human rights, freedom, or human dignity, only to poverty and misery for the majority.

Today, history has also placed human life in a precarious position – we face our own possible extinction if we do not save the planetary environment from collapsing or eliminate nuclear weapons from the face of the Earth. Today, we can no longer afford to tolerate the lies and distortions in the service of power, domination, and exploitation. Civilization, founded on immense integrity, can and must triumph.

The imperative for founding economics on the giant truths of our human situation has become a matter of life and death. Economics must be placed in the service of prosperity for the majority of persons, the protection of our planetary ecology, and the welfare of future generations. The alternative spells planetary suicide.

6.2 Nation-states, Monopoly Capitalism, and Violence

Chapter Four identified three fundamental forms of violence that permeate our world disorder today as institutionalized violence, imperial violence, and nihilistic violence. In Chapter Five we saw that the fourth and fifth forms of violence, revolutionary violence and religiously motivated violence, are insignificant in scope compared to the first three. Deeply intertwined with all of these forms of violence is the nation-state itself and its historically intimate partner, monopoly capitalism. In order to further understand the violence of our world in the early twenty-first century, let us continue to examine this relationship.

We have seen that a large portion of the war and terror arising from the nation-state system involves the use of military forces and other forms of coercion to keep in place a global system of institutionalized violence connected with global economic domination and exploitation of poor peoples and nations by wealthy peoples and nations. Historically the capitalist classes in nation-states have worked to maintain their political power over the law-making process in order to ensure the laws and cooperation of sovereign nation-states in the process of global accumulation.

Boswell and Chase-Dunn describe the origins of this relationship between capital and the *nation-state*:

The European interstate system was born in the Thirty Years' War (1618-1648) in which massive bloodletting and destruction forced imperial dynasties to become states sovereign over nations in order to survive.... Class relations expanded beyond the labor process to become institutionalized in state, colonial, and interstate structures. A system of sovereign states (i.e., with an overarching definition of sovereignty) is fundamental to the origins and reproduction of the capitalist world economy.... In the interstate system, unequally powerful states compete for resources by supporting profitable commodity production and by engaging in geopolitical and military competition.... Capital accumulation has always involved political power and coercion. (2000: 23-24)

Since the dawn of the modern world with the Spanish conquests of the Caribbean and Central America, the nation-state has worked hand in hand with the drive for capital accumulation on the part of ruling classes. The system of unequal exchange, resulting in the poverty of the weaker nations and peoples, must necessarily be kept in place through coercion. For the very system that deprives people of their basic needs is a system of institutionalized violence. Boswell and Chase-Dunn write:

Capitalism is the accumulation of resources by means of exploitation in the production and sale of commodities for profit. Capitalist exploitation is an unequal exchange wherein capitalists extract income from economic exchanges solely because they hold legal title to productive assets. There are two types of exploitation – primary and secondary. Primary exploitation, which takes the form of profit, is an unequal exchange with labor wherein capitalists appropriate all the "value added" in production, net of wages, because they own the business in which production takes place....

Secondary exploitation, which takes the form of rent and interest, is an unequal exchange between the capital-rich and the capital-poor, including between wealthy and poor countries....

As a result, at all points of exchange in production, capitalists have institutionalized *coercive power* as employers, bosses, lenders, and landlords. Both Adam Smith and Karl Marx considered exploitation to be the application of coercive power in markets to obtain an unequal exchange. (pp. 20-21)

Coercive power in markets is a result of domination for the sake of exploitation. The social-scientific definition of this relationship is not difficult. We have seen John Roemer, in *A General Theory of Exploitation and Class,* argue that one class can be said to be exploited by another class whenever "(1) There is a feasible alternative state in which coalition S would be better off than in its present situation; (2) Under this alternative, coalition S' would be worse off than at present; (3) Coalition S' is in relationship of dominance to S. This dominance enables it to prevent

coalition S from realizing the alternative" (1989:194-195).   All poor
peoples of the world today fall within this simple formula.

"Dominance" means one group (who are benefiting from a situation)
exist in a position to prevent the second group (who are being hurt by a
situation) from realizing alternative conditions. When nations have made a
break for independence from the system of domination (for example,
Guatemala before 1954, Cuba in 1959, Chile in 1970, and Nicaragua in
1979), the governments leading this break have been overthrown,
blockaded, or otherwise destroyed by the United States. Overt violence
ensures the continuation of institutionalized violence.

A similar process has been in place with every past hedgemon, from
Spain to Holland to Portugal to France to Great Britain. In the case of
"people's" dictatorships like the Soviet Union and China, the principle
remains similar. Powerful sovereign nations work in tandem with their
ruling classes to ensure the imperial system remains in place. However, the
world system for the past several centuries has been dominated not by the
distorted "communism" of the USSR or China, but by the system of
capitalism.

The result has been a world of immense poverty and suffering, kept in
place both by coercive economic and political forces and by overt military
interventions. In *When Corporations Rule the World*, David C. Korten
writes:

> In 1950, about the time the commitment was made to globalize the
> development process, the average income of the 20 percent of people living
> in the wealthiest countries was about thirty times that of the 20 percent
> living in the poorest countries. By 1989, this ratio had doubled to sixty
> times.
>
> Based on national averages, these figures represent disparities among
> countries and substantially understate the disparity among people. For
> example, all Americans are placed in the world's top income category,
> including the homeless, the rural poor, and the urban slum dwellers. When
> the UNDP estimated the global distribution based on individual incomes
> rather than on national averages, the average income of the top 20 percent
> was 150 times that of the lowest 20 percent. (pp. 110-111)

In *Millennium Dawn*, I described this world situation drawing on the
thought of Samir Amin:

> Economist Samir Amin has identified five features or "monopolies" that
> characterized today's capitalism, whose financial, commercial and productive
> markets now have a global reach: (1) monopoly over technology, chiefly
> through military research, (2) monetary control of worldwide financial
> markets, unprecedented in world history, (3) monopolistic access to the
> planet's natural resources, (4) media and communication monopolies that

have led to the "erosion of democratic practices in the West," and (5) monopolies over weapons of mass destruction....

"Advanced" capitalism is not only the neoliberal economic doctrine that forces "structural adjustment" on people who already have next to nothing, privatizing, into the hands of global capital, the few remaining public services to which the poor have access. It is not only the doctrine of third-world debt that forces billions of dollars in debt on ordinary citizens of third-world countries who never borrowed the money in the first place. It is also these five global monopolies, described by Amin, in which control of the fate of our planet and its resources has passed into fewer and fewer hands in the twentieth and twenty-first centuries. (2005a: 228)

Brazilian theologian Dominique Barbé asserts with reference to the international debt that poor countries have been forced to incur to the wealthy lending institutions of first-world countries: "Yes! It is institutional violence. The cheap sale of raw materials, our natural wealth, has paid for the debt. We have enriched the countries of the First-world through financial groups operating in Brazil. This type of institutional violence kills millions of persons, many more than a world war." (1989: 167) And Peter Marcuse writes:

> Capital that has extended its influence over these new territories knows its own interests, works together in its common interests even while individual capitals compete [and] coordinates its goals and its strategies in its common interest.... There will always be social inequality, because that increases profits; winners win more because losers lose more. Keeping the Third World in dependence and poverty is not an accident or failure of the world capitalist system, but part of its formula for success. (1990: 61)

The point here is very important because the ideology of capitalism in alliance with the nation-states claims the immense poverty in the world is the result of not enough capitalism, and that the well-known horror stories of entire societies economically collapsing are only incidental failures of the capitalist system. Economist J. W. Smith affirms that:

> Developed countries claim to be financing the developing world, but actually the poor countries are financing the rich through the wealthy world underpaying equally-productive developing world labor, paying far less than full value for natural resources, and through primarily investing in commodity production for the wealthy world. In this process, between 1980 and 1990 – when measured against the dollar... wage levels in Mexico declined by sixty percent...in Argentina by fifty percent and in Peru by seventy percent and again that was before the 1997-98 collapse of developing world currencies reduced wages on the periphery of empire by half.

The above appears to list IMF/World Bank/ GATT/NAFTA/WTO/ MAI/GATS/FTAA failures. However, they are not failures; they are the successes of financial and economic warfare. The prices of developing world commodities are lowered while the prices of developed world products are retained, siphoning every more wealth to the corporate imperialists. (2006: 20)

The "corporate imperialists" work hand in glove with imperial governments to create what the U.S. State Department refers to as a "stable investment climate," often by supporting brutal dictatorships in third-world countries. Political and military violence is used to protect the massive institutionalized violence of enforced poverty and depravation for the majority of humanity. The world system under sovereign nation-states involves "financial and economic warfare." The empirical result before us constitutes their success, not failure. It is only failure from the point of view of democracy, morality, ecology, and other fundamental human values.

Just as the nation-state system is inherently terrorist and inherently a war-system, so the nation-state system as we have known it for at least five centuries is inherently structurally violent. Absolute fragmentation under the concept of sovereign territories can have no other result, since, as we saw above, such fragmentation places the nations in "a state of nature," a condition in which there is no law but only the rule of the most powerful and a perpetual competition for power with its spoils in the form of controlling the resources of the planet in one's own interests.

However, unlike Hobbes, Kant, and other thinkers who understand this state of nature as the system of war between sovereign nations, it should now be clear that it is much more than that. The primary competition among sovereign nations involves struggles over wealth, as J.W. Smith has demonstrated at length in *Economic Democracy* (2005). The political and financial elite of nations and their multinational corporations vie for control of the wealth-producing process in relation to weaker countries (including control of production, services, natural resources, trade relations, and financial interactions). The modern world system has always had a vast periphery of poverty organized around several successive imperial centers, the last, since World War II, has been the United States.

Only democratic world law, enforceable over individuals, can bring us out of this system of "savagery and barbarism." It is not only war that is savage and barbaric, but the system of domination and exploitation marginalizing and impoverishing vast portions of the world's population. Only world law can legislate the dynamics of an economic system that will ensure the welfare of all: a system directed toward universal equity and prosperity instead of the present system of absolute winners and losers. This legislation by a World Parliament must be enforceable by civilian controlled world police and attorney generals. Only through genuine unification in relation to diversity can we free our planet from these disastrous consequences of fragmentation.

"Enforceable world law" here by no means connotes a new regime of violence to be substituted for the old. For a system of world laws, democratically legislated for the welfare and common good of all persons on Earth, can only be effectively enforced through nonviolent methods. To see how this can be the case, we will examine below (in this and the next chapter) the basic premises of the philosophy of nonviolence as contrasted with the inherent violence of today's dominant economic system.

6.3 Primitive Accumulation, Banking, and Corporations

6.3.1. *Primitive Accumulation and the Origins of Banking.* Economists often use the concept of "primitive accumulation" to characterize the early stages of capitalism when people were slaughtered and their wealth stolen in the service of a direct accumulation that became the concentrations of "capital" necessary for the system to begin. From these early accumulations of wealth "investments" were made in businesses and in developing the means of production. The profits from these investments would result in still greater concentrations of capital that could be again invested. Bartolomé de Las Casas describes the process of primitive accumulation in Nicaragua:

> Thus more than five hundred thousand Indians were torn out of this province and sold into slavery. And those Indians had been as free as I am. In the infernal wars waged by the Spaniards another five or six hundred thousand souls have perished up to the present time. And these ravages continue....
>
> Meanwhile the captain-general commanded the Indians to bring him gold, much gold, for that is mainly what he had come there for. The Indians replied that they would gladly provide the Spaniards with all the gold they possessed, and they gathered together a large quantity of copper axes overlaid with a coating of gold, giving them the aspect of solid gold. The captain had the gold assayed and when it was found that the axes were of copper, he exclaimed "To the devil with this land! There is no gold here," and he commanded his men to put the Indians that had served them in chains and branded as slaves. This was done and to all the Indians they could lay hands on, and I saw one of the sons of the ruler of that city being chained and branded. Some Indians escaped, and when the Indians of the land heard of this great misfortune, they gathered together and took up arms and in the battle that followed the Spaniards massacred and tortured a great number of Indians. (1998: 167-168)

From the gold and silver that flowed into Europe in great quantities, the cycle of productive growth and development could then provide "take off" in the endless productive expansion that is at the theoretical heart of capitalism. And, since "a rising tide floats all boats," as the contemporary practitioners of "trickle down theory" argue, the well-being of entire populations would be improved. The miracle of Adam Smith's "invisible hand" would be demonstrated empirically: a system predicated on private greed and self-interest would magically result in the greatest benefit for the greatest number of people.

The second innovation that developed during the Renaissance that was integral to the development of capitalism was the modern system of banking. Since money at that time largely took the form of gold and silver coins that were difficult to protect from theft and difficult to transport in the quantity necessary for large transactions, people found it convenient to deposit their money with the goldsmiths who had the most secure safes for the protections of such valuables. In exchange, the goldsmiths issued certificates of deposit that could be traded in place of the gold that backed them up.

The goldsmiths found that, as only perhaps a fifth of these receipts came back at any one time to be redeemed for the gold on deposit, they could lend out, at interest, monetary certificates ("backed by gold") worth several times the gold on deposit, thereby turning a handsome profit on gold that they did not own in the first place. They discovered that they could issue certificates worth four or five times the gold they had on reserve thus, in effect, creating money out of nothing. "If they were careful not to overextend this 'credit,' the goldsmiths could thus become quite wealthy without producing anything of value themselves" (E. Brown 2007: 27).

This "innovation" synchronized well with the vast influx of gold and silver coming into Europe through the process of "primitive accumulation." The owners of capital had discovered a way through which they could accumulate wealth and power through exploiting people and nature without having to work themselves. And the bankers had found ways to accumulate wealth and power for themselves through becoming facilitators and accessories to this system, eventually realizing that control of the money supply meant ultimate control over the system itself. Nathan Rothschild, head of the Rothschild banking cartel in the nineteenth century, wrote:

> I care not what puppet is placed upon the throne of England to rule the Empire on which the sun never sets. *The man who controls Britain's money supply controls the British Empire, and I control the British money supply.* (Ibid. p. 65)

Because the essence of capitalism involves *using* people and nature in the service of the private accumulation of wealth, the innermost character of the system has not changed since its beginnings in "primitive accumulation." In his book, *The Invention of Capitalism: Classical Political Economy and the Secret History of Primitive Accumulation* (2000), economist Michael Perelman shows that primitive accumulation has accompanied the history of capitalism in one form or another from its early beginnings down to the present. People and nature have always been robbed as things to be exploited and used up in the process of accumulation of private wealth for the few.

In *The Shock Doctrine,* Klein points out that the former "frontiers" possessing gold and other natural resources robbed by rapacious capitalism in the process of primitive accumulation no longer exist in today's world. Whereas the guru of capitalism, Adam Smith, spoke of seizing the wealth of frontier "waste lands" for "but a trifle," "today's multinationals see government programs, public assets and everything that is not for sale as terrain to be conquered and seized – the post office, national parks, schools, social security, disaster relief and anything else that is publicly administered" (2007: 242). "In much of the Southern Hemisphere, neoliberalism is frequently spoken of as 'the second colonial pillage': in the first pillage, the riches were seized from the land, and in the second they were stripped from the state" (ibid. p. 244). The world-wide pillage of other people's wealth continues unabated.

6.3.2. *Controlling the Total System.* Historically, the elite classes that dominated this system soon realized that the slaughter and extermination of populations in the pursuit of wealth was not the most effective use of human beings. As the Spaniards in Nicaragua realized, systems of slavery can put human beings to better use than simply exterminating them in the service of possessing their wealth. And, as systems of slavery evolved into colonial systems, the elite classes realized that great wealth is to be made not only in using people and nature in the process of production (as slaves are used) but that the fact that all people need food, clothing, and shelter can be an even better route to ever-greater wealth and power for the few.

Hence, the producers of wealth (who work for those who own the means of production) can also be exploited as the *consumers* of wealth. The fundamental concept of capitalism as *a system of trade* developed in which the wealthy control the entire process in their own interests from the forcing of human beings to serve the owners of the means of *production* to the process of *exchange and distribution* of the goods and services to the process of *consumption* of food, clothing, and shelter. Two other institutions evolved in tandem with this system of domination at every stage of the way: the global banking system and the system of sovereign nation-states.

With this insight into the totality of the wealth-producing process, the modern world system came into its mature stage of development. The systems of law, of the military might of nations, banking, mass media, and the organization of society under its ruling classes were all placed in the service of controlling the entirety of the wealth-producing process from beginning to end (cf. Draffan 2003). To control the wealth-producing process means to engage in a system of "trade," no longer (at least on the surface of things) in "primitive accumulation." The essence of capitalism, we are told today, is "free trade." But its deeper essence has always been the *use and exploitation of people and nature in the service of private accumulation of wealth.* The key to that process has always been to maintain *inequalities* of trade under the ideological cover of "free trade" and to use military force (war) and the power of the bankers (loans and debt) to ensure and enforce control of that process. J.W. Smith writes:

> When the blatant injustices of mercantilist imperialism became too embarrassing, the belief that mercantilism had been abandoned and true free trade was in place was expounded. In reality the same wealth confiscation went on, deeply buried within complex systems of subtle monopolies and unequal trade hiding under the cover of free trade. Many explanations have been given for wars between the imperial nations when there was really only one common thread: "Who will control resources and trade and the wealth produced through inequalities in trade?" This is proven by the inequalities of trade siphoning the world's wealth to *imperial-centers-of-capital* today just as when *plunder-by-trade* was learned centuries ago. The battles over the world's wealth have only kept hiding behind different protective philosophies each time the secrets of laying claim to the wealth of others have been exposed. (2003a: 85)

Capitalism lays claim to the wealth of others. The owners of the means of production do not have to work but get rich through extracting surplus value from the labor of their employees. The bankers do not have to work but get rich through lending out someone else's deposited money and extracting interest as well as repayment of the principal from the debtor. The transnational entrepreneur today looks for countries in economic collapse where public assets (belonging to the people of that country) can be picked up at fire-sale prices and turned into private property. In geopolitical terms, nation-states have gone to war and used their military and hegemonic might to control entire systems of the wealth-producing process in their own interest. The principle of operation is the same – pillaging the Earth and turning the common wealth of our bountiful planet into the private property of the few.

The global south has been colonized and exploited for five centuries by the ruling classes of the global northern imperial nations with complicity of the ruling elites in the subject domains and with no end in sight. Today's system of neocolonial domination and exploitation is no less brutal than that exercised by Spanish conquistadors or British imperial troops. And just as the Spanish government sponsored the conquistadors of primitive accumulation in Nicaragua and Latin America, and the mercantilist system coupled the laws and military might of imperial nations with the colonial systems of "trade" imposed upon subject peoples, so today the inseparability of the global economic system and the system of sovereign nation-states is manifest. Chase-Dunn writes:

> The state and the interstate system are not separate from capitalism, but rather are the main institutional supports of capitalist production relations. The system of unequally powerful and competing nation-states is part of the competitive struggle of capitalism, and thus wars and geopolitics are a systematic part of capitalist dynamics, not exogenous forces. (1998: 61)

The overt military violence used today is geometrically greater than that used by the conquistadors in Nicaragua and Latin America due to the development of modern weapons systems. In Vietnam, we have seen, the U.S. genocidally wiped out the civilian population through massive saturation bombing of their villages and cities, causing the deaths of three to four million persons. This was not an accident. Vietnam was part of the dynamic of global imperial domination in the service of capital exploitation of the cheap labor and resources of the entire world. If it had gone "Communist" this cheap labor and resources would have been denied them, and other nations might believe that they could break free as well. Nowhere on Earth is safe from attack if the people of some small nation want to take their economic destiny into their own hands (Chomsky 1993).

As Chapter Four demonstrated, this massive overt violence is used to enforce even more massive structural violence as the majority of the peoples of the world rot in a living hell of poverty, deprivation, disease, and death. "A rising tide floats all boats." Such simplistic slogans fly in the face of the empirical realities of our world disorder. In reality, the structural violence of the world exists for its victims as an order of things every bit as horrific as the era of "primitive accumulation." The wealth produced by their countries and through the sale of their cheap natural resources flows into the coffers of the wealthy, while the majority of people on the Earth sink ever-further into perdition. Brazilian politician Luis Ignacio Silva writes:

The Third World War has already started.... The war is tearing down Brazil, Latin America, and practically all the Third World. Instead of soldiers dying, there are children. It is a war over the Third World debt, one which has as its main weapon, interest, a weapon more deadly than the atom bomb, more shattering than a laser beam. (in E. Brown 2007: 202)

Christian theologian Jürgen Moltmann sums up the modern world system as follows:

There are political and economic structures which are unjust because they are used to enforce the domination of human beings over human beings, the exploitation of human beings by human beings, and the alienation of human beings from one another. Within these structures, violence is practiced, not directly and personally, but indirectly, by way of laws and prices. Through structures of this kind, violence is legitimated. Through them, violent death is spread. Today impoverishment, debt, and exploitation spread misery, disease and epidemics, and hence premature death, among the weakest of the weak in the Third-world. The mass death of children in Africa is just the beginning. There, the number of people dying a violent death through structural violence is greater than the number of soldiers killed by military violence in the great world wars. (1996: 95)

The imperial powers controlled this system under their ideology of sovereign nation-states and claimed imperial rights of domination over their colonies. The imperial nations also adopted the ideology of Adam Smith's "free trade" as a cover for their nationalistic competition to control the global wealth-producing process in their own interests (J.W. Smith, 2006: Chs. 1-4). They affirmed the ideology of unlimited capital expansion as the only possible route to development and prosperity, but simultaneously attempted to channel this process of expansion to the ruling classes of their respective nation-states.

With decolonization, we have seen, the newly "free" nations continued to be controlled from abroad as well as internally by multinational corporate wealth and private property, as well as foreign banks, whose monetary resources often exceeded the wealth of the host country itself (Korten 1995). Corporations today operate with relative impunity throughout the third world. Their loyalty is not to the people of these nations but solely to their foreign investors who expect them to maximize profit.

6.3.3. *Corporations.* In her 2007 book, *The Web of Debt – The Shocking Truth About Our Money System*, Ellen Hodgson Brown writes concerning corporations:

Corporations are feudalistic organizations designed in the structure of a pyramid, with an elite group at the top manipulating masses of workers below. Workers are kept marching in lockstep, passing received orders down from above, out of fear of losing their jobs, their homes, and their benefits if they get out of line. At the top of the pyramid is a small group of controllers who alone know what is really going on. Critics have noted that the pyramid with an overseeing eye at the top is also the symbol on the Federal Reserve Note, the privately issued currency that became the national monetary unit in 1913. (p. 104)

Brown correctly describes the twisted logic of the corporation that has become a legal monster devouring our world, just as has the international banking cartel that creates most of the world's money in the form of private debt (ibid. Sec. III). And she correctly describes this "legal monster" as totalitarian, the opposite of democracy. A recent documentary film, entitled *The Corporation* (2005), describes the legally created characteristics of these institutions solely devoted to the accumulation of private wealth at the expense of people and the environment as clinically insane.

A corporation is a "legal person" with all the freedoms and rights of persons, except that it is legally and institutionally bound *to maximize profits for its investors regardless of the consequences to the environment or other persons*. Hence, as a legal person, it also exhibits all the characteristics of a sociopath or psychopath: reckless disregard for the safety and well-being of others, chronic lying and deceiving of others in the service of its own advantage, inability to experience guilt or remorse, and failure to conform to social norms, morality, or obedience to the law.

The modern corporation as a "legal person" is the ultimate capitalist creation. It has all the legal rights and privileges of real human beings yet at the same time is constituted to be without a human moral dimension. Legally its concern is solely with accumulation of private profit with no concern for the environment or human beings who may be hurt in this process. This may technically qualify as insanity, but the system itself is anything but insane, for the laws that define corporations as sociopathic (that is, directed only toward self-interest without any human values or conscience), are carefully calculated by financiers, owners, bankers, and politicians to serve this system of domination.

In *The Divine Right of Capital* (2001), Marjorie Kelly draws an analogy between the older system of property rights in which a wife became her husband's property and all of her assets, even her clothing, passed into the possession of her husband and the modern corporation's ownership of its employees:

Today, the corporation is considered one legal entity, and that entity is equated with stockholders. Like wives, employees "disappear" into the corporation – where they have no vote. The property of the corporation is administered solely in the interests of stockholders, who, like husbands, claim the profits, and are required to render employees no accounting. We thus have a corporate marriage in which one party has sole domination. (p. 44)

It is this system that functions as the antithesis of planetary democracy and any vision of politics and economics predicated on human beings as ends in themselves. The system has three fundamental features, we have seen, all inherently undemocratic and destructive of the common good of the peoples of Earth: (1) the system of "sovereign" nation-states unaccountable to any law above themselves, (2) the system of transnational corporations unaccountable to any democratic rule of law or the common good of the Earth, and (3) the system of private banking that supplies the world with money in the form of interest-bearing debt, making the world dependent on the undemocratic and unaccountable control of these private financial cartels.

6.4 World Trade, International Banking, and the Threat of Global Totalitarianism

The world continues to move toward conditions of global totalitarianism under the control of the gigantic transnational corporations and financial institutions protected and promoted by the military might of the first world and the economic might of the World Trade Organization, World Bank, and IMF. The economic collapse that begin in 2007-8 was not sufficient to change the system itself. The dominant economic and political forces in the world are attempting to reactivate the same system.

The Director-General of the World Trade Organization in the 1980s wrote an article for the Wall Street Journal that began with the sentence "Globalization is a reality of our time." This globalization, as Vandana Shiva has pointed out, is a prescription for the dispossession of 80% of the planet's population (1997b; cf. Shiva 1997a). This "reality of our time" is not an accident, any more than the colonial exploitation and impoverishment of the majority of humankind was an accident, any more than centuries of slavery and violence against peoples of color were an accident. It is a carefully planned and constructed process of the most powerful economic and political forces in the world to continue converting the economies of the world to serve their own interests.

Today's rules of world trade (that continue even within the worldwide economic depression) require of nations (under the threat of severe economic penalties) to export and import the goods needed for their survival. The engines of globalization imposed by the World Bank and the IMF implement structural adjustment programs on economically weak nations, forcing them to open up to the exploitation by the transnational corporations and to convert from subsistence, self-sufficient forms of production, to dependence on international markets and the dominant transnational corporations. These principles, like powerful new rules of world intellectual property rights, were worked out in secret meetings between the giant corporations and the ruling elites of the most powerful nation-states and then imposed upon the rest of the approximately 120 nations within the WTO at the Uruguay Round of the General Agreement on Tariffs and Trade (GATT) that took place between 1986 and 1995. Both structural adjustment programs imposed by the World Bank and IMF and the rules of world trade formulated by the WTO are coercive instruments forced upon the poor of the world by its ruling elites.

At the International Food Summit in 1996, the U.S. Secretary of Agriculture announced that the U.S. would never accept food as a human right because this would constitute an unacceptable interference with "free trade" (Shiva 1997). People in the world today have no right to water, to healthcare, to sanitation, even to eat, unless some set of global corporations can profit from their basic human needs. This denial of the right to exist outside of the control of the powerful is not an inevitable or "natural" development of trade; it is a planned and coerced construction of the global economic system for the benefit of the few.

Under WTO rules, we have seen, corporations can now sue governments if laws enacted by those governments restrict their "free trade," cutting into their profit margins. The only forces capable of controlling the rapacity and destructive power of corporations, that is, governments with enforceable laws, are now superseded and capable of being attacked by the very forces that only government can control. Civilization has undergone centuries of political struggle by citizens longing for freedom in order to create the principles of democracy in which governments are responsible to their citizens and laws are required to be made for the common good of all. All this is today being wiped away by the economic elite of the world and their agents in the imperial nation-states. Klein's book *The Shock Doctrine* details this pattern of the destruction of democracy in the service of capitalism in country after country around the world.

The destruction of democracy and the authority of government to control domination and exploitation by the wealthy classes could not have taken place except through violence, precisely because real democracy itself is the quintessential form of nonviolent and non-coercive decision-making for society. Yet, today, rather than democracy being promoted and extended throughout the world, governments, we have seen, are being redefined as security forces for multinational investors (Shiva 1997). The traditional justifications for the authority of government – that it serve the needs, security, and common good of the people – have been reduced, within WTO regulations, to the protection of the private property of global investors. Under WTO protocols, governments are now to be solely concerned with their police and enforcement functions. Third world military and police are being trained by first-world imperial military forces to put down internal rebellion and subversion and to protect foreign economic assets within the host nations.

The world system today is dominated by international banking and corporate cartels whose aim, in the words of Dr. Carroll Quigley, President Bill Clinton's mentor, is "nothing less than to create a world system of financial control in private hands able to dominate the political system of each country and the economy of the world as a whole" (in E. Brown 2007: 2). In *When Corporations Rule the World*, Korten writes:

> These forces have transformed once-beneficial corporations and financial institutions into instruments of a market tyranny that reaches across the planet like a cancer, colonizing ever more of the planet's living spaces, destroying livelihoods, displacing people, rendering democratic institutions impotent, and feeding on life in an insatiable quest for money. (1995: 22)

Canadian economist Michel Chossudovsky states that:

> This manipulation of market forces by powerful actors constitutes *a form of financial and economic warfare.* No need to re-colonize lost territory or send in invading armies. In the later twentieth century, the outright "conquest of nations," meaning the control over productive assets, labor, and natural resources and institutions, can be carried out in an impersonal fashion from the corporate boardroom. (in E. Brown 2007: 255)

The experience of South Africa serves as a clear illustration of the hidden totalitarian power of an economic system that holds political power and the will of the people helpless within its grip. In *The Shock Doctrine*, Klein recounts the decades-long struggle of the non-white vast majority for freedom from the apartheid system of political domination by the tiny white minority. This system of domination was simultaneously a sector of the global capitalist system in which the white minority owned the industries, mines, investments, transportation systems, and banking and engaged in the international trade that made South Africa the most robust capitalist economy in Africa. While the vast non-white majority lived in astonishing poverty working for pitiful wages in these industries and mines, they lived both without political freedom and without electricity, running water, healthcare, or education.

Meanwhile, the ruling minority amassed immense fortunes from the exploitation of their cheap labor.

Klein chronicles the struggle for freedom in South Africa before and after the fall of apartheid under the leadership of the African National Congress (ANC) (2007:194-217). The struggle had long been guided by "the Freedom Charter," a document created through widespread participation of the people in 1955 that embodied their demands for land, healthcare, the right to work, decent wages, free education, freedom of movement, equality of citizenship, and a share in the immense wealth that had been amassed by the tiny white minority. Shortly before his release from 27 years of imprisonment, soon to be President of South Africa Nelson Mandela wrote to his followers from prison of his continuing commitment to the principles of the Freedom Charter: "The nationalization of the mines, banks and monopoly industries is the policy of the ANC, and the change or modification of our views in this regard is inconceivable. Black economic empowerment is a goal we fully support and encourage, but in our situation state control of certain sectors of the economy is unavoidable" (p. 195).

Soon Mandela and other ANC leaders were in negotiations with the apartheid government concerning the conditions for the transition of power. Probably unwittingly, they allowed the old economic system to remain in place since they were focused on attaining political democracy and political power for the first time, naively thinking that with political power, economic arrangements could be later addressed and corrected. Apartheid ended in South Africa, but the freedom described in the Freedom Charter never appeared. For real freedom is impossible for the majority under capitalism, just as the Freedom Charter had understood. Klein writes:

> After a decade of ANC rule, millions of people had been cut off from the newly connected water and electricity because they couldn't pay the bills. At least 40 percent of the new phone lines were no longer in service by 2003. As for the "banks, mines, and monopoly industry" that Mandela had pledged to nationalize, they remained firmly in the hands of the same four white-owned megaconglomerates that also control 80 percent of the Johannesburg Stock Exchange. In 2005, only 4 percent of the companies listed on the exchange were owned or controlled by blacks. Seventy percent of South Africa's land, in 2006, was still monopolized by whites, who are just 10 percent of the population. (p. 206).

Klein went to South Africa in 2005 to find out the story of what had happened. She interviewed a number of ANC antiapartheid activists and leaders, many of whom now understood that freedom had not been attained and that the majority of people in South Africa remained in slavery:

> A longtime antiapartheid activist, Rassool Snyman, described the trap to me in stark terms. "They never freed us. They only took the chain from around our neck and put it on our ankles." Yasmin Sooka, a prominent South African human rights activist, told me that the transition "was business saying, 'We'll keep everything and you [the ANC] will rule in name.... You can have political power, you can have the façade of governing, but real governance will take place somewhere else.'" It was a process of infantilization that is common to so-called transitional countries – new governments are, in effect, given the keys to the house but not the combination to the safe. (pp. 203-204)

The "financial and economic warfare" referred to by Michael Chossudovsky above is the *modus operandi* of the ruling capitalist elite in the world who know very well that political democracy without economic democracy is a substantially meaningless concept. "The man who controls the money supply controls the empire" exclaimed Nathan Rothschild. The financial and economic system needs government to supply police and security functions to protect its corporate property rights, maintain law and order, and provide a "stable investment climate." Democracy in name only is fine for this purpose. If not, then dictatorships or "authoritarian" governments will do just as well. The example of South Africa illustrates plainly that democracy is meaningless unless it includes economic democracy.

But South Africa's entrapment within the capitalist economic system was not simply internal to the country. The economic system of the world has been globalized. South Africa remains caught in a net that includes the World Bank, the IMF, international debt, global financial markets, international investment and banking, and world trade regulations. Nor was this net unplanned. One ANC activist described the process of "transition" to freedom:

> Key economic leaders were regularly ferried to the head offices of international organizations such as the World Bank and IMF, and during 1992 and 1993 several ANC staffers, some of whom had no economic qualifications at all, took part at abbreviated executive training programs at foreign business schools, investment banks, economic policy think tanks and the World Bank, where they were 'fed a steady diet of neo-liberal ideas.' It was a dizzying experience. Never before had a government-in-waiting been so seduced by the international community. (Ibid. p. 216)

The "warfare" waged by the wealthy ruling classes of the world is primarily waged by people in business suits with refined and cultivated manners whose calling cards proclaim advanced degrees from Harvard, Princeton, Yale, or the Chicago School of Economics. Propaganda and manipulation hidden within the façade of "education" serves as their stock and trade. However, if the ANC had really managed to nationalize "the mines, banks, and monopoly industries," it is likely the generous friendship of the "educators" would have been replaced by the hidden threat that really backs up their smiling regime – the South African government would have been the target of international military subversion and attack from the imperial centers of power who, we have seen, have attacked many countries of the world that have attempted to break free of global capitalism and take an independent economic course.

At present, the United States, as the absolute center of this imperial system now dominating much of the world's banking and trade, works tirelessly to militarize outer space and institute control of the entire globe so complete that no nation will be able to ever again rival its military dominance (Johnson 2006). The tiny elite of bankers, corporate captains, and ruling class elite who now control forty-seven percent of the world's wealth as well as the central policies of the United States government are working to end forever any hope of a just, decent, or equitable world order. This will not change under Barack Obama as President.

The system goes much deeper than the policies of any one President. As a group, they are cynical nihilists with no values apart from wealth, power, and domination. To them, any notions of intrinsic human dignity or human worth are a total illusion. The "charity" projects or non-profit foundations that some of them promote translate primarily to public relations ploys and tax deductions, a necessary part of "business as usual."

This tiny group of dominators uses every means at its disposal, from massive propaganda campaigns to smiling, educated business "advisors," to the largely fabricated "threat of terrorism," to the military might of first-world nations, to currency manipulation of entire countries, to World Trade Organization rules and sanctions in order to solidify its control and end forever the promise of freedom, democracy, and the dream of universal dignity on our planet. Global banking in the hands of unaccountable private interests, like transnational corporations and the governments of nation-states in these same hands, translates into slavery for the rest of the world and destruction of our planetary home that should be the inheritance of future generations. Today, it may appear that no power on Earth can control the ever-further concentration of the wealth of the world into ever-fewer private hands.

PART THREE

DAWN OF A HOLISTIC EARTH CIVILIZATION

Chapter Seven

A Nonviolent Democratic Community for the Earth

Authentic Political and Economic Democracy as Central to a Holistic World Order

The power to speak is not at our disposal, we are at its disposal....In this light our language becomes something more than a practical means of communication with others and of mastering things; when speaking becomes "saying"...then we have the experience of language as a gift and of thought as the recognition of this gift.

Paul Ricceur

A quantum shift *in the global brain is a sudden and fundamental transformation in the relations of a significant segment of the six and a half billion humans to each other and to nature –* a macroshift in society *– and a likewise sudden and fundamental transformation in cutting-edge perceptions regarding the nature of reality –* a paradigm shift in science. *The two shifts together make for a veritable "reality revolution" in society as well as in science.*

Ervin Laszlo

The transformative insight expressed by Ervin Laszlo in this quotation needs filling out in terms of the concrete institutions and relationships that will arise from the awakening of the "global brain," that is, from the awakening of human beings to their deeper species being and their intrinsic relatedness to one another. This chapter identifies two fundamental changes in human relationships: first the resurgence of community no longer based on a shared set of cultural, linguistic, or ethnic similarities but community as a sense of shared humanity and citizenship within the commonwealth of Spaceship Earth.

Second, related to the first, is the reinstatement of the concept of democratic socialism as the rational and moral alternative to monopoly capitalism. Socialism, we have seen, means economics with a sense of the community, of the value of its citizens, of their mutual trust and integrity, and their orientation to a common good. Hence, socialism means economics predicated on creating the good life for citizens precisely because economics should be in the service of human well-being, rather than human well-being sacrificed to the mercy of economics. Under genuine democracy, corporations can only be legal social constructs (not legal persons) responsible to the people and their common good.

Language comes to human beings as a gift, as Ricceur asserts, a gift that opens up for us alone an intelligible world: access to a world that is unitary, comprehensible, and structured as *unity in diversity*. The fundamental rationality of language reveals for human beings the foundations of knowledge, reality, and authentic values. The gift of language and openness to its call may well unveil for us other dimensions of giveness as well. It is very possible that a new awareness, a new sense of the depths of existence, will descend into human consciousness within the relatively near future. But for our purposes here we need only focus on the astonishing power of language to activate a holistic consciousness of dynamic *unity in diversity* that is that the heart of planetary democracy.

We have seen that twentieth-century science has effected a paradigm shift in our understanding in each of these dimensions. We are coming to comprehend knowledge as the holistic theoretic coherence and coordination arising from careful investigations of innumerable persons through time. We are beginning to comprehend the holistic structures of reality in which natural systems, biological systems, and human social systems manifest properties that are not reducible to the sum of their parts. And today we are in a position to derive authentic universal values that transcend the dogmatisms, cultural fixations, and biases of our parochial past.

7.1 The Human Community as a Moral Framework for Human Life

In his *Discourse on the Origins of Inequality*, Jean-Jacques Rousseau studies the origins of governments from out of that "state of nature" that existed when there were no governments and the Earth belonged in common to all persons. Rousseau recognizes that governments were originally instituted by those who had appropriated land for themselves and now wanted the collective force of society to legitimate and protect their stolen wealth. Governmental power, in this sense, has existed since earliest times and has nearly always been appropriated by the wealthy and unscrupulous as the most efficient means for protecting their criminal use and exploitation of the Earth and other people for their own selfish gain.

In this conception, government is a consolidation of power that uses the aura of legitimacy in the service of the private wealth and power of a few. It is, therefore, by and large a criminal enterprise that violates the ethical and spiritual principles of communicative reason, democracy, common morality, *unity in diversity*, and community. We understand these latter principles very well, for they are part of the experience of most people's lives in one way or another. Many people today also understand government as a criminal enterprise, often based on personal experience: since most governments today have been thus colonized.

Perhaps the first principle of good government is that it must represent the whole community, rather than special interests. The family, for example, often exists as a small community in which people care about one another and mutually respect one another's value and integrity. In families, it would not normally occur to the parents or the more powerful members of the family to exploit the weaker ones for private gain or allow them to die because they did not have the means to bring food, clothing, or shelter to themselves. A family, like a community, involves a set of relationships that bind people together in a variety of ways that transcend the use and exploitation of some for the advantage of others. Capitalist market relationships are not family or community relations based on communicative reason, democracy, or morality. They disintegrate the very basis of human communities.

In *21st Century Democratic Renaissance* (2008), Errol E. Harris discusses the tradition in political theory extending from Nazi theorist Carl Schmit to neoliberal guru Leo Strauss that understands government as revolving solely around the greedy struggle for control of power and manipulation of power. Harris contrasts this tradition with the mainstream tradition of democratic Western thinkers who have linked the legitimacy of government to the degree of freedom, equality, and community made possible for citizens. Harris shows the tremendous significance of the concepts of the community as a whole and the "common good" of the community that have been emphasized throughout the history of democratic theory.

One meaning of the concept of community involves a group of individuals beyond the level of the family who extend these relationships of communicative reason, democracy, morality, mutual concern, and respect to larger and larger social groupings. In larger social groupings, we may no longer be in face-to-face personal relationships as within a family. Nevertheless there can be bonds, customs, mores, feelings of solidarity, and traditions of communicative reasoning that permeate very large communities, as Hegel demonstrated at length. These become places where people can encounter strangers with a reasonable trust that one will not be used or manipulated but will be treated with respect and decency. A community in this sense embodies a moral reality permeated by a set of ethical, communal, and rational relationships that foster freedom, equality, dignity, and mutuality among its citizens.

Rousseau understood that government need not be a collective power appropriated by the unscrupulous few for their private gain at the expense of everyone else. He calls his conception of government as a moral reality within a community "the social contract." It is possible for citizens to unite under government in such a way that government represents the common force of them all in the service of liberty, equality, and authentic community. Government does not define the entirety of a community, but the political commitment of each to the mutual freedom and well being of all raises community to a higher level.

Government then takes on the qualities that we associate with genuine democracy, for democracy is most fundamentally a moral ideal predicated on the intrinsic dignity of each citizen within a framework of legitimate authority that simultaneously represents the common good of the community. And Rousseau insisted that such a moral community must be *founded*. It will not evolve naturally, precisely because the social contract arises from a founding legislative-moral act.

It may be that many existing governments exist as some combination of these two kinds of government. In the United States, the recent ascent of Barack Obama to power has elicited an outpouring of affirmations of the tradition of democracy in this country and its power to bind generation after generation within its ideals of mutual respect for human rights and a sense of mutual obligation for all citizens. This outpouring comes in stark contrast to the empowerment of the criminal element of the super-rich, the unscrupulous, the torturers, and the murderers who were encouraged under the George W. Bush administration.

However, popular affirmations of democracy alone will not change the system. The history of the United States is the largely the history of the failure of its founding principles (Zinn 1980). Philosopher David Ingram declares that the U.S. sytem (based on Lockean ideas of citizen distrust for the larger community) involves a "backward-looking notion" as opposed to Rousseau's "forward-looking notion" (2006: 55). Real democracy can only be institutionalized at the global level on political and economic principles consistent with a global community.

Rousseau's understanding of the meaning of the social contract as the creation of government as a moral reality permeating a human community was developed further by Kant and Hegel. Kant understood that the basic moral reality of legitimate government was identical with the basic imperative that confronts individual persons: the categorical imperative. The most basic moral command for any rational being is the command to universalize the maxim of one's proposed actions: "Can I make it a universal law that everyone act as I am about to act?" The moral individual legislates universal laws for him or herself. If an action is right, then it is right for everyone in these circumstances. If it is wrong, then I am making an exception for myself and saying, in effect, "To hell with everyone else, I am going to do what I (or my group) feel like doing regardless of their well-being."

When the categorical imperative is applied to society, Kant argued, we have the social contract of a constitutional "republican" state in which the freedom, equality, and independence of each citizen is guaranteed under the constitution and by the collective force of the entire community. The categorical imperative demands that we live under universal, democratically legislated laws, applying equally to all. Any alternative to this is immoral: to live in any situation where the stronger or more clever exploit or dominate the weaker is to live in a morally illegitimate situation, even if that situation if protected by some form of government.

Hegel brought Kant's abstract moral framework for society down into the concrete, particular relationships that permeate the whole of society at every level. The moral quality of a society resides in the on-going development and interaction of these relationships involving family, locality, civic organizations, business, and government. The totality is evolving toward an ever-greater integration of *unity in diversity*.

For Rousseau, Kant, and Hegel, and the democratic tradition following them and building upon their work, entire nations and even the world can be morally grounded communities in this sense. We have seen that Kant fully understood the implications of his thought in the sense that he realized that the system of sovereign nations itself was immoral because it was not a republican community guaranteeing the freedom, equality, and independence of all citizens everywhere. Even though *within* nations it was possible to have republican constitutions protecting everyone as a community, he thought, *between* nations there exists only a condition of actual or *defacto* war.

The only way for human beings to move out of this savage and barbaric international condition required, for Kant, creating an Earth Federation with a republican constitution uniting all the nations as states within the federation. Our planetary community can and should be grounded (as Rousseau, Kant, and Hegel understood) in the universal moral principles at the heart of democracy that must be actualized in the concrete relationships among people at all levels, including government. *Community, in the sense of a moral reality and framework for human interaction embodied in a planetary, democratic constitution and a global sense of solidarity, can and should encompass all humankind.* Indeed, we will see that it is only on this level that a genuine social contract and community can be realized. Without raising community to a universal level, elements such as sovereign nation-states, not bound by community relationships expressed in democratically legislated universal laws, will always destroy the moral framework of human life (cf. Martin 2008: Chs. 7 & 8). Our obligation, therefore, is to actualize this human community.

Religious insight confirms philosophical insight. Pope Benedict XVI's June 2009 encyclical, *Caritas in Veritate,* emphasizes the truth that there can be no global economic justice unless there is a global sense of "community," of "the common good." (e.g., in sections 7 and 9). Christian thinker Enrique Dussel concurs. In community, he writes "all individuals are persons for one another." The "sin" of turning people into "things" to be exploited, as instruments of labor or faceless consumers, is gone, "The community," he says, "is the real, concrete agent and mover of history. In community we are 'at home,' in safety and security, 'in common'" (1988, p. 11). Democracy can only be fully actualized within a genuine, universal community.

7.2 Eight Principles of Authentic Democracy

The moral framework of authentic democracy can be further clarified by itemizing the following principles at the heart of democracy. There may well be different legitimate formulations of these principles that emphasize some over others. However, together they articulate an overview of what must be the case if we are to actualize a holistic human social reality of liberty, equality, and community. As Kant emphasized, *only government* itself can actualize these, since the moral category of citizenship must be a *uniformly enforced legal category.* Such a legal category guarantees to every adult liberty, equality, and community under commonly enforceable, constitutionally mandated laws regardless of his or her social status, likeability, strength, race, political views, or other particular qualities.

The first seven principles discussed in this subsection are drawn from section 9.7 of *Ascent to Freedom* and reproduced here in quotation format. The eighth principle emphasizes the relationship of democracy with nonviolence emphasized in this book. All eight are applied within the context of our discussion of creating a nonviolent, holistic community upon the Earth. All these principles must be realized in some practically effective way if the claim of a government to democracy is to be legitimate. It should become clear that none of these principles can be truly realized on the level of sovereign nation-states.

> The first principle of authentic democracy *is the dignity of all persons as human beings*. This means persons cannot be manipulated, dominated, deceived, or dehumanized as if they were mere things. Torture is prohibited, as is imprisonment without proper due process of law, as are lying and deceit to the population. The deceitful use of people to achieve ends to which they are not a party is prohibited to any government that approximates genuine democracy. All these kinds of activities dehumanize people, turning them into mere things to be manipulated, and violate our inherent human dignity. This inherent dignity must be institutionalized in concrete systems of rights, due process procedures, and other democratic protections. Corporate entities do not have dignity and cannot be legal persons.

Under the system of militarized nation-states, it is inevitable that governments lie to their own people or withhold information from their own people under the guise of "national security." Military organization and strategy requires secrecy of logistics, planning, and information. These also require that the dignity of all those persons designated as "enemies" be ignored. The honest treatment of people necessary if their inherent dignity is respected, requires that government refuse to torture, manipulate, dominate or deceive. This shows that military organization is incompatible with authentic democracy. Only under the Earth Federation, in which a world peace system is established and all militarism abolished from the Earth, will authentic democracy be able to flourish. Commitment to this principle alone, is sufficient to solidify a global community spirit.

> The second principle of democracy is the idea that *all people have human rights that are inalienable*. This derives from our inviolable human dignity. It does not necessarily mean a Lockean idea of *a priori* attributes that somehow inhere in an individual from birth. It means, rather, that constitutions must specify those rights that are *beyond the power of government to touch*. The specific philosophical derivations are of secondary importance to the recognition of the inviolable dignity of persons

through recognition of inviolable rights. Democratic freedom is not worth much if government can suspend or alter fundamental protections of persons through the passage of laws or suspension of due process requirements.

The concept of inalienable rights need not, therefore, derive from metaphysical theories of *a priori* natural rights such as Locke's theory. Authentic democracy functions best if there is recognition that certain rights are beyond the scope of government or its legislative bodies to touch. This is the case with the *Constitution for the Federation of Earth* that designates the 18 rights in Article 12 as "inalienable." Under the plethora of nation-states, what is considered "inalienable" in one nation may be ignored in another nation, showing the absurdity of fragmentation under the nation-states. If "inalienable" is to have any meaning at all, it must refer to all persons and be protected for all persons, not merely a certain portion of humanity.

> The third principle of democracy *is universal political equality within a context of reasonable economic equality*. This is implicit in the first two principles and means that democracy cannot function unless all adult human beings, who are subject to laws and decisions that affect them, have a right to a basic political equality of voice allowing them to participate in this decision-making process. In cases of large populations, this participation often takes the form of voting for representatives who make decisions on behalf of the population, within a context of citizen oversight and transparency.

The development of computer and internet technologies have made possible much more participatory forms of citizen involvement in democratic decision-making. But the immense economic disparities now existing in the world make a mockery of the idea of political equality among citizen participants. Even if reasonable equality were achieved among citizens, as in today's Cuban society, democracy remains impossible when external rich and powerful nations interfere with Cuba's ability to function as a democracy. Even within societies, large concentrations of wealth inevitably translate into extremely undemocratic concentrations of political power and influence. Equality must be truly universal if democracy is to function, which can only mean some version of planetary market socialism under an *Earth Constitution*.

> The fourth principle of democracy is the existence of a *public space necessary for genuine communication*. The free exchange of ideas and the development of a genuinely communicative dimension are essential to any notion that the people are the source of legitimate authority in government. Communicative public space is to be distinguished from the early-modern liberal democratic idea, promoted by John Stuart Mill and others, of a "free

marketplace of ideas." Ideas do not fit well into the capitalist model of supply and demand, and their truth or wisdom certainly is not a matter of the whims of popular consumption and taste. Communicative public space requires institutionalized spaces for discussion that are free from dog-eat-dog political competition and sloganeering as well as from corporate public relations and advertising propaganda. The capacity for reasoned discourse and debate, intimately connected with our human dignity, must find ample space within any society claiming to be a democracy.

Under most present systems of government, even those calling themselves democratic, immense benefits accrue to those who win elections or who are appointed to power by others who win elections. These immense benefits (prominent contacts, government contracts, power and influence with respect to one's own interests) only accrue to the extent that governments are not genuinely democratic but are subject to manipulation in undemocratic ways. Under these circumstances public space is colonized by propaganda machines of concentrations of power like big, privately owned media, big business, or the military.

Genuine communication for mutual understanding, the pacification of existence, and promotion of the common good only effectively begin to the extent that such immense, undemocratic benefits are removed from the processes of governing. This can only be done effectively on a planetary scale when the planetary forces that distort democracy have been removed and public space is genuinely available for discourse rather than strategic manipulation. The technology exists today for worldwide dialogue and political participation within a globalized sense of a planetary community. The undemocratic forces of huge concentrations of wealth and huge military propaganda machines must be removed worldwide if there is ever to be democracy anywhere on Earth.

Indeed, today people from around the world dialogue with one another via the internet, but they profoundly lack the political and economic equality of voice that should be the foundation of democracy. Only a non-military Earth Federation operating with an economics of universal prosperity and reasonable equality can remove these factors that distort democracy and establish legitimate dialogue with a genuine public space for the people of Earth. Only such a legally protected and mandated global public space can undergird and make possible viable public spaces on the local level within nations. Here we have another foundation for a global community spirit – the universal commitment to honest dialogue rather than the use of deceit, propaganda, or force.

The fifth principle of democracy is the idea that *government only functions legitimately with the consent of the governed and active participation of the governed in formulating the laws under which they live.* Governmental authority to legislate and enforce laws is predicated on an unforced consent to these laws by the population. This means that consent must not be "manufactured" or engineered through government propaganda, intimidation, pressure to conformity, a corporate controlled media system, or any other method, but must be the product of free exchange of ideas within a democratic framework. As this is sometimes expressed, ultimate sovereignty belongs to the people, and only their free consent can create legitimate political obligation to respect and obey the laws. The people have the right to withdraw allegiance from any government that seriously violates their consent, dignity, equality, or human rights.

Consent of the governed is manifested in a multiplicity of ways that include participation in voting, in dialogue and debate, in protests or demonstrations, in communication with government officials or agencies, in willingness to pay taxes or serve society in other ways, etc. Under the present system of militarized nation-states, consent is not only manipulated by elite propaganda mechanisms, it is also falsely engineered through mechanisms of fear, making people accept governments because they believe these governments are working to keep them safe in a dangerous world (cf. Chomsky and Herman 2002). However, a dangerous, non-pacified world itself makes democracy impossible. Consent, therefore, today inevitably involves non-democratic elements that can only be removed at the planetary level.

The sixth principle of democracy is the existence of *citizenship within a community of rights and responsibilities*. When democracy exists in human affairs, the persons whose dignity, rights, equality, and consent are thus institutionalized are transformed from mere individuals forced to obey arbitrary laws by police or military authorities to *citizens* morally responsible to one another and to the society as a whole. A community of rights emerges that is a very special form of human association. Every one of one's rights becomes complemented by duties and obligations to the community.

To be part of an institutional framework that recognizes one's human dignity is to be politically recognized as a *citizen*, not merely a subject. Our rights embodied in a democratic political framework necessarily engender moral duties to society. We become co-participants in the ongoing development of events and morally responsible to our fellow citizens, the common good, and future generations. Loyalty to a genuine *community of rights* becomes a living force that binds the consent of the governed together within a community of mutual duties and obligations. Democracy not only recognizes our inalienable dignity as human beings, but it raises us to an even higher level of dignity by making us responsible to society and to our fellow citizens within a community of rights and duties.

This higher level of citizenship is the proper heritage of every person on Earth, for it draws together all the qualities of democracy and transforms people from isolated individuals into full-fledged members of a democratic community. The only way to create world peace is to include all the people of Earth in the *community of world citizenship* under an *Earth Constitution*. Citizenship secures the entire nexus of rights and responsibilities and transforms them from mere "ideals" into living, institutionally protected realities. It is the fulfillment of Article 28 of the U.N. Universal Declaration of Human Rights: "Everyone is entitled to a social and international order in which the rights and freedoms set forth in this Declaration can be fully realized."

The establishment of the reality of legal world citizenship simultaneously establishes a planetary community of rights and responsibilities and *binds all people together* into a framework within which their needs, problems, conflicts, misunderstandings, and differences can be effectively addressed. Outside of the embrace of full citizenship, these needs, problems, conflicts, misunderstandings, and differences remain largely *incommensurable* for lack of the effective institutions within which they can be addressed. A world peace system includes not only demilitarizing the lawless system of sovereign nation-states, it also necessarily means establishing the institutional framework for a genuine community of rights and responsibilities for the people of Earth.

> The seventh principle of democracy is *representation of the common good of the whole*. Within a framework of freedom, citizens soon develop a loyal community of rights and duties in which the common good of the whole becomes a matter of utmost importance. Democratic government that represents them must embody this concern. The notion of the common good of the whole logically includes the idea that the good of future generations must be taken into account. Legitimate government does not represent the interests of a segment of the population. Concern for the environment, for the prosperity of citizens, for preservation of resources for future generations, and for protecting the rights and political voice of all citizens equally are understood as representing the common good.

Within today's class societies radically divided between wealth and poverty, governments ignore the common good in favor of the good of the ruling classes. Second, within the framework of today's militarized nation-state system, there is no such thing as a democratic government acting for the common good of a whole nation. What appears to be the common good of one nation becomes the detriment to peoples of other nations. In a fragmented world order, a multiplicity of apparent common goods appears that necessarily become incommensurable with one another. The common good of the people of Earth and future generations evaporates as 193 national fragments all pursue incompatible common goods.

> The eighth principle of democracy requires a constitutional-legal framework and community spirit that *reduces as much as possible the use of force in human affairs.* It entirely eliminates war, which is always the antithesis of democracy and internally destroys the democracy of countries, but it also works to eliminate force in the form of political violence (such as repression or arrest of those with dissenting ideas). The legitimate use of force by democratic government requires effective legal restraints and systems of accountability for police and government officials. It also requires the principle of minimum use of necessary force in arresting lawbreakers and otherwise keeping order and careful avoidance of the use of force against any and all innocent bystanders. It absolutely prohibits the use or threat of force, fear, or intimidation as a form of political control of the population or against law-abiding nonviolent dissenters.

With each of these eight principles of authentic democracy it is clear that the principle of the common good is inherently universal and incapable of realization on the local level apart from federation within the whole of planet Earth. Democracy recognizes the dignity of *all* persons, just as it recognizes the inalienable rights of *all* persons, just as it demands for all persons universal equality, public space for dialogue, consent of the governed, the rights and duties of citizenship, the need for genuine representation of the common good, and the renunciation of violence in favor of the minimum uses of force. Each of these fundamental principles demands universality, and together they show clearly that democracy cannot function in today's world apart from its institutionalization at the planetary level.

Establishing a holistic, nonviolent planetary community is the only option for creating a decent future of ourselves and our children, and such a community can only be a real community of rights, responsibilities, and democratic participation if it can create reasonable prosperity for all the world's citizens and reasonable economic equality for all. The word "socialism" historically implies the idea of such a community and an economics based on the value of human beings as ends in themselves in ways that "capitalism" does not. Yet for all that, the word remains just a word. One could argue for an economics of "cooperative capitalism" or a conception of "economic democracy" and recommend basically the same framework.

Nevertheless, it should be clear that there will never be peace in the world, nor justice, nor democracy, as long as the world has not solved the problem of extreme poverty along with immense, unreasonable concentrations of private wealth. The *Earth Constitution* nowhere uses the word "socialism," nor the word "capitalism." However, for reasons that I hope to make clear, I have chosen to summarize the *Constitution's* economically democratic features, premised on the common good of all human beings, as "worldwide democratic market socialism."

7.3 Socialism: Economics Based on Fundamental Human Values

Perhaps the value-nihilism of today's world disorder under capitalism is most fundamentally the final result of the negation of our humanity by the imperative of capital accumulation. When all human values are negated – love, kindness, cooperation, sharing, community, and the value of people as ends in themselves – by an economic system that turns people into commodities whose labor and resources are exploited in the service of capital expansion, by a banking system that uses people's basic economic needs as an instrument of exploitation and domination, and by the military might of nation-states who place themselves in the service of capital accumulation of their respective ruling classes – then all values eventually appear to be relative (merely subjective) and the result is nihilism on the part of the ruling classes, their agents, their academic lackeys, and their militarized mandarins.

It is difficult to write convincingly about the deeper meanings of socialism in the face of a century and a half of propaganda in the service of the lords of the Earth directed at discrediting this concept. The concept arose as the diametrical opposite of capitalism – *instead of a system in which people and nature were used as a means to the private accumulation of wealth, some thinkers realized that we need a system in which people and the integrity of nature are the ends around which the economic and political systems of Earth were to be organized as means.* Capitalism inverts ends and means. It forces us to make economic survival the goal of our existence when this should be merely the means to self-fulfillment and the good life. Economic principles should be rationally developed as a means to human well-being rather than having human beings enslaved as to irrational economic institutions run for the benefit of the few.

Planetary social democracy would mean the triumph of civilization. It constitutes, in the words of Terry Eagleton, the fundamental "vision of humankind." It is based on our deepest ethical intuitions of *the way things should be*:

> Why, then, do some of us still cling to this political faith, in the teeth of what many would regard as reason and solid evidence? Not only, I think, because socialism is such an extraordinarily good idea that it has proved exceedingly hard to discredit, and this despite its own most strenuous

efforts. It is also because one cannot accept that this – the world we see groaning in agony around us – is the only way things could be, though empirically speaking this might certainly prove to be the case; because one gazes with wondering bemusement on those hard-headed types for whom all this, given a reformist tweak or two, is a good as it gets; because to back down from this vision would be to betray what one feels are the most precious powers and capacities of human beings; because however hard one tries, one cannot simply shake off the primitive conviction that *this is not how it is supposed to be.* (2009: 122-123)

Our deepest ethical sensibilities, our sense of our own higher human possibilities, and the heritage of nearly every civilization on Earth, cries out for this vision. The millions in every culture throughout history who have devoted their lives to the service of others and to the poor, the hundreds of thousands world-wide who have sacrificed their lives that the world might be a better place for others, and the untold hundreds of millions of victims tortured, starved, or murdered by modern capitalism and its imperial agents all cry out for this vision. What, then, is socialism?

Linguist and political thinker Noam Chomsky emphasizes the worker-oriented nature of socialist production. "One can debate the meaning of the term 'socialism,' he writes, "but if it means anything , it means control of production by the workers themselves, not owners and managers who rule them and control all decisions, whether in capitalist enterprises or an absolutist state" (1992: 97). Here again we see socialism linked with democracy and community. Neither an "absolutist state" like the former Soviet Union, nor totalitarian control of workers as in capitalist enterprises can give us either democracy or community, for Chomsky, for both of these require some form of socialism.

In his recent book on socialism, Michael Newman discusses the vast variety of socialisms that have existed historically, defying easy definition, and then goes on to write:

In my view, the most fundamental characteristic of socialism is its commitment to the creation of an egalitarian society. Socialists may not have agreed about the extent to which inequality can be eradicated or the means by which change can be effected, but no socialist would defend the current inequalities of wealth and power. In particular, socialists have maintained that, under capitalism, vast privileges and opportunities are derived from the hereditary ownership of capital and wealth at one end of the social scale, while a cycle of deprivation limits opportunities and influence at the other end. To varying extents, all socialists have therefore challenged the property relationships that are fundamental to capitalism, and have aspired to establish a society in which everyone has the possibility to seek fulfillment without facing barriers based on structural inequalities.

A second, and closely related, common feature of socialism has been a belief in the *possibility* of constructing an alternative egalitarian system based on the values of solidarity and cooperation. (2005: 2-3)

Implicit in Newman's description is the democratic commitment that people matter and that *all people matter equally*. And he explicitly recognizes that a *community* of "solidarity and cooperation" lives at the heart of the democratic socialist vision. Once again, we see that the three fundamental features of democracy – liberty, equality, and community – necessarily imply some form of socialism.

To any person who can think clearly, the globalized capitalist system that has led to the present global economic depression is deeply pathological, even insane. We have seen that corporations are constituted by law as "legal persons" who have all the rights of legal persons, yet at the same time are immortal and free of the responsibilities or moral qualities of real persons. These entities are run by boards of directors whose sole responsibility is to maximize profit for their investors regardless of the consequences for nature or other human beings. Such elitist, totalitarian organizations directed toward accumulation of profit for the few (the investors) then ravage the world in the quest for cheap natural resources and cheap labor, while colonizing governments to act in their service.

The obvious solution is to have people (the workers) democratically running corporate enterprises and businesses on behalf of their own welfare and the common good of society. Successful cooperative production is nothing new in economic history. There are many fine examples of socially cooperative arrangements producing common prosperity and well-being among populations. What is required for the conversion to economic democracy, however, is precisely an understanding of *democracy* and the ways in which democracy forms the social, political, and economic expression of our common humanity and rationality. As Boswell and Chase-Dunn express this:

Democracy encompasses political, social, and economic realms, rather than posing an artificial separation among them.... Our definition of socialism is a theory and a practice of progress toward the goals of steadily raising the living standards and ensuring the basic needs of the working class, expanding the public sphere and community life, and eliminating all forms of oppression and exploitation. Global democracy assumes a democratic and collective rationality that promotes great equality between as well as within countries, greater international cooperation and an end to war, and a more sustainable relationship with the biosphere.... Undemocratic socialism is simply not socialism regardless of the good intentions of its creators. (2000: 6)

For these social-scientists, the concept of democracy inherently implies fundamental human values that directly affect economic theory, and require the development of *planetary* cooperation and community. They recognize the moral basis of socialism with its implication that "undemocratic socialism is simply not socialism." The values implicit within the idea of democracy require global socialism understood in this way. Capitalist propaganda claiming that socialism is inherently undemocratic amounts to a massive lie.

Liberation thinker Jürgen Moltmann asserts these same principles using different categories. He uses "democracy" to refer to political democracy and "socialism" to refer to economic democracy or a system premised on "basic economic equality":

> If the political form of liberty is democracy, the economic form of equality is socialism or communitarianism. If all human beings are created free *and* equal, then the task of modern societies is to harmonize between the right to individual freedom and the right to social equality. Without equal conditions and equal opportunities for living no democracy can function. Without the development of individual freedom no system of social justice can function. The universalism of these declarations can be put into practice only in a worldwide community of states which make these human rights the fundamental rights of their citizens. (1996: 190-191)

Whether we call the result of a world order premised on respect for human beings "global democracy" or a "worldwide community of states," these thinkers perceive that democracy must be raised to the planetary level and that it must be premised on both economic equality and political freedom. Socialism embodies most fundamentally, therefore, *a moral theory* that develops a rational and coherent economics in relationship to its moral premises. It recognizes that economic principles and practices are *created by human beings* – that these are not "iron economic laws" akin to the laws of planetary motion or the equations for falling bodies. Since economic systems are socially constructed, they can and must be premised on rational moral principles.

Many independent thinkers in the history of economic theory have insisted that the economic organization of society must be inseparable from *a reflection on values, on the ends and meaning of human life.* Gerald Alonzo Smith reviews some of this history that includes such thinkers as Simeon Sismondi, John Ruskin, John Hobeson, R.H Tawney, Friedrich Soddy, and Thorstein Veblen (Daly & Townsend 1994: Ch. 10). More recent thinkers who have stressed the inseparability of economic institutions from the question of values intrinsic to being human are Lewis Mumford (1974), Mortimer J. Adler (1991), Erich Fromm (1996),

Herman E. Daly (1996), Michel Chossudovsky (1999), David C. Korten (2003), Stuart Chase (2005), Ellen H. Brown (2007), J. W. Smith (2008) and Richard C. Cook (2009). One of the greatest thinkers within this tradition was, of course, Karl Marx.

Reflection on this history and the thought of these scholars can lead to a deeper meaning of "socialism" that does not link the concept with any particular institutional arrangement but rather with the entire question of ends and means. Socialism, is not, as capitalist propaganda would have it, domination of some dictatorship of the proletariat, nor government ownership of all means of production. Nor does socialism mean government interference in the private lives, personal rights, or freedoms of individuals. Just the opposite. *Socialism, in its most basic sense, names any system in which economics (and politics) is predicated on people as ends in themselves and their cooperative economic and political action within social communities. It means institutions created to serve human beings and the integrity of the natural world. Socialism is, therefore, identical with genuine democracy.*

For this reason, a wide variety of institutional arrangements could serve under the heading of socialism. What in practice is best for human beings and nature might still need to be worked out in detail, since never in history has any such practice been implemented on a planetary scale, and the imperial capitalist nations of the world have worked to destroy it whenever people have attempted to establish socialism on a national scale (Boswell and Chase-Dunn 2000: 2). However, the broad parameters of all such possible arrangements are clear: government, banking, and production must serve the welfare of the vast majority of persons and the natural world, not the interests of the few at the expense of the many. Government, banking, and production must be legally organized to maximize democratic participation by the people themselves.

As sociologist Robert Blain declares, the essence of socialism is "good-will" for the "well being of all members of society."

> The socialist/communist cultures are inclusive, good-will motivated. People in the United States are culturally disposed to think of socialism and communism as *bad*. However, socialism emerged in Europe in the 1800s in opposition to the severe misery caused by industrial capitalism (World Book, Vol 18, pages 560-562). The name *socialism* implies concern for the well being of all members of society, whereas *capitalism* implies primary concern for personal accumulation of money. (2004: 115)

In *The Fate of Man in the Modern World*, Christian philosopher Nicholas Berdyaev links Christianity, which understands that human beings are ends in themselves, with the imperative for socialism:

Christianity is above all else a religion of life and liberty, but just because of this, the future is not determined by blind fate, either for good or for evil. Hence we move forward toward a tragic conflict. The new Christianity must rehumanize man and society, culture and the world....

The problem of man takes precedence over that of society or of culture, and here man is to be considered, not in his inner spiritual life, not as an abstract spiritual being, but as an integral being, as a being social and cosmic, as well. A new day is dawning for Christianity in the world. Only a form of Socialism, which unites personality and the communal principle, can satisfy Christianity. (1961: 130-131)

Socialism unites "personality and the communal principle," just as Herman E. Daly, in the quotation at the head of this chapter, says that each of us is an "individual within a community." The value of each person as an end in him or herself must be united with the cooperative working together to eliminate what Berdyaev calls the "bitter human need and the economic slavery of man" (ibid.) and create a world of peace, freedom, nonviolence, and prosperity for all persons. "Free" capitalist markets alone cannot bring these values into being. As Daly puts it: "Ecological criteria of sustainability, like ethical criteria of justice, are not served by markets" (1996: 32).

Berdyaev here correctly understands the meaning of socialism as the institutionalized political and economic form of love (cf. Martin 2005a: Ch. 7). Human spirituality (e.g., the *agape* of Christianity) understands that capitalism is inhuman (the denial of love that recognizes the intrinsic value of persons) and that the world must be "rehumanized," by reuniting the community and the value of the human personality. Socialism is the proper word for such a system, and that is why the capitalist propaganda system has attempted to demonize the term. If we had to imagine what institutions would most closely embody *agape,* it would be those that unite the value of personality with a communal principle.

In *The German Ideology,* Karl Marx puts the matter as follows: "Only in community [with others has each] individual the means of cultivating his gifts in all directions; only in community, therefore, is personal freedom possible.... In the real community the individuals obtain their freedom in and through their association" (1978: 197). Socialism puts economics in the service of human freedom and self-development. It understands that economics must build community (rather than disintegrate it through brutal competition), for from genuine communities flow democracy, human freedom, and reasonable prosperity for all.

We have seen Enrique Dussel link Christian religious insight with the idea of authentic community. In the same passage, he links community with Christian love (*agape*):

> In *community*, all individuals are persons for one another. Their relationships are "practical," and this praxis is that of the love that is charity: each serves the other for that other, in the friendship of all persons in all things. Everything is "common," then. What would an association of free persons be? It would be a community in which *individuality* is expressed in full and uncoerced communication. The community is the real, concrete agent and mover of history. In community we are "at home," in safety and security, "in common." (1988: 11)

Dussel is commenting here on the Gospel teachings of Jesus concerning *agape* and on St. Paul's statements that the early Christian communities held things "in common," for example, in Acts 2: 44-45 where Paul says "All the believers together had everything in common; they sold their possessions and their goods, and distributed among all in accordance with each one's need." It may well be that Marx had this passage in mind when he proclaimed the "banner" of communist society to be "from each according to his ability, to each according to his needs!" (1978, p. 531). Authentic socialism clearly represents be the political-economic embodiment of love.

Such statements by St. Paul are often taken to be a record of "early Christian socialism" (Cort 1988). However, Dussel places a deeper meaning on the phrase "in common." It reflects the intrinsic value of the individual human person within a community that recognizes this value. Socialism is founded on the reality of persons within community. It may have a variety of institutional arrangements as long as these embody this relation of the person within community. "Community" means an orientation toward the common good and equality of all within the whole while at the same time respecting the dignity of each. It means the recognition of moral obligations of each to the rest of the community. We have seen that the very possibility of genuine democracy requires the supporting matrix of a community of rights, freedoms, and shared understandings.

In contrast to the value of the individual within community, which is the relationship of *agape*, there is "idolatry," the sin condemned by Jesus for its lack of love and community. Dussel describes this as follows:

> The act by which one asserts oneself as the end of other persons – as factory owners they have a right to the factory's profit even though that profit be their worker's hunger transformed into money – is idolatry.... This is not a reality solely of the past. For example, as we shall see below, when the proprietors of capital forget that all the value of their capital is the labor of others objectified.... (Ibid. p. 19)

Our second theme, "Evil and Death"...leads us to consider the *principle of sin* that constitutes the perverse, negative point of departure of Christian ethics. That principle is an impediment to the constitution of community: it is the assertion of individuality *against* community. In authentic community, genuine individuality is fully actualized. In anticommunity, individuality is fetishized and ultimately destroys itself, by way of the death of the poor. (Ibid. p. 26)

We discern here the relationship between economics and the spirituality of *agape*. Socialism is the appropriate ethical and spiritual basis of economic institutions because it is concerned with the value of individuals as persons within communities. This concern, which *necessarily* involves the social relationships among persons, appropriately results in the conception of an authentic "community."

Capitalism destroys this ethical relationship. It affirms the individuality of the me-first attitude, the attitude of greed that *uses* other people and implicitly denies their intrinsic value. The capitalist, no matter how removed in time and space from the consequences of his or her "investments," is responsible for the death of the poor, just as the militarist, who protects the "stable investment climate" of the capitalist, is a murderer in the service of greed and domination.

In Chapter Three we examined a quotation from *The Meaning of Socialism* by philosopher Michael Luntley that bears recalling in this new context with some further commentary. "Socialism," Luntley wrote, "is a theory about how the good life is possible" because it focuses on the conditions necessary for "creating a society in which our lives are shaped by moral values." Capitalism, on the other hand, creates a society informed by forces that are destructive of the moral life (1990: 15). The amoral structure of capitalism results in the commodification of all existence, replacing our sense of community and our moral intuitions with a sense of insecurity and scarcity within a dog eat dog environment that pits human beings against one another.

Here again we find a recognition of the deeper meaning of socialism, which provides the institutions that make possible lives that are shaped by moral values. For under authentic socialism our politics, places of employment, and professions do not force us to exploit other persons and nature in ways that are inimical to the moral life. Because a socialist community embodies and encourages moral relationships, it makes possible the actualization of individual moral relationships among the people as a community. Because democratic socialism places moral values (such as the development of individual human potential within a framework of the common good of the community) into the economic equation, it empowers the development of moral values, rather than negating them.

Capitalism creates a society in which "our moral traditions have been erased by forces inimical to the moral life." That is why the lords of the

Earth are nihilists, why they care nothing for nature or human life. That is why *everything* is commodified, everything is for sale: trafficking in women and children, human bodily organs, sex slavery, dangerous drugs, rare animals, scarce resources, the genetic codes of living creatures, weapons, military contractors, ever-more wars and inevitable terrorist responses, torture, killer hit men, economic hit men (Perkins 2007) – nothing, under the amoral economics of capitalism, is not for sale. This is why millions in the first world live in utter hypocrisy, claiming to be Christians or Jews or Moslems while participating in institutions predicated on the exploitation of nature and other human beings.

That is why the contemporary world can live with the insanity and criminality of nuclear weapons (Boyle 2002) without rising up in outrage at their very existence and demanding their abolition. A great many today are nihilists, no longer recognizing any values that are not market values. Full recognition of human beings as ends in themselves within community – and moral living based upon this foundation – can only take place within the framework of socialist institutions. The institutionalization of greed, selfishness, and lack of concern for others under capitalism's false flag of "freedom" cannot stand.

This false flag routinely trumps and destroys all normal democratic rights and freedoms, as Chomsky points out. President Franklin Roosevelt famously declared that the U.S. and its allies would stand against the fascists on behalf of freedom of speech and worship and freedom from want and fear. In opposition to these four freedoms, Chomsky states that the only real loyalty of the ruling class and the U.S. government that it controls is:

> "The Fifth Freedom," understood crudely but with a fair degree of accuracy as the freedom to rob, to exploit and to dominate, to undertake any course of action to ensure that existing privilege is protected and advanced.... Dedication to the Fifth Freedom is hardly a new form of social pathology. Nor, of course, was it an invention of the "while hordes" who, "fortified in an aggressive spirit by an arrogant messianic Christianity" and "motivated by the lure of enriching plunder,....sallied forth from their western European homelands to explore, assault, loot, occupy, rule and exploit the rest of the world" during the nearly six centuries when "western Europe and its diaspora have been disturbing the peace of the world" –as the advance of European civilization is perceived, not without reason, by a perceptive African commentator. But this vocation of the powerful constantly assumes new forms – and new disguises, as the supportive culture passes through varying stages of moral cowardice and intellectual corruption. (1988: 1-3)

A constant barrage of propaganda from the capitalist ruling class through its coalition in the National Association of Manufacturers (NAM) and other sources falsely links the concept of freedom with capitalism, making, we have seen, genuine democracy effectively impossible (Caldicott 1992: Ch. 8). This propaganda transmutes into the dominant educational system through the moral cowardice and intellectual corruption of academic mandarins who earn their living by lending scholarly credibility to the system of domination and exploitation. If we begin to think deeply and seriously about the concept of freedom, we soon realize that freedom ultimately requires a universal community embodying to a significant degree the eight features of democracy summarized above, including freedom from want and reasonable economic equality.

Can we devise a system premised on human dignity in which hard work, creativity, or significant contributions to society are recognized and rewarded? Certainly. Can we devise a system premised on human dignity in which personal freedom is maximized insofar as this is compatible with the freedom of all others? Certainly. Can we devise a society in which those who have worked hard and obtained somewhat greater wealth than others do not colonize the political system in the service of their own interests? Certainly. Can we devise a society in which nation-states do not militarize themselves and act in conflict with other nation-states in a Machiavellian world of war and deceit often directed toward controlling the wealth-producing processes of the world? Certainly.

In is not difficult to imagine conditions under which all of these questions can be affirmatively answered. No lack of intellectual resources exist in either the history of economic thought or the history of democratic thought (cf. Harris 2008). We know very well what a decent economic and political system for the world would look like, in spite of the fact – or perhaps because of the fact – that such a system has remained largely a counterfactual ideal up to now. In the utter failure of everything that has been tried to date is revealed the one thing that has never been tried: economic and political systems predicated on the dignity, freedom, and equality of every person on Earth, in a word: planetary democracy.

Capitalism disintegrates community; socialism is predicated on it. The ideal of a "classless society" does not mean that everyone is economically or culturally the same. It means that human fraternity, community, has been substantially realized in society. Mortimer J. Adler writes:

> By democracy I mean the democratic constitution of a republic in which there is no division of the population into a ruling and subject class;

and...by socialism, I mean the economic counterpart of political democracy, achieved by the participation of all in the general economic welfare so that there is no division of the population into haves and have-nots. The socialist, democratic republic is only a first approximation of the new ideal of a classless society. A fuller realization of that ideal calls for the elimination of the other class divisions based on racial, ethnic, or other discriminations that create factional conflicts and result in injustice to one or another segment of society. (1991: 89-90)

Socialism, in the sense of fundamental economic equality and sufficiency for all, functions as the necessary complement of political democracy. One cannot effectively exist without the other. This will become the basis of eliminating other class divisions that divide and fragment human life. Adler continues:

The unity of peace which is the common good of all mankind cannot begin until the specious society of nations is transformed into a worldwide society of men. Until all men are citizens of the world, none will enjoy fully the citizenship granted by local and isolated democracies. Without unlimited fraternity, liberty and equality cannot reach their proper limits. (Ibid. p. 118)

Ultimately, democracy requires world citizenship, for within such a framework alone, that is, the framework of a world community or "unlimited fraternity," can liberty and equality also find their natural fulfillment. Democratic socialism is necessarily some form of market socialism, Adler points out, since a governmental controlled by a tiny managerial class cannot be democratic. When there is a proper community framework for free economic enterprise, then the market has an important role to play, especially to empower creativity, ingenuity, personal responsibility, local communities, and local producers.

It is not difficult to imagine the specific economic and political features of a moral community called social democracy. For example, if democracy means a commonwealth operating in the interests of the common good, then the central "natural monopolies" that make possible the common good must be largely in the democratic hands of the people. These include water-supply, major utilities, major transportation systems, major communications systems, health care systems, insurance systems, and the banking system (Smith 2008).

Since we have seen above that control of the money system in the interest of the common good is fundamental to democracy, there is no compelling reason for private banking at all. All banks should be public utilities, democratically controlled banks with appropriate citizen oversight. This basic idea of democracy – in which the people control their monetary system – is not new. Within the U.S., it was called by nineteenth-century Senator Henry Clay a system of "cooperative abundance" versus what he termed the British system of "competitive greed" (E. Brown 2007: 51 & 57). Ellen Brown points out many other historical initiatives and examples of democratically controlled banking (ibid).

This is the fundamental principle of socialism: not doing away with markets *but doing away with monopoly privileges that permit the few to monopolize markets and appropriate the wealth of others by the exploitation of people through monoply forces.* The key here is a socially owned banking system that equitably provides finance capital for whom ever has a sustainable creative, productive idea within the context of a legal framework empowering cooperative enterprises to implement these productive ideas. And in the wake of capitalism's current collapse, a socially owned banking system would eliminate the world of financial speculation and the casino aspect of economics that currently produces nothing but excessive wealth for unproductive people and companies along with ever-increasing risk of collapse.

A socially owned banking system would create *debt-free money* for infrastructure and development and supply capital at very low interest to individuals, nations, or groups with practical productive ideas. Economist J.W. Smith puts this as follows:

> Do away with the casino aspect of both money and stock markets and local needs can be easily financed. It would be a simple matter to calculate finance capital needs and assign a surcharge to all loans to go into a *socially-owned* capital accumulation fund kept in, and loaned from, local banks. Larger banks will have a department for financing large industries. Worker-owned businesses and cooperatives financed by those larger banks would be the economic ideal of labor employing capital. Everything is then local as opposed to an ethereal world of high finance. Capital needs of each federation region of the world, each nation, each state, each country, each region of a country, and each community can be calculated. So long as there are surplus labor and resources and real value is to be produced, finance capital can be obtained through printing money. Once established, that investment fund would replenish itself through loan repayments and interest rates high enough to cover loan losses. (2008: 39)

Cooperative abundance is exactly what democratic market socialism implies. As John Dewey insisted, the democratic ideal cannot be realized under monopoly capitalism, which always places an oligarchy of the rich into effective power (1993: 148-152). Unfettered capitalism obviates genuine democratic discussion (through control of the means of communication), social cooperation (through non-democratic workplaces), and abundance (through production directed at private profit for the few rather than satisfying basic human needs).

A socialized money supply means that government can create money for infrastructure or other essential projects without having to go into debt (or take its people into ever-greater national or mundial debt). It means that government can offer lines of credit at little or no interest for productive, socially beneficial projects and enterprises. It means prosperity for the majority rather than immense riches for the few.

In the globalized twenty-first century, however, effective democratic socialism must necessarily take the form of *planetary* democratic socialism under a worldwide civil Earth Federation. As the tragic example of South Africa illustrates, no single nation can break free within the worldwide economic system of globalized monopoly capitalism. Either democratic socialism becomes normative worldwide, or it will be destroyed by the global capitalist framework wherever it is attempted within individual nations, and intentionally so, as the many examples above clearly show.

The rule of democratically legislated laws predicated on equality, liberty, and community comprises the most fundamental principle of democracy. Nation-states demand that their citizens respect the rule of law. However, they refuse themselves to submit to the rule of law in their foreign policy, claiming to be "sovereign" and recognizing no superior authority beyond themselves while simultaneously promoting the interests of their ruling classes worldwide (cf. Martin 2008: Ch. 10; Boyle 2008). Within this international anarchy, the lawless vacuum created allows global monopoly capitalism to continue its criminal domination and exploitation of the Earth and its peoples.

The competitive system of lawless "sovereign nation-states" cannot possibly bring political equality, freedom, and dignity to every person on Earth, nor can it create a globalized economic system that ensures reasonable economic equality, freedom, and dignity for the majority. Planetary democracy must be founded first and foremost on the principle of *all*, *all human beings* have these rights and this dignity. This "all" is precisely what the fragmented competitive economics of capitalism and the fragmented, conflictive system of nation-states cannot bring to the people of Earth.

Either all are free, equal, with their dignity recognized and protected, or none are. If I have "democracy" in my little piece of the Earth, and people elsewhere are dominated and exploited, and I have *any* economic or political relationship with them that benefits me (e.g. I buy inexpensive goods made in China or pay taxes to build weapons that may be used against them), then I am complicit in their domination. I am part of an oligarchy exploiting them and cannot be said to live in a democracy.

Nor can the system of sovereign nation-states in conjunction with global monopoly capitalism deal with the collapsing planetary environment, worldwide depletion of essential resources, the scourge of nuclear weapons, ever increasing global poverty and disease, continuing climate collapse, or the coming militarization of space. The nexus of "global problems" that threaten human existence on this planet are by definition and experience beyond the scope of even the most powerful nation-states to solve. The only reasonable solution to these global crises that transcend the boundaries of all nations is a democratic world order with effective planetary planning and enforceable global law predicated on the freedom and common good of all people on Earth and the natural environment that sustains them.

7.4 Democracy Requires a Founded Earth Community under the *Earth Constitution*

Both monopoly capitalism and the sovereign nation-state system inhibit the universal principles that live at the foundations of democracy: communicative reason, basic moral principles, and human spiritualities such as kindness, compassion, or *agape*. Both foster the principle of privilege and lawlessness for the powerful. The rich, under capitalist societies, literally get away with murder. The death of their workers from poverty and disease, as Dussel points out, is on their hands. Similarly, powerful nations within the system of nation-states literally get away with mass murder in their efforts to maintain this system.

By contrast, the concepts of both democracy and socialism establish society on the genuine moral principles of human liberty, equality, and community. The principles (like all genuine moral principles) are inherently universal and cannot be effectively realized on a local level without a supporting universal framework. As Boswell and Chase-Dunn exclaim:

> Our starting point is one of *global democracy*. Global democracy has a dual meaning – democracy at the global level, with democratic institutions governing the ever more integrated world economy, and local democracy, with economic management and social administration as well as politics and the state open to democratic participation. Democracy includes civil and individual human rights, without which democratic institutions are meaningless. (2000: 5)

The only way the world can create a morally and practically successful social and political system is through the ascent to democratically legislated, non-military world law, that is, to global democracy. The only viable option by which the poor majority of the world can end the system of exploitation and have their dignity as human beings recognized is through the ascent to democratic world law. The only effective possibility for dealing with the global crises that are beyond the scope of nation-states is through the ascent to a democratic world law with the authority and resources to address these crises. This too involves a moral imperative. By not creating effective world law that can deal with these crises we are immorally cutting off the life prospects for our children and future generations.

The *Constitution for the Federation of Earth* provides the framework that makes possible a morally founded and practically successful world order. If the reader questions whether global social democracy could be practically successful, he or she is referred to Chapters Four to Six above. *The present world order is a complete disaster.* There is nothing whatsoever "practically successful" about global capitalism and the nation-state system. They have created together the immense violence and suffering of our planetary order as well as these global crises that threaten the very existence of life on our planet. Self-destruction, disintegration of the biosphere, and planetary suicide are not in the least "realistic" or "practical." The present world disorder represents total failure. Its failure is primarily due to deep misunderstanding of freedom, a corresponding deep social pathology, and a consequent lack of democracy on the Earth.

The Preamble to the *Earth Constitution* establishes the federation on the principle of the individual within community. The phrase used by the *Constitution* is *"unity in diversity,"* a concept we have seen in chapters above as fundamental not only to human spirituality and authentic religion but to planetary democracy itself. The Preamble states:

> Conscious that Humanity is One despite the existence of diverse nations, races, creeds, ideologies and cultures and that the principle of *unity in diversity* is the basis for a new age when war shall be outlawed and peace prevail; when the earth's total resources shall be equitably used for human welfare; and when basic human rights and responsibilities shall be shared by all without discrimination.

This paragraph (like the entire *Constitution* that follows it) founds the Earth Federation as *a universal human community.* The diversity of all is respected and protected precisely because the Earth Federation is a genuine community in which "basic human rights and responsibilities are shared by all without discrimination." The fact that the basic philosophical premise of the *Constitution* is that "Humanity is One" indicates that the authors understood the absolute need to establish humanity *as a community* if we are to survive much longer upon this Earth. Earlier in the Preamble the authors speak of humanity as having reached the "brink of disaster," of "the ever-increasing disparity between rich and poor," and of the moral obligation to "save Humanity from immanent and total annihilation" (see Appendix B).

The *Earth Constitution* converts the system of fragmented individualism and greed (the origin of governmental domination according to Rousseau) to a *global social contract* (for Rousseau, the beginning of community in which individuals are no longer fragments but are lifted up into a regime of equal rights and duties). A global social contract means all are included in the regime of collective empowerment. A planetary community is established on fundamental moral and practical principles thereby transforming (for many at the very least) self-interested individuals into responsible citizens.

Can there be *founded communities* just as there are natural, culturally defined communities? Absolutely. History is full of examples of founded societies, the founding of which generates the sense of being a cohesive community in their citizens. The United States is an example of one such founded society. The *Earth Constitution*, however, establishes the *community of Earth*. Are there enough commonalities among the peoples of Earth (as there were among the colonies of North America) to cement together the Earth as a founded community? Indeed.

The host of common threats that we face as global crises can alone serve as enough of an "enemy" to cement us together: war, militarism, WMDs, environmental collapse, pollution, resource depletion, poverty, terrorism, etc. Second, there is the universal communicative basis (and translatability) of all languages, within which, we have seen, the principles of universal democracy are inherent. We are already bound together on this Earth in a planetary community of discussion, debate, and dialogue. Third, we have a discovered a universal methodology for acquiring knowledge and understanding through the social and natural sciences. This has resulted in an immense heritage of works of science that have become the cultural legacy of every human being. Fourth, there is our universal human capacity for growth to higher levels of maturity.

Fifth, there are the dozens of "human universals" allowing us to recognize our common humanity everywhere on Earth (D. Brown 1991). These human universals can easily become deeper and more compelling than cultural differences as people realize ever-more clearly their world citizenship. Sixth, there also exists a large and growing *planetary cultural heritage* in documents like the *UN Universal Declaration of Human Rights*, the *Millennium Declaration*, *Agenda 21*, the *Earth Charter*, and the *Constitution for the Federation of Earth*.

Seventh, and perhaps most fundamentally, there is our universal human dignity and inviolability that is the foundation for universal moral principles. In *Ascent to Freedom*, I discussed at length a number of the great thinkers who have articulated this dignity and inviolability in a variety of ways right down to contemporary thinkers such as Habermas, Dewey, Dussel, and Gewirth. Perhaps the deepest and most compelling philosophical expression of this dignity and inviolability in our day can be found in the works of Emmanuel Levinas such as *Totality and Infinity, Ethics and Infinity,* and *Humanism of the Other*.

There is no time, nor is it particularly desirable, to try to naturally *evolve* an Earth community. Documents like the *Earth Charter, Agenda 21,* or the *Millennium Declaration*, while inspiring, are wholly inadequate to our present need. Human beings are self-aware creatures capable of operating according to *universal principles.* The *Constitution founds* the community of Earth upon just such universal principles, the most fundamental of which is the principle of *unity in diversity*. A founded community means real government, not just inspiring ideals.

It is not an accident that the Preamble states that this new community shall create a condition in which "the earth's total resources shall be equitably used for human welfare." The equitable use of resources is a necessary feature of social democracy. The absolute right of private property that can be used as a means to exploit and dominate others for the further private accumulation of that property with its attendant concentrations of power is destructive of not only of community, but democracy and the well-being of humanity. For the first time in history, the premise of *a universal social contract* establishes *the common good of all* as its fundamental regulative idea.

Our present world situation exhibits the very antithesis of the principle of equitable use of resources for the well-being of all. In creating a social contract for humanity, by founding "a new age" in which the legal relationships of all persons shall be determined by democratically legislated law, the framers were not taking away the right of private property from persons. They were creating *the moral foundation for genuine community* that could then democratically decide the best legal framework by which property relations could serve both the dignity of private persons (as distinct from corporations) and the reasonable welfare of all.

In fact, the *Constitution for the Federation of the Earth* explicitly provides for free enterprise and the right of private property (Articles 12.1 and 12.16). However, it prevents these rights from being used to exploit human beings and nature at the expense of the world community and its common good. We have seen that democratic socialism does not at all mean the abolition of these legal rights. Rather, it most fundamentally means that these legal rights must be exercised within the framework of the common good, individual legal personhood, and reciprocal moral duties. It is precisely these features that are denied by monopoly capitalism and the system of sovereign nations. These systems privilege the rich on the one hand and the militarily stronger on the other. Both systems are inherently totalitarian. They create structural situations in which the few have undemocratic power over the many. Such oligarchic systems constitute the major source of violence in human affairs.

The *Earth Constitution* creates a government *powerful enough to establish peace upon the Earth* and to effectively deal with global environmental crises and global poverty. However, its power derives from being the expression of the *community of Earth*, not from military domination. The power of democratic government resides in the common recognition of its legitimacy by the vast majority.

Such a government will necessarily significantly pacify today's militarized world. The non-military police under the *Constitution* will, of course, have the capability of using force to protect human beings and enforce the law worldwide. However, as we will see in Chapter Eight, the civilian based police force can and should operate in ways that are dynamically different from all forms of military violence.

Force, in this sense, is not the same as violence, as philosophers John Glenn Gray (1970) and Hannah Arendt (1970) have pointed out at length. Force can be used legitimately by a government rightly powerful as the representative of the sovereign people of Earth. The use of violence, on the other hand, necessarily *delegitimizes* a government and makes it less powerful. Arendt writes:

> Power needs no justification, being inherent in the very existence of political communities; what it does need is legitimacy.... Violence can be justifiable, but it never will be legitimate.... We saw that the current equation of violence with power rests on government's being understood as domination of man over man by means of violence.... To substitute violence for power can bring victory, but the price is very high: for it is not only paid by the vanquished, it is also paid by the victor in terms of his own power.... Power and violence are opposites; where the one rules absolutely, the other is absent. Violence appears where power is in jeopardy, but left to its own course it ends in power's disappearance. This implies that it is not correct to think of the opposite of violence as nonviolence; to speak of non-violent power is actually redundant. Violence can destroy power; it is utterly incapable of creating it. (pp. 52-55)

This expresses precisely why an Earth Federation under the *Constitution* will establish *a nonviolent democratic community* for the Earth. Its design, as well as its founding principles, direct the authority of government to the well-being of the people of Earth and the preservation of our planetary environment. The *Constitution* explicitly demilitarizes the Earth and establishes conflict resolution programs as well as organizations for the protection of human rights (such as the World Ombudsmus). It will necessarily maximize nonviolence in human affairs precisely because it establishes a government with real power and authority founded on the principle of a universal human community structured according to *unity in diversity.* Chapter Nine will examine this structure in greater detail.

Practically speaking, how can a world community and a new social contract for humanity come into being? The only way to implement democratic world law under the *Earth Constitution* is for the people of the world to decide that they no longer want to live under these totalitarian systems of domination, exploitation, and misery. The vast majority of the people of the world (the 90% or so who have nothing to lose and everything to gain from the ascent to democratic world law) must ratify the *Earth Constitution* according to the criteria set forth in Article 17. Article 17 gives practical and very possible steps by which the world can move from totalitarianism and self-destruction to democracy. It can begin with a portion of humanity (under Article 17) and quickly spread to the rest. If the majority want it to happen, it can happen tomorrow.

Only under the *Constitution for the Federation of Earth,* in which each nation receives its rightful place as an equal member of the Earth Federation under the rule of enforceable non-military democratic world law, can there ever be both peace and prosperity on the Earth (cf. Martin 2005b). This arrangement takes away the power of imperialism from the nations, disarms them, and makes them cooperating units within a whole, very much like the coexistence of the states within the United States today. The diversity of nations is precious and important to preserve as long as it is embraced within a unity that overcomes the brutal fragmentation of today's near-absolute sovereignty.

This arrangement allows productive free enterprise while taking away the power of exploitation and domination from the wealthy and the corporations. It also makes them cooperating units within a democratic whole, requiring environmental sustainability and attention to the common good. Free enterprise is a wonderful thing if it contributes not only to creativity and personal success but to the common good of society and the preservation of nature. Truly free enterprise, we shall see, requires the creation of a global commons of banking, technology, communications, and resources, no longer controlled by the tiny elite who now dominate global economics. Today's so-called "free enterprise," without integration within a democratic community representing the common good, becomes an immoral nightmare of human and environmental desecration.

It is the act of uniting as a democratic whole, as a community of Earth, that effects these transformations. The foreign policy of nations becomes no longer one of naked self-interest but is integrated within the framework of the common good of the Earth and humankind. The economic activities of transnational corporations no longer operate from a self-interest that denies the intrinsic goods of nature and other people but becomes by law an effective promoter of the common good and prosperity of all people and future generations. Planetary democracy means real democracy for the first time on Earth, for the necessary conditions behind real democracy are for the first time satisfied: *all persons – equality, freedom, and community for all persons.*

Ultimately, the only fully appropriate economic and political community is the human community. Anything of lesser scope remains within the fragmentation of mere parts that are inherently a war system and a system of power relationships with those beyond incommensurable borders, rather than a system of moral relationships under an enforceable social contract. This answers the profound concern raised by Karl Jaspers: "It is a question of the manner in which the unity of mankind becomes a concrete reality for us" (1953: 21). This unity only becomes concrete within a genuine social contract. *The triumph of civilization finds its fullest expression in the founding of a universal human community.*

The rule of enforceable democratic law in the world then makes possible the *restoration of democracy within each nation-state* for a number of reasons. (1) It ends the chaos of militarism in all nations, which destroys democracy internally as well as externally. (2) World law effectively deals with global crises beyond the capacity of *nation-states* such as climate-collapse, exhaustion of natural resources, world population expansion, and militarism – and hence restores to each nation the ability to protect the common welfare of its citizens. (3) World law under the *Earth Constitution* nationalizes (mundializes) the key resources, transportation, banking, and communications systems of the world to the point where private wealth can no longer interfere with the democratic processes of humankind. For this reason, again, democracy is restored within individual nation-states because the rich will no longer be able to control the law-making process in their own interests.

Finally, and perhaps most fundamentally, the *Earth Constitution* (4) mundializes the global monetary system and converts it to a debt-free system of money creation and government-issued credit. Government is taken out of a system of indebtedness to private banking cartels and placed, for the first time in history, in a position to transform these cartels in the service of the common good. The money system is fundamental to all human transactions and to the common welfare of people everywhere. Unless it is democratically controlled, it will necessarily be used for private interests and totalitarian control in the service of private interests. It is a "natural monopoly" of the people and, if used as a public utility (administered at the local level) for the common good of the people, can transform the present horrific world of unsustainable and painful debt into a world of prosperity for the vast majority.

Similarly, transnational corporations, like the transnational financial institutions, today operate beyond the control of any nation-state, even the United States. They amass their hedge-funds and other assets in the Cayman Islands or other off-shore havens, avoiding not only taxes but national legislation that might control their activities in the interest of the common good. Like the nation-states that refuse to recognize any law above themselves, the transnational corporations and global financial institutions write their own rules of world trade and financial interactions. A clandestine global totalitarian order arises beyond the ability of even sovereign nations to control. Only a morally-founded Earth community under enforceable world law can redeem the nightmare of today's world and establish a decent future for humanity.

The *Constitution for the Federation of Earth* was developed and ratified by thousands of world citizens in four international Constituent Assemblies held between 1968 and 1991 (see Appendix A). The collective wisdom of these world citizens has given us one of the most important and legitimate public documents that we possess today on this planet. The eloquent Preamble to the *Constitution* reminds one of Thomas Jefferson's visionary writings and of his statement that constitutions are not to be written in stone for all time but are to be enlarged and transcended to suit the times. Today, we must enlarge our conception of what is necessary for the democratic rule of law to the planetary level. Anything less remains preliminary and inadequate. A founded Earth community remains our only real and reasonable option.

7.5 Monetary Reform: Its Basic Agreement and Fatal Flaw

The global economic meltdown continuing into 2009 and beyond has led to a chorus of voices from economists and monetary theorists who believe that human welfare and the welfare of our planet should be the central premise of economics. We have seen that such a focus has been the central theme of democratic market socialism from its inception. Whether these thinkers use the forbidden "S-word," or speak in terms of some form of "cooperative capitalism," or of economics premised on the "public good" is irrelevant to their consensus. There are two central alternatives: either have money and the economy controlled by huge private financial monopolies structured around the accumulation of ever-greater private wealth for themselves (the present world-system) or place money, much production, and the economy democratically in the hands of the people through a socialized banking system.

Economist Michael Hudson describes the latter alternative in contradistinction to the bailout proposal currently being proffered by the Obama administration:

> The alternative is a century and a half old, and emerged out of the ideals of the classical economic doctrines of Adam Smith, David Ricardo, John Stuart Mill, and the last great classical economist, Marx. Their common denominator was to view rent and interest as extractive, not productive. Classical political economy and its successor Progressive Era socialism sought to nationalize the land (or at least to fully tax its rent as the fiscal base). Governments were to create their own credit, not leave this function to wealthy elites via a bank monopoly on credit creation. So today's neoliberalism paints a false picture of what the classical economists envisioned as free markets. They were markets free of economic rent and interest (and taxes to support an aristocracy or oligarchy). Socialism was to free economies from these overhead charges. Today's Obama-Geithner rescue plan is just the reverse.... The Treasury is paying off the gamblers and billionaires by supporting the value of bank loans, investments and derivative gambles, leaving the Treasury in debt. (2009)

The issue is not the abolition of all private property. This idea functions as a red herring promoted by dominant elites to terrorize populations into not examining the present system carefully and honestly. The real issue involves the question as to whether *the economic infrastructure that provides the means for all business and trade* will be democratically owned by the people as a public utility to be used in the service of universal prosperity or whether it will be privately owned to be used in the service of private accumulation of wealth for the rich. The central issues are banking, money creation, and the structure of property laws in general.

This is as much an infrastructure question as are roads and streets. Government normally builds and maintains roads, streets, electrical systems, sewage systems, and other vital infrastructure because these *make possible the free exchange of goods and services* that constitute a healthy economy. You cannot have all streets and roads the private property of individuals or corporations to be used for private interests without throwing the society into chaos. But this is precisely what the dominant monopoly capitalist ethos advocates: the monetary system must be privately owned by giant financial interests and government must raise money through taxes on the people and debt enslavement of the public to these private interests.

Monetary theorist Stephen Zarlenga describes this alternative common sense basis for any genuine democracy:

> Lack of money to pay for crucial programs is again not a fiscal but a monetary problem caused ultimately by the false idea that government must get money only by taxation or borrowing....
>
> Behind these problems is the fact that the nation is controlled more from behind the scenes by financial institutions than by citizens through elections. *When society loses control over its money system it loses whatever control it might have had over its own destiny.* It can no longer set priorities and the policies for achieving them. It can't solve problems, which then develop into crises and continually mount up....
>
> This book has shown that it is historically self-evident that the best monetary systems have been controlled and monitored through law, by public authority. Leaving money power in private hands has invited, even assured, disastrous results. This is also consistent with the logic of money: since the money system is a creature of law, it rightfully belongs within government, just as the law courts do. (2002: 655-657)

The overwhelming agreement among economists and monetary theorists who are not indentured as propagandists for the monopoly capitalist system focuses on a socially-owned banking system. As Zarlenga points out, democracy is effectively gutted when private interests control its financial infrastructure for society loses control over its own destiny. As monetary theorist Ellen Hodgson Brown (2008) shows in detail, financial elites who control the money system use their control not to fund the productive economy but to maximize their wealth through the financial manipulation of markets and casino investments directed toward speculative windfalls. As Hudson says above, both classical economics and its successor progressive era socialism understood that "governments were to create their own credit, not leave this function to wealthy elites via a bank monopoly on credit creation."

Monetary theorist Richard C. Cook (2008) agrees. The ability of financial elites to speculate in the unproductive economy must be abolished by law and capital markets should be regulated to maximize the productive economy in which real goods and services are produced to serve human needs. All of these thinkers advocate the same basic principle. Money and its democratic creation and regulation should be treated as a "public utility," available to all citizens as part of their social heritage and human rights. Cook itemizes the key points:

- Private creation of credit for speculative purposes should be abolished, and capital markets should be regulated to assure fairness, openness, and freedom from predatory practices.

- Every national government should have the right to spend low cost credit directly into existence for public purposes—including infrastructure, environmental protection, education, and health care—without incurring new debt.
- The physical backing for every currency in existence should be the actual production of national economies.
- National governments should treat credit as a public utility — like clean air, water, or electricity — and should assure its availability to all citizens as their social heritage and as a basic human right. (Ibid.)

Economist J.W. Smith also agrees. The banking system must be "socially owned" and financial speculation by private financial interests must be abolished at the same time that public investment is made in the real productive economy that supplies goods and services to the people. "Due to a *socially-owned* banking system being more powerful than armies...." he writes, "that power is denied a private banking system because their *property rights* are designed for maximum rights to monopolists and minimum rights for all others" (2009: 169-170). Smith affirms that:

> Monopolies claim a large share of the wealth produced, waste enormous amounts of resources, capital, and labor, restrict the efficiencies of an economy, claim unearned wealth, and all this doubles the cost of production.... In an efficient economy, with *full and equal rights for all*, there are no unearned values. Instead of financing unearned monopoly-created values, touchable and usable *use values* are financed, created, and bought and sold. Both planning and financial control are primarily regional and local. (Ibid. pp. 144-146)

Smith shows that the structure of property laws today actively prevents both social equality and a fully efficient economy. A socially owned banking system not only enables production of the general wealth that substantially eliminates poverty and creates universal prosperity, it democratizes society, placing the power back in the hands of the people's democratically elected government rather than in the hands of financial elites to whom the government is debt ridden and beholden. The key to an economically transformed world order and democratically run community in the service of the common good is clear and simple. Banking must be a public utility in the service of the people and the community, and property laws must be modified so that people gain full rights to the fruits of their labor and creative ingenuity.

This fundamental agreement among monetary theorists is marred, however, by a fatal flaw in their thought: many of these theorists remain trapped within the conceptual straightjacket of the sovereign nation-state. They have liberated themselves from the concept of a privately owned monopoly banking system as well as the property laws supporting this system and have shown the path toward a real salvation for humanity from poverty, misery, disease, and war. However, they fail to realize that there can be no such salvation under the planetary war-system of sovereign nations each operating its own central bank on its own behalf. Cook (2008), for example, writes:

- Monetary systems should be controlled by sovereign national governments, not the central banks which mainly serve private finance. The main economic function of the monetary system should be to assure adequate purchasing power to consume an environmentally sustainable and optimal level of production whereby the basic needs of every person in the world community are satisfactorily met.
- Income security, including a basic income guarantee and a national dividend, should be a primary responsibility of national governments in the economic sphere. A right to adequate purchasing power should be part of every national constitution. (www.richardccook.com/articles/)

Cook's excellent and sound monetary principles are undercut by his naïve assumption that each sovereign government of the 193 or so worldwide must have its locally controlled socially owned monetary system. His motivations are clearly in the right place, since socially owned monetary systems will create "an optimum level of production whereby the basic needs of every person in the world community are satisfactorily met." Yet one cannot liberate human beings through sound economic principles coupled with flawed political principles. We have seen the many ways in which the system of sovereign nation-states has devastated democracy, human rights, and peace for more than four centuries, existing, as they do, in a system that is intrinsically a war system.

Exceptions among these monetary thinkers are Ellen Hodgson Brown and J.W. Smith, both of whom acknowledge the need for a global monetary system under some form of an Earth Federation of nations, even though they both see this in the future and do not recognize its immediate necessity and viability. With regard to solutions to the world's financial mess, Brown writes:

That sort of model has been proposed by an organization called the World Constitution and Parliament Association, which postulates an Earth Federation working for equal prosperity and well-being for all the Earth's citizens. The global funding body would be authorized not only to advance credit to nations but to issue money directly, on the model of Lincoln's Greenbacks and the IMF's SDRs [special drawing rights]. These funds would then be disbursed as needed for the Common Wealth of Earth.

Some such radical overhaul might be possible in the future; but in the meantime, global trade is conducted in many competing currencies, which are vulnerable to speculative attack by pirates prowling in a sea of floating exchange rates. The risk needs to be eliminated. But how? (2007, p. 440)

Brown ignores that fact that the Earth Federation Movement has *already* designed a universal currency to replace the "many competing currencies" in their "sea of floating exchange rates." She ignores the fact that the founding of the Earth Community is not a "radical overhaul" of the present broken system (which cannot be repaired because it is based on false premises). Rather, the establishment of the Earth community actualizes the very heart of our civilizational project. Its founding on universal principles is *the only possible way out* of today's mess.

Smith puts the matter as follows:

The once powerless are getting stronger and they recognize that the imperial centers are getting weaker. Their many alliances and federations are forming a power that will be difficult to challenge and they can serve notice to the historic imperial nations that the UN be restructured into a democratic and moral forum or they will form their own world governing body, effectively a federation of 80% of the world....

World federalist organizations have been working to have a constitution ready for that momentous day. The World Constitution and Parliament Association (WCPA), as does others, has one ready for revision and acceptance by just such an alliance of nations.... With a name picked and a constitution for that governing body in place, the first order of business should be on how best to move forward on world development and alleviation of both poverty and global warming. (2009: 155-156)

Smith sees more clearly that the immediate solution requires global transformation through a "world governing body," although he fails to recognize how unlikely it is that the flawed premises of the U.N. system can be "restructured" into such a body.

While Brown and Smith appear to be far ahead of Hudson, Zarlenga, and Cook in their recognition that a solution to the world's immense economic inequality and instability will ultimately require an Earth Federation, neither of them sees clearly that a solution to today's economic nightmare is *effectively impossible without a real democratic world governing body under the Earth Constitution* having genuine legal authority to operate the monetary and banking systems, reform property laws, alleviate poverty, deal with global warming, and end war and militarism forever. We have seen above some of the ways that all these problems are interconnected and interdependent within the modern world system. They cannot be solved piecemeal by changes within some of the 193 sovereign nations. An effective Earth Federation is a *necessary condition* for a decent world order.

7.6 Specific Economic Arrangements under the *Earth Constitution*

Human liberation requires spiritual awakening to compassion, effective development of our common communicative rationality, financial transformation to economic democracy, and political transformation to democratic world law. Ratification of the *Earth Constitution* can accomplish the third and fourth of these objectives, but it will also set the stage for the first two. In Chapter One we saw Erich Fromm point out that "a change in the human heart is possible only to the extent that drastic economic and social changes occur that give the human heart the chance for change and the courage and vision to achieve it" (1996: 10). Founding a truly democratic community on the Earth will *provide the framework* for humanity to ascend to planetary maturity, which includes development of communicative rationality with its concomitant sense of a planetary community, as well as spiritual awakening to *agape* and compassion.

By abolishing the present war system of the Earth and bringing the nations together to deal with terrorism, human rights, poverty, disease, education, resource depletion, population explosion, and global warming, the *Earth Constitution* creates a planetary community that is the only possible basis for a general ascent to planetary maturity. A fragmented humanity lacking effective political, social, and economic unity cannot serve as the ground for the widespread transformation of human consciousness. Both communicative rationality and compassion require *system changes* that both make possible and activate their general development.

Article 1 of the *Earth Constitution* specifies the "Broad Functions of the World Government." These six broad functions form the central responsibilities of the Earth Federation and are the central justification for its creation: (1) To prevent war and secure disarmament; (2) To protect universal human rights, including life, liberty, security, and democracy; (3) To obtain equitable economic and social development for all peoples on Earth; (4) To regulate world trade, communications, transportation, currency, standards, and use of resources; (5) To protect the global environment and the ecological fabric of life; and (6) To devise solutions to all problems beyond the capacity of national governments.

Each of these articles addresses a global crisis that is clearly "beyond the capacity of national governments": (1) the problem of global militarism and wars; (2) the problem of nearly universal human rights violations; (3) the problem of global poverty and misery; (4) the problem of inequitable trade, uses of resources, etc.; (5) the problem of a collapsing planetary ecosystem; and (6) the problem of no planetary authority capable of protecting the people of Earth and planning for the future.

The *Earth Constitution* creates a democratic world commonwealth directed to the common good of humanity and future generations. It is non-military by law (Article 2) and democratic at every level, leaving economic and political self-determination to the nations insofar as these conform to universal human rights and world law (Article 14). Hence, the three non-democratic sources of the deep violence of today's world outlined above – sovereign nation-states, transnational corporations, and global banking cartels – are brought under the democratic control of the people of Earth through enforceable world law.

All nations joining the Earth Federation must demilitarize within a coordinated and carefully orchestrated procedure. Under Article 17, half of the immense wealth saved by this process is then used to fund the newly formed Earth Federation, the other half kept by the nations to empower sustainable development. All transnational corporations are refranchised in the service of human welfare by the World Parliament. And global banking is mundialized – socially owned by the people of Earth – to be administered through peoples' banks in localities worldwide.

The Earth Federation now coordinates the international actions of demilitarized nation-states through world laws legislated by the World Parliament. Conflicts are settled through the world court system and violators are subject to arrest and prosecution by the World Attorneys General and the World Police. Similarly, transnational corporations are regulated through the democratic legislation of the World Parliament. Their expertise and organizational infrastructures can now be used to promote universal prosperity while protecting the environment.

Finally, the Earth Federation issues debt-free, interest-free money to promote the prosperity, free trade, and well-being of the people of Earth while protecting the planetary environment. Individuals, corporations, state and local governments may all take advantage of very low cost development loans and lines of credit that are not premised on exploitation of the debtors in the service of private profit. In addition, primary created (dept-free) money will be judiciously spent for global infrastructure needs by the World Parliament. Money and banking are now used in the service of the common good of the people of Earth and in protection of the "ecological fabric of life" on our planet. The rich can no longer exploit the poor through a system of loans and debt that has so far created such misery for the peoples and nations of Earth.

Three features of the corrupt oligarchy that now dominates the world economy are eliminated from the start. *First,* military Keynesianism (or militarism used to artificially pump up the economies of nations) is eliminated, since under Article 2 all militaries worldwide become illegal.

Second, legal corporate personhood is abolished, which has turned the once beneficial corporations of the world into monstrous, immortal super-humans, who use their billions of dollars and super-human legal rights to dominate the economy of our planet. *Third,* the *Constitution* also removes the ability of these corporate entities to influence politics, judges, and government officials through massive campaign contributions or other forms of monetary influence. Hence, the key steps necessary to founding a truly democratic and prosperous world order take place with the ratification of the *Constitution*: the hold of the military oligarchies now dominating the planet is broken along with the hold of their associates, the banking, corporate, and massive financial oligarchies, and the monetary system of the world is placed in the service of the people of Earth. The founding of world democracy under the *Earth Constitution* accomplishes all this from the very beginning.

Article 4 of the *Earth Constitution,* entitled "Grant of Specific Powers to World Government," item number 17, reads: "Establish and operate world financial, banking, credit and insurance institutions designed to serve human needs; establish, issue and regulate world currency, credit and exchange." To do this effectively, Article 8 of the *Constitution* establishes the "World Financial Administration." Section G. 1. F. reads:

> Pursuant to specific legislation enacted by the World Parliament, and in conjunction with the Planetary Banking System, to establish and implement the procedures of a Planetary Monetary and Credit System based upon useful productive capacity and performance, both in goods and services. Such a monetary and credit system shall be designed for use with the Planetary Banking System for the financing of the activities and projects of the World Government, and for all other financial purposes approved by the World Parliament, without requiring the payment of interest on bonds, investments or other claims of financial ownership or debt.

Our global monetary system today is 99% composed of privately created debt-money (Brown 2007). Because of this we live in a world of global scarcity and desperation requiring, as we have seen, massive military training for counter-insurgency warfare and massive military interventions by imperial nations designed to protect and promote the present world domination by a tiny corporate and financial elite. The *Earth Constitution* is explicit that money must be created by the Federation as *debt-free money* addressed to the common good and planetary prosperity.

Under the authority of Article 19 of the *Earth Constitution,* a Provisional World Parliament has begun operating since 1982. The most recent session of the Parliament took place in Nainital, India in July 2009.

During its eleven sessions to date, the Provisional World Parliament has passed some 47 World Legislative Acts designed to implement and develop the infrastructure of the Earth Federation under both the spirit and letter of the *Constitution for the Federation of Earth.* These acts are not binding on the final world parliament once the *Constitution* is ratified. However, they serve to elaborate and elucidate the content and spirit of the *Constitution,* and they will likely serve as a compelling model for the final World Parliament.

These acts include the creation of a World Economic Development Organization (WLA 2), an Earth Financial Funding Corporation (WLA 7), a Provisional Office for World Revenue (WLA 17), a World Patents Act (WLA 21), a World Equity Act (WLA 22), a World Public Utilities Act (WLA 38), and an act for a World Guaranteed Annual Income (WLA 42). Together they are laying the economic foundations for a global market economy based on human rights, promotion of the common good, and a democratic world order that benefits everyone, not just the present 10 percent of humanity who today own 85 percent of all the global wealth (E. Brown 2007: 271).

As early as the first session of the Parliament in 1982, when WLA 2 was passed creating the World Economic Development Organization (WEDO), the Parliament saw through the deception of debt-based money creation. Among the means of funding for WEDO is the directive to develop the financing potential and procedures defined under Article 8, Section G, paragraphs (d), (e), (f) of *Earth Constitution to base finance on people's potential productive capacity in both goods and services,* rather than on past savings.

From this principle of funding under the *Earth Constitution,* that is, the creation of debt-free fiat money and credit based on the potential of those funded to produce goods and services, follow all the other principles of the Provisional World Parliament that are building the infrastructure for an equitable and just world order. With government-issued debt-free money, the Earth Federation will hire tens of millions of unemployed people in the Third World to restore the environment, replant the forests of the Earth, and restore the degraded agricultural lands of the Earth. This massive effort is absolutely necessary if we are to deal effectively with global warming. Even though the *Constitution* gives Parliament the right to levy taxes, no such process is necessary within the sound monetary policy formulated by WEDO.

The Earth Federation will have a common currency valued the same everywhere, ending speculation in currencies and the domination of "hard" over "soft" currencies. It will institute the principle of "equal pay for equal work," ending the exporting of production to low-wage areas of the world in order to maximize the rate of exploitation and profit. It will encourage in numerous ways worker investment and cooperative management in the firms within which they often spend their working lives. It will distribute the work burden among the working population more equitably, and empower people at the grassroots level worldwide.

In short, it provides a genuinely "New Deal" for the people of Earth. The tens of millions hired to restore the environment will have money to exchange in their local economies. In conjunction with interest-free loans or grants for building infrastructure, sanitation systems, education, healthcare, and many private and public sustainable new enterprises, local economies will "take off" in that dynamic circulation of money within communities that economists speak of as economic health. Once the militarized *nation-state* is removed (today pouring one trillion U.S. dollars per year down the toilet of militarism) along with gigantic corporate and banking institutions dedicated to extracting private profit from localities into foreign banks of the rich, economic well-being will not be difficult to achieve.

The *Constitution* guarantees everyone on Earth a minimum wage entirely sufficient to live with dignity and freedom (under Article 13). It ensures sanitation systems, essential resources, and educational systems for everyone. It provides every person on Earth with free health care, free education, and ample insurance in case of accident or old age. Provisional world legislation enacted by the Provisional World Parliament under the authority of Article 19 of the *Constitution* provides every person over age 18 with a guaranteed annual income sufficient to eliminate extreme poverty and starvation from the Earth (WLA 42).

The world order can be fairly easily transformed into one of planetary peace with justice and prosperity. The present world-system of scarcity and domination is a result of the principle inherent in money created as public debt to private financial elites and on a global system of maximizing private profit at the expense of the common good of the people of Earth. Perhaps the most fundamental secret is in "democratic money": money issued debt-free in the name of the productive capacity of the citizens of Earth to produce goods and services.

But this global transformation cannot be accomplished without the ratification of the *Earth Constitution* and the basing of our world order on its fundamental principles of democratic market socialism and enforceable democratic world law. Socialism understands that individual freedom must be correlative with the common good of all within a community that recognizes the dignity of each person and promotes a reasonable equity and parity among all persons. We arrive once more at the central meanings of "planetary democracy" and the "triumph of civilization" for these concepts simply articulate our progressive civilizational understanding of who and what we are as human beings.

These principles cannot work, we have seen, unless we take this "all" seriously and universalize democracy to every person on Earth. This universalization process is the fundamental imperative of our time. Yet there is a concomitant aspect of our moral obligation today that requires us to abjure violence, war, and military service altogether. This aspect, too, shows the moral impossibility of sovereign nation-states and military service on their behalf. Let us now turn to an exposition of this related dimension of the fundamental moral imperative of our time.

Chapter Eight

Nonviolence and World Order

The Moral Impossibility of Military Service or Sovereign Nation-states under the Genuine Rule of Law

We consider people to be "religious" because they say they believe in God. Is there any difficulty in saying this? Is there any reality in it, except that the words are uttered? Obviously I am speaking here about an experience which should constitute the reality behind the words. What is this experience? It is one of recognizing oneself as part of humanity, of living according to a set of values in which the full experience of love, justice, truth, is the dominant goal of life to which everything else is subordinated; it means a constant striving to develop one's powers of life and reason to a point at which a new harmony with the world is attained; it means striving for humility, to see one's identity with all beings, and to give up the illusion of a separate, indestructible ego.

Erich Fromm

'There is no thing in the world which does not point a way to the fear of God and to the service of God. Everything is commandment.' By no means, however, can it be our true task in the world into which we have been set, to turn away from the things and beings that we meet on our way and that attract our hearts; our task is precisely to get in touch, by hallowing our relationship with them, with what manifests itself in them as beauty, pleasure, enjoyment. Hasidism teaches that rejoicing in the world, if we hallow it with our whole being, leads to rejoicing in God.

Martin Buber

Moral growth involves growth in personal autonomy concomitant with a growing connection with the whole of humanity and with the whole of the cosmos. Unless individuals can legislate universal principles for themselves on the grounds expressed so well and consistently by Noam Chomsky, Alan Gewirth, Leonard Nelson, Immanuel Kant, and others, the appeal to "moral rules" is merely conventional and socially conformist. Actions taken by individuals or groups from a unilateral perspective, not truly universalized, proclaim, in effect, "to hell with everyone else, we will do just what we want because we have the power to do so."

As the quotations above from Erich Fromm and Martin Buber suggest, the capacity for moral insight, universality, autonomy, and action is inseparable from authentic religion, that is, from attunement to the "voice of God" within human life. And both thinkers insist that this voice is progressively revealed the more we rejoice in this world, the more we love the world and life itself in "beauty, pleasure, and enjoyment." Life in the service of war and destruction is no longer a legitimate option.

We experience morality as a demand inherent in our human situation. As Paul Tillich expresses this, we find inherent in our situation an unconditional demand that the future be different from the past, that we hear and respond to the "ought" commanding us to a world of community, love, and justice (1987: 143-144). Once this is understood, as John Hick (2004) elucidates at length, the diversity of particular scriptural demands that make it appear as if the religions have conflicting truth-claims, begins to lose its force and the universality of our human condition becomes clear.

What I am calling "authentic religion" need not mean that persons practice any particular religion or follow any particular rituals. It means that our human condition, our lifeworld, manifests as a whole, experienced by many as sacred. Authentic, mature morality actualizes within us the same universal principles and insights as do authentic religion and authentic spirituality. This holism inheres within our situation from the very beginning. It simply needs to be actualized in our lives and in history. Both morality and religion demand that we actualize the holism of our situation in the form of a global community of peace, freedom, and justice.

For these reasons, we have seen above, membership within community is not in the slightest incompatible with moral autonomy. Genuine moral autonomy is simply the expression of human maturity, entirely distinct from the false individualism of liberalism. Lack of moral autonomy, on the other hand, leaves persons open to collectivism, to mass hysteria, conformity, bigotry, nationalism, militarism, or ethnocentrism. We find the most basic moral principle expressed in religions around the world as some form of the golden rule, as John Hick demonstrates at length (2004: Ch. 18). The principle of doing to others what you would want done to yourself can also be expressed as a principle of universality: applying the same moral standards to oneself as one applies to others.

This basic moral demand inherent in our situation as expressed in the writings of Noam Chomsky has two aspects to it: (1) *Universality: apply the same standards to others as you apply to yourself.* If moral principles are appealed to (and the most fundamental of these express some form of the golden rule), they must be universalized so that all persons or groups are measured equally by the same norm. (2) *Persons or groups are responsible for the likely consequences of their actions.* Persons or groups acting unilaterally from their own national, ethnic, religious, or personal perspectives routinely cause immense harm to others. The refusal to universalize the principles out of which one acts is simultaneously a refusal to accept the likely consequences of one's actions.

Yet people will not adhere to these simple principles, nor demand that their leaders adhere to them, unless they have reached a level of autonomy that allows them to see through the systematic privileging of a partial point of view in the service of group solidarity, system imperatives, power, domination, or exploitation. As Christian thinker Thomas Merton puts it, "a mature political consciousness" involves the insight that "our evils are common and the solution of them can only be common" (1964: 16). The solution to our common problems, morally speaking, involves the simple application of genuine universality of ethical standards and taking responsibility for the likely consequences of one's actions.

The "legislation of universal principles" by persons growing in autonomy is not incompatible with the openness in silence to the eschatological call emerging from the depths of our human situation. Autonomy does not mean being closed off from other human beings or the depths of existence. It means the growth of self-awareness in us to the point where we no longer take our values exclusively from the social matrix into which we happen to have been born but, rather, act from universal principles deriving from our freedom and deeper intuitions. We have seen Tillich name the unconditional demand arising from self-awareness and freedom as *the demand for justice.* Without moral autonomy, we cannot experience this demand in a clear and compelling way as the transformative demand for a planetary form of social democracy ensuring peace, freedom, and reasonable prosperity for every citizen of Earth.

8.1 The Kantian Principle of Moral Autonomy

I am not concerned in this section to defend the controversial aspects of Kant's ethical philosophy such as his radical separation of duty from desire, nor his outdated justifications for how freedom of the will is possible in the light of the (now discredited) Newtonian physics. Instead, I am using his formulations of the fundamental principle of morality, which he calls the *categorical imperative*, to elucidate the principle of moral autonomy and its implications with respect to the issue of violence. Once we have understood the implications of the categorical imperative with respect to violence, we will be able to discern the very real possibility of establishing a substantially nonviolent world order.

Neither do I see this "fundamental principle of morality" as incompatible with a properly understood utilitarian ethics (discussed below), nor with virtue ethics, nor with so-called justice ethics of fairness and equality, nor with a developing ethics of ecological holism. It may well be that all these approaches to ethics are attempting to articulate similar pre-theoretical intuitions in ways that ultimately complement one another. The approach below does not attempt to present a complete ethical theory. It merely attempts to isolate the dimension of moral autonomy in relation to militarism and violence. For unless there are compelling grounds for persons asserting their individual right and duty to abjure militarism and violence, the very possibility of ending these horrific practices is forfeited.

We saw above in Chapter Three that Jürgen Habermas (1979) fundamentally agrees with psychologist Lawrence Kohlberg (1984) concerning the actualization of moral autonomy in the higher stages of moral development. For both thinkers there is a basic pattern to moral development (paralleling the actualization of cognitive development) leading from morality as social conformity to critically examined community mores to morality as individual autonomy operating under universal principles. They both associate the latter "stage 6" moral realization with the categorical imperative of Kant.

This is absolutely crucial for comprehending our moral situation as human beings. There must come a point in the growth of each adult in which we realize that authentic moral principles cannot be derived exclusively from our native culture, religion, nation, or tradition but can only be chosen, embraced, or affirmed though the rational good will of each individual on grounds of their universality, coherence, and consistency. Kohlberg sees this moral autonomy as a necessary condition for the realization of a "stage 7" holistic ethics in which "moral principles are not seen as arbitrary human inventions; rather, they are seen as principles of justice that are in harmony with broader laws regulating the evolution of human nature and the cosmic order" (1984: 250)

A morally autonomous person is capable, if necessary, of morally standing in opposition to his or her culture, religion, or tradition. Such a person is capable of thinking for him- or herself and asking a question transcending culture, religion, or tradition: "Is this right?" The only possible authentic answer to this question is the rational, subjective affirmation and personal comprehension that this is indeed right or wrong. This "inwardness" of authentic morality was emphasized by Kant and understood by Kierkegaard, Wittgenstein, Leonard Nelson, Habermas, Kohlberg, and many others.

The second of Chomsky's principles identified above is not necessarily a utilitarian principle in contradiction to the so-called "deontological" first principle. Kant, who first formulated these principles in an explicit and systematic way, *never* says that we should not consider the consequences of our actions when we act according to a universalized maxim of a proposed action. Of course we should. *Every reasonably considered action will necessarily include an evaluation of that action and its consequences together.* It would be absurd to assert the morality of an action that was blindly performed regardless of any deleterious consequences that might reasonably ensue. Rational people normally take consequences into account in their every decision, and Kant understood this, as we will see below, and assumed that we understand it as well.

When Kant says that the morality of an action is assessed in terms of its faithfulness to the categorical imperative alone, he means that the *source of the rightness of an action* (the sense of moral obligation itself) is not dependent on some estimate of consequences. For moral obligation involves an "absolute command" of reason in the present to do what is right. What Kant wishes to avoid is the loss of the "categorical" character of moral principles to some morass of vague calculations of possible consequences. A morally alive person experiences absolute imperatives best summed up in the general principle: "Always do what is right regardless of your inclinations." If my inclinations refer to the many aspects of my self-interest and the many vagaries of my emotional life, then these must be excluded, for what is right must be universal – equally applicable to all regardless of any self-interest or contingent emotions.

In virtue ethics, it is precisely these "inclinations" that must be molded and shaped through education, discipline, understanding and action into habitual modes of excellence that might also include the abjuring of war and violence. However, Kant's principle remains central, for unless I have the moral autonomy to do what is right regardless of such inclinations as anger, rage, hate, fear, cruelty, greed, or lust, then I lose my human dignity as a free, self-determining agent and become nothing more than an automaton not responsible for acting on these impulses. As Errol Harris puts it: "Morality consists in respect for an objective imperative that imposes obligation in despite of inclination" (2000b: 81).

Since Kant formulated these principles in the eighteenth century, they have been reformulated by a number of thinkers in language that has adapted to our growing understanding of our human situation. As discussed above with respect to Habermas, for example, the mutuality or social character of the human self and the implications of this for our sense of moral obligation lead us to express the categorical imperative in more interactive, communicative, and socially holistic terms. A late twentieth century formulation of this is presented by philosopher John Hick:

> Since morality is thus generated by the inter-personal nature of personality, its basic principle is mutuality, or acceptance of the other as another person, someone else of the same nature as oneself. The fundamental moral claim is accordingly to treat others as having the same value as myself. This is in effect a transcription of the Golden Rule found in the Hindu, Buddhist, Confucian, Taoist, Zoroastrian, Jain and Christian scriptures and in the Jewish *Talmud* and the Muslim *Hadith*...and is likewise a translation of Kant's concepts of a rational person as an end and of right action as action which our rationality, acknowledging a universal rationality transcending individual desires and aversions, can see to be required. (2004: 149)

The recognition of human mutuality (the other as a *Thou* having the same value as myself), one of the great emphases of twentieth-century thinkers such as Paul Ricceur (1969), Martin Buber (1971), Emmanuel Levinas (1985), and Habermas, "is likewise a translation of Kant's concepts of the rational person as an end." This "fundamental moral claim" is another way of stating that there is, in Kant's language, an absolute or categorical imperative that is always with us as rational creatures – to treat other persons as persons, that is, as ends in themselves. In his *Groundwork to the Metaphysics of Morals* (1964), first published in 1783, Kant attempts to awaken insight into our fundamental moral duty through formulating several versions of this categorical imperative focusing on the sense of moral obligation that pervades our rational lives. In each version, the universal rational principle functions as an absolute imperative independently of the fact that we also normally can and do estimate the consequences of our actions, and regardless of our compulsive self-interested and fluctuating emotional lives.

The several formal principles by which we try to decide what is right in a complex world, as presented by Kant, have overlapping similarities and within a range of differences that attempt to give us an insight into the general categorical imperative for human life. But the central idea remains that the maxim of my proposed action must ask this question: "Can I make a universal principle that everyone act as I propose to act in this situation?" This necessarily involves a rational estimate of consequences of the action.

One could not even formulate a maxim of action if it did not include a rational and immediate estimate of consequences. If I am acting rightly in this situation, my comprehension of this situation *and* its circumstances involves immediate comprehension of concrete long and short term consequences. It would be absurd and bizarre if it did not. This is the way the human mind works, and Kant had no need to remind us about the most obvious and basic functioning of the human mind in creating maxims of action. His focus was on the formal "absolute command" aspect of the moral imperative. What does it mean for a free, rational being to experience the absolute command to do what is right regardless of his or her inclinations?

I take it that this is what Noam Chomsky emphasizes when he asserts that persons or groups are responsible for the likely consequences of their actions. It is not that the morality of actions *depends* on a utilitarian calculation. For the primary moral command, Chomsky asserts, is to apply the same standards to others as one applies to oneself, in other words, to recognize persons as persons with the same equality, dignity, and freedom as oneself and the likely consequences of one's actions with regard to them as persons. The key to morality, in the words of Mortimer Adler quoted at the beginning of Chapter One, involves the ability to say "all" and really mean "all" for the first time, that is, to truly universalize both the principle of our actions *and* its likely consequences.

Even in John Stuart Mill's classic formulation in *Utilitarianism* (1957), first published in 1861, the fundamental *equality* of all human beings is assumed along with the emphasis on mutuality and progressive recognition of the common good. The criterion of morality, for Mill, is the *principle of utility* which states that "actions are right in proportion as they tend to promote happiness; wrong as they tend to produce the reverse of happiness" (p. 10). This principle appears to require an estimate of the consequences of actions in order to assess their rightness or wrongness. Kant finds this problematic for reasons we shall further discuss. However, it also links our actions with society and the welfare of others, a connection that Kant strongly endorses.

Mill continues: "Not only does all strengthening of social ties, and all healthy growth of society, give to each individual a stronger personal interest in practically consulting the welfare of others, it also leads him to identify his *feelings* more and more with their good, or at least with an even greater degree of practical consideration for it" (p. 41). Mill here emphasizes the interface between "feelings" and rationality (unlike Kant, who separates these two) in part because he does not hold a metaphysics that allows for "free will." Nevertheless, this passage reveals his assumption of the equality and universality of all human beings that remains on target, as well as the need to modify our feelings and emotions ever-more closely with the rational demands of morality, a process also endorsed by virtue ethics (for example, in Aristotle's *Nichomachean Ethics*).

Kant's fundamental difference with Mill lies in his recognition of the absolute character of the moral imperative that is always with us in virtue of our freedom and rationality. The moral imperative cannot and should not *depend on* the cultivation of moral feelings, although such cultivation remains for Kant a desirable goal. Nor should it *depend on* a calculation of the possible consequences of one's action, although accurate calculation of consequences remains a desirable goal.

Kant presents at least four versions of the categorical imperative to describe a range of ways that the sense of absolute obligation in human life can be understood and formulated. *The first is the "formula of universal law"* that Kant immediately reformulates as the "formula of the law of nature." The examples Kant gives to illustrate the operation of this first principle (whether to commit suicide, whether to borrow money and pay it back, and whether to cultivate a natural talent) all involve a rational estimate of the consequences of the proposed action.

It could not be otherwise. Kant's central point is that the universalization of a conception of a proposed action *and its likely consequences* must give us an absolute (categorical) imperative to do or not to do the action. The principle of utility by itself omits this "absolute command" aspect of morality. It may be that there is a sense in which (as the quotation from Martin Buber at the head of this chapter suggests) "everything is commandment." Emmanuel Levinas expresses this sense of obligation in terms of the human face: "The first word of the face is the 'Thou shalt not kill.' There is a commandment in the appearance of the face, as if a master spoke to me" (1985: 89). Kant, like Levinas, focuses on our *relation* to other persons, which itself involves this sense of an absolute command.

This idea is borne out in the *second formulation of the categorical imperative, the formula of the end in itself:* "Act in such a way that you always treat humanity, whether in your own person or in the person of any other, never simply as a means, but always at the same time as an end." In other words, always treat persons as ends in themselves, never merely as a means. Here again we find Kant's main point that moral principles are categorically commanded. The principle of utility cannot generate this fundamental aspect of morality. One cannot cultivate feelings to provide an absolutely consistent, universal command, nor can you calculate the imagined, complex consequences of actions to provide such a command.

This aspect of morality as presented by Kant, once again, would be nonsense if we could not reasonably predict the consequences of our actions as part of assessing the maxim of our proposed actions. If the World Bank facilitates exploitation of a country on behalf of its investors to the point where the economy of that country collapses and desperate, starving people descend into social chaos and civil war, then, in the very first place, it is clear that these decision makers acted immorally. For economically exploiting people, even apart from the consequences I have described, violates the principle of treating them as ends in themselves. (These consequences have, of course, literally happened in the case of Rwanda and a number of other countries, cf. Chossudovsky 1999, Klein 2007.)

Nor have the decision makers at the World Bank acted morally in the second place: for the *likely consequences* of their actions were implicit in the principle of exploitation by which they operated in the first place. One cannot exploit people (use them as a means for enrichment at the expense of their impoverishment) without *anticipating consequences* (my enrichment and their impoverishment with its attendant social chaos). Similarly, I cannot use someone by lying to him or her for my advantage without *anticipating* my advantage. I cannot express propaganda on network TV as if it were news without *anticipating* that I am controlling people's opinions and reactions in the service of dominant interests. Unless I distinguish the likely consequences of using people in contrast to treating them with dignity (as ends in themselves), the categorical imperative can have no meaning at all.

The third formulation of the categorical imperative expresses the "formula of autonomy" in contrast to all principles that appeal to "heteronomy," that is, principles that require certain self-interests, certain feelings, or certain consequences to be valid. Kant says that the only valid moral laws are laws that are legislated by each of us as a rational being and yet at the same time are universal. He remarks that the failure to discover the foundation of moral principles throughout the history of philosophy lies precisely in that no thinker ever identified this principle of autonomy as the basis of valid moral law.

Any moral law or principle deriving from a "heteronomous" source, that is, a source outside the rational self, is compromised because the self requires incentives, some form of self-interest, to be induced to obey it. One of the greatest twentieth-century philosophers, Ludwig Wittgenstein, agrees with the insight that Kant is attempting to evoke in his readers. Wittgenstein says: "As soon as one gives me a command that this or that is right to do, my first thought is 'What if I disobey it?'" External sources of obligation mean nothing unless they are legislated from our rational freedom itself, unless we affirm the rightness of the action as morally autonomous persons.

The absolute command of ethics and its autonomous legislation (only possible through "inner" rational freedom) distinguishes the moral source of ethics so clearly that Wittgenstein could write:

> I can only describe my feeling by the metaphor, that, if a man could write a book on Ethics which really was a book on Ethics, this book would, with an explosion, destroy all the other books in the world. Our words used as we use them in science, are vessels capable only of containing and conveying meaning and sense, natural meaning and sense. Ethics, if it is anything, is supernatural and our words will only express facts; as a teacup will only hold a teacup full of water even if I were to pour out a gallon over it. (1965: 7)

This means that no book on ethics is possible because no external set of words or sentences can capture the inner rational freedom of a human being and our awareness of the absolute imperative of morality. Ethics, in this sense, is "supernatural." From an objectivating (naturalistic) view of a human being, we can easily comprehend inclinations as a sort of inner causality motivating behavior. My hunger serves as an inclination impelling me to eat something; my exhaustion serves as an inclination impelling me to sleep, etc. The principle of utility was formulated by Mill as an attempt to ground ethics precisely in these naturalistic feelings, in our pleasure-pain responses, and sense of consequences of our actions in terms of such pleasures and pains.

However, the objectivating point of view leaves out rational freedom and comprehends a human being under the category of causality that we normally apply to external events in nature. Rational freedom cannot be comprehended from such an externalizing point of view. An absolute moral imperative to do what is right regardless of inclinations or self-interest is incomprehensible to the objectivating point of view. For it requires the free rational decision of an autonomous moral person. As Søren Kierkegaard exclaimed, *the observer always misses the point.*

This underlines exactly Kant's point. To obey a heteronomously imposed rule or command, I require some incentive, something that appeals to my self-interest, for example, the approval of my community, the fear of punishment by the legal system, satisfying my needs in some way, expressing my feelings of kindness or compassion, acting on my desire for reward in heaven or my fear of hell. These incentives external to the rightness of the action make the action comprehensible as an inclination, an internal "cause" of my behavior. But precisely these factors do not make the command right. What can be the source of this rightness?

If it is God, then we have an anthropomorphically conceived God who, like a stern (or loving) father, gives moral commands. But to obey these commands because they are right in themselves means I have to affirm (legislate) this rightness for myself and act because it is right to do so and not for the motive of some reward (e.g., pleasing God, avoiding hell, or winning heaven). Kant's point is that the only valid source of an absolute command must be my own rational affirmation of this as an absolute command, worth doing because I affirm its intrinsic rightness.

If what God commands is by definition right, then I affirm that rightness (objectively universalize the commands) myself and follow these commands because they are right, not for some external reward or fear of punishment. This is what Kant means by "autonomy." If good is simply what God commands regardless of whether or not we can affirm its rightness (as some, such as Duns Scotus and William of Ockham have argued), then we find ourselves once again in heteronomy, needing some external or internal incentives for obeying the commands of morality. However, there can be no such valid source of moral laws unless I can simultaneously rationally affirm the law as valid by legislating it (affirming it) for myself (independently of such incentives). Valid moral laws for human beings arise only from freedom, reason, and autonomy. As adults, we are tasked to aspire to the progressive actualization of these unique features of our humanity.

In addition, the law is only valid if I recognize it as objectively valid independent of any interest I might have in acting according to my proposed maxim. The issue raised by Habermas and others as to whether Kant is unnecessarily a "dualist" by ascetically excluding any self-interest (such as feelings or inclinations) from morality misses the main point. An objectively valid principle may or may not coincide with my interests. But its objective validity can obviously never rest on my interests or even consider my interests or feelings, for, if it did so, it would no longer be universal (equally applicable to all). Universality requires autonomy, that is, exclusion of all self-interest or personal inclinations in the affirmation of the moral rightness of a law. The fact that in practice we only approximate this principle and very often compromise it with hidden forms of self-interest does not invalidate the principle.

This possibility, linked with the rational freedom in all of us, is what gives human beings our exalted status of ends in ourselves (in Kant's words, our intrinsic *dignity beyond all price*). It is precisely our ability as rational beings to exclude self-interest from our evaluation of moral principles. If we only acted wholly or partially from self-interest, we would be merely creatures of opportunity, chance, taste, or whim. But we have the capacity in principle to legislate objective universal laws. Thus each human being is more than an empirical creature pursuing his or her own inclinations, feelings, and interests. We are each vehicles of objectively valid, universal moral laws, for we possess rational freedom. In my formulation (2008: Ch. 2), as human beings we are best described as "rational freedom oriented toward wholeness."

There is no need to attribute some superhuman power to persons with regard to the formula of autonomy. There is no need to point out that it may be next to impossible for the ordinary person to exclude all interest from his or her actions. The point is that each of us can and often does make the distinction between our subjective tastes, needs, and inclinations and what we can meaningfully affirm as morally objectively valid. Every normal person can distinguish his or her feelings, needs, and inclinations from what that person takes to be objectively right. Since we can do this in principle, the possibility of doing this in practice in any particular moral decision is always there. As long as we are aware of this possibility (by distinguishing our own subjectivity from what might be objectively valid) then our dignity as human beings (who have the capacity to legislate objective moral laws for themselves) is assured.

The fourth formulation of the Categorical Imperative is the "formula of the kingdom of ends." If we abstract from the personal differences of persons and from their multiplicity of private ends, we are left with all human beings as ends in themselves. Insofar as all human beings have the dignity of being able to universalize the maxims of their actions under the idea of objectively right principles, then *human beings are the same in their dignity,* as ends in themselves. From this arises the idea of a systematic union of ends in themselves, the idea of a kingdom or society where people treat one another as ends in themselves, never merely as means.

The idea of a kingdom of ends is a necessary aspect of the concept of the categorical imperative because implied in the very idea of morality is the idea of other people (as well as oneself) as ends in themselves. All morality implies a kingdom, a society. This society encompasses a universal (worldwide) society insofar as all human beings share the same dignity. As a society, as a potential Kingdom of Ends, the categorical imperative demands that legislation be enacted (positive laws be formed) that maximize the freedom of each person (and hence enable autonomy) insofar as this is consistent with the freedom and autonomy of every other person.

Nation-states and local governments may legislate for their localities, but if they claim a sovereignty that allows recognition of no law above themselves, then they are in violation of the universality of the societal categorical imperative (the kingdom of ends) that commands universal legislation applying equally to all persons everywhere. Only democratic world law can universalize the principle that all persons are ends in themselves and eliminate the absurdity that protection of human dignity stops at some arbitrarily drawn political border that asserts "over this line persons are no longer protected by our democratic constitution." There is no such legitimate line, for the absolute social imperative is the command that all persons be subject to universally legislated democratic laws and have their rights equally protected before that law.

In the formula of the kingdom of ends it becomes clear that moral principles cannot be separated from the moral foundations of society. One cannot live morally within an immoral society without one's principles simultaneously demanding transformation of that society. Authentic moral principles demand political, social, and economic transformation. Our world society of nation-states and global capitalism is immoral, for inherent in our individual freedom and reason is *the demand to create the kingdom of ends on Earth,* a kingdom in which every person is treated as an end in his or herself. In a planetary kingdom of ends there could be no involuntary poverty, no exploitation, and no war. We encounter once more the intrinsic holism of our human situation.

8.2 Military Service is both Contradictory and Immoral

In August 2006, the U.S. Military began preliminary proceedings toward a court martial for First Lieutenant Ehren Watada for refusing to deploy to the war in Iraq, a country that had been invaded by the United States in 2003. Lieutenant Watada was charged with missing movement, contempt toward officials, and conduct unbecoming an officer and a gentleman (for making comments critical of the war and President Bush). He faced possible dishonorable discharge, forfeiture of all pay, and seven years imprisonment (Boyle 2008: 196-197).

Military lawyers cross-examined Professor Francis A. Boyle, an expert witness on International Law called by the defense. Professor Boyle testified extensively concerning the many violations of international law committed by the U.S. by this invasion and its aftermath: violations of the laws of war, the treatment of prisoners, the treatment of civilians, and the aggressive use of force by the United States as these are enumerated in the Geneva Conventions and the Nuremburg Charter, Judgment, and Principles. All of these treaties also constitute the law of the land in the U.S. according to Article VI of the U.S. Constitution, and they all state that soldiers are *required to disobey orders* that involve them in a crime in any of these areas. Soldiers, commanders, and civilians participating in any of these crimes are held individually responsible under these international laws. According to these laws, the defense that claims one was only "obeying orders of a superior" is not acceptable. Here is a brief section of the lengthy testimony and cross-examination of Professor Boyle:

> Boyle: The Nuremberg Judgment made it quite clear that where a soldier knows to a moral certainty, as he sees it, that an order is illegal, he has to disobey that order.
>
> Question: And that's subjective for each individual service member.
>
> Answer: Yes. It's subjective.
>
> Question: Good order and discipline is important for the military, of course. Do you agree with that?
>
> Answer: Sure. My father, after Pearl Harbor, enlisted in the Marine Corps. He invaded Saipan, Tinian, and Okinawa.
>
> Question: So Congress, and the country as a whole, has a vested interest in maintaining good order and discipline within the ranks of the military?
>
> Answer: Yes....
>
> Question: So with respect to some other military action which has been property authorized, if in that context some individual soldier subjectively decides for himself or herself not to participate...that would be a problem for discipline and good order in the military, which could properly be prosecuted; isn't that fair to say? (pp. 215 & 220)

For the military questioner, the personal moral decisions of a solider are *merely* "subjective" and hence incomparably secondary to the "objective" situation that the solder has been called to duty because a war is going on and the necessity of the military to maintain "good order and discipline." You simply cannot have every soldier subjectively deciding whether or not he or she wants to participate in a particular war. It is clear that the concern of the military lawyer is to maintain this "discipline" to the point where severe penalties and the threat of possible severe penalties can be applied to those who might consider their commanded duties to violate international laws against torture, war crimes, crimes against civilians, crimes against peace, or, alternatively, the moral prohibition against murdering one's fellow human beings. The weight, threat, and immediacy of these possible penalties normally far outweighs, in the minds of most soldiers, any question of a possibly immoral action for which they are unlikely to be held accountable by some future international court.

In Lieutenant Watada's case, the Judge declared a mistrial, according to Francis Boyle, because it looked as if the military jury might acquit Watada which "would be a great blow to the Pentagon, to the Bush administration, and to the continuation of the Iraq war" (ibid. p. 199). Military courts of any country are there to intimidate and cover up the profoundly questionable character of military service for the very reason that all military service involves *training in blind obedience*. It cannot be otherwise. To encourage the development of moral autonomy or conscience in soldiers would be disaster for the military of any country. Soldiers must be willing to kill and destroy whomever they are told to kill and destroy, and to do so in obedience to secretly formulated plans in the chain of command above them. This is the essence of war and military organization. Soldiers are not expected to morally evaluate the orders given to them as to whether these command criminal actions according to international law.

Training in blind obedience is, therefore, an essential feature of military training. A military must maintain "good order and discipline" and cannot allow soldiers to subjectively decide the rightness or wrongness of what they are called upon to do. This is a necessary prerequisite for training in working with others to kill those designated as "the enemy," to destroy their homes, properties, and life-support systems, without asking questions, blindly obeying the orders secretly formulated high up in the chain of command.

Human beings in civilian life are ordinarily somewhat slack in their personal habits. In the military they receive training in "discipline." But the core of this disciplinary training is the absolute, blind obedience to the orders of commanders. In the military form of social organization, training must necessarily be this way, for the military must (1) maximize efficiency in the destruction of people and property, (2) condition its soldiers to do things and endure hardships they would not ordinarily dream of doing or enduring in civilian life, and (3) overcome the natural resistance normal human beings have to killing and destroying other human beings.

These goals of military service wherever it is found on Earth require recruiting soldiers who have not yet grown in maturity to the point of moral autonomy. The interest of the military questioner in the above quoted dialogue involves the need to maintain "discipline" over masses of persons enrolled as soldiers and trained to kill and destroy an enemy in objective situations of war or conflict. But such "discipline" can only be maintained if the vast majority of these soldiers have not yet reached moral maturity, that is, moral autonomy. They must be recruited and trained at the pre-autonomous stages of morality (primarily when they are young) in which moral principles are seen as deriving externally from one's nation, culture, religion, or tradition.

The killing and destruction of designated enemies according to secret orders formulated above oneself in some chain of command in itself violates the principle of moral autonomy. Lieutenant Watada was morally advanced enough to apply the principle of personal ethical decision within which he understood the clear conflict between the Nuremburg and Geneva principles and the order to deploy to Iraq. He understood that it was his inward perception of the immorality of the deployment (his conscience) that determines his responsibility.

The masses of soldiers deployed in wars such as Vietnam, Iraq, or Afghanistan have never reached this level of moral autonomy. They take their behavioral guidelines from external sources. The culture and regulations of militarism and war form one such external source, as does the nationalism that gives priority to the interests of one's own nation at the expense of all other peoples and nations. The system itself encourages the abdication of personal moral responsibility.

As psychologist Stanley Milgram has shown, persons in the military routinely transfer responsibility for their actions to their commanders, to the military organization, and to service on behalf of their nation (1974: 179-187). Milgram interviewed at length many military personnel who had routinely committed atrocities in Vietnam. "There is fragmentation of the total human act;" he writes, "no one man decides to carry out the evil act and is confronted with its consequences. The person who assumes full responsibility for the act has evaporated. This is the most common characteristic of socially organized evil in society" (p. 11).

We begin to discern here another aspect of the "good order and discipline" promoted by the military questioner in the above quoted dialogue. The military system itself is designed to evaporate personal responsibility for one's actions. It fosters nearly the opposite of what is required of civilized persons living under the rule of democratically legislated laws. *For under the rule of law all persons are held personally accountable for their actions.* Civilized living thus encourages the development of morally mature persons who can be held accountable for their actions. The institution of the military encourages the opposite of this. It can only exist by using immature persons who have not yet reached moral maturity and whose responsibility has evaporated into the bowels of the "socially organized evil."

We have seen above that the fundamental principle of morality is the universalization of the maxim of one's proposed action (a maxim that includes a reasonable estimate of the likely consequences of the action). The ability to do this is the fundamental source of our dignity as human beings. This ability is called "autonomy," the capacity to distinguish my needs, interests, and inclinations from what is right. Human beings are human because they are an ends in themselves through participating in this moral dimension of human life. To use someone, to treat them solely as a means, for example, to lie to them or threaten violence as a means of control, involves dehumanizing them. All such actions turn human beings into things, rather than respecting them as persons with dignity.

Military service violates every principle in the preceding paragraph and therefore is an utterly immoral occupation, set of activities, or way of life. *First,* it violates the principle of autonomy. If my dignity as a person derives from my ability to legislate (or affirm) universal moral principles and act on them, the military makes this nearly impossible. If I am trained and constrained to blindly obey orders, then I have given up my moral autonomy as a human being. I am dehumanized and demeaned. In the military it is impossible for individuals to legislate universal moral principles on the basis of respect for other persons' dignity, to estimate the likely consequences of their actions, or to autonomously affirm that it is right to take these actions.

Second, the blind obedience to orders necessarily exists within a context in which only the few on top in the military know the strategy and intent behind the conflict. Soldiers are denied the ability to estimate the likely consequences of their actions. They are trained simply to do what they are told (kill and destroy or aid and abet those who kill and destroy) in the dark, so to speak. Their ability to rationally assess their actions both in terms of universalizing principles and estimating the likely consequences of actions is removed from the vast majority of participants in military organizations. Hence, once again, they (no less than their victims) are dehumanized and debased as human beings.

Third, soldiers are reduced to being *used* solely as a means for other people's (the commanders and those who command the commanders) purposes. To live a life under the command of others, where one blindly obeys orders, is to allow someone else to turn you into a thing, a mere instrument of someone else's purposes. This is a moral impossibility for human beings. The principle of autonomy demands first and foremost that we take responsibility for ourselves. Each adult person exists as a morally responsible center of action and our very humanity demands that we focus on our duties (our self-legislated moral obligations) in contradistinction to our inclinations. Military life makes this nearly impossible. Moral decision-making is taken out of the hands of soldiers who must blindly obey orders. Soldiers are dehumanized as mere things. They have wittingly or unwittingly abdicated their dignity as human beings.

Fourth, the principle of morality (the categorical imperative) demands recognition that all persons are ends in themselves. All persons have an immeasurable dignity in virtue of being persons. To be part of an organization which has as its effective goal the destruction of persons and their life-support systems is to make every aspect of one's life immoral. Every statement of inalienable human rights, from the U.S. Declaration of Independence to the French Declaration of the Rights of Man, includes the basic principles also articulated in Article 3 of the U.N. Universal Declaration of Human Rights: "every person has the inalienable right to life, liberty, and security of person."

One might attempt to make arguments for the death penalty or for the right to take a life in immediate self-defense if one is attacked. Under very limited and special circumstances, one might argue, individual persons can give up their inherent dignity by their actions. And whether or not the death penalty is instituted or personal self-defense is absolved *must necessarily decided by the courts*, not according to who has the most power or the latest weapons.

But there can be no legitimate arguments for dropping bombs from airplanes, for launching missiles against some "target" that one does not see, for setting a land mine that might blow up an innocent person, or for destroying the life-support systems of entire groups of people by targeting, for example, their water, electricity, or food supplies. (By and large, so called "just war theory," going all the way back to the Fourth Century writings of St. Augustine, has always served as an ideological cover for the injustice and corruption of war.)

Similarly, there can be no legitimate arguments for being a non-combatant military person aiding and abetting those who do kill. Obviously, among groups targeted by any military action there may be one or some (such as women and children) who have not given up their right to be treated as ends in themselves by their actions, those who are blithely dismissed by military authorities as "collateral damage." If there exists even a chance of there being such persons at the other end of one's lethal actions (and in war this is always the case), then all military actions and involvement with military organizations is immoral. No one can be legitimately deprived of their rights to life, liberty, or security of person without rigorous due process under democratically legislated laws.

Even supposing one could make the case that a human life could be taken, for example, by the state in the case of the death penalty, the argument would logically require a description of due process of law to which accused persons are entitled. Because the taking of the life of someone considered an end in themselves is so serious, a rigorous process of trial by jury, careful weighing of evidence, and right of the person to counsel, access to medical care and family, and other aspects reflecting the seriousness of the proposed action (taking of a human life) must be required.

Similarly, if there is an immediate life-threatening attack on myself or my family that must be defended against and does not afford the option of any due process involving outside authorities such as the police, an argument could be made that the attacker has forfeited his or her status as a protected end in him or herself. In such rare cases, people have made arguments that should be seriously considered and weighed against the absolute prohibition of morality to violate a person's dignity and intrinsic rights as a human being. However, war and the military dispense with all of this.

In the military, commanders have expertise precisely in eliminating due process and respect for the intrinsic dignity of persons considered "the enemy" in favor of strategy and tactics for maximizing the killing of people and destroying their life-support systems. In the military, the object is to cause pain and suffering to a perceived (collectively envisioned) enemy until that enemy (in virtue of many deaths and much destruction) capitulates. Military training and organization necessarily ignore human beings as ends in themselves. It could not be any other way. This is one reason why Kant, in his essay *Perpetual Peace*, referred to the *defacto state of war* among sovereign nations as "barbaric" and "savage." War (and all military organization that supports it or engages in it) is necessarily immoral, that is, "barbaric" and "savage" in Kant's sense of these words.

On these four grounds, then, at the very least, military service is both contradictory and immoral. In terms of the arguments in this book for democratic world law, it should be clear that one absolutely serious imperative behind the demand for democratic world law involves the need to eliminate war and militarism from human affairs entirely. It is not only the survival of the human race in the face of possible nuclear war or other weapons of mass destruction that is the basis of the argument. It is the simple fact that war and militarism constitute a moral scourge on human existence that obligates all of us to work for a democratic world government in which these become legally and effectively impossible.

The fact that the *Earth Constitution* abolishes war and all military is not, therefore, a merely contingent matter. The first principle of the *Constitution* is that all persons are responsible to the law as individuals. The excuse is no longer available that I was acting under the orders of my corporation, boss, nation, church, or commanding officer. All design, production, testing, possession, transport, and use of weapons of war have been made illegal under both the Provisional World Parliament and the *Constitution for the Federation of Earth*. Individuals are held accountable at every step of the way. This principle is absolutely fundamental to establishing a *peace system* for the Earth. The war system necessarily evaporates personal moral responsibility.

The abolition of war and the securing of disarmament is one of the six broad functions for which the Earth Federation was created as specified in Article 1 of the *Earth Constitution*. War is logically and morally abominable. Neither war nor military preparation and service should exist. Both are institutionalized violations of human dignity and personhood, of morality, and of mature, civilized human behavior.

The Earth Federation rightly makes all activities related to war and militarism illegal, with stiff penalties, under due process of law, assigned to those convicted of violating these statutes. In doing so it raises the human project to a higher order of existence, into a new era in human history. All forms of militarism involve criminal behavior, and the *Constitution for the Federation of Earth* and Provisional World Parliament recognize this fact. The barbarism and savagery of military institutions is abolished from the Earth forever. Human institutions are premised for the first time on universal moral foundations − which necessarily means individual moral responsibility and accountability.

8.3 The Sovereign Nation-state System as Inherently Terrorist

The deeper assumptions behind our institutions and world order remain unquestioned and unthought by even highly educated people. If humankind is to survive much longer we must examine these unquestioned assumptions. The basic presuppositions guiding our institutions thwart the best-intentioned actions and efforts to achieve a peaceful and just world order. People commit their life-energies to peace and the result is violence, war, and terror. People work to eradicate poverty, misery, and disease and the result is ever-deepening poverty, misery, and disease.

Nearly all people wish to eradicate terrorism, yet terrorism continues to grow and flourish within and between nations and groups. Without a deeper level of thought, without deep insight and understanding into what Martin Buber called "the perversity of what is perverted," we continue to rush headlong toward ever-greater planetary disaster. What are the deeper assumptions behind our present world order that foment the terrorist mentality and terrorist forms of organization?

Today books and articles pour forth about terrorism, its causes and consequences. Conferences are held, governmental agencies formulate definitions, systems of monitoring and investigation are formed. Yet terrorism continues to increase. People in many places in the world lack a sense of security, peace, and well-being. They live with a vague sense of terror, in fear, regardless of whether they have had any direct experience of terrorism. Yet we will see that the foundations of a peaceful and secure world order are entirely within our grasp if we correctly diagnose the causes and remedies for world terrorism.

The 1999 FBI definition of terrorism can serve as a working definition for understanding this phenomenon. Terrorism, according to the FBI, is "the unlawful use of force or violence committed by a group or individual, who has some connection to a foreign power or whose activities transcend national boundaries, against persons or property to intimidate or coerce a government, the civilian population or any segment thereof, in furtherance or political or social objectives" (Blum 2000: 32). The essential points of this definition are that terrorism is (1) connected with violence or the threat of violence that transcends national boundaries and (2) it is the "unlawful" use of violence to achieve political or social objectives.

One important principle that astute thinkers have pointed out repeatedly in our time involves the distinction between non-governmental forms of terrorism and government-sponsored terrorism. We have come to understand that nation-states also engage in terrorism. It becomes more and more difficult to distinguish between private terrorism and terrorism routinely engaged in by nation-states. Military violence or the threat of violence by nation-states fits this FBI definition perfectly.

The use of military power to achieve international political objectives in a world of isolated "sovereign" nation-states is inevitable on a planet where there is no true, enforceable world law. If a nation uses its military resources to economically blockade the people of Cuba, for example, because it objects to their form of government, then it has used violence or the threat of violence, transcending national boundaries, to achieve political or social objectives. This is terrorism plain and simple according to the FBI definition.

As the issue of terrorism continues to be discussed, the history of interventions by the imperialist powers has once again come to light. One discovers a history of interventions, surprise bombings, assassinations, support for death squads, overthrowing of small nations, subversion of democracy, mining of harbors, blowing up of facilities, covert actions, drug smuggling, torture, arbitrary execution of political enemies, and outright aggression through invasions or military attacks. Every such instance fits the FBI definition of terrorism. It could not be otherwise, for under the system of sovereign nation-states, recognizing no effective law above themselves, the primary resources they have for international action is lawless terrorism: to use violence or the threat of violence to achieve political or social objectives.

Under the world system of the past five centuries, all imperial nations have engaged in such terrorism. Author William Blum describes this process with respect to the United States: "From 1945 to the end of the century, the United States attempted to overthrow more than 40 foreign governments, and to crush more than 30 populist-nationalist movements struggling against intolerable regimes. In the process the U.S. caused the end to life for several million people, and condemned many millions more to a life of agony and despair" (2000: 2). The selling of weapons to foreign regimes, the training and equipping of foreign military machines, and outright military interventions in foreign countries, all of which have been major policies of the U.S. throughout this period in order to politically manipulate or control the world order in its own interests, fit perfectly this FBI definition of terrorism.

Indeed, since the advent of the United Nations there have been some 150 wars resulting in some 25 million deaths. Most of these deaths were civilians. Compared to this, the number of people killed by non-governmental terrorists through car bombings, suicide bombings, assassinations, etc., is minuscule. Only massive ideological manipulation by the huge, profit-making media corporations of the world can obscure these obvious facts from the majority of people. Why is it that the vast preponderance of the terror of our world throughout the past fifty years has come from nation-state terrorism, not private terrorism? And why has this been covered up so effectively?

The majority of countries in the U.N. have called for study of the basic causes of terrorism, and to convene conferences on terrorism to define it and differentiate it from the [legitimate] struggles of people for national liberation. The U.S. has vetoed such actions by the U.N. for the obvious reason that its own unlawful and violent foreign policy to achieve global political objectives would be exposed and condemned by such conferences. Nevertheless, much excellent, independent work has been done on the real causes and conditions that foster terrorism.

The causes of private terrorism are often identified as extreme poverty, exploitation, imperial domination, and the humiliation that some nations, groups, or religions impose on others. Terrorists think of themselves as being in a war against such forces. State terrorism is often understood in this literature as being the mirror of private terrorism, since it is the use of state military power to enforce a system resulting in extreme poverty for the majority, exploitation, domination, and humiliation. However, despite the important insights presented here, the real sources of terrorism lie deeper than this.

The real source of terrorism is the nation-state system itself, structured, as it is, to be inseparable from global monopoly capitalism. The modern system of nation-states first developed out of the Renaissance, beginning at the same time the capitalist economic system developed in fifteenth-century Italy and culminating at the Peace of Westphalia in 1648. Some scholars define the "sovereign" nation-state as a political entity that has complete control over its internal affairs and complete independence with regard to other nation-states in its external affairs. The world today has about 193 of these territorial entities, all claiming to be "sovereign" and independent of all the others. A moment's reflection reveals this system as not only extremely irrational but morally perverse as well.

None of these "sovereign" entities lives under the rule of law. None of them lives under democracy. None of them in effect recognizes the equality, rights, and sovereignty of peoples outside their borders, since any such principles can only be enforced within nations. So-called "international law" is not law but a misnomer, since it is not democratically legislated, is not enforceable, and compliance with it is merely voluntary or else is enforced, not by the due process of law, but by military action from the Security Council.

According to the U.N. Charter, if the Security Council feels some nation has violated "international law" and international peace, the Council may authorize war ("by land, sea, or air") to reestablish peace. The contradiction is explicit and inevitable under the system of sovereign nations: peace is maintained by means of war or the threat of war. This is because there is no genuine law in international affairs. Relations between "sovereign" nation-states are mere treaties, that is, voluntary, unenforceable agreements that can be renounced or subverted at any time the nations party to these treaties feel it is in their self-interest to do so. The only alternative under such a system is war.

The representatives of nations comprising the Security Council vote according the perceived self-interest of their respective nations as do all nations within the U.N. They do not vote according to whether international law has been violated by some genocidal dictator in Africa or elsewhere, but according to whether it is in their geopolitical interest to intervene. And it has been rare that all of the five permanent members of this Council who possess the veto have agreed to attempt to protect human rights. (They are all massive violators of human rights themselves.) And when they have agreed, it was often much too late.

Hence, in spite of the contradiction in the U.N. Charter in which peace is maintained by means of war or the threat of war, since even when not engaged in war, the relations among the U.N. nations is one of *de facto war* (i.e. acting out of self-interest with no law above themselves), human rights atrocities and dozens of wars proceed unabated worldwide. The U.N. is not "powerless" to act as is often proclaimed. *The U.N. is intrinsically a war system.* Whatever "power" it has comes from the military might of members nations to decide to act militarily according to the dictates of their own self-interest. In the sense of political and moral legitimacy, we have seen, it has no legitimate power at all (only the ability to use violence), since it is not in any sense a democratic government.

Therefore, even though some nations claim to be "democracies" within their borders, and claim to believe in "democracy" as the only legitimate form of government, their defense of this bizarre concept of "national sovereignty" shows this to be false. They do not want to live under the rule of democratically legislated law but want to be entirely "independent" in a lawless, chaotic world of "international relations." If we redefine "sovereignty" to mean integrity and independence with respect to the internal affairs of a particular national territory under the rule of world law, then the concept becomes harmless. But "sovereignty" as external independence from any enforceable democratically legislated world law remains the main root of our present terroristic world order.

With modern weapons systems the absurdity of this arrangement has been underlined over and over again as intercontinental ballistic missiles have been developed capable of bringing nuclear weapons to any city on earth in the space of twenty minutes. Today, U.S. Trident nuclear submarines patrol the bottom of the oceans of the world, each submarine capable of launching nuclear warheads sufficient to destroy 123 cities worldwide, upon being given the order to do so or as the consequence of some horrible error. The criminal nature of this arrangement, a direct consequence of the absurd system of sovereign nation-states, is surely apparent to anyone who cares to think objectively.

Under this system every nation is thought to have the right to militarize itself for "self-defense" purposes. Nearly all of these 193 entities, living in a lawless world, arm themselves to the utmost, costing their citizens a large portion of the wealth they produce and causing other nations to perpetually renew their armaments to keep up with the possible threat from other sovereign nations, all independent and claiming the right to operate as they please in their foreign affairs and internal affairs.

Under this system a nation can violate human rights within its borders almost with impunity. Indeed, the imperial nations, led by the U.S. since WW II, have supported brutal, repressive regimes around the world in the interest of both international political struggles (e.g. against Communism) and creating, as they put it, "a stable investment climate." World private arms dealing and official government "military aid" to repressive regimes perceived to be "friendly" amounts to many billions of dollars per year. All told, the world spends close to a trillion U.S. dollars per year on militarism and weapons, while less than half of this amount could provide clean water and sanitation for every person on the planet. This entire system of militarization, we have seen, amounts to violence or the threat of violence. The world system, as it exists today, is clearly immoral, inherently terroristic, and completely absurd.

For example, the claim was made in 1998 by NATO that Yugoslavia was committing massive human rights violations (a claim never made against the official client states of the imperial powers whose human rights records were equally as bad or worse – for example, Turkey, itself a NATO member). In order to remove the Yugoslavian President and stop these violations, the supposed suffering of the people from their government then had to be compounded by militarily attacking them with cruise missiles and cluster bombs, destroying citizens and their factories, bridges, homes, and hospitals. In the FBI definition of terrorism, this was clearly the "unlawful" use of violence to achieve political or social objectives. Neither was this attack even legitimated under existing "international law," since it was never approved by the U.N. Security Council.

Whether these objectives are thought to be noble is irrelevant, since all terrorists believe their objectives are noble. When there is no independent or objective system in place to evaluate the uses of violence in claimed "self-defense," then both terrorists and nation-states will justify their own violent actions as noble, as justified, or as necessary. The nation-state system is nothing if not terrorist to its very foundations. Even the recently formed International Criminal Court designed to try individuals accused of war crimes and crimes against humanity must hopelessly dilute its procedures and authority in deference to this system of sovereign nations. This is certainly a step forward, but a pitifully weak one within an overwhelmingly terroristic world disorder.

The international system of militarized violence is based on a false analogy that the propaganda machines of the imperial powers do not wish us to examine too closely. It is an analogy with the individual's right of self-defense under the rule of law. Under democratically legislated law within nations, individuals and groups are prohibited from using violence against one another to achieve political or social objectives. Mechanisms such as arbitration, courts, the right of political participation, and freedom of expression are created by law to allow for the nonviolent adjudication of differences and the achieving of political or social goals. This is almost a definition of what it means to be "civilized."

If one is threatened or attacked, therefore, the law requires that citizens call the police or otherwise handle the provocation nonviolently. On the rare occasion that one's bodily integrity, family, property, or life is threatened and it is impossible to call the police, then the law provides for "the right of self-defense." Under these narrowly defined circumstances, it is legal to use violence or the threat of violence to protect oneself, one's property, or family. But the action must be later justified before the courts and the law. The rule of civilized law means precisely this: that our actions are not justified merely by our own subjective judgment, but must be justified before an objective, independent tribunal.

To project this "right of self-defense" onto the system of nation-states, therefore, is entirely fallacious. For under the world system of "sovereign" nations, there is no rule of law, no democracy, no due process, no independent court system, and no police protection of nations, groups, or individuals. Without the rule of enforceable law in the world, we have nothing left but the "savage" and "barbaric" condition of the world without the rule of law. Under the system of "sovereign" nations, the big nations do what they please (and subjectively justify their actions as noble or necessary) and the weaker nations suffer accordingly. For under this system, each nation *may decide for itself* what constitutes legitimate self-defense and act accordingly.

If I live under the rule of law *within* a nation, I may not machine-gun all the people in the next neighborhood, claiming preemptive self-defense, because I surmise they might some day attack or threaten me. The courts and enforceable laws decide what is legitimate self-defense and what is not. Within a nation, I may not commence bombing a neighboring county because I surmise that the government of that county is violating human rights. Under the rule of law, all such claims must be subjected to due process, protecting the rights of the accused to be considered innocent until proven guilty.

However, in international affairs, there is no superior force (democratic government and law) that can decide the legitimacy of any particular nation's claim to self-defense or its accusations against another nation. The powerful do what they please and use the "self-defense" argument or the "defending human rights" argument to justify whatever they perceive to be in their self-interest. That is why Kant described this nation-state system as manifestly immoral. It is not only the actions of individual nations that may be immoral, but the system itself is immoral.

Even the very existence of a military organization within nations is a terrorist consequence of the present world system as the FBI definition quoted above makes clear. Nations create a military for self-defense. The very existence of these military organizations constitutes a "threat of violence" to other nations, saying that if you attack us we will use violence to defend ourselves. In a world without genuine law (which is inevitable under the system of "sovereign" nation-states) the existence of such militaries constitutes the threat of the use of violence to achieve political or social objectives, namely, the protection and preservation of this government *vis-à-vis* all other "sovereign" governments.

A world order without democratically legislated, enforceable law over everyone is inherently terrorist, that is, the use of violence or threat of violence to achieve political or social objectives is built into the system itself. As long as nations claim there that there can be no world law above themselves (because they are "sovereign") and as long as they claim the "right of self-defense" in a world without law, then the use of violence or the threat of violence to achieve political or social objectives is inevitable. It is built into the very system of lawlessness itself. The triumph of civilization will mean bringing world law enforceable over all individuals to every person on Earth. Only then, will the "self-defense" argument begin to have cogency and legitimacy.

For nearly five decades the World Constitution and Parliament Association has offered the world a practical alternative – the creation of nonmilitary, democratic world government under the *Constitution for the Federation of Earth*. The ascent to democratically legislated world law under this *Constitution* is not just another arbitrary possibility among the many peace proposals offered today by the U.N. and NGOs. For only democratic world law can move us beyond the barbaric condition of international lawlessness and terrorism to a morally legitimate world of peace and security. There is no other option. Without the rule of democratically legislated enforceable law over all nations and individuals, we continue in the immoral mode of the rule of violence and the threat of violence to achieve political or social objectives.

Sentimental appeals to peace and respect for human rights such as the Hague Appeal for Peace in the year 2000 will not make a substantial difference. Neither will attempts to reform the U.N. achieve peace or put an end to terrorism. The U.N. charter is explicitly premised on the preservation of the system of sovereign nation-states. Treaties among sovereign nations controlling weapons of mass destruction or other militarized systems will not be successful. For none of these *addresses the root cause of most terrorism*, which is the system of "sovereign" nations itself. Only non-military world law under a *Constitution for the Federation of Earth* can give us a world of peace.

For only democratic world government creates enforceable rights for all people and nations under the rule of law. We move out of the barbaric world system of the past five centuries that was predicated on the use of violence or the threat of violence in international affairs. We move forward to a new world order that is the only morally legitimate order. For the use of violence for reasons of self-defense is only justifiable in extreme circumstances under the rule of democratically legislated laws with guaranteed due process, freedom of expression, and equal rights for all peoples and nations. No longer will there be the rule of power in world affairs but the rule of right, law, and due process. Individual responsibility is no longer evaporated by system imperatives, whether corporate or military. Moral autonomy and maturity in the population is empowered.

There is no other way beyond terrorism, since terrorism is predicated on the lawlessness of a world order that abjures democracy, law, and universal human rights in favor of the rule of violence and the threat of violence. The present system of so-called "sovereign" nation-states is inherently terroristic. Terrorism can only be overcome through democracy and a democratic world order. Terrorism can only be overcome through ratification of the *Constitution for the Federation of Earth*.

(Note: a version of section 8.3 was first published in *Culture and Quest: Issue on Violence, Nonviolence, and World Peace,* Kolkata, India: ISISAR, 5 January 2005, pp. 53-58)

8.4 The Moral Vacuum of Today's International System

One of the debates that the September 11, 2001 attacks on the World Trade Center and Pentagon engendered in the United States was whether a military response was appropriate to a criminal act. The government of the U.S. tended to treat these attacks as an act of war and correspondingly assumed it had a right to invade Afghanistan and later Iraq as an act of self-defense at least partly on the grounds that the governments of these countries were connected in some way with the attacks. However, no nation-state had attacked the World Trade Center and Pentagon, and, even then, it was extremely doubtful that the governments of Afghanistan or Iraq had anything to do with the attacks. (I am discussing the dynamics of the nation-state system here and leave aside the important question of whether the government of the United States had secretly helped engineer or orchestrate these attacks for its own political purposes: see Tarpley 2008; Griffin 2004 and 2008; Morgan and Henshall 2005.)

Critics of this policy claimed that the attacks were a criminal act, not an act of war. They argued that a military response was both useless and ill-conceived. The proper response, they said, was for many national governments to work together to investigate, arrest, and prosecute those responsible for these terrible attacks. They argued that going to war would not only obscure the real issue, it might well create the emotional and political grounds for more such terrorist attacks in the future.

However, neither side pointed out that the grounds for attacks by nation-states (war) and the grounds for violent attacks by criminals (usually called terrorism) are *built into* the chaos of a world without democratic law applying to everyone. We have seen that when there are disagreements among nation-states or discontent among groups anywhere in the world with international implications, there is no binding legal framework from which to adjucate these disagreements. And there is no binding legal framework for holding national leaders and their followers legally accountable for their actions if they initiate war or violent crimes such as kidnapping or assassination. For this reason, wars, kidnappings, or assassinations are simply options that autonomous nation-states have in their repertoire of strategies for pursuing their national interests in a lawless world vis-à-vis all other autonomous nation-states.

Discontented groups within nations having the rule of law cannot go to war with other groups within these nations. The enforceable legal framework prevents this, and if violence (even militarized violence) is perpetrated by some group, this is treated properly as a criminal act, as a violation of the legitimate rule of law within the nation. *War is only possible where the rule of law is lacking,* that is, in the legal vacuum between "sovereign" nation-states or in cases of civil war when a democratic government does not have the effectiveness to treat violence as the criminal act that it often is.

However, on these same grounds, the international forms of violence called "terrorism" cannot be readily labeled as "criminal acts." A criminal act is a violation of the legitimate rule of law. But in the legal vacuum between "sovereign" nations there is no such thing as the legitimate rule of law. So-called international law, we have seen, involves merely voluntary agreements and promises that the signatories to the treaties will abide by what the treaties say, just as Al-Qaeda might sign some document promising no more terrorist attacks. But voluntary promises, unenforceable and non-judicable, have little resemblance to law.

We have seen that terrorist behavior is no different from autonomous nation-state behavior. In the legal and moral vacuum between autonomous nations, people, organizations, and nations simply do whatever they like. They kidnap, assassinate, or bomb as they think necessary. One can label the behavior of any of these actors as "criminal" in a moral sense. But in a legal sense, there is no such thing. However, what is criminal in a moral sense (without legal definition and courts to decide upon the applicability of such definition) becomes largely a matter of subjective accusations: "The attacks on the Pentagon and World Trade Center were criminal" – The Invasion of Iraq was criminal" – "The economic blockade against Cuba is criminal," etc., without end.

The lawlessness of the international arena not only spawns morally reprehensible criminal behavior with regard to political violence (terrorism and so-called "counter-terrorism"). It fosters a host of horrendous activities that would be criminal under any system of democratically legislated law. The world sex-trade, a major component of which is sex-slavery, is a multi-billion dollar activity. The sale, exploitation, and slavery of children is similarly a multi-billion dollar activity flourishing in legal vacuum between nations.

In *When Corporations Rule the World*, David Korten writes:

> There are an estimated 500,000 child prostitutes in Thailand, Sri Lanka, and the Philippines alone. Millions migrate from their homes and families in search of opportunity and a means of survival. In addition to the 25 to 30 million people working outside their own countries as legal migrants, an estimated 20 to 40 million are undocumented migrant workers, economic refugees without legal rights and with little access to basic services. Some,

especially women, are confined and subjected to outrageous forms of sexual, physical, and psychological abuse. (p. 29)

In addition, the worldwide drug trade also flourishes in this vacuum and is approached by those fighting "wars on drugs" in militaristic ways (poisoning people's crops, disappearing people, paramilitary attacks on suspected processing centers, etc.) that are just as morally criminal as those producing lethal drugs for international sale. The multi-billion dollar trade in black-market weapons similarly flourishes within this international legal vacuum, as does money-laundering, illegal off-shore banking, trafficking in bodily organs, and other corrupt practices. Multi-national corporations capitalize on this chaos through destroying the environment, dumping toxic wastes as they please, bribing local officials, violating the human rights of their employees, and employing their own criminalized security forces in the pursuit of profit maximization.

The modern world has globalized itself in communications, travel, trade, and many other ways. Yet it has not globalized in terms of law, of a legitimate legal order applying to all persons guaranteeing due process and based on a regulative ideal of universal justice. In the legal vacuum between nations created by this antiquated system, a huge panoply of morally criminal practices flourish. The rule of legitimate law is mocked and its legitimate ideal of civilized living is debunked and demeaned as citizens see before them a world of lawlessness and corruption acting with relative impunity.

This disastrous situation is one direct consequence of our collective failure to question the nation-state as the legitimate locus of the rule of civilized law. The nation-state only becomes legitimate as a bearer of the rule of law when it is federated with all other nations under democratic world law. Otherwise, the consequences of this monumental conceptual error give us the morally reprehensible world of international criminal activity that we see before us today. Even the belief in the rule of law among decent men and women within nations is undermined by this absurd system.

Law, as we have seen in many of ways throughout this book, is inherently universal. To voluntarily support fragmentation of the rule of law into dozens of sovereign entities with a yawning, abysmal legal vacuum among them spawning war, terrorism, toxic dumping, drugs, sex-slavery, child-slavery, black market weapons sales, and the corruption of legitimate work and business through manipulation of this system is to embrace the darkest intellectual and moral blinders. At this point in the twenty-first century there is little philosophical reason to continue to support this out-dated system that has its origins in a very different world of four to five centuries ago.

The self-determination of peoples is perfectly compatible with the universal rule of law. Indeed, it can be protected and legalized by an Earth Federation based on the principle of *unity in diversity*. Under the present system of fragmentation, self-determination is only for the militarily and economically stronger peoples, in which case it is never *legitimate* self-determination. The weaker succumb in a world of violent struggle, threats, economic manipulation, and endless destruction. The inherently universal rule of law is only legitimately formulated when it protects individuals and groups who are smaller or weaker through rigorous systems of due process and justice. Such protection is manifestly impossible under the system of sovereign nation-states.

8.5 The Locus of Legitimate Democratic Government

If military organization and service is both contradictory and immoral, as I have shown, then no legitimate democratic government can have a military organization. A military, by its very nature, violates the most basic principles of democracy. There may be a "military code" authorized by law within a certain nation, but the very nature of that code states that soldiers will obey orders directed to the destruction of people and their life-support systems as directed by commanders. In addition, as we have also seen, a system of autonomous nation-states is inherently terroristic. One cannot conceptually distinguish terrorist acts from legitimate military acts by nation-states. The two share exactly the same premises: denial of the rule of enforceable democratic law as the framework for addressing problems of human conflict and community.

Democracy means precisely the protection of all people, their rights, property, and life-support systems, under the rule of democratically legislated laws. To kill an "enemy" under orders from a commander, whether as a terrorist fighter or a military soldier, violates those people's right to due process under democratically legislated laws. No one may be arbitrarily killed in violation of their rights to arrest, habeas corpus, fair trial, and due protection of the law. Military organization therefore intrinsically violates the principle of democracy and any "democratic" nation possessing a military engages in a performative contradiction – they contradict in practice what they claim to believe in principle.

The pretence among nearly all nations today is that one can have democracy within arbitrary national boundaries while "defending democracy" with a military beyond those boundaries. But not only does this contradict the very principle of democracy, as we have seen, any military organization inculcating blind obedience in a segment of the population destroys the very moral autonomy that is required for a mature adult population within a democracy.

We have seen that legitimate democracy can only flourish when a large enough portion of the population has reached the degree of maturity that frees people from the adolescent emotions of religious fundamentalism, racism, bigotry, rabid nationalism, etc. Training in blind obedience inhibits the development of the critical rational capacity that remains vital to functioning democracy. The blind obedience in which military personnel are trained is required precisely to convert them from citizens (required to think critically, with moral autonomy, and participate in governing themselves) to violators of human rights: to kill, without due process of law, whomever they are commanded to kill.

We have also seen above that the founding of a social community of mutual recognition, rights, and trust is fundamental to authentic democracy with its promise of positive freedom. Only when such a sense of community develops (what Rousseau called the "general will") does the common good of the society begin to interface with the particular goods of the free individuals within society. Without the development of the democratic community, individual freedom remains a negative and severely truncated freedom of resistance to the threats of governmental and/or majority tyrannies.

Democracy and a world peace system are, therefore, coextensive concepts. *You cannot have democracy without the institutionalization of a world peace system and you cannot have a world peace system that is not democratic.* The very meaning of democracy in our time is planetary in scope, requiring civilian police and abjuring all military organization.

In *Ascent to Freedom*, I identified five "effectiveness" criteria for legitimate government, all of which have to do with the orientation to the common good that is fundamental to legitimate democracy. The five principles required of democratic government mandate that it reasonably provide (1) social stability and good order so citizens can live their lives reasonably well, (2) security and safety of citizens from external and internal threats, (3) proper management of the economy to ensure widespread prosperity, (4) maintenance of environmental integrity and good management of resources, and (5) effective popular enfranchisement and maximization of the role of citizens in governing.

Without repeating the detailed arguments and examples here, I will summarize by saying that none of these features of the common good could possibly have been sufficiently realized within the system of sovereign nation-states within the past sixty or so years. With high speed weapons, WMDs, terrorist threats, global economic instability, global environmental breakdown, and the other crises beyond the scope of nation-states that have arisen in the past sixty years, no government on Earth can any longer provide these features of the common good reasonably well to its citizens.

The problems that undermine the ability of nations to protect the common good of their citizens are primarily the *global problems* that have come to world attention during the past sixty years. These are by definition beyond the scope of individual nations to deal with and, we have seen, are the central functions of the Earth Federation government as defined in Article 1 of the *Earth Constitution. History, therefore, has irrevocably changed the meaning and scope of the democratic idea from nation-states to planetary democracy.* As Errol Harris states, nations have become the illegitimate locus for democracy not only because their ethical legitimacy is called into question (they can no longer protect the common good of their populations) but also because their "juristic" legitimacy (or rightful power) is negated:

> National sovereign independence therefore has proved fatally inimical to the solution of world problems. Yet it is on the resolution of these global difficulties that the welfare of peoples and the very survival of humankind depends. The national sovereign state can no longer effectively protect its citizens from devastation in war, nor can it protect their living standards and maintain the amenities of life in the face of environmental deterioration.... In short, the national state now lacks the one and only justification for the exercise of sovereign power, the fostering of national prosperity and security. Its ethical character has been undermined, and its title to be juristically supreme is no longer valid. (2000a: 70-71)

With terrorist attacks possible any time or place, with high speed weapons like cruise missiles capable of evading radar and slamming into population centers at any time, with developing space-based weapons, with nuclear weapons capable of being launched half way around the world into space and raining down on a country within a twenty minute space of time, the claim of sovereign nations to be ethically and juristically supreme is entirely falsified. Only a pacified world order can restore democracy to the internal governments of the nations. And this can happen only if the nations federate under planetary democracy and abandon militarism for the due-process rule of law.

Chapter Nine

A Nonviolent Peace System for Spaceship Earth

The Anatomy of a Holistic World Community

The ultimate problem of production is the production of human beings. To this end, the production of goods is intermediate and auxiliary. It is by this standard that the present system stands condemned. "Security" is a means, and although an indispensable social means it is not the end....The means have to be implemented by a social-economic system that establishes and uses the means for the production of free human beings associating with one another on terms of equality. Then and only then will these means be an integral part of the end, not frustrated and self-defeating, bringing new evils and generating new problems.

John Dewey

Democracy and violence can go ill together. The States that are today nominally democratic have either to become frankly totalitarian or, if they are to become truly democratic, they must become courageously nonviolent. It is a blasphemy to say nonviolence can be practiced only by individuals and never by nations which are composed of individuals.

Mahatma Gandhi

The philosophy of nonviolence that has been developed through much of the twentieth century has made an indispensable contribution to all theories of legitimate transformative social change. Yet the implications of the philosophy of nonviolence are often not well understood. Nonviolence is integral to the realization of authentic democracy on our planet, just as it is integral to creating a global economics of universal prosperity rather than today's agonizing scarcity for sixty percent of the Earth's people. It is also, of course, integral to the process of world demilitarization and the activation of a civilized world order for the first time in history.

9.1 The Philosophy of Nonviolence and World Law

Neither Mahatma Gandhi nor most of the subsequent philosophers of nonviolent transformative social change repudiated all use of force. Gandhi himself said that if one lacked the courage to fight injustice through nonviolent means, one should pick up a gun. Worse than using a gun to fight injustice is cowardice: doing nothing, refusing to act: "I have been repeating over and over again that he who cannot protect himself or his nearest and dearest or their honor by nonviolently facing death may and ought to do so by violently dealing with the oppressor" (1987: 144).

What Gandhi advocates in this and similar passages is not violence "as a last resort" or a "slippery slope" that opens the door to militarized violence. Rather, he is pointing out that nonviolence means an activation of the universal potential of our humanity that is within us all. Nonviolence is the actualization of true courage, honor, faithfulness, integrity, and loyalty to truth and justice. It is not that the use of force is always prohibited, but rather that our selves and our institutions must be premised on clinging to gigantic Truth (*Satyagraha*). If we do this, then the use of force will nearly always be the *minimum necessary* to protect everyone involved. It can be the actions of a civilian police force or individual self-defense, but it can never be militarized violence, which always intentionally seeks to harm a perceived "enemy."

The philosophy of nonviolence is not a utopian ideal of starry-eyed "pacifists" placing their bodies for slaughter before implacable military machines. It remains a pragmatic and common-sense understanding directed toward breaking the infamous "cycle of violence" that has characterized most human history to date and toward activating our higher human possibilities. It understands, as Gandhi did, that the use of force is sometimes necessary, despite the fact that every human being has inalienable rights and an inviolable dignity. We live in a concrete world filled with dangerous institutions, dangerous forces, and occasionally dangerous people. The task is to deal practically and justly with all these dangers without ourselves sinking into the cycle of violence and the corruption it entails and to move ourselves and the world forward substantially beyond these dangers. The task placed upon all of us is to deal with these dangers morally and pragmatically while transforming the world system beyond its present nightmare of violence and corruption.

Legitimate social change within truly democratic societies, of course, is always necessarily nonviolent. Democratic societies institutionalize provisions (through numerous channels) for citizen participation: discussion, public debate, freedom of information, public demonstrations, referendums, election of officials, and both individual and collective forms of action. Societies that are not truly democratic (all national governments today) institutionalize empty forms of citizen participation as a propaganda mechanism for legitimating their authority while in reality relegating decision-making to special interest groups like corporations, the rich, dominant elites, those with "security clearances," etc.

The rule of universally applicable and fairly enforced laws is the foundation for a largely nonviolent society. Gandhi identified the institutional violence of Indian society with those features that did not conform to this pattern: the vast disparity between rich and poor, colonial privilege for a certain group, untouchability, etc. But in an interdependent world possessing horrendous high speed weapons, as well as vast inequalities, there can be no democratically run, nonviolent society anywhere unless there is the rule of democratic world law that ends most institutional violence everywhere on Earth. Only such world law can eliminate the primary causes of imperialism, militarism, subversive violence, state terrorism, and private terrorism.

For Gandhi, and for the philosophy of nonviolence, genuine democracy very definitely requires a tremendous reduction in the gap between rich and poor. In this, he agrees with John Dewey who argued, we saw, that progress in democracy necessarily required a democratization of the sphere of economic decision-making as well as the sphere of politics. The *Earth Constitution* is premised on both these aspects of genuine democracy, one that institutionalizes real provisions for citizen participation and nonviolent change and the other that creates a global economics of prosperity and removes the possibility of massive exploitation of the poor by the rich.

We have seen that the *Earth Constitution* is premised on the moral foundations of the sovereignty of the people of Earth, universal human rights, the principle of *unity in diversity*, human equality, and the right of all to a freedom compatible with the equal freedom of everyone else. For this reason, establishing a genuine world democracy requires removing the institutional violence of economic scarcity, manipulation, and exploitation: "That economics is untrue," Gandhi writes, "which ignores or disregards moral values" (1972: 118).

In *The Morality of Law* (1969), Professor Lon L. Fuller raises sharp objections to all those theories of law that assert or assume "that the distinguishing mark of law consists in the use of coercion or force" (p. 108). He argues correctly that coercion is a necessary feature of law but only insofar as there needs to be some "efficacy" in which people are encouraged to behave in cooperative law abiding ways and discouraged from behaving in socially destructive ways (pp. 108-109). He points out that the mechanisms by which people can be induced to behave in certain ways are vastly larger than the threat of coercion. In a world society united around our common humanity and the principle that the diversity of all can only be effectively protected through the solidarity of all under world law, the incentives for obedience to the law can be very broad and creative indeed.

Nonviolence includes the activation of universal moral values in every sphere of life, since it is premised on the foundation of nearly all moral values, that is, the inviolable dignity of the human person. Those moral values that claim to respect this dignity yet try to legitimize war, economic relations that allow mass poverty and misery, or "security" arrangements that protect dominant elites from social change are false and hypocritical. Nonviolence does not abjure all use of force, but insists that social arrangements be transformed so that the use of force becomes the absolute minimum of what is necessary (within rigorous due process restraints) for the protection of everyone equally.

"The extension of the law of nonviolence in the domain of economics," Gandhi writes, "means nothing less than the introduction of moral values as a factor to be considered when regulating international commerce" (1972: 118). This must be true on a global scale. "Immediately as the spirit of exploitation is gone," he asserts, "armaments will be felt as a positive unbearable burden. Real disarmament cannot come unless the nations of the world cease to exploit one another" (1972: 112).

All militarism under the world system, like all terrorism, derives from the same undemocratic root. For when genuine democracy does not exist (and it cannot exist without democratic world government), then the only alternative is to institutionalize violence: to use the police and the law to repress the poor, to protect the privileged, to institutionalize lying and deceit to the public, to militarize society with the bogus threat of implacable enemies everywhere, to imperialistically control the wealth-producing processes of the world to the advantage of the already wealthy and powerful in the imperial centers of capital (Smith 2005a).

World revolution through world law means founding genuine universal democracy for the first time in history. This necessarily entails not only activating citizen participation in governing but modifying global economics to a system of truly universal prosperity. "If the recognized leaders of mankind," Gandhi writes, "who have control over the engines of destruction were wholly to renounce their use, with full knowledge of the implications, permanent peace can be obtained. This is clearly impossible without the Great Powers of the Earth renouncing their imperialistic design. This again seems impossible without great nations ceasing to believe in soul-destroying competition and to desire to multiply wants and, therefore, increase their material possessions" (1972: 111).

The "Great Powers" can only achieve this if they are federated within democratic world government and subject to demilitarization within an economic system that maintains their prosperity while also creating prosperity for everyone else on the planet. They can only achieve this if their mutual security is assured by effective, enforceable world law that demilitarizes all nations and organizations equally. And they can only achieve this if it is demanded by the people of Earth.

Gandhi introduced a resolution to the Indian National Congress that was passed on 5 August 1942. It read:

> While the Indian National Congress must primarily be concerned with independence and defense of India in this hour of danger, the Committee is of the opinion that the future peace, security, and ordered progress of the world demand a world federation of free nations, and on no other basis can the problems of the modern world be solved. Such a world federation would ensure the freedom of its constituent nations, the prevention of aggression and exploitation by one nation over another, the protection of national ministries, the advancement of all backward areas and peoples, and the pooling of the world's resources for the common good of all (Hudgens 1986: 14)

This is a very close description of what the *Constitution for the Federation of Earth* offers. Gandhi understood that a nonviolent world order is not only a spiritual commitment on the part of persons everywhere but must be institutionalized both politically and economically in the form of democratic world government that is federated at all levels of governing.

"The entire social order has got to be reconstructed," he says, "a society based on nonviolence cannot nurture any other ideal" (1972: 120). "Democracy and violence can ill go together," he writes, "it is a blasphemy to say that nonviolence can only be practiced by individuals and never by nations which are a compound of individuals" (ibid. p. 134). Given the cycle of violence today that also protects massive institutionalized violence, founding a demilitarized democratic world government is the most practical and common sense course of action for humanity.

A reconstructed social order of this kind would necessarily be founded on truth, freedom of speech, inquiry, and press, rather than on manipulation of the public by dominant elites through deception and propaganda. Its democratic framework and its ways of dealing with law-breaking: with police practices, with due process procedures, with court practices, with sentencing, forms of punishment, and imprisonment would all cultivate the spirit of nonviolence in the population. People would see for themselves that their rights were respected and that equality, freedom, and justice were promoted. Such government would by no means eliminate conflict. Rather, it would institutionalize nonviolent ways of dealing with conflict on all levels. Nonviolence does not eliminate conflict, Gandhi asserts. It eliminates the intention to harm one's opponent:

> To say or write a distasteful word is surely not violent especially when the speaker or writer believes it to be true. The essence of violence is that there must be a violent intention behind a thought, word, or act, i.e., an intention to do harm to the opponent so-called. False notions of propriety or fear of wounding susceptibilities often deter people from saying what they mean and ultimately land them on the shores of hypocrisy. But if nonviolence of thought is to be evolved in individuals or societies or nations, truth has to be told, however harsh or unpopular it may appear to be at the moment. (1972: 91)

Can police be trained to arrest lawbreakers with the intention of using the minimum force necessary to secure the safety of themselves, the suspect, and any innocent bystanders? Of course. In some European nations, police are already being trained in such methods of apprehension and arrest. Conflict can be democratically institutionalized in a way that minimizes both violence and the tendency to violence in dissidents and lawbreakers. North American philosopher Robert Holmes advocates a similar practical understanding of the philosophy of nonviolence:

> This doesn't require changing human nature or transforming the world into a community of saints. It does require recognizing that if we don't cherish the human person, there is no point to the many other activities and strivings that consume our time; no point to saving the environment unless we value the beings that inhabit it; no virtue in self-sacrifice when at the expense of the lives and happiness of others. It does require a massive commitment of time, energy, and moral and financial resources to exploring nonviolent ways of getting along in the world.

The aim should not be to end conflict. That would be utopian and might not even be desirable. The aim should be to develop nondestructive ways of dealing with conflict. Violence by its very nature cannot do that. Nonviolence can. As Gandhi demonstrated, rather than approaching conflict with a view to trying to prevail at any cost, it's possible to approach it with a view to trying to see that the truth prevail – trying to see that the best solution emerge, whether or not it be one to which you were predisposed at the outset. People can learn this. They can be trained in techniques to implement it. They can incorporate it in their institutions. (1990: 139)

Given the truth that nonviolence can be institutionalized to minimize the use of force in human relations, what will the nonviolent democratic world government look like? How will its police behave? How will it deal with terrorism, killers, or violent dissidents? The *Constitution for the Federation of Earth* provides the framework for a nonviolent world order. We have seen that this framework requires both genuine democracy and general economic prosperity with an end to economic exploitation. Article 10, "The Enforcement System," makes the following declaration concerning enforcement by the World Police force:

(1) The enforcement of world law and world legislation shall apply directly to individuals, and individuals shall be held responsible for compliance with world law and world legislation regardless of whether the individuals are acting in their own capacity or as agents or officials of governments at any level or of the institutions of governments, or as agents or officials of corporations, organizations, associations or groups of any kind.
(2) When world law or world legislation or decisions of the world courts are violated, the Enforcement System shall operate to identify and apprehend the individuals responsible for violations.
(3) Any enforcement action shall not violate the civil and human rights guaranteed under this World Constitution.
(4) The enforcement of world law and world legislation shall be carried out in the context of a non military world federation wherein all member nations shall disarm as a condition for joining and benefitting from the world federation, subject to Article X VII, Sec. C 8 and D 6. The Federation of Earth and World Government under this World Constitution shall neither keep nor use weapons of mass destruction.
(5) Those agents of the enforcement system whose function shall be to apprehend and bring to court violators of world law and world legislation shall be equipped only with such weapons as are appropriate for the apprehension of the individuals responsible for violations.
(6) The enforcement of world law and world legislation under this World Constitution shall be conceived and developed primarily as the processes of effective design and administration of world law and world legislation to serve the welfare of all people on Earth, with equity and

justice for all, in which the resources of Earth and the funds and the credits of the World Government are used only to serve peaceful human needs, and none used for weapons of mass destruction or for war making capabilities.

This set of six principles defines the framework for the operation of the World Police and the possession of weapons. No legitimate government or democracy requires a military apparatus, since all democratic legislation applies to individuals, not governments, institutions, or corporations. Militaries are organized for mass destruction of some perceived "enemy," not for the apprehension of individuals according to the due process of law.

Once the international anarchy and chaos of the system of "sovereign" nation-states is replaced with real world law and a federation of nations, militaries will no longer be necessary. "Nations will no longer lift up their sword against nations." At this point, enforcement will only need to apply to individuals. Therefore, the police under democratic world law "shall be equipped only with such weapons as are appropriate for the apprehension of the individuals responsible for violations." They will possess no weapons of war. The triumph of civilization will have begun.

Since a constitution provides a framework, not a body of specific laws, the question of what weapons allowed the World Police is left to the World Parliament to decide. However, they must be only those necessary to apprehend individuals. All tanks, warships, warplanes, bombs, missiles, etc., are necessarily excluded since these are military weapons, not those necessary to apprehend individuals using a minimum of force while protecting the rights and safety of all concerned. The philosophy of nonviolence implies exactly this social transformation to the point where the use of force is minimized in human relations.

(Note: a version of section 9.1 was first published as part of Chapter Six of *World Revolution Through World Law*, IED Press, 2005.)

9.2 Civilian Police versus Military Force

It is very important here to distinguish between the role of civilian police and the role of military force, including a militarized police force. Military institutions destroy democracy and freedom both within and without individual nation-states, as we have seen, for democracy itself requires a nonviolent institutional framework that is incompatible with militarism. This is why the world government cannot be militarized, not because of some utopian idea that human beings will be without conflict or without requiring the occasional use of force.

The innermost meaning of democracy as a world society organized as a community of rights on the principle of *unity in diversity* is only possible under non-military democratic world government. Any militarized society will inhibit the solidarity and mutual respect among all people that as at the heart of genuine democracy. Military doctrine and practice, we have seen, are incompatible with with the principles of both due process of law and individual accountability.

Civilian police, on the other hand (the only kind of police allowed under the *Constitution*) are accountable to the citizens for their behavior, their obedience to the law, their use of force, and their job security. We already have a measure of this in many cities that require a civilian review board to monitor police behavior. Civilian police are normally mandated to use (and can be trained to use) the minimum force necessary to apprehend individuals suspected of crimes. But these police under the Earth Federation will operate on a qualitatively different basis from that of police within traditional sovereign nation-states.

The World Police are required to respect the rights of all citizens, to "protect and serve." A nonviolent set of governmental institutions would insist that police are highly trained and educated in the proper function of a civilian police force. Police within a genuine democracy are mandated to use the minimum necessary force, and to make every effort to use non-lethal force. Their role will be that of peacemakers and community builders, in addition to being merely law enforcers.

It only makes sense that their weapons would be more and more *non-lethal* as technology in non-lethal weaponry advances. Stun guns, propelled body nets, non-lethal darts, and other technology of non-lethal weaponry yet to be developed will likely become the stock and trade of the World Police. It may well be that in most instances the World Police will not find it necessary to carry weapons at all. There is much evidence that de-escalation of the readiness for violence tends to result in the de-escalation of violence. The World Police are under mandate to weaken and ultimately break the cycle of violence.

A civilian police force within a framework of real democratic justice, respect for individual rights, and freedom will be tasked to continually examine how it can accomplish its mission of effectively apprehending criminals while at the same time continually maximizing the safety of themselves, those apprehended, and innocent bystanders. Very high quality training and education will necessarily supplement whatever weapons are authorized by the World Parliament. Police will be trained in nonviolent techniques of apprehension and arrest (and in self-defense techniques such as judo) as well as in the techniques of minimum use of necessary force, de-escalation, and conflict resolution.

The *Constitution* also leaves open for the World Parliament to legislate what weapons are acceptable for *private individuals*. A constitution is not a blueprint. Many decisions must be made through the democratic processes set up by the *Constitution*. However, the Provisional World Parliament has already passed provisional world laws in this regard specifying that individuals may posses only those weapons also permitted to the World Police.

Provisional world laws are not binding on the established World Parliament once it has been activated. They serve as guidelines, models, and a preliminary groundwork. This particular provisional world law of the Provisional Parliament was controversial and by no means unanimous, yet it appears consistent with the *Constitution*'s founding premise of the dignity and inviolable rights of every individual on Earth, including the right to self-defense. We saw above that Gandhi affirmed even the use of force in defense of one's self and loved-ones if a person lacked the capacity to do this nonviolently.

The Provisional World Parliament has followed the *Constitution* closely by outlawing the design, development, sale, transportation, or possession of all weapons of war for individuals, groups, corporations, governments, and even the world government. Weapons of war are illegal under the *Constitution* even though the World Parliament will define what personal weapons are available to world citizens and the World Police. If the established World Parliament sees fit to follow the Provisional World Parliament in allowing individuals the same weapons as it allows the World Police, this may serve as an incentive for the World Police to develop ever-more and better non-lethal forms of apprehension and arrest and to progressively eliminate lethal weapons. Article 12 of the *Constitution* gives each citizen of the Earth Federation the following rights:

- Safety of person from arbitrary or unreasonable arrest, detention, exile, search or seizure; requirement of warrants for searches and arrests.
- Prohibition against physical or psychological duress or torture during any period of investigation, arrest, detention or imprisonment, and against cruel or unusual punishment.
- Right of habeas corpus; no ex post facto laws; no double jeopardy; right to refuse self incrimination or the incrimination of another.
- Prohibition against private armies and paramilitary organizations as being threats to the common peace and safety.
- Safety of property from arbitrary seizure; protection against exercise of the power of eminent domain without reasonable compensation.
- Right of privacy of person, family and association; prohibition against surveillance as a means of political control.

The security, safety, and freedom of citizens is clearly a primary focus of the *Constitution*. And, given what we have seen in this volume, it should be clear that the Earth Federation will be nonviolent regardless of whatever stun-guns, handguns, pepper spray canisters, or rifles citizens are allowed to possess. If people feel they need to possess these items, they will do so. But given the framework of a deeply nonviolent society that is built by the *Constitution* (in which true democracy is realized and institutionalized violence and exploitation are eliminated), it is unlikely that many will feel this need.

The law could easily maximize their freedoms in this regard without the fear that there would be many people using such weapons to break the law or do violence. This list of rights possesses a fundamental difference from the U.N. Universal Declaration of Human Rights that duplicates many of the rights in Article 12. For the U.N. Declaration is "merely symbolic." It has no legal force. Whereas under the *Earth Constitution*, the people of Earth have an enforceable legal right to these protections, and numerous effective legal options through which to ensure these protections are carried out.

As Gandhi made clear, if we will create real democracy on Earth, and real economic justice and prosperity on Earth, then we must *institutionalize nonviolence*. With today's system of militarized "sovereign" nation-states and vast disparities between extreme wealth and extreme poverty, we have *institutionalized violence*. This violence requires the military to enforce its global system of injustice and exploitation. But if we ratify the *Constitution for the Federation of Earth* and create world institutions premised on the dignity, freedom, and equality of every person on Earth, we will eliminate the perceived need not only for the military but also for most personal or terrorist violence. And what is even more fundamental, we will have laid the groundwork for a transformation of the human spirit.

Today, the human spirit is distorted by the violent institutions that pervade our lives. The process of realizing a democratic world order under the *Constitution* may be marred by having to contend with the violence of the nation-states that currently eat, sleep, and breathe violence through their every institution. As we have seen above, the people of Earth (and each of us insofar as we act from what is universal in ourselves) not only have the right, but the duty to create democratic world government and exit the immoral state of *defacto* war and institutionalized violence under which we are currently forced to live.

Under Article Nineteen of the *Constitution*, the people of Earth have the mandate to elaborate the institutions of *provisional world government* until such time as the *Constitution* has been formally ratified according to the provisions set forth in Article Seventeen. This means we are building what is sometimes called a "parallel government" to the ones currently falsely claiming legitimacy in the world. This "parallel government" is not a competing claim to nation-statehood, of course, but includes the invitation to all national governments to reclaim their legitimacy and integrity by becoming part of the emerging Earth Federation. In this regard, it is not "parallel" at all but the entity representing the sovereignty of the people of Earth capable of restoring the legitimacy of the national governments as well as eliminating their violent and unjust characteristics.

Yet in our efforts to elaborate the infrastructure of world government, members of the emerging Earth Federation avail themselves of many of the techniques of nonviolent action. Professor Gene Sharp in Part Two of *The Politics of Nonviolent Action* entitled *The Methods of Nonviolent Action*, lists 198 techniques or methods of nonviolent struggle. Number 198 is listed as "dual sovereignty and parallel government." Sharp writes:

> This method involves the creation of a new government, or continued loyalty to an existing rival government to that of the opponent. If the parallel government receives overwhelming support from the populace, it may replace the opponent's established government....This general phenomenon has occurred in a variety of situations and is by no means a product of twentieth century revolutions. (1985: 423)

Sharp goes on to describe historical examples of when this method was used, often without conscious intent as a nonviolent method. He describes the Netherlands struggle against the Spanish king in 1575-77, the conflict in England between Charles and the Long Parliament during the 1640s, the struggle during U.S. revolutionary times between the Continental Congress and British rule, "Door's Rebellion" in Rhode Island in 1841-42, the Russian Revolution of 1905, and again of 1917, the general strike in Winnipeg, Canada, in 1919, the Indian struggle against the British, especially during the 1930-31 campaign, and the contest in China between the Japanese and the "Border Government" during the 1930s.

Given this long history of transformative movements developing an alternative government to replace or parallel an existing government, one can say that the work of the Provisional World Parliament and the members of the emerging Earth Federation are definitely engaged with time-honored methods of nonviolent action. As the institutions of the Federation develop (assuming the *Constitution* has not yet been ratified by the people and nations of Earth) we will be elaborating the world ministries, the World Parliament, the world courts, and the world enforcement system of police and attorneys general.

The World Police may be called upon to apprehend criminals (for example, any persons engaged in weapons research, design, manufacture, transport, sale, purchase, or deployment, which are all criminal activities under existing provisional world law). From what has been said above, it should be clear that even the provisional World Police will be well trained in what it means to be a civilian police officer within a genuine democracy. That is, they will be trained to use the minimum force necessary to apprehend the suspect, protect themselves, ensure the safety of innocent bystanders, and follow due-process procedures ensuring the rights of all.

In addition, citizens (as well as the World Ombudsmus) will be free to monitor the behavior of the police to be sure that they fulfill their function of reducing the use of force to a minimum. Provisional World Legislative Act 14.3 reads in part as follows:

Civil Empowerment. Behavior of World Police Officers while on duty may be freely audited by both non-interfering private Earth citizens and by the World Ombudsmus, to assure compliance to least necessary force and to appropriate behavior on the part of the Enforcement System. The World Ombudsmus and Earth Citizens may file legal complaints or legal charges, and seek rectification for damages arising from the improper use of weapons. At which time the World Police begins its formation and forever thereafter, the World Police Force may develop, use and possess only weapons legal to the citizens of the Earth Federation without requirement of permit, registration or disclosure.
(http://www.worldproblems.net/english/legislation/full_texts)

The World Police under the Earth Federation will be truly servants and protectors of the people as this passage states. Under provisional world law as it now stands, world citizens may possess any weapons possessed by the world police "without requirement of permit, registration or disclosure." Nonviolence, as well as the right of citizens to self-defense, is therefore institutionalized within both the *Constitution* and Provisional World Law.

This is practical and commonsense nonviolence in action. It does not demand some *utopian* abjuring of all reasonable use of force. It clearly forbids an "intention to do harm to the opponent" that Gandhi says is a defining characteristic of violence. It does not assume some "peaceful human nature" or conflict-free future for humanity. Human intelligence can build communities of rights and solidarity. "Human nature" is extremely flexible. When the levels of violence, fear, and tension are reduced, the level of violence is also reduced.

Nonviolence involves action in the service of authentic democracy, which is necessarily nonviolent to every extent possible. It is also action in the service of the nonviolent method of developing a "parallel government" that appeals to the allegiance to the people of Earth precisely because it is democratic, just, liberating, and nonviolent. Just as "violent means" inevitably lead to violent results (as the institutionalized violence of today's world illustrates), so nonviolent means are the only legitimate transformative strategy to realize a truly new and fundamental goal: a nonviolent world democracy of justice, freedom, equality, and peace.

9.3 Principles of Nonviolence behind the Institutionalization of Peace

In sections 1 and 2 of Chapter Eight, we examined the philosophical principles expounded by Immanuel Kant concerning human freedom, morality, and the categorical imperative. The key form of all moral principles is precisely their universality. They must be in principle valid for all persons confronted with this particular situation. The principle of universality implies the equality and dignity of all human beings. Therefore, Kant asserts that every person should be treated as an end in themselves, never merely as a means. Every person has intrinsic value: the dignity from which their inalienable human rights flow and their inviolability as a human being.

We saw that these principles are equivalent to the principle of autonomy in which valid moral principles are seen to flow from a free decision of one's practical reason or rational will. It is this subjective rational affirmation that makes them valid and is the reason why they cannot come from any heteronomous source. This, we saw, is a fundamental reason why military service is self-contradictory. One cannot universalize giving up one's rational autonomy, for this undercuts the very possibility of moral action and our intrinsic dignity as human beings.

Finally, the universality of the categorical imperative implies the kingdom of ends: a world society in which all human beings treat one another as ends and in which government is premised on the fundamental reality that all human beings are intrinsically valuable and should be socially related to one another as such. The kingdom of ends is a society of peace, just as it is also necessarily a society of freedom, since free rational choice is the foundation of all moral principles and human dignity. In these principles we have the philosophical basis for the institutionalization of peace and the moral impossibility of our present world system of institutionalized violence and war.

It is this inviolability of all human beings, together with the gigantic truth that we are all one in our fundamental humanity or species-being, that is at the heart of the philosophy and practice of nonviolence. Above we have seen some of the principles that Mahatma Gandhi elaborated as the principles behind *satyagraha* as a "clinging to truth" or "soul-force." Similar principles are expressed by Martin Luther King, Jr., in *Stride Toward Freedom* and other works. King identifies seven principles at the heart of the philosophy of nonviolence on which I will draw here to articulate the principles that must be institutionalized if government is ever to be constructed on the basis of nonviolence.

The *first* is that nonviolence is active resistance to evil and injustice, whereas military service may be active physically but is passive spiritually. This principle relates to Kant's formula of autonomy. To be active spirituality is to legislate the maxims of one's actions on universal grounds. Military service places the individual under a command structure in which this power is largely given up. In practice, responsibility is deferred upward to commanders and the most horrible actions are performed by those obeying orders.

To institutionalize peace in the first place must be to make military service illegal so that all citizens can be held accountable for their actions. Military service in nation-states is not "service to one's country" under the rule of democratic law. It is a function of the lawlessness that exists between nations and the refusal of nation-states to recognize any law above themselves. Non-military community service for the common good, on the other hand, is a perfectly reasonable requirement of government and can be the subject of democratically legislated laws.

The *second* principle of nonviolent action outlined by King involves effort directed toward reconciliation and redemption of the conflict, not toward the defeat and domination of the perceived enemy. Human life is filled with conflict among religions, ethnic groups, nations, races, cultures, and individuals. Is it possible to create governmental structures built around an inclusiveness that respects all who are party to conflicts? There are many programs in conflict resolution that exist today, some of them associated with national governments. These programs serve as a model for building world government structures. A world government premised on truly universal human rights and directed toward the institutionalization of peace would necessarily act from such an inclusive orientation.

Third, nonviolence seeks to defeat injustice, not people, whereas militarized violence seeks the destruction of people and their life-support systems. Under good government, the distinction between justice and injustice need not be a vague slogan used to cover up an oppressive reality. If justice is the primary consideration, rather than military or some other "victory," then conflicts can be dealt with effectively rather than repressed or manipulated from the motivation of strategic interests.

Fourth, nonviolence involves voluntary suffering or willingness for self-sacrifice (*tapasya*), whereas military action attempts to inflict suffering on others in ways that often make reconciliation impossible. Article 12 of the *Earth Constitution* gives citizens "freedom of assembly, association, organization, petition, and peaceful demonstration." When people deeply believe that injustice has taken place and are willing to nonviolently suffer to stop the injustice, these factors can and must be included in the recognition of those governmental institutions responsible for dealing with the conflict: courts, police, prosecutors, Ombudsmus, etc. A bill was passed at the Eleventh Session of the Provisional World Parliament in July, 2009, in Nainital, India, that legally empowers and protects nonviolent civil disobedience for the citizens of the Earth Federation – ensuring that the *reasoning* behind this disobedience be heard in court. Civil disobedience involving voluntary suffering is clearly worthy of respect by government institutions. The concerns of citizens willing to take risks by breaking the law deserve careful government attention.

Fifth, nonviolence treats the opponent as a "thou," whereas military and violent action treats the "enemy" as an "it." We have seen that this is why military service cannot be included in any government that wishes to institutionalize peace, since to obey orders to kill strangers who one does not know regardless of their due process rights necessarily includes a denial of their personhood and their dignity as human beings. A world government based on universal human rights solves crime, violence, and conflict through investigation, apprehension, and trial by due process of law for all citizens. Such practices can be premised on the human rights of all suspects. Unlike military service, they are capable of treating all persons as a "thou" while still enforcing the laws.

Sixth, Martin Luther King, Jr. says that the person of nonviolence acts from oneness with God, the source of being, or a sense of the sacredness of justice, etc. Government for all human beings cannot, of course, legitimately affirm any particular religious beliefs or religions. However, government can fulfill King's principle insofar as it recognizes the inviolability of the human person and human rights. The commitment to human rights affirms our human dignity in a way that requires no religious beliefs but functions with the same absoluteness and sacredness as traditional religious commitments. Utilitarian grounds or pragmatic grounds are not sufficient to establish inviolability of human rights (cf. Martin 2008: Ch. 7).

People in government need not believe in a transcendent ground for these rights but must be committed, under the *Earth Constitution*, to treat them as inviolable. The *Constitution*, therefore, calls these rights "inalienable." It is this commitment to a set of inalienable rights that can be institutionalized. The prologue to the Article 12 Bill of Rights of the

Earth Constitution makes this commitment and hence the determination to institutionalize peace:

> The inhabitants and citizens of Earth who are within the Federation of Earth shall have certain inalienable rights defined hereunder. It shall be mandatory for the World Parliament, the World Executive, and all organs and agencies of the World Government to honor, implement, and enforce these rights, as well as for national governments of all member nations in the Federation of Earth to do likewise. Individuals or groups suffering violation or neglect of such rights shall have full recourse through the World Ombudsmus, the Enforcement System and the World Courts for redress of grievances.

Seventh, nonviolence is based on truthfulness, honesty, and openness whereas violence and militarism require secrecy, lies, propaganda, and deceit. A world filled with the institutionalized violence of domination and exploitation by the ruling elites in the imperial centers of capital will necessarily be permeated by the *spiritual violence* of lies, deceit, propaganda, and distortion. The same multinational corporations who operate in league with imperial governments to control the wealth-producing process in their own interest at the expense of the poor worldwide also control, own, or influence the mass media in the imperial centers. Just as imperial governments spew forth an ideology that justifies and covers up what is really going on so the privately owned corporate mass media spew forth similar ideological constructions. A world of institutionalized violence and overt (military) violence is necessarily complemented by the spiritual violence of massive propaganda and deceit.

The conversion to institutionalized peace eliminates the need for government and the media to lie. Just as the advocate of nonviolence insists on truthfulness and openness (since if one is not trying to destroy or exploit an opponent, one has no need to lie) so government must be committed to truth and institutionally predicated on truthfulness. To set up a system on this basis (that includes even privately-owned media) is not difficult. The corporation must be stripped of its artificial legal personhood (now common under the system of violence) and have transparency required by law. Corporations must not be allowed to illegitimately influence elections or otherwise legally put government officials in their debt. Freedom of information, research, and knowledge of government actions must be citizen rights under law. These are indeed the arrangements under the *Earth Constitution* and the acts of the Provisional World Parliament to date.

All seven of these principles embodied within democratic world government constitute a transformation of the old order of institutionalized violence into a new order structurally organized for peace. They are not utopian ideals but the practical consequences of the way we organize our institutions and the basic premises from which we operate. Philosophically, the framers of the *Earth Constitution* realized this fact. The Preamble to the *Earth Constitution* includes the following statements:

> Aware that the traditional concept of security through military defense is a total illusion both for the present and for the future;
> Aware of the misery and conflicts caused by ever increasing disparity between rich and poor;
> Conscious of our obligation to posterity to save Humanity from imminent and total annihilation....
> We, citizens of the world, hereby resolve to establish a world federation to be governed in accordance with this constitution for the Federation of Earth.

As we saw in Chapter Seven, the Preamble abolishes war and the institutional violence of the disparity between rich and poor on behalf of "a new age, when war shall be outlawed and peace prevail; when the earth's total resources shall be equitably used for human welfare; and when basic human rights and responsibilities shall be shared by all without discrimination." The founding philosophical principles of the Earth Federation involve nonviolent social structures, nonviolent economics, and the establishing of a nonviolent human community for the Earth. The triumph for civilization demands nothing less.

9.4 The Institutionalization of Peace

Just as war is *institutionalized* within the nation-state system and in the economics of global capitalism so peace, if it is ever to occur, must be institutionalized. We are often under a misunderstanding regarding "law." Law is not a necessary coercion placed over human beings who have a tendency to violence and require its force to keep them in order. Rather, human beings without law are already in a state of *defacto* violence with respect to one another, for they have no objective, common universal principles through which to relate to one another as equals: nonviolently and democratically. By entering into civil society under democratic government, John Locke asserts, men "have excluded force" (1963: 464). Peace and nonviolence can only be institutionalized through democratically legislated, universally enforceable laws.

Exactly the same holds true regarding nation-states. As we saw in Chapters Four through Six, the sovereign nation-state system is inherently violent, for there is no common set of objective universal principles over sovereign nations by which they might relate to one another nonviolently and democratically. The few small, weak nations that do not have a military in today's world have security arrangements with states that do have a military and rely on these states for protection within an intrinsically violent world. But they themselves, insofar as they are not willing to recognize universal law over themselves in the form of Earth Federation, remain part of the violence – scorners of law, freedom, and democratic equality for everyone on Earth.

Peace not only requires that we all place ourselves under universal democratically legislated laws, it requires that we address the vast inequalities of the world, eliminating poverty, disease, and deprivation as far as possible. Only an Earth Federation can accomplish this, eliminating from the world imperial and exploitative relationships among nations. Peace requires that we preserve our global environment and that we equitably share the hardships that destruction of the environment is rapidly bringing upon humankind.

Indeed, the institutionalization of peace under world government will require substantially solving all the multidimensional global crises that today plague humankind: to prevent war and secure disarmament, to protect universal human rights and equal opportunities in life, to obtain for all people the conditions for equitable economic and social development, to regulate the use of world resources and other international processes, to protect the environment and the ecological fabric of life, and to solve any unforeseen problems that transcend national boundaries.

This list, we have seen, recounts the six broad functions of the world government listed in Article 1 of the *Constitution for the Federation of Earth*. Poverty and exploitation can only be eliminated by law, but the interdependent planetary crises of our day make it clear that poverty can only be solved if the problem of the environment is also solved, and only if militarism is solved, and only if human rights and freedom are protected. The world order is deeply interrelated and interdependent. Just as all the planetary crises are interdependent (e.g. poverty, militarism, environmental degradation, etc.) and are consequences of the fragmented system of nation-states in conjunction with monopoly capitalism so democratic world government must address all these aspects of the world order *simultaneously* in order to institutionalize peace. The solution must be holistic.

We have seen above that all military service is both immoral and self-contradictory for individuals. These principles are now embodied in law, as they should be. Citizens of Earth within the Federation are protected by law from having to do any form of military service. They cannot legally be conscripted by their nations or localities. As the Bill of Rights in Article 12 makes clear, people have the *right to peace*, just as they have the right to a healthy planetary environment, quality healthcare, and educational opportunities. Article 12.11 makes all military conscription illegal. Article 12.15 prohibits all private armies and paramilitary organizations. Article 17 requires all nations joining the Earth Federation to begin the process of demilitarization with simultaneous conversion of their economy and social order toward peace.

In the first stages of the emerging world government when all nations are not yet under the aegis of the Earth Federation, external nations will undoubtedly remain militarized. However, under the *Constitution* it is not possible for the Federation itself to militarize in response to these threats (Federation nations need not fully demilitarize until the second stage). Otherwise peace can never be established. The Earth Federation must deal with external militarized nations in the early stages of world government by showing the people of Earth (including those in the militarized nations) that it has established a new order that is to *everyone's* benefit. The purpose is to break the cycle of violence and war that has characterized all human history and that is intrinsic to the system of sovereign nation-states. This cycle can never be broken through military action, nor through the mouthing of pious ideals. It can only be broken through the *institutionalization* of peace.

One aspect of this effort has been the establishment of the World Disarmament Agency (WDA) that is tasked to eliminate all weapons of mass destruction from the Earth. The first session of the Provisional World Parliament in Brighton, England, (1982) created the World Disarmament Agency as World Legislative Act Number 1 (WLA 1). The act criminalizes not only possession of WMDs but their research, design, testing, transport, installation, maintenance, storage, buying, selling, or detonating. This is what is meant by the institutionalization of peace: the entire framework that made war and exploitation possible is transformed by the simple act of uniting human beings under a single constitution and legislating for peace across the spectrum of human activities.

The World Disarmament Agency is tasked to work with nations to systematically and methodically reduce and eliminate WMDs so that no nation feels vulnerable or threatened by the disarmament process. However, the systematic reduction and elimination of these horrendous inventions is not a voluntary process. The reason why no significant progress has been made in this direction under the current world system, despite many attempts and many treaties, is because under the nation-state system all treaties are voluntary.

The WDA is a governmental agency with the authority behind it of the World Parliament, the World Police, and the World Court System. Those not cooperating are held accountable as individuals. Those found designing, researching, transporting or otherwise involved with WMDs are arrested by the World Police and arraigned in court. Only the genuine rule of law can institutionalize peace, just as is now done *within* the borders many nation-states. Within stable nations with effective governments people are *disarmed* by law, that is, what weapons they are allowed to posses is regulated by law. To have the weapons one is allowed to possess regulated by law is to be effectively disarmed. As a private individual, I cannot buy a cruise missile or a nuclear submarine. In the chaos of sovereign nations, however, nations can be destabilized by having weapons smuggled in from outside. Criminal groups within the present international legal vacuum attempt to buy missiles or even nuclear weapons.

The Provisional World Parliament has also activated the Global Ministry of the Environment (WLA 9) within the framework of the *Earth Constitution* and created an Emergency Earth Rescue Administration (WLA 6) to work with the Global Ministry in reversing the process of climate collapse and environmental destruction. An Earth Federation Funding Corporation (WLA 7) has been created to fund the operations of these agencies. The global war system can only be transformed through changing the very premises of the system from sovereign nation-states to *unity in diversity* under world government. This requires dealing with the world system as a whole, which only world government can do. Peace can never be institutionalized unless the entire interconnected panoply of global problems can be dealt with simultaneously.

The Provisional World Parliament in its second session in New Delhi, India, (1985) created the World Commission on Terrorism to study terrorism, its causes, the specific complaints of groups behind terrorism, and to work with the World Police and the World Economic Development Organization (WLA 2), not only in prosecuting terrorists, but in eliminating the major causes of terrorism through creating a free, just, and equitable world order. The Commission on Terrorism carefully examines both local conflicts where terrorism has occurred and larger economic, social, and political causes of terrorism. It works with other governmental agencies not in a "war on terrorism" but to institutionalize a world of peace where the causes of most terrorism have been eliminated.

The World Peace Act (WLA 13), adopted by the sixth session of the Provisional World Parliament in Bangkok, Thailand, in 2003, extends the provisions of the WMDs prohibition passed in WLA 1. The act prohibits United Nations Security Council veto power so that the work of institutionalizing peace cannot be interfered with by the system that has institutionalized war (the U.N.). The act also initiates a worldwide minesweeping operation for the millions of mines that plague the civilian populations of the Earth, establishes incentives for conversion to less lethal munitions, and administers the disbanding of military forces.

Similarly, WLA 26, passed at the eighth session of the Provisional World Parliament in Lucknow, India, in 2004, delineates and establishes the educational system of the Earth Federation. The act establishes a broad set of curricular criteria for all public schools and institutes that receive support or funding from the Earth Federation. (Free public education through the pre-university level is a universal right under Article 13 of the *Earth Constitution*.) Within a broad, flexible framework geared to the level of students, all schools must require: study of the *Earth Constitution*, reflection on, and development of, their own "quality of life index," reflection on the requirements for world peace, development of their own *unity in diversity* index, and, similarly, development of a good government index.

In other words, students everywhere will be required to thoughtfully consider the *Earth Constitution*, what *unity in diversity* means, what constitutes a real quality of life (certainly not only material wealth), and the meaning of world peace and good government. Once again we see the multidimensional character of the institutionalization of peace. It cannot be done by disarmament alone if the economic, educational, and other systems are left untouched. It can only be accomplished by a unified effort directed to all major aspects of our presently failed world order. No ideology is imposed or suggested, for serious reflection alone will confirm the valid philosophical premises at the heart of the *Earth Constitution*.

The ninth session of the Provisional World Parliament in Tripoli, Libya, in 2006 passed WLA 32: enabling legislation for a Department of Conflict Resolution within the Federation of Earth. The Preamble to the act states that:

> A basic condition for preventing outbreaks of violence which the Enforcement System shall facilitate in every way possible, shall be to assure a fair hearing under nonviolent circumstances for any person or group having a grievance, and likewise to assure a fair opportunity for a just settlement of any grievance with due regard for the rights and welfare of all concerned.
> (http://www.worldproblems.net/english/legislation/full_texts_en_htm/wla_32_conflict_resolution_act.htm)

A central function of the Department of Conflict Resolution, with offices mandated in every part of the world, will be to give a fair hearing in a non-courtroom setting for all groups or persons having a serious grievance that might lead to violent conflict. Of course, under Article 11 of the *Earth Constitution*, all such groups already have available to them the Office of the World Ombudsmus, charged with protecting human rights everywhere on Earth. And under Article 9 they have available the World Court System that can legally address and enforce grievances involving a violation of law. But the institutionalization of peace requires a manifold of governmental organizations and programs designed to make peace a reality in human affairs: not just the temporary absence of war (so-called "negative peace") and not simply repression of the aspirations of oppressed groups. The Department of Conflict Resolution uses experts trained in conflict resolution worldwide to further ensure a world order premised on peace.

This clearly does not mean that the Earth Federation government will be weak or wishy-washy in the face of the immense conflicts tearing our world apart. On the contrary; we have seen that the *Earth Constitution* creates a planetary government and democratic community with sufficient authority to pacify the multi-dimensional violence of today's world disorder. As Hannah Arendt says "power needs no justification, being inherent in the very existence of political communities; what it does need is legitimacy," and she describes the way in which legitimacy in any form is *eroded* by violence. A nonviolent Earth Federation can and should be powerful.

When Dr. Robert Muller (later U.N. Assistant Secretary-General for 18 years) was a young law student in France of 1947, living amidst the devastation wrought by the World War, he won an essay contest on the subject of "world government" in which he wrote:

> It must be comprised of all the organs characteristic of government – legislative, executive, and judicial. It must have all humans as subjects. World government is very different from international government, which has been a bankruptcy, unable to provide humans with peace. There are needs that are common to all humanity.
>
> World government must not be a slave. It must be the master, and the State its servant. The notion of an army must be reduced to its true meaning, that of a police. Only this world police would be allowed to intervene and impose the sanctions of world rules. Many voices have been raised and have grown over the past 50 years, proof that the challenge is not utopian. (In Gillies 2003: 224)

The nation-states must be the "servants," and the people of Earth "the master." This principle is "not utopian," but the most fundamental common sense. The *Earth Constitution* and the Provisional World Parliament have taken many concrete steps to accomplish just that: a common sense way to eliminate structural violence and found a system that institutionally embodies peace, which can only mean effective democracy at the planetary level.

Chapter Ten

Conclusion: The Twenty-first Century Triumph of Civilization

Planetary Maturity, Nonviolent Institutions, and a Holistic Earth Community

The earth is the place that touches our skin, the place where we make our dwelling, our ecology. This is the origin of the dialectic of person and cosmos, the phenomenon of nature, as habitat.

From this earth, then, we gather wood, for we have discovered fire: wood is warmth now, and safety, and light.... Nourishing, welcoming, protecting, motherly earth! Earth, lively nature, splendor of dawns and sunsets, beauty of mountain streams, of the singing of the nightingales, of the terrible, bounding sea! Earth, mother of the sweet smelling rose.

Sin is the destruction of the work created by God. God's most perfect deed is the human person. But the earth, too, is the work of God. Its destruction is the annihilation of the locus of human history, of humanity, of the incarnation, and hence the gravest of ethical misdeeds.

Enrique Dussel

*The state of peace among men living side by side is not the natural state (status naturalis); the natural state is one of war. This does not always mean open hostilities, but at least an unceasing threat of war. A state of peace, therefore, must be **established**, for in order to be secured against hostility it is not sufficient that hostilities simply not be committed; and, unless this security is pledged to each by his neighbor (a thing that can occur only in a civil state), each may treat his neighbor, from whom he demands this security, as an enemy.*

Immanuel Kant

The "utopian surplus" that spills over into our awareness from art, literature, philosophy, morality, spiritual practices, religion, critical thought, and everyday living firmly establishes the insight that things do not have to be the way they are. There are reasons, causes, behind the way things are that can be modified, changed, or transformed. Our human situation is informed by "real and objective possibility" that has yet to be actualized. It is this insight that animated the framers of the *Earth Constitution* who offer us the practical possibility of a new age. *The triumph of civilization* lives at the heart of our common human potential. It requires the *founding* of a holistic Earth community.

10.1 Ascent to the Freedom of Holism

We have reached the limits of our adolescent condition of personal and collective immaturity as well as the limits of our outdated and fractured institutions – global capitalism and the system of sovereign nation-states, along with the racism, bigotry, ethnocentrism, and technocracy that intertwine with these global institutions. Philosopher H. L. Finch states "that some major change in the way we live is beginning to manifest itself is evident from the many signs of our times, not the least of which is the exhaustion of the principles by which we have been living" (1995: 5). We have seen at length how this exhaustion operates throughout our world today – in the massive exploitation of peoples, in the on-going destruction of our planetary ecosystem, in unremitting violence everywhere on the planet.

We need, and live in the midst of, a renaissance, a rebirth. Such major changes in human thought and attitudes have happened a few times in history, not the least of which was the Renaissance that gave birth to the modern world during the fifteenth and sixteenth centuries. Just as new "modern" political and economic institutions emerged during the Renaissance to replace older "feudal" institutions so new political and economic institutions need to emerge in the twenty-first century. However, the stakes are higher today because our immediate actions *will determine forever* either the flourishing or destruction of human beings and our planetary ecology.

There are many books, articles, and social movements in our day working for a transformation of our largely failed world order. But the general public worldwide has yet to see and affirm the significance of their work on behalf of a planetary renaissance. The renaissance we need goes beyond the grasping of an abstract holism of wholes and parts discerned by the contemporary sciences to a new concreteness, a new immediacy in which we discover the living experience in which "the earth is the place that touches our skin, the place where we make our dwelling, our ecology. This is the origin of the dialectic of person and cosmos, the phenomenon of nature, as habitat."

"Democracy" must no longer function as a mere abstraction for people who accept as "realistic" profoundly undemocratic structures and processes. To live from our rootedness in the Earth, in its beauty, its smells, the way it feels, the breath of fresh air, the immense sky with its multiplicity of ecstatic colors and moods, is to begin to discern our democratic equality in which we all inherit this magical planet at the same level. The Earth belongs to us all, and we must create the common, sustainable political, social and economic structures that embody this equiprimordial truth.

The ascent to the freedom of holism in our lives not only liberates us from hate, fear, compulsions, and idolatries, it links us with others in communities of positive freedom and hopeful vision. To live from the equiprimordial truth of our common joy in living in touch with our Earth invokes a great responsibility toward all other people and nature. We experience the moral imperative to transform our planetary institutions from fragmentation to holism, from violence to nonviolence, from competitive destructiveness to a holistic Earth community. Such an Earth community can only be founded if we unite under a common constitution.

The title of Errol E. Harris' recent book conveys this possibility: *21ˢᵗ Century Democratic Renaissance*. This title captures precisely what will save us from a complete disaster for human civilization. As we have seen, the renaissance of the twenty-first century, according to Harris, must include democratic world government:

> In the world today the only form of democracy that could aspire to the ideals of the traditional philosophical conception would have to be global, one that could legislate to implement global measures to deal with global problems (as sovereign nation-states cannot) and could maintain the Rule of Law worldwide (which the exercise of sovereign rights by independent nations prevents). Accordingly, the only effective democracy would have to take the form of World Government, and that can be truly democratic only if it is federal, because federalism assures the right of member states to autonomy with respect to their own internal affairs, while it consigns to the federal administration control over issues, the interest in which is common to all its peoples, and which the several member states cannot regulate within their own jurisdiction. (2008: 135)

"Planetary democracy," it should be clear, means both real democracy and world democracy. It means "Earth Federation." It means that we begin paying attention to the deeper implications of our common humanity and realize that our institutions and practices must be premised on our emergent human characteristics as indicated not only by spirituality and morality, but by rational common sense and practical action to save ourselves from disaster. It means that we begin to understand the meaning of *holism* much more deeply as applied to human life and relationships.

What is not permitted is postponement, the liberal and non-transformative notion that we have sufficient time to "evolve" toward a genuine democratic world community. We need a *renaissance*, a nonviolent revolution, not an incremental "evolution." According to environmental scientist John Cairns, Jr., (2008) quoted in Chapter Six, we have "as little as ten years" left to make deep, fundamental changes. There is no one at the helm: no responsible persons constructing a decent future and acting to avoid unspeakable disaster. We must act now from our love of the Earth and our love of life, and we must actualize the moral obligation that we have to all other persons and the Earth's other living creatures.

Civilized human beings live under the rule of democratically legislated, enforceable laws. The triumph of civilization will mean bringing this simple fact of civilized living to planet Earth. There are no good or evil nations (as there may be sometimes leaders of nations who do evil acts), there is simply a system of relatively autonomous nation-states that abjures the rule of law in the world. The horrors we see all around us are by and large a direct consequence of this system, in tandem with an economic system that must, like a cancer, grow or die, and so necessarily eats up the biosphere of our planet in its quest for endless increase in private profit for a few. Acting now can save our planet from self-destruction. It only really requires that we fully grasp the fundamental principle that *civilized human beings live under the rule of democratically legislated, enforceable laws.*

10.2 Planetary Maturity

It is sometimes said that the spirit of the fifteenth-century Renaissance was captured in the *Oration on the Dignity of Man* by Pico Della Mirandola. In his oration, Pico links the great dignity of human beings with the fact that we do not have a predetermined nature like the other creatures that limits what we may become. Rather, we can move to higher or lower levels of existence according to our own choices and free will. This insight again manifests in our own day as fundamental. We are indeed not predetermined by some hard-wired, corrupt human nature to self-destruct on planet Earth, perhaps as a failed experiment in God's evolutionary upsurge within creation.

At present we are often choosing what is lower in ourselves, what is bestial: hatred, fear, greed, preying upon one another economically, ideologically, and militarily. We are moving to lower levels of existence by making ourselves into robots rather than free persons. We are willingly submitting to national security domination, military domination, and the dominations of fear, hate, and insecurity, as well as the dominations of greed and egoistic self-interest at the expense of others. We are confusing fragmentation and our fragmented identities with realism. At best, we have settled down in this botched and broken world order and accepted its absurdity as "practical realism," as "facing the hard facts." We keep our heads down, indulge our private satisfactions, and let the world be damned.

All these phenomena destroy other human beings and nature and exhibit the sense of nihilism in values and illusion of immortality often characteristic of adolescents. Only adolescents are solely concerned with their private satisfactions regardless of all others. Only adolescents think the tiny set of religious and cultural identities of their childhood are the only true identities. Only adolescents fool themselves into thinking that this absurd, socially constructed nightmare of a world gives us the "hard facts" or what is "practically realistic."

The reality of our universe has been revealed by twentieth-century science as an astonishing holistic plenum of dynamic *unity in diversity*. The reality of our humanity has been revealed by psychologists and spiritual thinkers as a host of higher human potentialities involving the same structures of *unity in diversity* that are today inhibited and crushed by our fragmented economic and political systems. The reality of the universe does not deny our childhood religious and cultural identities but *embraces* them within a series of ever-larger holistic fields.

All of these phenomena destroy *community*: the mutual recognition and trust that lives at the foundation of authentic democracy. They all destroy the active commitment to others and our common human project that is at the heart of human maturity. They destroy the *holism* of the human species and our sustaining biosphere living on spaceship Earth.

This self-dehumanization will also mean our self-destruction and the destruction of the precious and beautiful Earth, which is an intimate part of our selves. We fail to comprehend the direct, interdependent relationship between community, love, and mutual cooperation and the fulfillment of each of our selves as individuals. We need to rapidly ascend to a deep understanding of planetary maturity and global democracy.

The immense record of human spirituality, philosophy, political thought and intercultural common sense indicates that we can think and act differently, that we can recognize "the exhaustion of the principles by which we have been living" and begin to live from healthier, more universal, more life-affirming principles. The "utopian surplus" characterizing our lives reflects our potential as human beings, the sense that we are unfinished animals that can become greater and do better than we have done in the past. The emergence of democracy as a moral ideal and transformative force throughout the past 2500 years of human history points to this higher human potential in all of us.

We have seen the simple expression of this ideal in the holistic slogan: "liberty, equality, and fraternity." We can embody our higher human potential for mutual freedom by *founding* truly democratic institutions for our planet. These institutions will necessarily embody *freedom* through protection of our inviolable human rights and dignity, meaningful *equality* that makes possible the political and economic participation of every citizen to the point where citizens recognize in government a reflection of their general will, and *community* in which positive liberty arises from a mutual recognition and trust predicated on the common good of all.

We have understood that democracy is not just another form of government among other possible forms. It is the fundamental moral framework for human association, encompassing our experience of human dignity, rights, freedom, and equality. Democracy manifests, therefore, much of *our higher rational potential* as human beings that is finally coming to fruition in the twenty-first century. It also manifests our *universal* human potential and therefore can only effectively be planetary democracy – a manifestation, as well as condition of, our growing planetary maturity. It signals the coming great transformation from a fragmented world of adolescent ego-struggles to a mature world of holistic reciprocity, mutual respect, and real institutional unity within the world's diversity.

Planetary democracy and community institutionalized under an *Earth Constitution* also means the activation of *positive freedom* rather than mere negative freedom for the peoples of Earth. The mutual recognition and trust of genuine community under authentic democracy are what make freedom possible at all. The perpetual struggle of those who embrace *negative freedom*, believing that they must perpetually resist governmental authority and resist tyranny of the majority in order to maximize their private license to do what they please, radically restricts their life possibilities.

All our resources derive from present and past communities: our technology, our wealth, our education, our opportunities, and our common inheritance of the surface of the Earth. The creation of planetary democracy empowers us to positive freedom and multiplies our life-possibilities. Instead of a perpetual struggle to defend our private freedom, we find vastly enlarged opportunities to expand our deeper life opportunities. Our conception of the common good matures into an empowering holism.

Growth out of adolescence comes in spurts and abrupt changes: one moment a wise-ass kid, the next moment a responsible young adult. Something similar is happening with the development of our species: the Greeks and other ancient cultures were like beautiful, innocent children; the moderns with their macho capitalism and militarized nation-state system are like wild adolescent boys, defining "freedom" as their right to do whatever they damn well please. But the dawning awareness of our global crises has placed immense pressure on our consciousness to grow to another level.

Our problems will not magically disappear, but they will look entirely different and fundamentally manageable from the point of view of a united humanity and a federated Earth. We are beginning to transcend the false, fragmented individualism and understand our fundamental relatedness to one another. Soon we will be capable of nonviolently operating our Spaceship Earth.

10.3 A Founded Society

Will we slowly *evolve* to planetary maturity in time in the face of the immense forces and institutions opposing that growth? This is not likely since tremendous powers resist the growth of that maturity. *Peace must be established.* In the quotation at the outset of this chapter, Kant has proclaimed the most fundamental of principles. Peace can only derive from a *founded* society, just as the United States is a founded nation, and India is a founded nation. A founded global civil society, an Earth community, is one established according to principles embodied in a founding document, a constitution. Once we have established peace through founding an Earth community under democratic institutions, the continued development of maturity can and will happen rapidly.

From the outset the principles embodied in that constitution work to control the forces opposed to those principles, or, better, the founding principles simply reorganize society to substantially reduce forces that subvert universal peace, justice, and prosperity. The *Constitution for the Federation of Earth* establishes a global government according to the federal principle of shared sovereignty, from the local to national, to world levels. No longer can the institution of the lawless sovereign nation-state destroy the peace, freedom, and justice of the people of Earth. The *Earth Constitution* also organizes the framework of world economics according to market socialist principles of reasonable equality of all persons and freedom from exploitation and domination by gigantic banking, corporate, and nation-state forces.

Finally, the immense power of the wealthy classes of Earth to inhibit democracy and the growth of human maturity through their ownership of the mass media and other means is carefully circumscribed by the *Earth Constitution*, as it also does regarding the powers of nationalism, racism, ethnocentrism, sexism, or religious bigotry that interfere with the peace or the development of planetary maturity. Under the *Constitution* elections cannot be bought, and the power of big media to undermine democracy is intelligently curtailed.

Without *establishing peace* through the creation of a global body politic in which the general will of the people of Earth prevents by law war, exploitation, and injustice, the gigantic forces ranged against peace will continue to subvert the best efforts of peace activists or non-governmental organizations to evolve the world toward maturity and decency. The war system of sovereign nations and the oligarchic power system of monopoly capitalism (reaping huge profits from the violence and injustice of the present system) must be transformed through the founding of global democracy. The *Earth Constitution* establishes the essential elements for a genuinely peaceful planetary community.

This reveals the immense flaw of many writers cited in this book who work for a holistic world order. Writers such as Ervin Laszlo, David Korten, Brian Swimme, Thomas Berry, Vandana Shiva, Sally Goener, Robert Dyck, Dorothy Lagerroos, and a number of others correctly argue for a holistic Earth civilization. However, they argue on a cultural level trying to convince the peoples of the world to embrace a culture of holism before it is too late (including the holisms of freedom, justice, and sustainable economic equity). *They fail to understand that a war-system cannot culturally evolve into a peace-system.*

Not only are gigantic institutions ranged against peace (such as the militarized nation-state, a huge military-industrial complex, and the immense forces of disaster capitalism) but the system of sovereign nation-states itself is an anti-holistic war system defeating peace at every turn. They fail to understand that the system of sovereign nation-states as it now stands cannot embrace holism. Its very structure embodies fragmentation, division, conflict, and violence. It might "evolve" over hundreds of years, but by that time the Earth will be uninhabitable for any form of life above the level of cockroaches.

The establishing of peace creates a global body politic under the authority of the people of Earth that prohibits war, disarms the nations, protects human rights worldwide, moderates economics for the common good of all, protects the environment, converts the world to sustainable production and consumption, and shares the resources of the planet equitably for all people and for future generations. A holistic Earth civilization can only be *founded.* It necessarily includes establishing a genuine democratic government for Spaceship Earth. The founding itself will activate an immense step forward in human maturity.

There can be no genuine holism, and no peace, without the *establishment* of a global body-politic. Our higher human potential is actualized in significant measure in this awakening – not only the understanding of holism itself but in the understanding that holism for human beings requires the just rule of law for the whole of humanity. Our equiprimordial freedom, equality, and community as human beings inheriting the ecstatic beauty and marvel of life on this planet must be embodied in our social, economic, and political institutions.

10.4 Common Sense Political and Economic Arrangements

There is nothing particularly mysterious about this understanding of our higher human potential, and much of it can be summed up in the concept of nonviolence that has been a major theme of this book: nonviolent society, government, and economics. Gandhi writes:

> The world of tomorrow will be, must be, a society based on nonviolence. That is the first law; out of it all other blessings will flow. It may seem a distant goal, an impractical Utopia. But it is not in the least unobtainable, since it can be worked for here and now. An individual can adopt the way of life of the future – the nonviolent way – without having to wait for others to do so. And if an individual can do it, cannot whole groups of individuals? Whole nations? Men often hesitate to make a beginning because they feel that the objective cannot be achieved in its entirety. This attitude of mind is precisely the greatest obstacle to progress – an obstacle that each man, if he only wills it, can clear away. Equal distribution – the second great law of tomorrow's world as I see it – grows out of nonviolence.... I see no poverty in the world of tomorrow, no wars, no revolutions, no bloodshed. (1987: 458-460).

Gandhi's vision is not naïve. *Satyagraha* (clinging to Truth) is an expression of holism, the holism shown by science to inform every dimension of our universe. The truth that Gandhi sees is the truth of the whole (which he also calls 'God'). He understands the implications of holism for human life, reflecting our "utopian surplus" of "real and objective possibility."

We have seen that Gandhi advocated a world federation to actualize this nonviolent world of tomorrow. The Earth Federation that he advocated would also be responsible to end poverty and create a substantially equitable world order. "Equal distribution" does not mean enforced sameness, for Gandhi, nor for the emerging Earth Federation, as we have seen, but rather the ending of a system in which "the few ride on the backs of the millions." We have seen that this can only effectively happen through a democratic Earth Federation that represents everyone, whose mandate is to represent the common good of everyone, and whose institutions allow an effective determination of the general will of the people of Earth.

For Gandhi, the world of the future will of necessity be an Earth Federation characterized by "socialism" since this combines respect for each individual with meaningful equality and a sense of the human community as a whole under the rule of enforceable law. A nonviolent world order is a logical consequence of the fact that each of us can adopt the nonviolent way of life here and now and work to embody this in nonviolent institutions. For Gandhi as well – peace must be *established*, even though it can also be adopted by any individual at any time and at any place. "Clinging to truth" (*Satyagraha*) includes clinging to the holism of our human situation.

The principles behind the new, nonviolent, holistic economic and political democracy are simple and clear. They are all embodied in the *Constitution for the Federation of Earth*, establishing a peace system. A united Earth could easily implement these common sense principles:

- Take banking, money creation, and a few other key aspects of the economy out of the hands of the oligarchy that now controls the economics of the Earth and place these under the democratic control of the people of Earth.

- Empower local communities and economies through interest-free lines of credit and job creation for restoring the environment and building the infrastructure (including clean water, sanitation, eco-friendly industry, free quality health care, social security, and education) for a decent economy for all.

- Empower people from the bottom up to take political control of their lives, communities, and businesses and to contribute their voices to the general will for governing of Spaceship Earth. The vast majority desire only freedom, peace, and reasonable prosperity.

- Undertake worldwide programs to restore and clean-up the environment: including replanting forests, providing fresh water for all, restoration of farming land, clean oceans, etc., paying for these projects by primary created Earth Federation money that will activate local economies worldwide.

- Eliminate weapons of war (including all weapons of mass destruction) from the Earth and prevent their further production by enforceable world law.

- Represent, and dialogue with, all groups and peoples equally, taking grievances seriously and dealing thoughtfully and fairly with conflicts so that no group feels it has to turn to war, violence, or terrorism.

- Protect and enforce equal human rights (both political and economic rights) equitably for all people on Earth within the context of worldwide conflict resolution programs designed to promote mutual understanding and security as well as reduce the felt need to resort to violence.

- Provide the democratic agencies and institutions for monitoring the health of the planet, assessing new technologies, and planning for a sustainable future for our entire planet with all its people, ecosystems, and animals.

All of these principles are simple and quite common sense. Yet none of this can be done without uniting our planet under a single democratic government. It is precisely the federation of the many nations and communities of the Earth under the rule of democratically legislated enforceable world law that creates *the holistic dynamic of unity in diversity essential to our survival.* To speak of a holism of human relationships on Earth without the universal democratic rule of law constitutes a naïve idealism of the worst kind. Holism must be institutionalized and embodied in our political and economic systems, just as presently fragmentation and division are institutionalized in our non-democratic planetary systems.

Science has understood that there is no atom without a field, that an atom is *incomprehensible* without a field, which ultimately includes the field of the whole universe. Similarly no human being is comprehensible apart from the field of our entire human community on the Earth. The fact alone that we have a "language instinct" and that we are universally genetically structured as language-speaking beings (Pinker 1994) indicates the field character of our human community. Holism implies both planetary democracy and nonviolence. The *triumph of civilization* means a conversion, not only of thought, but of economics and politics to holistic principles. It means the *founding* of an Earth community.

Proper economics involves the means by which the basic necessities of life can be obtained by all human beings under conditions of freedom and community without the violence of involuntary poverty, exploitation, or domination. We have seen that our present global economic system has utterly failed in this regard. For a nonviolent world order to become a reality requires that we put an end to the *irredeemable fragmentation* fostered by today's global economics. We must unite together under the *unity in diversity* of democratic world law. Only then will the intimations of our "utopian surplus," that is, our mature human potential, become actualized in the daily life of humankind.

10.5 Rationality and Spirituality

The communicative rationality that has been shown by Habermas and others to live at the heart of our universal human ability to use language (and that is therefore fundamental to human civilization itself) must be activated and promoted in every venue. Communicative rationality must supersede our present obsession with manipulative *instrumental* rationality as the primary mode of human interaction. Only adolescents lack the healthy sense of self that drives them to use language manipulatively and project a false image of their selves to the world. As we grow, our use of language becomes more and more communicative.

Communicative rationality immediately implies a world community, worldwide respect for human rights, global democracy, and the beginnings of planetary maturity. It reveals the equality, dignity, and fundamental rights of every human being and provides the rational foundations for global democracy. We understand that the presuppositions of the very possibility of language, as Habermas points out, in addition to its universal intelligibility, include "truth, truthfulness, and normative rightness" (1979).

These are also the presuppositions of democracy. There can be no democracy without communicative interaction directed toward *truth*, without a framework encouraging *honesty and integrity* in communication, nor without mutual recognition of legitimate *rights and responsibilities*. We are very close to that maturity which allows us to recognize our common *species-being*.

The communicative core of language is the living source of *both* our continually developing autonomy as unique persons and our bonding in community with other persons. Habermas, building on and quoting the work of Wilhelm von Humboldt, emphasizes that our fundamental communicative rationality *simultaneously individuates and unites*. The same is true of cultures, nations, and groups: "And what holds true for individuals holds to an even greater degree for nations: 'In its capacity for dividing peoples, language unifies the difference between individualities without detracting from them in any way, by means of the mutual understanding of foreign speech.' Language compels the individuation of peoples and individual persons, 'but in such a wonderful way that, precisely in dividing, it awakens a feeling of unity; it appears indeed as a means of creating unity'" (1998h: 187-188). Our language instinct both progressively binds us together as one species and one Earth civilization, and actualizes our individualities as persons, members of cultures, groups, religions, and nations. *The field embraces and unites the parts while simultaneously enhancing their uniqueness as parts.*

Similarly, the spiritualities of compassion, kindness, *agape*, and holistic intuition can no longer live merely as the luxury of a few saints or mystics. We have seen that these spiritualities exist as characteristics of human maturity rather than as esoteric or mysterious irrelevancies. Today, they have become necessities for our survival. They operate in our lives unnamed every time we respect another person simply because they are a person, every time we feel another's suffering, and every time we intuit that things could be different, that the future could be one of peace, freedom, and prosperity. They operate unnamed today in the lives of millions of mindful, thoughtful, and mature human beings. They also operate within the human potential of every normal human being.

The Fourteenth Dalai Lama, Tenzin Gyatso, never tires of asserting this primordial truth: "Love, compassion and tolerance are necessities, not luxuries; without them, humanity cannot survive" (1990: 3). Human spirituality on its most fundamental level does not direct us to exotic sensibilities realized through yoga or contemplative prayer. It draws on what is utterly common and most universally human – our ability to live with gentleness, compassion, kindness, love, and holistic intuition. We must establish a holistic Earth community that allows these primordial truths to flourish.

In every way (in our teaching, writing, speaking, acting, and learning) these should be promoted, although not necessarily named as I have named them. Racism, ethnic discrimination, sexism, nationalism, class elitism, and religious fundamentalism are all forms of collective egoism, positing the superiority of one group over another and violating the face to face of personal respect due to every person and the imperative to develop a living community on the Earth. Our recognition of the personhood of each is *simultaneously* our understanding that the world could be transformed on this basis. Personhood is both utterly unique and deeply universal. This recognition is simply the next step in human maturity.

10.6 Nonviolence

Insofar as we overcome these egoistic compulsions we become ever-more nonviolent. Violence is incompatible with the spiritualities of compassion, kindness, *agape*, or holistic intuition, just as it is incompatible with communicative rationality and democracy. Nonviolence lies at the heart of integral liberation. There is nothing mysterious or utopian in the negative sense about these insights. They only appear utopian because they exist in conflict with our fragmented institutions and immature attitudes blocking their full actualization.

Nonviolent social relationships simply mean economic and political democracy on Earth, something everyone can understand. Creating these nonviolent relationships will mean the eschatological fulfillment of the human project. This simply means that we are capable of establishing a world order of peace, freedom, justice, and reasonable prosperity for all. To put this in the religious language from which it derives, it will mean the gentle prelude to the Kingdom of God on Earth. Again, nearly everyone can easily understand the meaning of this symbolism, whether or not they come from a religious tradition.

Nonviolence, therefore, need not and cannot be limited to a personal orientation to life. We saw that it can be and must be substantially institutionalized, that authentic democracy itself involves an embodiment of nonviolence, and that even Gandhi envisioned this as an earth federation. With the political will to create a decent world order for ourselves and our children, we can rapidly institutionalize a nonviolent economics premised on reasonable prosperity for all rather than great wealth for a few with suffering and death for the vast majority. We can create nonviolent institutions protecting social change, human rights, and nonviolent conflict resolution. We can institutionalize nonviolent law enforcement through an Earth Federation that protects the life, liberty, and security of each, and oppresses none.

Global democracy flows from the universal communicative rationality in which all language speaking creatures participate as well as from the spiritualities of compassion, *agape*, and holistic intuition alive within all of us. It will promote global solidarity and global community within which the Earth Federation will be able to respond to the general will of the people of Earth. We are at the end of the line. Postponement is no longer an option.

Planetary democracy and human maturity also mean a new ecological and holistic relationship to the biosphere and our planet's other living creatures. Just as democracy requires genuine community among human beings, so it transforms our attitude toward nature from one of domination to one of balance and harmony. The community spirit and the ecological spirit are two sides of the same orientation that overcomes egoism, destructive individualism, and the spirit of competitive domination. The concern with a healthy human community mirrors the concern for healthy ecological communities. It reflects the desire to live holistically, in harmony with one's environment, rather than atomistically within a fragmented world disorder.

Planetary maturity means the realization of what is most fundamental and significant about each of us – our common humanity arising from the deep mystery of existence and portending unlimited possibilities for beautiful forms of transformation and self-realization. The more that we concretely and effectively realize that we are citizens of Spaceship Earth, first and foremost, the more our wonderful diversities and unique individualities can be appreciated and protected. Unity and diversity arise together throughout this marvelous universe. Planetary maturity means they arise together on Earth as well. "Thy will be done on Earth, as it is in heaven" – if "heaven" means the deepest foundations or the basic meaning of existence, then human beings have yet to fulfill this hope implicit in our potential for planetary maturity.

10.7 The Triumph of Civilization

But we have seen in some detail that all of this remains empty rhetoric unless embodied in concrete institutions and democratic procedures that effectively translate our human potential into democratic world law that applies equally to all. Without a concrete Earth Federation under a

Constitution for the Federation of Earth, the oppressors and exploiters and postponers can say "Oh yes, I very much agree with these ideals that we are all working toward in the future." The claim to hold ideals that we are working toward in the future reflects an inauthentic and dishonest response to our human situation when those ideals could and should be effectively institutionalized *now* within a concrete world democracy.

The *Renaissance of the Twenty-first Century*, the triumph of civilization on planet Earth, must necessarily include non-military, civilian democratic Earth Federation. The renaissance cannot be merely cultural. It cannot be an evolution in mere global "governance" as some economists and political leaders like Al Gore (2006) appear to urge. It must include real civil *government*, with the ability to enforce democratic laws over even the heads of nation-states and transnational corporations. As with the Enlightenment of the Eighteenth Century, it must result in a concrete democratic constitution – with a founding document that can both enhance and lay the groundwork for continuing growth in planetary maturity and a peaceful, prosperous, and free human existence on Spaceship Earth. Everything is ready for us to take this next step toward a higher human civilization.

The next step must be a real step, a genuine transformation of our fundamental assumptions and premises. It cannot be the pretence of change that attempts to deal with our planetary crises from the same outmoded set of assumptions. We have seen the disastrous effects of assumptions such as the fragmented system of sovereign nation-states, the economics of monopoly capitalism, a United Nations that is in no sense "united," the false notion of a "clash of civilizations," or the naïve assumption of the incommensurability of the world's religions. We must ascend to genuine *unity in diversity*, institutionalized under an *Earth Constitution*, which is indeed the foundation stone for a holistic planetary community of freedom, sustainability, and prosperity.

Planetary democracy and human maturity go together. We have understood that political and economic democracy serves as *both ends and means*. More than a political system, democracy lives as a moral ideal for human relationships, demanding that economic and political liberty, equality, and community become the norm in human relationships, that we begin relating to one another as *persons*, not as things. Institutionalizing democracy constitutes the *means* to mature, sustainable living in peace on planet Earth as well as the ultimate *end* to be sought through all our activities. Ends and means at last achieve harmony. The end or goal of democratic liberty, equality, and community on Earth is also the means to that ideal.

Our present non-democratic and immature world system of neoliberal capitalism, sovereign nation-states, and other forms of social and moral fragmentation surges forward, like an immense raging river, toward planetary disaster. We face the final crossroad. Either we create a truly democratic renaissance for the twenty-first century by founding a holistic Earth civilization or we go down to perdition – and the immense promise of our common human project may be lost forever on our failed planet. The choice is still ours if we summon the courage and political will for immediate action to ratify an *Earth Constitution* and found a holistic Earth community.

To think, act, and live in terms of the concept and ideal of planetary democracy is to become a catalyst for a rebirth for humanity that prepares a glorious future for our children. We no longer live from the divisive ego but from our deeper common reality, actualizing our higher human potential for a pacified and just world community. Only this transformative action can lead to a triumph for civilization – uniting all peoples under the equal protection of democratically legislated laws. We see before us the possibility of a new dawning for humanity. This is our highest hope, our most beautiful dream, our most rational conclusion, and our most fundamental moral obligation.

Appendix A
The Development of the *Earth Constitution* and Provisional World Parliament
A Brief History

1958. Agreement to Call a World Constitutional Convention initiated by four persons, circulated worldwide for signatures, requesting both national governments and people of each country to send delegates.

1959-1960. World Committee for a World Constitutional Convention formed. Thousands sign the Agreement, including many prominent leaders. Organizers of this action travel around the world to enlist support.

1961-1962. Definitive Call to the World Constitutional Convention adopted. Many persons sign, including Heads of five national governments.

1963-1964. First Preparatory Congress held Denver, Colorado, USA, with delegates from five continents. Call to the World Constitutional Convention is publicly issued, then circulated for more signers and response.

1965-1966. Second Preparatory Congress held at Milan, Italy. Outline for Debate and Drafting of a World Constitution is formulated, on basis on alternative choices. Plan agreed for a Peoples' World Parliament to meet concurrently.

1967. Decision made at Third Preparatory Congress to begin Convention in 1968, even if no government sends delegates. 300 Peoples Delegates pledged.

1968. First working sessions of World Constitutional Convention and Peoples' World Convention held at Interlaken, Switzerland, and Wolfach, W. Germany, with 200 Peoples Delegates from 27 countries, of five continents. Work begun on drafting the World Constitution.

1969-1971. Strategy for Reclaiming Earth for Humanity is circulated. Emergency Council of World Trustees meets, Santa Barbara, Calif., and issues First Decree for Protection of Life, outlawing nuclear weapons. Directions given to drafting commission.

1972. World Constitution drafting commission of four persons works for two months, almost completes first draft of *Constitution for the Federation of Earth*.

1973-1975. First draft finished, printed in 1974, then circulated worldwide for comment, together with Call to the second session in 1977, now defined as the World Constituent Assembly. Comments on first draft complied.

1976-1977. Drafting Commission meets again. Second draft completed, circulated, 1977. Second Session of World Constituent Assembly held in June, Innsbruck, Austria. *Earth Constitution* debated paragraph by paragraph, amended, then adopted with 138 original signers from 25 countries of 6 continents. Call for ratification by the nations and peoples of Earth is issued. *Constitution* is sent to U.N. General Assembly and to all national governments.

1978-1980. *Earth Constitution* is circulated worldwide for debate and ratification. Third session of World Constituent Assembly held January, 1979, Colombo, Sri Lanka; adopts Rationale For a World Constituent Assembly, defining right of people to convene Assembly, draft constitution, and obtain ratification. Appeal issued for national parliaments to ratify.

1981. World Constitution & Parliament Assn. meets at New Delhi, India. Call issued for Provisional World Parliament to convene in 1982 under terms of Article 19 of the *Earth Constitution*. Honorary Sponsor list of 150 prominent persons enrolled.

1982. First Session of Provisional World Parliament meets at Brighton, England. Delegates form 25 countries of 6 continents. Five world Legislative Acts are adopted: for World Disarmament Agency, World Economic Development, Ownership of Oceans & Seabeds, Graduate School of World Problems, and World Courts.

1983-1984. First Provisional District World Court organized in Los Angeles; takes up case of outlawing nuclear weapons. Plans for Provisional World Parliament in Sudan and Nigeria thwarted by military coups.

1985. Second Session of Provisional World Parliament held New Delhi, India. Opened by President of India, presided by speaker of Lok Sabha. Three more World Legislative Acts adopted: for Emergency Earth Rescue Administration, World Government Funding, and Commission on Terrorism.

1986. Campaign continued for "provisional" ratification of the *Constitution for the Federation of Earth*, pending review at next World Constituent Assembly.

1987. Third session of Provisional World Parliament held Miami Beach, Florida. Three more World Legislative Acts are adopted: for Global Finance System, Environment Protection, and Hydrogen Energy. Provisional World Cabinet begun.

1988-1989. Plan launched for collaboration by many organizations to prepare next session of World Constituent Assembly. 150 organizations join in Preparatory Committee. Two meetings held in New York with UN

Ambassadors, to explain and solicit help. List of Honorary Sponsors reconfirmed and expanded.

1990. Government of Egypt agrees to host Assembly. Three preparatory meetings held. Call circulated for Governments and People to send delegates.

1991. Location of 4th session World Constituent Assembly abruptly changed due to the 1991 Gulf War. Held at Troia, Portugal, in May. Delegates adopt 59 minor amendments to the *Earth Constitution*. New ratification campaign begun, appealing to both people and governments. Most Honorary Sponsors personally ratify.

1992. Global Ratification & Elections Network organized, including several hundred organizations, to promote ratification of the *Constitution for the Federation of Earth*, then election of delegates to World Parliament. Government heads should also ratify.

1996. The Fourth Session of the Provisional World Parliament held at Barcelona, Spain, in September. A number of resolutions passed as well as a "Manifesto" declaring the oceans the property of the people of Earth under the authority of the *Earth Constitution*.

2000. The Fifth Session of the Provisional World Parliament is held on the Island of Malta, November 22nd to 27th. One Omnibus legislative act and a number of resolutions passed.

2003. The Sixth Session of the Provisional World Parliament held in Bangkok, Thailand, March 23rd to 28th. Several important legislative acts passed: a World Peace Act, a World Security Act, a Provisional Office of World Revenue Act, a Hydrocarbon Resource Act, and a Statute for the World Court on Human Rights. The Commission for Legislative Review is formed. Parliamentary law format commences with the Sixth Session.

2003. The Seventh Session of the Provisional World Parliament is held at Chennai, India, December 23-29. Several important legislative acts passed: a Criminal Penalty Code, Rules for Procedure and Evidence, a World Bench for Criminal Cases Act, a World Patents Act, a Global Accounting and Auditing Standards Act, and a Preservation of World Government Records Act. The *Manifesto of the Earth Federation* and the "Pledge of Allegiance to the *Earth Constitution*" are unanimously ratified by the Parliament.

2004. The Eighth Session of the Provisional World Parliament held at Lucknow, India, in August. Several important legislative acts passed, including creation of a World Bench for Juvenile Cases, a Child Rights Act, an Elections Act, and a Water Act. The International Criminal Court in the Hague is empowered by world legislation. A global Education Act is passed as well as a World Economic Equity Act establishing the Earth Currency on an independent and fully democratic basis. A Global People's Assembly is created to activate grass roots participation in the House of Peoples. The "Declaration on the Rights of Peoples" is unanimously ratified.

2006. The Ninth Session of the Provisional World Parliament held in Tripoli, Libya, in April. Eight World Legislative Acts are passed, an enabling act for the World Ombudsmus, the creation of a Department of Conflict Resolution for the Earth Federation, a ban on the production of fissile materials for weapons, a nuclear weapons elimination protocol, a nuclear contamination act prohibiting the use of depleted uranium and other weapons, a quit Guantanamo directive, an agreement on world privileges and immunities (revising the weaker version of the Assembly of States Parties), and a public utilities act. The former "Global Ratification and Elections Network (GREN)" is transformed into the Earth Federation Movement (EFM).

2007. The Tenth Session of the Provisional World Parliament held in Kara, Togo, in June. Four world legislative acts are passed: an act prohibiting unauthorized destruction of illegal financial instruments, an act creating a system of divestment from illegal weapons manufacture, an act requiring posting of the world illegal stock law in stock exchanges around the world, and an act providing a guaranteed annual income for all adults within the Earth Federation.

2009. The Eleventh Session of the Provisional World Parliament held in Nainital, India, in July. Several world legislative acts passed, including one describing the procedure for dismantling nuclear weapons, another proscribing and penalizing all forms of human trafficking, a law protecting the right of civil disobedience for citizens of the Earth, and a law protecting citizens of Earth from excessive bureaucracatic regulations within the Earth Federation.. A translation of the *Constitution* into its 23rd language (Bengali) was presented to the Parliament by the delegation from Bangladesh.

Note: Most of the above legislative acts can be found on the websites of WCPA (www.wcpa.biz) and IOWP (www.worldproblems. net). The full texts of all, along with summaries and analyses, can also be found in the forthcoming three volume series: *Emerging World Law*, Eugenia Almand and Glen T. Martin, eds., Sun City, AZ: Institute for Economic Democracy Press, 2009.

Appendix B

A Constitution for the Federation of Earth

As Amended at the

World Constituent Assembly

in Troia, Portugal, 1991

NOW BEING CIRCULATED

WORLDWIDE

FOR RATIFICATION

BY THE NATIONS

AND PEOPLE OF EARTH

PREAMBLE

Realizing that Humanity today has come to a turning point in history and that we are on the threshold of an new world order which promises to usher in an era of peace, prosperity, justice and harmony;

Aware of the interdependence of people, nations and all life;

Aware that man's abuse of science and technology has brought Humanity to the brink of disaster through the production of horrendous weaponry of mass destruction and to the brink of ecological and social catastrophe;

Aware that the traditional concept of security through military defense is a total illusion both for the present and for the future;

Aware of the misery and conflicts caused by ever increasing disparity between rich and poor;

Conscious of our obligation to posterity to save Humanity from imminent and total annihilation;

Conscious that Humanity is One despite the existence of diverse nations, races, creeds, ideologies and cultures and that the principle of unity in diversity is the basis for a new age when war shall be outlawed and peace prevail; when the earth's total resources shall be equitably used for human welfare; and when basic human rights and responsibilities shall be shared by all without discrimination;

Conscious of the inescapable reality that the greatest hope for the survival of life on earth is the establishment of a democratic world government;

We, citizens of the world, hereby resolve to establish a world federation to be governed in accordance with this constitution for the Federation of Earth.

CONSTITUTION FOR THE FEDERATION OF EARTH

Article 1. Broad Functions of the World Government

The broad functions of the Federation of Earth shall be:

1. To prevent war, secure disarmament, and resolve territorial and other disputes which endanger peace and human rights.

2. To protect universal human rights, including life, liberty, security, democracy, and equal opportunities in life.

3. To obtain for all people on earth the conditions required for equitable economic and social development and for diminishing social differences.

4. To regulate world trade, communications, transportation, currency, standards, use of world resources, and other global and international processes.

5. To protect the environment and the ecological fabric of life from all sources of damage, and to control technological innovations whose effects transcend national boundaries, for the purpose of keeping Earth a safe, healthy and happy home for humanity .

6. To devise and implement solutions to all problems which are beyond the capacity of national governments, or which are now or may become of global or international concern or consequence.

Article 2. Basic Structure of World Federation and World Government

1. The Federation of Earth shall be organized as a universal federation, to include all nations and all people, and to encompass all oceans, seas and lands of Earth, inclusive of non-self governing territories, together with the surrounding atmosphere.

2. The World Government for the Federation of Earth shall be non-military and shall be democratic in its own structure, with ultimate sovereignty residing in all the people who live on Earth.

3. The authority and powers granted to the World Government shall be limited to those defined in this Constitution for the Federation of Earth, applicable to problems and affairs which transcend national boundaries, leaving to national governments jurisdiction over the internal affairs of the respective nations but consistent with the authority of the World Government to protect universal human rights as defined in this World Constitution.

4. The basic direct electoral and administrative units of the World Government shall be World Electoral and Administrative Districts. A total of not more than 1000 World Electoral and Administrative Districts shall be defined, and shall be nearly equal in population, within the limits of plus or minus ten percent.

5. Contiguous World Electoral and Administrative Districts shall be combined as may be appropriate to compose a total of twenty World Electoral

and Administrative Regions for the following purposes, but not limited thereto: for the election or appointment of certain world government officials; for administrative purposes; for composing various organs of the world government as enumerated in Article IV; for the functioning of the Judiciary, the Enforcement System, and the Ombudsmus, as well as for the functioning of any other organ or agency of the World Government.

6. The World Electoral and Administrative Regions may be composed of a variable number of World Electoral and Administrative Districts, taking into consideration geographic, cultural, ecological and other factors as well as population.

7. Contiguous World Electoral and Administrative Regions shall be grouped together in pairs to compose Magna-Regions.

8. The boundaries for World Electoral and Administrative Regions shall not cross the boundaries of the World Electoral and Administrative Districts, and shall be common insofar as feasible for the various administrative departments and for the several organs and agencies of the World Government. Boundaries for the World Electoral and Administrative Districts as well as for the Regions need not conform to existing national boundaries, but shall conform as far as practicable.

9. The World Electoral and Administrative Regions shall be grouped to compose at least five Continental Divisions of the Earth, for the election or appointment of certain world government officials, and for certain aspects of the composition and functioning of the several organs and agencies of the World Government as specified hereinafter. The boundaries of Continental Divisions shall not cross existing national boundaries as far as practicable. Continental Divisions may be composed of a variable number of World Electoral and Administrative Regions.

Article 3. Organs of the World Government

The organs of the World Government shall be:
1. The World Parliament.
2. The World Executive.
3. The World Administration.
4. The Integrative Complex.
5. The World Judiciary.
6. The Enforcement System.
7. The World Ombudsmus.

Article 4. Grant of Specific Powers to the World Government

The powers of the World government to be exercised through its several organs and agencies shall comprise the following:
1. Prevent wars and armed conflicts among the nations, regions, districts, parts and peoples of Earth.

2. Supervise disarmament and prevent re-armament; prohibit and eliminate the design, testing, manufacture, sale, purchase, use and possession of weapons of mass destruction, and prohibit or regulate all lethal weapons which the World Parliament may decide.

3. Prohibit incitement to war, and discrimination against or defamation of conscientious objectors.

4. Provide the means for peaceful and just solutions of disputes and conflicts among or between nations, peoples, and/or other components within the Federation of Earth.

5. Supervise boundary settlements and conduct plebiscites as needed.

6. Define the boundaries for the districts, regions and divisions which are established for electoral, administrative, judicial and other purposes of the World Government.

7. Define and regulate procedures for the nomination and election of the members of each House of the World Parliament, and for the nomination, election, appointment and employment of all World Government officials and personnel.

8. Codify world laws, including the body of international law developed prior to adoption of the world constitution, but not inconsistent therewith, and which is approved by the World Parliament.

9. Establish universal standards for weights, measurements, accounting and records.

10. Provide assistance in the event of large scale calamities, including drought, famine, pestilence, flood, earthquake, hurricane, ecological disruptions and other disasters.

11. Guarantee and enforce the civil liberties and the basic human rights which are defined in the Bill of Rights for the Citizens of Earth which is made a part of this World Constitution under Article 12.

12. Define standards and promote the worldwide improvement in working conditions, nutrition, health, housing, human settlements, environmental conditions, education, economic security, and other conditions defined under Article 13 of this World Constitution.

13. Regulate and supervise international transportation, communications, postal services, and migrations of people.

14. Regulate and supervise supra-national trade, industry, corporations, businesses, cartels, professional services, labor supply, finances, investments and insurance.

15. Secure and supervise the elimination of tariffs and other trade barriers among nations, but with provisions to prevent or minimize hardship for those previously protected by tariffs.

16. Raise the revenues and funds, by direct and/or indirect means, which are necessary for the purposes and activities of the World Government.

17. Establish and operate world financial, banking, credit and insurance institutions designed to serve human needs; establish, issue and regulate world currency, credit and exchange.

18. Plan for and regulate the development, use, conservation and re-cycling of the natural resources of Earth as the common heritage of Humanity; protect the environment in every way for the benefit of both present and future generations.

19. Create and operate a World Economic Development Organization to serve equitably the needs of all nations and people included within the World Federation.

20. Develop and implement solutions to transnational problems of food supply, agricultural production, soil fertility, soil conservation, pest control, diet, nutrition, drugs and poisons, and the disposal of toxic wastes.

21. Develop and implement means to control population growth in relation to the life-support capacities of Earth, and solve problems of population distribution.

22. Develop, protect, regulate and conserve the water supplies of Earth; develop, operate and/or coordinate transnational irrigation and other water supply and control projects; assure equitable allocation of trans- national water supplies, and protect against adverse trans-national effects of water or moisture diversion or weather control projects within national boundaries.

23. Own, administer and supervise the development and conservation of the oceans and sea-beds of Earth and all resources thereof, and protect from damage.

24. Protect from damage, and control and supervise the uses of the atmosphere of Earth.

25. Conduct inter-planetary and cosmic explorations and research; have exclusive jurisdiction over the Moon and over all satellites launched from Earth.

26. Establish, operate and/or coordinate global air lines, ocean transport systems, international railways and highways, global communication systems, and means for interplanetary travel and communications; control and administer vital waterways.

27. Develop, operate and/or coordinate transnational power systems, or networks of small units, integrating into the systems or networks power derived from the sun, wind, water, tides, heat differentials, magnetic forces, and any other source of safe, ecologically sound and continuing energy supply.

28. Control the mining, production, transportation and use of fossil sources of energy to the extent necessary to reduce and prevent damages to the environment and the ecology, as well as to prevent conflicts and conserve supplies for sustained use by succeeding generations.

29. Exercise exclusive jurisdiction and control over nuclear energy research and testing and nuclear power production, including the right to prohibit any form of testing or production considered hazardous.

30. Place under world controls essential natural resources which may be limited or unevenly distributed about the Earth. Find and implement ways to reduce wastes and find ways to minimize disparities when development or production is insufficient to supply everybody with all that may be needed.

31. Provide for the examination and assessment of technological innovations which are or may be of supranational consequence, to determine possible hazards or perils to humanity or the environment; institute such controls

and regulations of technology as may be found necessary to prevent or correct widespread hazards or perils to human health and welfare.

32. Carry out intensive programs to develop safe alternatives to any technology or technological processes which may be hazardous to the environment, the ecological system, or human health and welfare.

33. Resolve supra-national problems caused by gross disparities in technological development or capability, capital formation, availability of natural resources, educational opportunity, economic opportunity, and wage and price differentials. Assist the processes of technology transfer under conditions which safeguard human welfare and the environment and contribute to minimizing disparities.

34. Intervene under procedures to be defined by the World Parliament in cases of either intra-state violence and intra-state problems which seriously affect world peace or universal human rights.

35. Develop a world university system. Obtain the correction of prejudicial communicative materials which cause misunderstandings or conflicts due to differences of race, religion, sex, national origin or affiliation.

36. Organize, coordinate and/or administer a voluntary, non-military World Service Corps, to carry out a wide variety of projects designed to serve human welfare.

37. Designate as may be found desirable an official world language or official world languages.

38. Establish and operate a system of world parks, wild life preserves, natural places, and wilderness areas.

39. Define and establish procedures for initiative and referendum by the Citizens of Earth on matters of supra-national legislation not prohibited by this World Constitution.

40. Establish such departments, bureaus, commissions, institutes, corporations, administrations, or agencies as may be needed to carry out any and all of the functions and powers of the World Government.

41. Serve the needs of humanity in any and all ways which are now, or may prove in the future to be, beyond the capacity of national and local governments.

Article 5. The World Parliament

Sec. A. Functions and Powers of the World Parliament

The functions and powers of the World Parliament shall comprise the following:

1. To prepare and enact detailed legislation in all areas of authority and jurisdiction granted to the World Government under Article IV of this World Constitution.

2. To amend or repeal world laws as may be found necessary or desirable.

3. To approve, amend or reject the international laws developed prior to the advent of World Government, and to codify and integrate the system of world law and world legislation under the World Government.

4. To establish such regulations and directions as may be needed, consistent with this world constitution, for the proper functioning of all organs, branches, departments, bureaus, commissions, institutes, agencies or parts of the World Government.

5. To review, amend and give final approval to each budget for the World Government, as submitted by the World Executive; to devise the specific means for directly raising funds needed to fulfill the budget, including taxes, licenses, fees, globally accounted social and public costs which must be added into the prices for goods and services, loans and credit advances, and any other appropriate means; and to appropriate and allocate funds for all operations and functions of the World Government in accordance with approved budgets, but subject to the right of the Parliament to revise any appropriation not yet spent or contractually committed.

6. To create, alter, abolish or consolidate the departments, bureaus, commissions, institutes, agencies or other parts of the World Government as may be needed for the best functioning of the several organs of the World Government, subject to the specific provisions of this World Constitution.

7. To approve the appointments of the heads of all major departments, commissions, offices, agencies and other parts of the several organs of the World Government, except those chosen by electoral or civil service procedures.

8. To remove from office for cause any member of the World Executive, and any elective or appointive head of any organ, department, office, agency or other part of the World Government, subject to the specific provisions in this World Constitution concerning specific offices.

9. To define and revise the boundaries of the World Electoral and Administrative Districts, the World Electoral and Administrative Regions and Magna Regions, and the Continental Divisions.

10. To schedule the implementation of those provisions of the World Constitution which require implementation by stages during the several stages of Provisional World Government, First Operative Stage of World Government, Second Operative Stage of World Government, and Full Operative Stage of World Government, as defined in Articles XVII and XIX of this World Constitution.

11. To plan and schedule the implementation of those provisions of the World Constitution which may require a period of years to be accomplished.

Sec. B. Composition of the World Parliament

1. The World Parliament shall be composed of three houses, designated as follows:

a. The House of Peoples, to represent the people of Earth directly and equally;

b. The House of Nations, to represent the nations which are joined together in the Federation of Earth; and

c. A House of Counselors with particular functions to represent the highest good and best interests of humanity as a whole.

2. All members of the World Parliament, regardless of House, shall be designated as Members of the World Parliament.

Sec. C. The House of Peoples

1. The House of Peoples shall be composed of the peoples delegates directly elected in proportion to population from the World Electoral and Administrative Districts, as defined in Article 2-4.

2. Peoples delegates shall be elected by universal adult suffrage, open to all persons of age 18 and above.

3. One peoples delegate shall be elected from each World Electoral and Administrative District to serve a five year term in the House of Peoples. Peoples delegates may be elected to serve successive terms without limit. Each peoples delegate shall have one vote.

4. A candidate for election to serve as a peoples delegate must be at least 21 years of age, a resident for at least one year of the electoral district from which the candidate is seeking election, and shall take a pledge of service to humanity.

Sec. D. The House of Nations

1. The House of Nations shall be composed of national delegates elected or appointed by procedures to be determined by each national government on the following basis:

a. One national delegate from each nation of at least 100,000 population, but less than 10,000,000 population.

b. Two national delegates from each nation of at least 10,000,000 population, but less than 100,000,000 population.

c. Three national delegates from each nation of 100,000,000 population or more.

2. Nations of less than 100,000 population may join in groups with other nations for purposes of representation in the House of Nations.

3. National delegates shall be elected or appointed to serve for terms of five years, and may be elected or appointed to serve successive terms without limit. Each national delegate shall have one vote.

4. Any person to serve as a national delegate shall be a citizen for at least two years of the nation to be represented, must be at least 21 years of age, and shall take a pledge of service to humanity.

Sec. E. The House of Counselors

1. The House of Counselors shall be composed of 200 counselors chosen in equal numbers from nominations submitted from the twenty World Electoral and Administrative Regions, as defined in Article II-5 and II-6, ten from each Region.

2. Nominations for members of the House of Counselors shall be made by the teachers and students of universities and colleges and of scientific academies and institutes within each world electoral and administrative region.

Nominees may be persons who are off campus in any walk of life as well as on campus.

3. Nominees to the House of Counselors from each World Electoral and Administrative Region shall, by vote taken among themselves, reduce the number of nominees to no less than two times and no more than three times the number to be elected.

4. Nominees to serve as members of the House of Counselors must be at least 25 years of age, and shall take a pledge of service to humanity. There shall be no residence requirement, and a nominee need not be a resident of the region from which nominated or elected.

5. The members of the House of Counselors from each region shall be elected by the members of the other two houses of the World Parliament from the particular region.

6. Counselors shall be elected to serve terms of ten years. One-half of the members of the House of Counselors shall be elected every five years. Counselors may serve successive terms without limit. Each Counselor shall have one vote.

Sec. F. Procedures of the World Parliament

1. Each house of the World Parliament during its first session after general elections shall elect a panel of five chairpersons from among its own members, one from each of five Continental Divisions. The chairpersons shall rotate annually so that each will serve for one year as chief presiding officer, while the other four serve as vice-chairpersons.

2. The panels of Chairpersons from each House shall meet together, as needed, for the purpose of coordinating the work of the Houses of the World Parliament, both severally and jointly.

3. Any legislative measure or action may be initiated in either House of Peoples or House of Nations or both concurrently, and shall become effective when passed by a simple majority vote of both the House of Peoples and of the House of Nations, except in those cases where an absolute majority vote or other voting majority is specified in this World Constitution.

4. In case of deadlock on a measure initiated in either the House of Peoples or House of Nations, the measure shall then automatically go to the House of Counselors for decision by simple majority vote of the House of Counselors, except in the cases where other majority vote is required in this World Constitution. Any measure may be referred for decision to the House of Counselors by a concurrent vote of the other two houses.

5. The House of Counselors may initiate any legislative measure, which shall then be submitted to the other two houses and must be passed by simple majority vote of both the House of Peoples and House of Nations to become effective, unless other voting majority is required by some provision of this World Constitution.

6. The House of Counselors may introduce an opinion or resolution on any measure pending before either of the other two houses; either of the other houses may request the opinion of the House of Counselors before acting upon a measure.

7. Each house of the World Parliament shall adopt its own detailed rules of procedure, which shall by consistent with the procedures set forth in this World Constitution, and which shall be designed to facilitate coordinated functioning of the three houses.

8. Approval of appointments by the World Parliament or any house thereof shall require simple majority votes, while removals for cause shall require absolute majority votes.

9. After the full operative stage of World Government is declared, general elections for members of the World Parliament to the House of Peoples shall be held every five years. The first general elections shall be held within the first two years following the declaration of the full operative stage of World Government.

10. Until the full operative stage of World Government is declared, elections for members of the World Parliament to the House of Peoples may be conducted whenever feasible in relation to the campaign for ratification of this World Constitution.

11. Regular sessions of the House of Peoples and House of Nations of the World Parliament shall convene on the second Monday of January of each and every Year.

12. Each nation, according to its own procedures, shall appoint or elect members of the World Parliament to the House of Nations at least thirty days prior to the date for convening the World Parliament in January.

13. The House of Peoples together with the House of Nations shall elect the members of the World Parliament to the House of Counselors during the month of January after the general elections. For its first session after general elections, the House of Counselors shall convene on the second Monday of March, and thereafter concurrently with the other two houses.

14. Bi-elections to fill vacancies shall be held within three months from occurrence of the vacancy or vacancies.

15. The World Parliament shall remain in session for a minimum of nine months of each year. One or two breaks may be taken during each year, at times and for durations to be decided by simple majority vote of the House of Peoples and House of Nations sitting jointly.

16. Annual salaries for members of the World Parliament of all three houses shall be the same, except for those who serve also as members of the Presidium and of the Executive Cabinet.

17. Salary schedules for members of the World Parliament and for members of the Presidium and of the Executive Cabinet shall be determined by the World Parliament.

Article 6. The World Executive

Sec. A Functions and Powers of the World Executive

1. To implement the basic system of world law as defined in the World Constitution and in the codified system of world law after approval by the World Parliament.

2. To implement legislation enacted by the World Parliament.

3. To propose and recommend legislation for enactment by the World Parliament.

4. To convene the World Parliament in special sessions when necessary.

5. To supervise the World Administration and the Integrative Complex and all of the departments, bureaus, offices, institutes and agencies thereof.

6. To nominate, select and remove the heads of various organs, branches, departments, bureaus, offices, commissions, institutes, agencies and other parts of the World Government, in accordance with the provisions of this World Constitution and as specified in measures enacted by the World Parliament.

7. To prepare and submit annually to the World Parliament a comprehensive budget for the operations of the World Government, and to prepare and submit periodically budget projections over periods of several years.

8. To define and propose priorities for world legislation and budgetary allocations.

9. To be held accountable to the World Parliament for the expenditures of appropriations made by the World Parliament in accordance with approved and longer term budgets, subject to revisions approved by the World Parliament.

Sec. B. Composition of the World Executive

The World Executive shall consist of a Presidium of five members, and of an Executive Cabinet of from twenty to thirty members, all of whom shall be members of the World Parliament.

Sec. C. The Presidium

1. The Presidium shall be composed of five members, one to be designated as President and the other four to be designated as Vice Presidents. Each member of the Presidium shall be from a different Continental Division.

2. The Presidency of the Presidium shall rotate each year, with each member in turn to serve as President, while the other four serve as Vice Presidents. The order of rotation shall be decided by the Presidium.

3. The decisions of the Presidium shall be taken collectively, on the basis of majority decisions.

4. Each member of the Presidium shall be a member of the World Parliament, either elected to the House of Peoples or to the House of Counselors, or appointed or elected to the House of Nations.

5. Nominations for the Presidium shall be made by the House of Counselors. The number of nominees shall be from two to three times the number to be elected. No more than one-third of the nominees shall be from the

House of Counselors or from the House of Nations, and nominees must be included from all Continental Divisions.

6. From among the nominees submitted by the House of Counselors, the Presidium shall be elected by vote of the combined membership of all three houses of the World Parliament in joint session. A plurality vote equal to at least 40 percent of the total membership of the World Parliament shall be required for the election of each member to the Presidium, with successive elimination votes taken as necessary until the required plurality is achieved.

7. Members of the Presidium may be removed for cause, either individually or collectively, by an absolute majority vote of the combined membership of the three houses of the World Parliament in joint session.

8. The term of office for the Presidium shall be five years and shall run concurrently with the terms of office for the members as Members of the World Parliament, except that at the end of each five year period, the Presidium members in office shall continue to serve until the new Presidium for the succeeding term is elected. Membership in the Presidium shall be limited to two consecutive terms.

Sec. D. The Executive Cabinet

1. The Executive Cabinet shall be composed of from twenty to thirty members, with at least one member from each of the ten World Electoral and Administrative Magna Regions of the world.

2. All members of the Executive Cabinet shall be Members of the World Parliament.

3. There shall be no more than two members of the Executive Cabinet from any single nation of the World Federation. There may be only one member of the Executive Cabinet from a nation from which a Member of the World Parliament is serving as a member of the Presidium.

4. Each member of the Executive Cabinet shall serve as the head of a department or agency of the World Administration or Integrative Complex, and in this capacity shall be designated as Minister of the particular department or agency.

5. Nominations for members of the Executive Cabinet shall be made by the Presidium, taking into consideration the various functions which Executive Cabinets members are to perform. The Presidium shall nominate no more than two times the number to be elected.

6. The Executive Cabinet shall be elected by simple majority vote of the combined membership of all three houses of the World Parliament in joint session.

7. Members of the Executive Cabinet either individually or collectively may be removed for cause by an absolute majority vote of the combined membership of all three houses of the World Parliament sitting in joint session.

8. The term of office in the Executive Cabinet shall be five years, and shall run concurrently with the terms of office for the members as Members of the World Parliament, except that at the end of each five year period, the Cabinet

members in office s hall continue to serve until the new Executive Cabinet for the succeeding term is elected. Membership in the Executive Cabinet shall be limited to three consecutive terms, regardless of change in ministerial position.

Sec. E. Procedures of the World Executive

1. The Presidium shall assign the ministerial positions among the Cabinet members to head the several administrative departments and major agencies of the Administration and of the Integrative Complex. Each Vice President may also serve as a Minister to head an administrative department, but not the President. Ministerial positions may be changed at the discretion of the Presidium. A Cabinet member or Vice President may hold more than one ministerial post, but no more than three, providing that no Cabinet member is without a Ministerial post.

2. The Presidium, in consultation with the Executive Cabinet, shall prepare and present to the World Parliament near the beginning of each year a proposed program of world legislation. The Presidium may propose other legislation during the year.

3. The Presidium, in consultation with the Executive Cabinet, and in consultation with the World Financial Administration, (see Article VIII, Sec. G-1-i) shall be responsible for preparing and submitting to the World Parliament the proposed annual budget, and budgetary projections over periods of years.

4. Each Cabinet Member and Vice President as Minister of a particular department or agency shall prepare an annual report for the particular department or agency, to be submitted both to the Presidium and to the World Parliament.

5. The members of the Presidium and of the Executive Cabinet at all times shall be responsible both individually and collectively to the World Parliament.

6. Vacancies occurring at any time in the World Executive shall be filled within sixty days by nomination and election in the same manner as specified for filling the offices originally.

Sec. F. Limitations on the World Executive

1. The World Executive shall not at any time alter, suspend, abridge, infringe or otherwise violate any provision of this World Constitution or any legislation or world law enacted or approved by the World Parliament in accordance with the provisions of this World Constitution.

2. The World Executive shall not have veto power over any legislation passed by the World Parliament.

3. The World Executive may not dissolve the World Parliament or any House of the World Parliament.

4. The World Executive may not act contrary to decisions of the World Courts.

5. The World Executive shall be bound to faithfully execute all legislation passed by the World Parliament in accordance with the provisions of this World Constitution, and may not impound or refuse to spend funds appropriated by the

World Parliament, nor spend more funds than are appropriated by the World Parliament.

6. The World Executive may not transcend or contradict the decisions or controls of the World Parliament, the World Judiciary or the Provisions of this World Constitution by any device of executive order or executive privilege or emergency declaration or decree.

Article 7. The World Administration

Sec. A. Functions of the World Administration

1. The World Administration shall be organized to carry out the detailed and continuous administration and implementation of world legislation and world law.

2. The World Administration shall be under the direction of the World Executive, and shall at all times be responsible to the World Executive.

3. The World Administration shall be organized so as to give professional continuity to the work of administration and implementation.

Sec. B. Structure and Procedures of the World Administration

1. The World Administration shall be composed of professionally organized departments and other agencies in all areas of activity requiring continuity of administration and implementation by the World Government.

2. Each Department or major agency of the World Administration shall be headed by a Minister who shall be either a member of the Executive Cabinet or a Vice President of the Presidium.

3. Each Department or major agency of the World Administration shall have as chief of staff a Senior Administrator, who shall assist the Minister and supervise the detailed work of the Department or agency.

4. Each Senior Administrator shall be nominated by the Minister of the particular Department or agency from among persons in the senior lists of the World Civil Service Administration, as soon as senior lists have been established by the World Civil Service Administration, and shall be confirmed by the Presidium. Temporary qualified appointments shall be made by the Ministers, with confirmation by the Presidium, pending establishment of the senior lists.

5. There shall be a Secretary General of the World Administration, who shall be nominated by the Presidium and confirmed by absolute majority vote of the entire Executive Cabinet.

6. The functions and responsibilities of the Secretary General of the World Administration shall be to assist in coordinating the work of the Senior Administrators of the several Departments and agencies of the World Administration. The Secretary General shall at all times be subject to the direction of the Presidium, and shall be directly responsible to the Presidium.

7. The employment of any Senior Administrator and of the Secretary General may be terminated for cause by absolute majority vote of both the

Executive Cabinet and Presidium combined, but not contrary to civil service rules which protect tenure on grounds of competence.

8. Each Minister of a Department or agency of the World Administration, being also a Member of the World Parliament, shall provide continuous liaison between the particular Department or agency and the World Parliament, shall respond at any time to any questions or requests for information from the Parliament, including committees of any House of the World Parliament.

9. The Presidium, in cooperation with the particular Ministers in each case, shall be responsible for the original organization of each of the Departments and major agencies of the World Administration.

10. The assignment of legislative measures, constitutional provisions and areas of world law to particular Departments and agencies for administration and implementation shall be done by the Presidium in consultation with the Executive Cabinet and Secretary General, unless specifically provided in legislation passed by the World Parliament.

11. The Presidium, in consultation with the Executive Cabinet, may propose the creation of other departments and agencies to have ministerial status; and may propose the alteration, combination or termination of existing Departments and agencies of ministerial status as may seem necessary or desirable. Any such creation, alteration, combination or termination shall require a simple majority vote of approval of the three houses of the World Parliament in joint session.

12. The World Parliament by absolute majority vote of the three houses in joint session may specify the creation of new departments or agencies of ministerial status in the World Administration, or may direct the World Executive to alter, combine, or terminate existing departments or agencies of ministerial status.

13. The Presidium and the World Executive may not create, establish or maintain any administrative or executive department or agency for the purpose of circumventing control by the World Parliament.

Sec. C. Departments of the World Administration

Among the Departments and agencies of the World Administration of ministerial status, but not limited thereto and subject to combinations and to changes in descriptive terminology, shall be those listed under this Section. Each major area of administration shall be headed by a Cabinet Minister and a Senior Administrator, or by a Vice President and a Senior Administrator.

1. Disarmament and War Prevention.
2. Population.
3. Food and Agriculture.
4. Water Supplies and Waterways.
5. Health and Nutrition.
6. Education.
7. Cultural Diversity and the Arts.
8. Habitat and Settlements.
9. Environment and Ecology.

10. World Resources.
11. Oceans and Seabeds.
12. Atmosphere and Space.
13. Energy.
14. Science and Technology.
15. Genetic Research and Engineering.
16. Labor and Income.
17. Economic and Social Development.
18. Commerce and Industry.
19. Transportation and Travel.
20. Multi-National Corporations.
21. Communications and Information.
22. Human Rights.
23. Distributive Justice.
24. World Service Corps.
25. World Territories, Capitals and Parks.
26. Exterior Relations.
27. Democratic Procedures.
28. Revenue.

Article 8. The Integrative Complex

Sec. A. Definition

1. Certain administrative, research, planning and facilitative agencies of the World Government which are particularly essential for the satisfactory functioning of all or most aspects of the World Government, shall be designated as the Integrative Complex. The Integrative Complex shall include the agencies listed under this Section, with the proviso that other such agencies may be added upon recommendation of the Presidium followed by decision of the World Parliament.

a. The World Civil Service Administration.
b. The World Boundaries and Elections Administration.
c. The Institute on Governmental Procedures and World Problems.
d. The Agency for Research and Planning.
e. The Agency for Technological and Environmental Assessment.
f. The World Financial Administration.
g. Commission for Legislative Review.

2. Each agency of the Integrative Complex shall be headed by a Cabinet Minister and a Senior Administrator, or by a Vice President and a Senior Administrator, together with a Commission as provided hereunder. The rules of procedure for each agency shall be decided by majority decision of the Commission members together with the Administrator and the Minister or Vice President.

3. The World Parliament may at any time define further the responsibilities, functioning and organization of the several agencies of the Integrative Complex,

consistent with the provisions of Article VIII and other provisions of the World Constitution.

4. Each agency of the Integrative Complex shall make an annual report to the World Parliament and to the Presidium.

Sec. B. The World Civil Service Administration

1. The functions of the World Civil Service Administration shall be the following, but not limited thereto:

a. To formulate and define standards, qualifications, tests, examinations and salary scales for the personnel of all organs, departments, bureaus, offices, commissions and agencies of the World Government, in conformity with the provisions of this World Constitution and requiring approval by the Presidium and Executive Cabinet, subject to review and approval by the World Parliament.

b. To establish rosters or lists of competent personnel for all categories of personnel to be appointed or employed in the service of the World Government.

c. To select and employ upon request by any government organ, department, bureau, office, institute, commission, agency or authorized official, such competent personnel as may be needed and authorized, except for those positions which are made elective or appointive under provisions of the World Constitution or by specific legislation of the World Parliament.

2. The World Civil Service Administration shall be headed by a ten member commission in addition to the Cabinet Minister or Vice President and Senior Administrator. The Commission shall be composed of one commissioner from each of ten World Electoral and Administrative Magna-Regions. The persons to serve as Commissioners shall be nominated by the House of Counselors and then appointed by the Presidium for five year terms. Commissioners may serve consecutive terms.

Sec. C. The World Boundaries and Elections Administration

1. The functions of the World Boundaries and Elections Administration shall include the following, but not limited thereto:

a. To define the boundaries for the basic World Electoral and Administrative Districts, the World Electoral and Administrative Regions and Magna-Regions, and the Continental Divisions, for submission to the World Parliament for approval by legislative action.

b. To make periodic adjustments every ten or five years, as needed, of the boundaries for the World Electoral and Administrative Districts, the World Electoral and Administrative Regions and Magna-Regions, and of the Continental Divisions, subject to approval by the World Parliament.

c. To define the detailed procedures for the nomination and election of Members of the World Parliament to the House of Peoples and to the House of Counselors, subject to approval by the World Parliament.

d. To conduct the elections for Members of the World Parliament to the House of Peoples and to the House of Counselors.

e. Before each World Parliamentary Election, to prepare Voters' Information Booklets which shall summarize major current public issues, and shall list each candidate for elective office together with standard information about each candidate, and give space for each candidate to state his or her views on the defined major issues as well as on any other major issue of choice; to include information on any initiatives or referendums which are to be voted upon; to distribute the Voter's Information Booklets for each World Electoral District, or suitable group of Districts; and to obtain the advice of the Institute on Governmental Procedures and World Problems, the Agency for Research and Planning, and the Agency for Technological and Environmental Assessment in preparing the booklets.

f. To define the rules for world political parties, subject to approval by the World Parliament, and subject to review and recommendations of the World Ombudsmus.

g. To define the detailed procedures for legislative initiative and referendum by the Citizens of Earth, and to conduct voting on supra- national or global initiatives and referendums in conjunction with world parliamentary elections.

h. To conduct plebiscites when requested by other Organs of the World Government, and to make recommendations for the settlement of boundary disputes.

i. To conduct a global census every five years, and to prepare and maintain complete demographic analyses for Earth.

2. The World Boundaries and Elections Administration shall be headed by a ten member commission in addition to the Senior Administrator and the Cabinet Minister or Vice President. The commission shall be composed of one commissioner each from ten World Electoral and Administrative Magna-Regions. The persons to serve as commissioners shall be nominated by the House of Counselors and then appointed by the World Presidium for five year terms. Commissioners may serve consecutive terms.

Sec. D. Institute on Governmental Procedures and World Problems

1. The functions of the Institute on Governmental Procedures and World Problems shall be as follows, but not limited thereto:

a. To prepare and conduct courses of information, education and training for all personnel in the service of the World Government, including Members of the World Parliament and of all other elective, appointive and civil service personnel, so that every person in the service of the World Government may have a better understanding of the functions, structure, procedures and inter-relationships of the various organs, departments, bureaus, offices, institutes, commissions, agencies and other parts of the World Government.

b. To prepare and conduct courses and seminars for information, education, discussion, updating and new ideas in all areas of world problems, particularly for Members of the World Parliament and of the World Executive, and for the chief personnel of all organs, departments and agencies of the World Government, but open to all in the service of the World Government.

c. To bring in qualified persons from private and public universities, colleges and research and action organizations of many countries, as well as other qualified persons, to lecture and to be resource persons for the courses and seminars organized by the Institute on Governmental Procedures and World Problems.

d. To contract with private or public universities and colleges or other agencies to conduct courses and seminars for the Institute.

2. The Institute on Governmental Procedures and World Problems shall be supervised by a ten member commission in addition to the Senior Administrator and Cabinet Minister or Vice President. The commission shall be composed of one commissioner each to be named by the House of Peoples, the House of Nations, the House of Counselors, the Presidium, the Collegium of World Judges, The World Ombudsmus, The World Attorneys General Office, the Agency for Research and Planning, the Agency for Technological and Environmental Assessment, and the World Financial Administration. Commissioners shall serve five year terms, and may serve consecutive terms.

Sec. E. The Agency for Research and Planning

1. The functions of the Agency for Research and Planning shall be as follows, but not limited thereto:

a. To serve the World Parliament, the World Executive, the World Administration, and other organs, departments and agencies of the World Government in any matter requiring research and planning within the competence of the agency.

b. To prepare and maintain a comprehensive inventory of world resources.

c. To prepare comprehensive long-range plans for the development, conservation, re-cycling and equitable sharing of the resources of Earth for the benefit of all people on Earth, subject to legislative action by the World Parliament.

d. To prepare and maintain a comprehensive list and description of all world problems, including their inter-relationships, impact time projections and proposed solutions, together with bibliographies.

e. To do research and help prepare legislative measures at the request of any Member of the World Parliament or of any committee of any House of the World Parliament.

f. To do research and help prepare proposed legislation or proposed legislative programs and schedules at the request of the Presidium or Executive Cabinet or of any Cabinet Minister.

g. To do research and prepare reports at the request of any other organ, department or agency of the World Government.

h. To enlist the help of public and private universities, colleges, research agencies, and other associations and organizations for various research and planning projects.

i. To contract with public and private universities, colleges, research agencies and other organizations for the preparation of specific reports, studies and proposals.

j. To maintain a comprehensive World Library for the use of all Members of the World Parliament, and for the use of all other officials and persons in the service of the World Government, as well as for public information.

2. The Agency for Research and Planning shall be supervised by a ten member commission in addition to the Senior Administrator and Cabinet Minister or Vice President. The commission shall be composed of one commissioner each to be named by the House of Peoples, the House of Nations, the House of Counselors, the Presidium, the Collegium of World Judges, the Office of World Attorneys General, World Ombudsmus, the Agency for Technological and Environmental Assessment, the Institute on Governmental Procedures and World Problems, and the World Financial Administration. Commissioners shall serve five year terms, and may serve consecutive terms.

Sec. F. The Agency for Technological and Environmental Assessment

1. The functions of the agency for Technological and Environmental Assessment shall include the following, but not limited thereto:

a. To establish and maintain a registration and description of all significant technological innovations, together with impact projections.

b. To examine, analyze and assess the impacts and consequences of technological innovations which may have either significant beneficial or significant harmful or dangerous consequences for human life or for the ecology of life on Earth, or which may require particular regulations or prohibitions to prevent or eliminate dangers or to assure benefits.

c. To examine, analyze and assess environmental and ecological problems, in particular the environmental and ecological problems which may result from any intrusions or changes of the environment or ecological relationships which may be caused by technological innovations, processes of resource development, patterns of human settlements, the production of energy, patterns of economic and industrial development, or other man-made intrusions and changes of the environment, or which may result from natural causes.

d. To maintain a global monitoring network to measure possible harmful effects of technological innovations and environmental disturbances so that corrective measures can be designed.

e. To prepare recommendations based on technological and environmental analyses and assessments, which can serve as guides to the World Parliament, the World Executive, the World Administration, the Agency for Research and Planning, and to the other organs, departments and agencies of the World

Government, as well as to individuals in the service of the World Government and to national and local governments and legislative bodies.

f. To enlist the voluntary or contractual aid and participation of private and public universities, colleges, research institutions and other associations and organizations in the work of technological and environmental assessment.

g. To enlist the voluntary or contractual aid and participation of private and public universities and colleges, research institutions and other organizations in devising and developing alternatives to harmful or dangerous technologies and environmentally disruptive activities, and in devising controls to assure beneficial results from technological innovations or to prevent harmful results from either technological innovations or environmental changes, all subject to legislation for implementation by the World Parliament.

2. The Agency for Technological and Environmental Assessment shall be supervised by a ten member commission in addition to the Senior Administrator and Cabinet Minister or Vice President. The commission shall be composed of one commissioner from each of ten World Electoral and Administrative Magna-Regions. The persons to serve as commissioners shall be nominated by the House of Counselors, and then appointed by the World Presidium for five year terms. Commissioners may serve consecutive terms.

Sec. G. The World Financial Administration

1. The functions of the World Financial Administration shall include the following, but not limited thereto:

a. To establish and operate the procedures for the collection of revenues for the World Government, pursuant to legislation by the World Parliament, inclusive of taxes, globally accounted social and public costs, licenses, fees, revenue sharing arrangements, income derived from supra-national public enterprises or projects or resource developments, and all other sources.

b. To operate a Planetary Accounting Office, and thereunder to make cost/benefit studies and reports of the functioning and activities of the World Government and of its several organs, departments, branches, bureaus, offices, commissions, institutes, agencies and other parts or projects. In making such studies and reports, account shall be taken not only of direct financial costs and benefits, but also of human, social, environmental, indirect, long-term and other costs and benefits, and of actual or possible hazards and damages. Such studies and reports shall also be designed to uncover any wastes, inefficiencies, misapplications, corruptions, diversions, unnecessary costs, and other possible irregularities.

c. To make cost/benefit studies and reports at the request of any House or committee of the World Parliament, and of the Presidium, the Executive Cabinet, the World Ombudsmus, the Office of World Attorneys General, the World Supreme Court, or of any administrative department or any agency of the Integrative Complex, as well as upon its own initiative.

d. To operate a Planetary Comptrollers Office and there under to supervise the disbursement of the funds of the World Government for all purposes, projects and activities duly authorized by this World Constitution, the World Parliament, the World Executive, and other organs, departments and agencies of the World Government.

e. To establish and operate a Planetary Banking System, making the transition to a common global currency, under the terms of specific legislation passed by the World Parliament.

f. Pursuant to specific legislation enacted by the World Parliament, and in conjunction with the Planetary Banking System, to establish and implement the procedures of a Planetary Monetary and Credit System based upon useful productive capacity and performance, both in goods and services. Such a monetary and credit system shall be designed for use within the Planetary Banking System for the financing of the activities and projects of the World Government, and for all other financial purposes approved by the World Parliament, without requiring the payment of interest on bonds, investments or other claims of financial ownership or debt.

g. To establish criteria for the extension of financial credit based upon such considerations as people available to work, usefulness, cost/benefit accounting, human and social values, environmental health and esthetics, minimizing disparities, integrity , competent management, appropriate technology, potential production and performance.

h. To establish and operate a Planetary Insurance System in areas of world need which transcend national boundaries and in accordance with legislation passed by the World Parliament.

i. To assist the Presidium as may be requested in the technical preparation of budgets for the operation of the World Government.

2. The World Financial Administration shall be supervised by a commission of ten members, together with a Senior Administrator and a Cabinet Minister or Vice President. The commission shall be composed of one commissioner each to be named by the House of Peoples, the House of Nations, the House of Counselors, the Presidium, the Collegium of World Judges, the Office of Attorneys General, the World Ombudsmus, the Agency for Research and Planning, the Agency for Technological and Environmental Assessment, and the Institute on Governmental Procedures and World Problems. Commissioners shall serve terms of five years, and may serve consecutive terms.

Sec. H. Commission for Legislative Review

1. The functions of the Commission for Legislative Review shall be to examine World Legislation and World Laws which the World Parliament enacts or adopts from the previous Body of International Law for the purpose of analyzing whether any particular legislation or law has become obsolete or obstructive or defective in serving the purposes intended; and to make recommendations to the World Parliament accordingly for repeal or amendment or replacement.

2. The Commission for Legislative Review shall be composed of twelve members, including two each to be elected by the House of Peoples, the House of

Nations, the House of Counselors, the Collegium of World Judges, the World Ombudsmus and the Presidium. Members of the Commission shall serve terms of ten years, and may be re-elected to serve consecutive terms. One half of the Commission members after the Commission is first formed shall be elected every five years, with the first terms for one half of the members to be only five years.

Article 9. The World Judiciary

Sec. A. Jurisdiction of the World Supreme Court

1. A World Supreme Court shall be established, together with such regional and district World Courts as may subsequently be found necessary. The World Supreme Court shall comprise a number of benches.

2. The World Supreme Court, together with such regional and district World Courts as may be established, shall have mandatory jurisdiction in all cases, actions, disputes, conflicts, violations of law, civil suits, guarantees of civil and human rights, constitutional interpretations, and other litigations arising under the provisions of this World Constitution, world legislation, and the body of world law approved by the World Parliament.

3. Decisions of the World Supreme Court shall be binding on all parties involved in all cases, actions and litigations brought before any bench of the World Supreme Court for settlement. Each bench of the World Supreme Court shall constitute a court of highest appeal, except when matters of extra-ordinary public importance are assigned or transferred to the Superior Tribunal of the World Supreme Court, as provided in Section E of Article IX.

Sec. B. Benches of the World Supreme Court

The benches of the World Supreme Court and their respective jurisdictions shall be as follows:

1. Bench for Human Rights: To deal with issues of human rights arising under the guarantee of civil and human rights provided by Article XII of this World Constitution, and arising in pursuance of the provisions of Article XIII of this World Constitution, and arising otherwise under world legislation and the body of world law approved by the World Parliament.

2. Bench for Criminal Cases: To deal with issues arising from the violation of world laws and world legislation by individuals, corporations, groups and associations, but not issues primarily concerned with human rights.

3. Bench for Civil Cases: To deal with issues involving civil law suits and disputes between individuals, corporations, groups and associations arising under world legislation and world law and the administration thereof.

4. Bench for Constitutional Cases: To deal with the interpretation of the World Constitution and with issues and actions arising in connection with the interpretation of the World Constitution.

5. Bench for International Conflicts: To deal with disputes, conflicts and legal contest arising between or among the nations which have joined in the Federation of Earth.

6. Bench for Public Cases: To deal with issues not under the jurisdiction of another bench arising from conflicts, disputes, civil suits or other legal contests between the World Government and corporations, groups or individuals, or between national governments and corporations, groups or individuals in cases involving world legislation and world law.

7. Appellate Bench: To deal with issues involving world legislation and world law which may be appealed from national courts; and to decide which bench to assign a case or action or litigation when a question or disagreement arises over the proper jurisdiction.

8. Advisory Bench: To give opinions upon request on any legal question arising under world law or world legislation, exclusive of contests or actions involving interpretation of the World Constitution. Advisory opinions may be requested by any House or committee of the World Parliament, by the Presidium, any Administrative Department, the Office of World Attorneys General, the World Ombudsmus, or by any agency of the Integrative Complex.

9. Other benches may be established, combined or terminated upon recommendation of the Collegium of World Judges with approval by the World Parliament; but benches number one through eight may not be combined nor terminated except by amendment of this World Constitution.

Sec. C. Seats of the World Supreme Court

1. The primary seat of the World Supreme Court and all benches shall be the same as for the location of the Primary World Capital and for the location of the World Parliament and the World Executive.

2. Continental seats of the World Supreme Court shall be established in the four secondary capitals of the World Government located in four different Continental Divisions of Earth, as provided in Article XV.

3. The following permanent benches of the World Supreme Court shall be established both at the primary seat and at each of the continental seats: Human Rights, Criminal Cases, Civil Cases, and Public Cases.

4. The following permanent benches of the World Supreme Court shall be located only at the primary seat of the World Supreme Court: Constitutional Cases, International Conflicts, Appellate Bench, and Advisory Bench.

5. Benches which are located permanently only at the primary seat of the World Supreme Court may hold special sessions at the other continental seats of the World Supreme Court when necessary, or may establish continental circuits if needed.

6. Benches of the World Supreme Court which have permanent continental locations may hold special sessions at other locations when needed, or may establish regional circuits if needed.

Sec. D. The Collegium of World Judges

1. A Collegium of World Judges shall be established by the World Parliament. The Collegium shall consist of a minimum of twenty member judges, and may be expanded as needed but not to exceed sixty members.

2. The World Judges to compose the Collegium of World Judges shall be nominated by the House of Counselors and shall be elected by plurality vote of the three Houses of the World Parliament in joint session. The House of Counselors shall nominate between two and three times the number of world judges to be elected at any one time. An equal number of World Judges shall be elected from each of ten World Electoral and Administrative Magna-Regions, if not immediately then by rotation.

3. The term of office for a World Judge shall be ten years. Successive terms may be served without limit.

4. The Collegium of World Judges shall elect a Presiding Council of World Judges, consisting of a Chief Justice and four Associate Chief Justices. One member of the Presiding Council of World Judges shall be elected from each of five Continental Divisions of Earth. Members of the Presiding Council of World Judges shall serve five year terms on the Presiding Council, and may serve two successive terms, but not two successive terms as Chief Justice.

5. The Presiding Council of World Judges shall assign all World Judges, including themselves, to the several benches of the World Supreme Court. Each bench for a sitting at each location shall have a minimum of three World Judges, except that the number of World Judges for benches on Continental Cases and International Conflicts, and the Appellate Bench, shall be no less than five.

6. The member judges of each bench at each location shall choose annually a Presiding Judge, who may serve two successive terms.

7. The members of the several benches may be reconstituted from time to time as may seem desirable or necessary upon the decision of the Presiding Council of World Judges. Any decision to re-constitute a bench shall be referred to a vote of the entire Collegium of World Judges by request of any World Judge.

8. Any World Judge may be removed from office for cause by an absolute two- thirds majority vote of the three Houses of the World Parliament in joint session.

9. Qualifications for Judges of the World Supreme Court shall be at least ten years of legal or juristic experience, minimum age of thirty years, and evident competence in world law and the humanities.

10. The salaries, expenses, remunerations and prerogatives of the World Judges shall be determined by the World Parliament, and shall be reviewed every five years, but shall not be changed to the disadvantage of any World Judge during a term of office. All members of the Collegium of World Judges shall receive the same salaries, except that additional compensation may be given to the Presiding Council of World Judges.

11. Upon recommendation by the Collegium of World Judges, the World Parliament shall have the authority to establish regional and district world courts below the World Supreme Court, and to establish the jurisdictions thereof, and the procedures for appeal to the World Supreme Court or to the several benches thereof.

12. The detailed rules of procedure for the functioning of the World Supreme Court, the Collegium of World Judges, and for each bench of the World

Supreme Court, shall be decided and amended by absolute majority vote of the Collegium of World Judges.

Sec. E. The Superior Tribunal of the World Supreme Court

1. A Superior Tribunal of the World Supreme Court shall be established to take cases which are considered to be of extra-ordinary public importance. The Superior Tribunal for any calendar year shall consist of the Presiding Council of World Judges together with one World Judge named by the Presiding Judge of each bench of the World Court sitting at the primary seat of the World Supreme Court. The composition of the Superior Tribunal may be continued unchanged for a second year by decision of the Presiding Council of World Judges.

2. Any party to any dispute, issue, case or litigation coming under the jurisdiction of the World Supreme Court, may apply to any particular bench of the World Supreme Court or to the Presiding Council of World Judges for the assignment or transfer of the case to the Superior Tribunal on the grounds of extra-ordinary public importance. If the application is granted, the case shall be heard and disposed of by the Superior Tribunal. Also, any bench taking any particular case, if satisfied that the case is of extra-ordinary public importance, may of its own discretion transfer the case to the Superior Tribunal.

Article 10. The Enforcement System

Sec. A. Basic Principles

1. The enforcement of world law and world legislation shall apply directly to individuals, and individuals shall be held responsible for compliance with world law and world legislation regardless of whether the individuals are acting in their own capacity or as agents or officials of governments at any level or of the institutions of governments, or as agents or officials of corporations, organizations, associations or groups of any kind.

2. When world law or world legislation or decisions of the world courts are violated, the Enforcement System shall operate to identify and apprehend the individuals responsible for violations.

3. Any enforcement action shall not violate the civil and human rights guaranteed under this World Constitution.

4. The enforcement of world law and world legislation shall be carried out in the context of a non-military world federation wherein all member nations shall disarm as a condition for joining and benefiting from the world federation, subject to Article X VII, Sec. C-8 and D-6. The Federation of Earth and World Government under this World Constitution shall neither keep nor use weapons of mass destruction.

5. Those agents of the enforcement system whose function shall be to apprehend and bring to court violators of world law and world legislation shall be equipped only with such weapons as are appropriate for the apprehension of the individuals responsible for violations.

6. The enforcement of world law and world legislation under this World Constitution shall be conceived and developed primarily as the processes of effective design and administration of world law and world legislation to serve the welfare of all people on Earth, with equity and justice for all, in which the resources of Earth and the funds and the credits of the World Government are used only to serve peaceful human needs, and none used for weapons of mass destruction or for war making capabilities.

Sec. B. The Structure for Enforcement: World Attorneys General

1. The Enforcement System shall be headed by an Office of World Attorneys General and a Commission of Regional World Attorneys.

2. The Office of World Attorneys General shall be comprised of five members, one of whom shall be designated as the World Attorney General and the other four shall each be designated an Associate World Attorney General.

3. The Commission of Regional World Attorneys shall consist of twenty Regional World Attorneys.

4. The members to comprise the Office of World Attorneys General shall be nominated by the House of Counselors, with three nominees from each Continental Division of Earth. One member of the Office shall be elected from each of five Continental Divisions by plurality vote of the three houses of the World Parliament in joint session.

5. The term of office for a member of the Office of World Attorneys General shall be ten years. A member may serve two consecutive terms. The position of World Attorney General shall rotate every two years among the five members of the Office. The order of rotation shall be decided among the five members of the Office.

6. The Office of World Attorneys General shall nominate members for the Commission of twenty Regional World Attorneys from the twenty World Electoral and Administrative Regions, with between two and three nominees submitted for each Region. From these nominations, the three Houses of the World Parliament in joint session shall elect one Regional World Attorney from each of the twenty Regions. Regional World Attorneys shall serve terms of five years, and may serve three consecutive terms.

7. Each Regional World Attorney shall organize and be in charge of an Office of Regional World Attorney. Each Associate World Attorney General shall supervise five Offices of Regional World Attorneys.

8. The staff to carry out the work of enforcement, in addition to the five members of the Office of World Attorneys General and the twenty Regional World Attorneys, shall be selected from civil service lists, and shall be organized for the following functions:

    a. Investigation.
    b. Apprehension and arrest.
    c. Prosecution.
    d. Remedies and correction.

e. Conflict resolution.

9. Qualifications for a member of the Office of World Attorneys General and for the Regional World Attorneys shall be at least thirty years of age, at least seven years legal experience, and education in law and the humanities.

10. The World Attorney General, the Associate World Attorneys General, and the Regional World Attorneys shall at all times be responsible to the World Parliament. Any member of the Office of World Attorneys General and any Regional World Attorney can be removed from office for cause by a simple majority vote of the three Houses of the World Parliament in joint session.

Sec. C. The World Police

1. That section of the staff of the Office of World Attorneys General and of the Offices of Regional World Attorneys responsible for the apprehension and arrest of violators of world law and world legislation, shall be designated as World Police.

2. Each regional staff of the World Police shall be headed by a Regional World Police Captain, who shall be appointed by the Regional World Attorney.

3. The Office of World Attorneys General shall appoint a World Police Supervisor, to be in charge of those activities which transcend regional boundaries. The World Police Supervisor shall direct the Regional World Police Captains in any actions which require coordinated or joint action transcending regional boundaries, and shall direct any action which requires initiation or direction from the Office of World Attorneys General.

4. Searches and arrests to be made by World Police shall be made only upon warrants issued by the Office of World Attorneys General or by a Regional World Attorney.

5. World Police shall be armed only with weapons appropriate for the apprehension of the individuals responsible for violation of world law.

6. Employment in the capacity of World Police Captain and World Police Supervisor shall be limited to ten years.

7. The World Police Supervisor and any Regional World Police Captain may be removed from office for cause by decision of the Office of World Attorneys General or by absolute majority vote of the three Houses of the World Parliament in joint session.

Sec. D. The Means of Enforcement

1. Non-military means of enforcement of world law and world legislation shall be developed by the World Parliament and by the Office of World Attorneys General in consultation with the Commission of Regional World Attorneys, the Collegium of World Judges , the World Presidium, and the World Ombudsmus. The actual means of enforcement shall require legislation by the World Parliament.

2. Non-military means of enforcement which can be developed may include: Denial of financial credit; denial of material resources and personnel; revocation of licenses, charters, or corporate rights; impounding of equipment;

fines and damage payments; performance of work to rectify damages; imprisonment or isolation; and other means appropriate to the specific situations.

3. To cope with situations of potential or actual riots, insurrection and resort to armed violence, particular strategies and methods shall be developed by the World Parliament and by the Office of World Attorneys General in consultation with the Commission of Regional World Attorneys, the Collegium of World Judges, the Presidium and the World Ombudsmus. Such strategies and methods shall require enabling legislation by the World Parliament where required in addition to the specific provisions of this World Constitution.

4. A basic condition for preventing outbreaks of violence which the Enforcement System shall facilitate in every way possible, shall be to assure a fair hearing under non-violent circumstances for any person or group having a grievance, and likewise to assure a fair opportunity for a just settlement of any grievance with due regard for the rights and welfare of all concerned.

Article 11. The World Ombudsmus

Sec. A. Functions and Powers of the World Ombudsmus

The functions and powers of the World Ombudsmus, as public defender, shall include the following:

1. To protect the People of Earth and all individuals against violations or neglect of universal human and civil rights which are stipulated in Article 12 and other sections of this World Constitution.

2. To protect the People of Earth against violations of this World Constitution by any official or agency of the World Government, including both elected and appointed officials or public employees regardless of organ, department, office, agency or rank.

3. To press for the implementation of the Directive Principles for the World Government as defined in Article 13 of this World Constitution.

4. To promote the welfare of the people of Earth by seeking to assure that conditions of social justice and of minimizing disparities are achieved in the implementation and administration of world legislation and world law.

5. To keep on the alert for perils to humanity arising from technological innovations, environmental disruptions and other diverse sources, and to launch initiatives for correction or prevention of such perils.

6. To ascertain that the administration of otherwise proper laws, ordinances and procedures of the World Government do not result in unforeseen injustices or inequities, or become stultified in bureaucracy or the details of administration.

7. To receive and hear complaints, grievances or requests for aid from any person, group, organization, association, body politic or agency concerning any matter which comes within the purview of the World Ombudsmus.

8. To request the Office of World Attorneys General or any Regional World Attorney to initiate legal actions or court proceedings whenever and wherever considered necessary or desirable in the view of the World Ombudsmus.

9. To directly initiate legal actions and court proceedings whenever the World Ombudsmus deems necessary.

10. To review the functioning of the departments, bureaus, offices, commissions, institutes, organs and agencies of the World Government to ascertain whether the procedures of the World government are adequately fulfilling their purposes and serving the welfare of humanity in optimum fashion, and to make recommendations for improvements.

11. To present an annual report to the World Parliament and to the Presidium on the activities of the World Ombudsmus, together with any recommendations for legislative measures to improve the functioning of the World Government for the purpose of better serving the welfare of the People of Earth.

Sec. B. Composition of the World Ombudsmus

1. The World Ombudsmus shall be headed by a Council of World Ombudsmen of five members, one of whom shall be designated as Principal World Ombudsman, while the other four shall each be designated as an Associate World Ombudsman.

2. Members to compose the Council of World Ombudsmen shall be nominated by the House of Counselors, with three nominees from each Continental Division of Earth. One member of the Council shall be elected from each of five Continental Divisions by plurality vote of the three Houses of the World Parliament in joint session.

3. The term of office for a World Ombudsman shall be ten years. A World Ombudsman may serve two successive terms. The position of Principal World Ombudsman shall be rotated every two years. The order of rotation shall be determined by the Council of World Ombudsmen.

4. The Council of World Ombudsmen shall be assisted by a Commission of World Advocates of twenty members. Members for the Commission of World Advocates shall be nominated by the Council of World Ombudsmen from twenty World Electoral and Administrative Regions, with between two and three nominees submitted for each Region. One World Advocate shall be elected from each of the twenty World Electoral and Administrative Regions by the three Houses of the World Parliament in joint session. World Advocates shall serve terms of five years, and may serve a maximum of four successive terms.

5. The Council of World Ombudsmen shall establish twenty regional offices, in addition to the principal world office at the primary seat of the World Government. The twenty regional offices of the World Ombudsmus shall parallel the organization of the twenty Offices of Regional World Attorney.

6. Each regional office of the World Ombudsmus shall be headed by a World Advocate. Each five regional offices of the World Ombudsmus shall be supervised by an Associate World Ombudsman.

7. Any World Ombudsman and any World Advocate may be removed from office for cause by an absolute majority vote of the three Houses of the World Parliament in joint session.

8. Staff members for the World Ombudsmus and for each regional office of the World Ombudsmus shall be selected and employed from civil service lists.

9. Qualifications for World Ombudsman and for World Advocate shall be at least thirty years of age, at least five years legal experience, and education in law and other relevant education.

Article 12. Bill of Rights for the Citizens of Earth

The inhabitants and citizens of Earth who are within the Federation of Earth shall have certain inalienable rights defined hereunder. It shall be mandatory for the World Parliament, the World Executive, and all organs of the World Government to honor, implement and enforce these rights, as well as for the national government of all member nations in the Federation of Earth to do likewise. Individuals or groups suffering violations or neglect of such rights shall have full recourse through the World Ombudsmus, the Enforcement System and the World Court for redress of grievances. The inalienable rights shall include the following.

1. Equal rights for all citizens of the Federation of Earth, with no discrimination on grounds of race, color, caste, nationality, sex, religion, political affiliation, property or social status.

2. Equal protection and application of world legislation and world laws for all citizens of Earth.

3. Freedom of thought and conscience, speech, press, writing, communication, expression, publication, broadcasting, telecasting, and cinema, except as an overt part of or incitement to violence, armed riot or insurrection.

4. Freedom of assembly, association, organization, petition and peaceful demonstration.

5. Freedom to vote without duress and freedom for political organization and campaigning without recrimination.

6. Freedom to profess, practice and promote religion or religious beliefs or no religion or religious beliefs.

7. Freedom to profess and promote political beliefs or no political beliefs.

8. Freedom for investigation, research and reporting.

9. Freedom to travel without passport or visas or other forms of registration used to limit travel between, among, or within nations.

10. Prohibition against slavery, peonage, involuntary servitude and conscription of labor.

11. Prohibition against military conscription.

12. Safety of person from arbitrary or unreasonable arrest, detention, exile, search or seizure; requirement of warrants for searches and arrests.

13. Prohibition against physical or psychological duress or torture during any period of investigation, arrest, detention or imprisonment, and against cruel or unusual punishment.

14. Right of Habeas Corpus; no ex-post facto laws; no double jeopardy; right to refuse self-incrimination or the incrimination of another.

15. Prohibition against private armies and paramilitary organizations as being threats to the common peace and safety.

16. Safety of property from arbitrary seizure; protection against exercise of the power of eminent domain without reasonable compensation.

Right to family planning and free public assistance to achieve family planning objectives.

18. Right of privacy of person, family and association; prohibition against surveillance as a means of political control.

Article 13. Directive Principles for the World Government

It shall be the aim of the World Government to secure certain other rights for all inhabitants within the Federation of Earth, but without immediate guarantee of universal achievement and enforcement. These rights are defined as Directive Principles, obligating the World Government to pursue every reasonable means for universal realization and implementation and shall include the following:

1. Equal opportunity for useful employment for everyone, with wages or remuneration sufficient to assure human dignity.

2. Freedom of choice in work, occupation, employment or profession.

3. Full access to information and to the accumulated knowledge of the human race.

4. Free and adequate public education available to everyone, extending to the pre-university level; equal opportunities for elementary and higher education for all persons; equal opportunity for continued education for all persons throughout life; the right of any person or parent to choose a private educational institution at any time.

5. Free and adequate public health services and medical care available to everyone throughout life under conditions of free choice.

6. Equal opportunity for leisure time for everyone; better distribution of the work load of society so that every person may have equitable leisure time opportunities

7. Equal opportunity for everyone to enjoy the benefits of scientific and technological discoveries and developments.

8. Protection for everyone against the hazards and perils of technological innovations and developments.

9. Protection of the natural environment which is the common heritage of humanity against pollution, ecological disruption or damage which could imperil life or lower the quality of life.

10. Conservation of those natural resources of Earth which are limited so that present and future generations may continue to enjoy life on planet earth.

11. Assurance for everyone of adequate housing, of adequate and nutritious food supplies, of safe and adequate water supplies, of pure air with protection of oxygen supplies and the ozone layer, and in general for the continuance of an environment which can sustain healthy living for all.

12. Assure to each child the right to the full realization of his or her potential.

13. Social Security for everyone to relieve the hazards of unemployment, sickness, old age, family circumstances, disability, catastrophe of nature, and technological change, and to allow retirement with sufficient lifetime income for living under conditions of human dignity during old age.

14. Rapid elimination of and prohibitions against technological hazards and man-made environmental disturbances with are found to create dangers to life on Earth.

15. Implementation of intense programs to discover, develop and institute safe alternatives and practical substitutions for technologies which must be eliminated and prohibited because of hazards and dangers to life.

16. Encouragement for cultural diversity; encouragement for decentralized administration.

17. Freedom for peaceful self-determination for minorities, refugees and dissenters.

18. Freedom for change of residence to anywhere on Earth conditioned by provisions for temporary sanctuaries of residence to anywhere on Earth conditioned by provisions for temporary sanctuaries in events of large numbers of refugees, stateless persons, or mass migrations.

19. Prohibition against the death penalty.

Article 14. Safeguards and Reservations

Sec. A. Certain Safeguards

The World Government shall operate to secure for all nations and peoples within the Federation of Earth the safeguards which are defined hereunder:

1. Guarantee that full faith and credit shall be given to the public acts, records, legislation and judicial proceedings of the member nations within the Federation of Earth, consistent with the several provisions of this World Constitution.

2. Assure freedom of choice within the member nations and countries of the Federation of Earth to determine their internal political, economic and social systems, consistent with the guarantees and protections given under this World Constitution to assure civil liberties and human rights and a safe environment for life, and otherwise consistent with the several provisions of this World Constitution.

3. Grant the right of asylum within the Federation of Earth for persons who may seek refuge from countries or nations which are not yet included within the Federation of Earth.

4. Grant the right of individuals and groups, after the Federation of Earth includes 90 percent of the territory of Earth, to peacefully leave the hegemony of the Federation of Earth and to live in suitable territory set aside by the Federation neither restricted nor protected by the World Government, provided that such territory does not extend beyond five percent of Earth's habitable territory, is

kept completely disarmed and not used as a base for inciting violence or insurrection within or against the Federation of Earth or any member nation, and is kept free of acts of environmental or technological damage which seriously affect Earth outside such territory.

Sec. B. Reservation of Powers

The powers not delegated to the World Government by this World Constitution shall be reserved to the nations of the Federation of Earth and to the people of Earth.

Article 15. World Federal Zones and the World Capitals

Sec. A. World Federal Zones

1. Twenty World Federal Zones shall be established within the twenty World Electoral and Administrative Regions, for the purposes of the location of the several organs of the World Government and of the administrative departments, the world courts, the offices of the Regional World Attorneys, the offices of the World Advocates, and for the location of other branches, departments, institutes, offices, bureaus, commissions, agencies and parts of the World Government.

2. The World Federal Zones shall be established as the needs and resources of the World Government develop and expand. World Federal Zones shall be established first within each of five Continental Divisions.

3. The location and administration of the World Federal Zones, including the first five, shall be determined by the World Parliament.

Sec. B. The World Capitals

1. Five World Capitals shall be established in each of five Continental Divisions of Earth, to be located in each of the five World Federal Zones which are established first as provided in Article 15 of this World Constitution.

2. One of the World Capitals shall be designated by the World Parliament as the Primary World Capital, and the other four shall be designated as Secondary World Capitals.

3. The primary seats of all organs of the World Government shall be located in the Primary World Capital, and other major seats of the several organs of the World Government shall be located in the Secondary World Capitals.

Sec. C. Locational Procedures

1. Choices for location of the twenty World Federal Zones and for the five World Capitals shall be proposed by the Presidium, and then shall be decided by a simple majority vote of the three Houses of the World Parliament in joint session. The Presidium shall offer choices of two or three locations in each of the twenty World Electoral and Administrative Regions to be World Federal Zones, and shall offer two alternative choices for each of the five World Capitals.

2. The Presidium in consultation with the Executive Cabinet shall then propose which of the five World Capitals shall be the Primary World Capital, to be decided by a simple majority vote of the three Houses of the World Parliament in joint session.

3. Each organ of the World Government shall decide how best to apportion and organize its functions and activities among the five World Capitals, and among the twenty World Federal Zones, subject to specific directions from the World Parliament.

4. The World Parliament may decide to rotate its sessions among the five World Capitals, and if so, to decide the procedure for rotation.

5. For the first two operative stages of World Government as defined in Article 17, and for the Provisional World Government as defined in Article 19, a provisional location may be selected for the Primary World Capital. The provisional location need not be continued as a permanent location.

6. Any World Capital or World Federal Zone may be relocated by an absolute two-thirds majority vote of the three Houses of the World Parliament in joint session.

7. Additional World Federal Zones may be designated if found necessary by proposal of the Presidium and approval by an absolute majority vote of the three Houses of the World Parliament in joint session.

Article 16. World Territories and Exterior Relations

Sec. A. World Territory

1. Those areas of the Earth and Earth's moon which are not under the jurisdiction of existing nations at the time of forming the Federation of Earth, or which are not reasonably within the province of national ownership and administration, or which are declared to be World Territory subsequent to establishment of the Federation of Earth, shall be designated as World Territory and shall belong to all of the people of Earth.

2. The administration of World Territory shall be determined by the World Parliament and implemented by the World Executive, and shall apply to the following areas:

a. All oceans and seas having an international or supra-national character, together with the seabeds and resources thereof, beginning at a distance of twenty kilometers offshore, excluding inland seas of traditional national ownership.

b. Vital straits, channels, and canals.

c. The atmosphere enveloping Earth, beginning at an elevation of one kilometer above the general surface of the land, excluding the depressions in areas of much variation in elevation.

d. Man-made satellites and Earth's moon.

e. Colonies which may choose the status of World Territory; non-independent territories under the trust administration of nations or of the United

Nations; any islands or atolls which are unclaimed by any nation; independent lands or countries which choose the status of World Territory; and disputed lands which choose the status of World Territory.

3. The residents of any World Territory, except designated World Federal Zones, shall have the right within reason to decide by plebiscite to become a self-governing nation within the Federation of Earth, either singly or in combination with other World Territories, or to unite with an existing nation with the Federation of Earth.

Sec. B. Exterior Relations

1. The Government shall maintain exterior relations with those nations of Earth which have not joined the Federation of Earth. Exterior relations shall be under the administration of the Presidium, subject at all times to specific instructions and approval by the World Parliament.

2. All Treaties and agreements with the nations remaining outside the Federation of Earth shall be negotiated by the Presidium and must be ratified by a simple majority vote of the three Houses of Parliament.

3. The World Government for the Federation of Earth shall establish and maintain peaceful relations with the other planets and celestial bodies where and when it may become possible to establish communications with the possible inhabitants thereof.

4. All explorations into outer space, both within and beyond the solar system in which Planet Earth is located, shall be under the exclusive direction and control of the World Government, and shall be conducted in such a manner as shall be determined by the World Parliament.

Article 17. Ratification and Implementation

Sec. A. Ratification of the World Constitution

This World Constitution shall be submitted to the nations and people of Earth for ratification by the following procedures:

1. The World Constitution shall be transmitted to the General Assembly of the United Nations Organization and to each national government on Earth, with the request that the World Constitution be submitted to the national legislature of each nation for preliminary ratification and to the people of each nation for final ratification by popular referendum.

2. Preliminary ratification by a national legislature shall be accomplished by simple majority vote of the national legislature.

3. Final ratification by the people shall be accomplished by a simple majority of votes cast in a popular referendum, provided that a minimum of twenty-five percent of eligible voters of age eighteen years and over have cast ballots within the nation or country or within World Electoral and Administrative Districts.

4. In the case of a nation without a national legislature, the head of the national government shall be requested to give preliminary ratification and to submit the World Constitution for final ratification by popular referendum.

5. In the event that a national government, after six months, fails to submit the World Constitution for ratification as requested, then the global agency assuming responsibility for the worldwide ratification campaign may proceed to conduct a direct referendum for ratification of the World Constitution by the people. Direct referendums may be organized on the basis of entire nations or countries, or on the basis of existing defined communities within nations.

6. In the event of a direct ratification referendum, final ratification shall be accomplished by a majority of the votes cast whether for an entire nation or for a World Electoral and Administrative District, provided that ballots are cast by a minimum o f twenty-five percent of eligible voters of the area who are over eighteen years of age.

7. For ratification by existing communities within a nation, the procedure shall be to request local communities, cities, counties, states, provinces, cantons, prefectures, tribal jurisdictions, or other defined political units within a nation to ratify the World Constitution, and to submit the World Constitution for a referendum vote by the citizens of the community or political unit. Ratification may be accomplished by proceeding in this way until all eligible voters of age eighteen and above within the nation or World Electoral and Administrative District have had the opportunity to vote, provided that ballots are cast by a minimum of twenty-five percent of those eligible to vote.

8. Prior to the Full Operative Stage of World Government, as defined under Section E of Article XVII, the universities, colleges and scientific academies and institutes in any country may ratify the World Constitution, thus qualifying them for participation in the nomination of Members of the World Parliament to the House of Counselors.

9. In the case of those nations currently involved in serious international disputes or where traditional enmities and chronic disputes may exist among two or more nations, a procedure for concurrent paired ratification shall be instituted whereby the nations which are parties to a current or chronic international dispute or conflict may simultaneously ratify the World Constitution. In such cases, the paired nations shall be admitted into the Federation of Earth simultaneously, with the obligation for each such nation to immediately turn over all weapons of mass destruction to the World Government, and to turn over the conflict or dispute for mandatory peaceful settlement by the World Government.

10. Each nation or political unit which ratifies this World Constitution, either by preliminary ratification or final ratification, shall be bound never to use any armed forces or weapons of mass destruction against another member or unit of the Federation of Earth, regardless of how long it may take to achieve full disarmament of all the nations and political units which ratify this World Constitution.

11. When ratified, the Constitution for the Federation of Earth becomes the supreme law of Earth. By the act of ratifying this Earth Constitution, any

provision in the Constitution or Legislation of any country so ratifying, which is contrary to this Earth Constitution, is either repealed or amended to conform with the Constitution for the Federation of Earth, effective as soon as 25 countries have so ratified. The amendment of National or State Constitutions to allow entry into World Federation is not necessary prior to ratification of the Constitution for the Federation of Earth.

Sec. B. Stages of Implementation

1. Implementation of this World Constitution and the establishment of World Government pursuant to the terms of this World Constitution, may be accomplished in three stages, as follows, in addition to the stage of a Provisional World Government as provided under Article 19:

    a. First Operative Stage of World Government.
    b. Second Operative Stage of World Government.
    c. Full Operative Stage of World Government.

2. At the beginning and during each stage, the World Parliament and the World Executive together shall establish goals and develop means for the progressive implementation of the World Constitution, and for the implementation of legislation enacted by the World Parliament.

Sec. C. First Operative Stage of World Government

1. The first operative stage of World Government under this World Constitution shall be implemented when the World Constitution is ratified by a sufficient number of nations and/or people to meet one or the other of the following conditions or equivalent :

    a. Preliminary or final ratification by a minimum of twenty-five nations, each having a population of more than 100,000.

    b. Preliminary or final ratification by a minimum of ten nations above 100,000 population, together with ratification by direct referendum within a minimum of fifty additional World Electoral and Administrative Districts.

    c. Ratification by direct referendum within a minimum of 100 World Electoral and Administrative Districts, even though no nation as such has ratified.

2. The election of Members of the World Parliament to the House of Peoples shall be conducted in all World Electoral and Administrative Districts where ratification has been accomplished by popular referendum.

3. The Election of Members of the World Parliament to the House of Peoples may proceed concurrently with direct popular referendums both prior to and after the First Operative Stage of World Government is reached.

4. The appointment or election of Members of the World Parliament to the House of Nations shall proceed in all nations where preliminary ratification has been accomplished.

5. One-fourth of the Members of the World Parliament to the House of Counselors may be elected from nominees submitted by universities and colleges which have ratified the World Constitution.

6. The World Presidium and the Executive Cabinet shall be elected according to the provisions in article VI, except that in the absence of a House of Counselors, the nominations shall be made by the members of the House of Peoples and of the House of Nations in joint session. Until this is accomplished, the Presidium and Executive Cabinet of the Provisional World Government as provided in Article 19, shall continue to serve.

7. When composed, the Presidium for the first operative stage of World Government shall assign or re-assign Ministerial posts among Cabinet and Presidium members, and shall immediately establish or confirm a World Disarmament Agency and a World Economic and Development Organization.

8. Those nations which ratify this World Constitution and thereby join the Federation of Earth, shall immediately transfer all weapons of mass destruction as defined and designated by the World Disarmament Agency to that Agency. (See Article 19, Sections A-2-d, B-6 and E-5). The World Disarmament Agency shall immediately immobilize all such weapons and shall proceed with dispatch to dismantle, convert to peacetime use, re-cycle the materials thereof or otherwise destroy all such weapons. During the first operative stage of World Government, the ratifying nations may retain armed forces equipped with weapons other than weapons of mass destruction as defined and designated by the World Disarmament Agency.

9. Concurrently with the reduction or elimination of such weapons of mass destruction and other military expenditures as can be accomplished during the first operative stage of World Government, the member nations of the Federation of Earth shall pay annually to the Treasury of the World Government amounts equal to one-half the amounts saved from their respective national military budgets during the last year before joining the Federation, and shall continue such payments until the full operative stage of World Government is reached. The World Government shall use fifty percent of the funds thus received to finance the work and projects of the World Economic Development Organization.

10. The World Parliament and the World Executive shall continue to develop the organs, departments, agencies and activities originated under the Provisional World Government, with such amendments as deemed necessary; and shall proceed to establish and begin the following organs, departments and agencies of the World Government, if not already underway, together with such other departments, and agencies as are considered desirable and feasible during the first operative stage of World Government:

  a. The World Supreme Court;
  b. The Enforcement System;
  c. The World Ombudsmus;
  d. The World Civil Service Administration;
  e. The World Financial Administration;
  f. The Agency for Research and Planning;
  g. The Agency for Technological and Environmental Assessment;

h. An Emergency Earth Rescue Administration, concerned with all aspects of climate change and related factors;

i. An Integrated Global Energy System, based on environmentally safe sources;

j. A World University System, under the Department of Education;

k. A World Corporations Office, under the Department of Commerce and Industry;

l. The World Service Corps;

m. A World Oceans and Seabeds Administration.

11. At the beginning of the first operative stage, the Presidium in consultation with the Executive Cabinet shall formulate and put forward a proposed program for solving the most urgent world problems currently confronting humanity.

12. The World Parliament shall proceed to work upon solutions to world problems. The World Parliament and the World Executive working together shall institute through the several organs, departments and agencies of the World Government whatever means shall seem appropriate and feasible to accomplish the implementation and enforcement of world legislation, world law and the World Constitution; and in particular shall take certain decisive actions for the welfare of all people on Earth, applicable throughout the world, including but not limited to the following:

a. Expedite the organization and work of an Emergency Earth Rescue Administration, concerned with all aspects of climate change and climate crises;

b. Expedite the new finance, credit and monetary system, to serve human needs;

c. Expedite an integrated global energy system, utilizing solar energy, hydrogen energy, and other safe and sustainable sources of energy;

d. Push forward a global program for agricultural production to achieve maximum sustained yield under conditions which are ecologically sound;

e. Establish conditions for free trade within the Federation of Earth;

f. Call for and find ways to implement a moratorium on nuclear energy projects until all problems are solved concerning safety, disposal of toxic wastes and the dangers of use or diversion of materials for the production of nuclear weapons;

g. Outlaw and find ways to completely terminate the production of nuclear weapons and all weapons of mass destruction;

h. Push forward programs to assure adequate and non-polluted water supplies and clean air supplies for everybody on Earth;

i. Push forward a global program to conserve and re-cycle the resources of Earth.

j. Develop an acceptable program to bring population growth under control, especially by raising standards of living.

Sec. D. Second Operative Stage of World Government

1. The second operative stage of World Government shall be implemented when fifty percent or more of the nations of Earth have given either preliminary or final ratification to this World Constitution, provided that fifty percent of the total population of Earth is included either within the ratifying nations or within the ratifying nations together with additional World Electoral and Administrative Districts where people have ratified the World Constitution by direct referendum.

2. The election and appointment of Members of the World Parliament to the several Houses of the World Parliament shall proceed in the same manner as specified for the first operative stage in Section C-2,3,4 and 5 of Article 17.

3. The terms of office of the Members of the World Parliament elected or appointed for the first operative stage of World Government, shall be extended into the second operative stage unless they have already served five year terms, in which case new elections or appointments shall be arranged. The terms of holdover Members of the World Parliament into the second operative stage shall be adjusted to run concurrently with the terms of those who are newly elected at the beginning of the second operative stage.

4. The World Presidium and the Executive Cabinet shall be re-constituted or reconfirmed, as needed, at the beginning of the second operative stage of World Government.

5. The World Parliament and the World Executive shall continue to develop the organs, departments, agencies and activities which are already underway from the first operative stage of World Government, with such amendments as deemed necessary; and shall proceed to establish and develop all other organs and major departments and agencies of the World Government to the extent deemed feasible during the second operative stage.

6. All nations joining the Federation of Earth to compose the second operative stage of World Government, shall immediately transfer all weapons of mass destruction and all other military weapons and equipment to the World Disarmament Agency, which shall immediately immobilize such weapons and equipment and shall proceed forthwith to dismantle, convert to peacetime uses, recycle the materials thereof, or otherwise destroy such weapons and equipment. During the second operative stage, all armed forces and para-military forces of the nations which have joined the Federation of Earth shall be completely disarmed and either disbanded or converted on a voluntary basis into elements of the non-military World Service Corps.

7. Concurrently with the reduction or elimination of such weapons, equipment and other military expenditures as can be accomplished during the second operative stage of World Government, the member nations of the Federation of Earth shall pay annually to the Treasury of the World Government amounts equal to one-half of the amounts saved from their national military budgets during the last year before joining the Federation and shall continue such payments until the full operative stage of World Government is reached. The World Government shall use fifty percent of the funds thus received to finance the work and projects of the World Economic Development Organization.

8. Upon formation of the Executive Cabinet for the second operative stage, the Presidium shall issue an invitation to the General Assembly of the United Nations Organization and to each of the specialized agencies of the United Nations, as well as to other useful international agencies, to transfer personnel, facilities, equipment, resources and allegiance to the Federation of Earth and to the World Government thereof. The agencies and functions of the United Nations Organization and of its specialized agencies and of other international agencies which may be thus transferred, shall be reconstituted as needed and integrated into the several organs, departments, offices and agencies of the World Government.

9. Near the beginning of the second operative stage, the Presidium in consultation with the Executive cabinet, shall formulate and put forward a proposed program for solving the most urgent world problems currently confronting the people of Earth.

10. The World Parliament shall proceed with legislation necessary for implementing a complete program for solving the current urgent world problems.

11. The World Parliament and the World Executive working together shall develop through the several organs, departments and agencies of the World Government whatever means shall seem appropriate and feasible to implement legislation for solving world problems; and in particular shall take certain decisive actions for the welfare of all people on Earth, including but not limited to the following:

a. Declaring all oceans, seas and canals having supra-national character (but not including inland seas traditionally belonging to particular nations) from twenty kilometers offshore, and all the seabeds thereof, to be under the ownership of the Federation of Earth as the common heritage of humanity, and subject to the control and management of the World Government.

b. Declare the polar caps and surrounding polar areas, including the continent of Antarctica but not areas which are traditionally a part of particular nations, to be world territory owned by the Federation of Earth as the common heritage of humanity, and subject to control and management by the World Government.

c. Outlaw the possession, stockpiling, sale and use of all nuclear weapons, all weapons of mass destruction, and all other military weapons and equipment.

d. Establish an ever-normal granary and food supply system for the people of Earth.

e. Develop and carry forward insofar as feasible all actions defined under Sec. C-10 and C-12 of the First Operative Stage.

Sec. E. Full Operative Stage of World Government

1. The full operative stage of World Government shall be implemented when this World Constitution is given either preliminary or final ratification by meeting either condition (a) or (b):

a. Ratification by eighty percent or more of the nations of Earth comprising at least ninety percent of the population of Earth; or

b. Ratification which includes ninety percent of Earth's total population, either within ratifying nations or within ratifying nations together with additional World Electoral and Administrative Districts where ratification by direct referendum has been accomplished, as provided in Article 17, Section A.

2. When the full operative stage of World Government is reached, the following conditions shall be implemented:

a. Elections for Members of the House of Peoples shall be conducted in all World Electoral and Administrative Districts where elections have not already taken place; and Members of the House of Nations shall be elected or appointed by the national legislatures or national governments in all nations where this has not already been accomplished.

b. The terms of office for Members of the House of Peoples and of the House of Nations serving during the second operative stage, shall be continued into the full operative stage, except for those who have already served five years, in which case elections shall be held or appointments made as required.

c. The terms of office for all holdover Members of the House of Peoples and of the House of Nations who have served less than five years, shall be adjusted to run concurrently with those Members of the World Parliament whose terms are beginning with the full operative stage.

d. The second 100 Members of the House of Counselors shall be elected according to the procedure specified in Section E of Article 5. The terms of office for holdover Members of the House of Counselors shall run five more years after the beginning of the full operative stage, while those beginning their terms with the full operative stage shall serve ten years.

e. The Presidium and the Executive Cabinet shall be reconstituted in accordance with the provisions of Article VI.   f. All organs of the World Government shall be made fully operative, and shall be fully developed for the effective administration and implementation of world legislation, world law and the provisions of this World Constitution.

g. All nations which have not already done so shall immediately transfer all military weapons and equipment to the World Disarmament Agency, which shall immediately immobilize all such weapons and shall proceed forthwith to dismantle, convert to peaceful usage, recycle the materials thereof, or otherwise to destroy such weapons and equipment.

h. All armies and military forces of every kind shall be completely disarmed, and either disbanded or converted and integrated on a voluntary basis into the non-military World Service Corps.

i. All viable agencies of the United Nations Organization and other viable international agencies established among national governments, together with their personnel, facilities and resources, shall be transferred to the World Government and reconstituted and integrated as may be useful into the organs, departments, offices, institutes, commissions, bureaus and agencies of the World Government.

j. The World Parliament and the World Executive shall continue to develop the activities and projects which are already underway from the second operative stage of World Government, with such amendments as deemed necessary; and shall proceed with a complete and full scale program to solve world problems and serve the welfare of all people on Earth, in accordance with the provisions of this World Constitution.

Sec. F. Costs of Ratification

The work and costs of private Citizens of Earth for the achievement of a ratified Constitution for the Federation of Earth, are recognized as legitimate costs for the establishment of constitutional world government by which present and future generations will benefit, and shall be repaid double the original amount by the World Financial Administration of the World Government when it becomes operational after 25 countries have ratified this Constitution for the Federation of Earth. Repayment specifically includes contributions to the World Government Funding Corporation and other costs and expenses recognized by standards and procedures to be established by the World Financial Administration.

Article 18. Amendments

1. Following completion of the first operative stage of World Government, amendments to this World Constitution may be proposed for consideration in two ways:

a. By a simple majority vote of any House of the World Parliament.

b. By petitions signed by a total of 200,000 persons eligible to vote in world elections from a total of at least twenty World Electoral and Administrative Districts where the World Constitution has received final ratification.

2. Passage of any amendment proposed by a House of the World Parliament shall require an absolute two-thirds majority vote of each of the three Houses of the World Parliament voting separately.

3. An amendment proposed by popular petition shall first require a simple majority vote of the House of Peoples, which shall be obliged to take a vote upon the proposed amendment. Passage of the amendment shall then require an absolute two-thirds majority vote of each of the three Houses of the World Parliament voting separately.

4. Periodically, but no later than ten years after first convening the World Parliament for the First Operative Stage of World Government, and every 20 years thereafter, the Members of the World Parliament shall meet in special session comprising a Constitutional Convention to conduct a review of this World Constitution to consider and propose possible amendments, which shall then require action as specified in Clause 2 of Article XVIII for passage.

5. If the First Operative Stage of World Government is not reached by the year 1995, then the Provisional World Parliament, as provided under Article XIX, may convene another session of the World Constituent Assembly to review the Constitution for the Federation of Earth and consider possible amendments according to procedure established by the Provisional World Parliament.

6. Except by following the amendment procedures specified herein, no part of this World Constitution may be set aside, suspended or subverted, neither for emergencies nor caprice nor convenience.

Article 19. Provisional World Government

Sec. A. Actions to be Taken by the World Constituent Assembly

Upon adoption of the World Constitution by the World Constituent Assembly, the Assembly and such continuing agency or agencies as it shall designate shall do the following, without being limited thereto:

1. Issue a Call to all Nations, communities and people of Earth to ratify this World Constitution for World Government.

2. Establish the following preparatory commissions:

   a. Ratification Commission.

   b. World Elections Commission.

   c. World Development Commission.

   d. World Disarmament Commission.

   e. World Problems Commission.

   f. Nominating Commission.

   g. Finance Commission.

   h. Peace Research and Education Commission.

   i Special commissions on each of several of the most urgent world problems.

   j. Such other commissions as may be deemed desirable in order to proceed with the Provisional World Government.

3. Convene Sessions of a Provisional World Parliament when feasible under the following conditions:

   a. Seek the commitment of 500 or more delegates to attend, representing people in 20 countries from five continents, and having credentials defined by Article 19, Section C;

   b. The minimum funds necessary to organize the sessions of the Provisional World Parliament are either on hand or firmly pledged.

   c. Suitable locations are confirmed at least nine months in advance, unless emergency conditions justify shorter advance notice.

Sec. B. Work of the Preparatory Commissions

1. The Ratification Commission shall carry out a worldwide campaign for the ratification of the World Constitution, both to obtain preliminary ratification by national governments, including national legislatures, and to obtain final

ratification by people, including communities. The ratification commission shall continue its work until the full operative stage of World Government is reached.

2. The World Elections Commission shall prepare a provisional global map of World Electoral and Administrative Districts and Regions which may be revised during the first or second operative stage of World Government, and shall prepare and proceed with plans to obtain the election of Members of the World Parliament to the House of Peoples and to the House of Counselors. The World Elections Commission shall in due course be converted into the World Boundaries and Elections Administration.

3. After six months, in those countries where national governments have not responded favorable to the ratification call, the Ratification Commission and the World Elections Commission may proceed jointly to accomplish both the ratification of the World Constitution by direct popular referendum and concurrently the election of Members of the World Parliament.

4. The Ratification Commission may also submit the World Constitution for ratification by universities and colleges throughout the world.

5. The World Development Commission shall prepare plans for the creation of a World Economic Development Organization to serve all nations and people ratifying the World Constitution, and in particular less developed countries, to begin functioning when the Provisional World Government is established.

6. The World Disarmament Commission shall prepare plans for the organization of a World Disarmament Agency, to begin functioning when the Provisional World Government is established.

7. The World Problems Commission shall prepare an agenda of urgent world problems, with documentation, for possible action by the Provisional World Parliament and Provisional World Government.

8. The Nominating Commission shall prepare, in advance of convening the Provisional World Parliament, a list of nominees to compose the Presidium and the Executive Cabinet for the Provisional World Government.

9. The Finance Commission shall work on ways and means for financing the Provisional World Government.

10. The several commissions on particular world problems shall work on the preparation of proposed world legislation and action on each problem, to present to the Provisional World Parliament when it convenes.

Sec. C. Composition of the Provisional World Parliament

1. The Provisional World Parliament shall be composed of the following members:

  a. All those who were accredited as delegates to the 1977 and 1991 Sessions of the World Constituent Assembly, as well as to any previous Session of the Provisional World Parliament, and who re-confirm their support for the Constitution for the Federation of Earth, as amended.

  b. Persons who obtain the required number of signatures on election petitions, or who are designated by Non-Governmental Organizations which adopt approved resolutions for this purpose, or who are otherwise accredited according to terms specified in Calls which may be issued to convene particular sessions of the Provisional World Parliament.

       c. Members of the World Parliament to the House of Peoples who are elected from World Electoral and Administrative Districts up to the time of convening the Provisional World Parliament. Members of the World Parliament elected to the House of Peoples may continue to be added to the Provisional World Parliament until the first operative stage of World Government is reached.

       d. Members of the World Parliament to the House of Nations who are elected by national legislatures or appointed by national governments up to the time of convening the Provisional World Parliament. Members of the World Parliament to the House of Nations may continue to be added to the Provisional World Parliament until the first operative stage of World Government is reached.

       e. Those universities and colleges which have ratified the World Constitution may nominate persons to serve as Members of the World Parliament to the House of Counselors. The House of Peoples and House of Nations together may then elect from such nominees up to fifty Members of the World Parliament to serve in the House of Counselors of the Provisional World Government.

       2. Members of the Provisional World Parliament in categories (a) and (b) as defined above, shall serve only until the first operative stage of World Government is declared, but may be duly elected to continue as Members of the World Parliament during the first operative stage.

Sec. D. Formation of the Provisional World Executive

       1. As soon as the Provisional World Parliament next convenes, it will elect a new Presidium for the Provisional World Parliament and Provisional World Government from among the nominees submitted by the Nominating Commission.

       2. Members of the Provisional World Presidium shall serve terms of three years, and may be re-elected by the Provisional World Parliament, but in any case shall serve only until the Presidium is elected under the First Operative Stage of World Government.

       3. The Presidium may make additional nominations for the Executive Cabinet.

       4. The Provisional World Parliament shall then elect the members of the Executive Cabinet.

       5. The Presidium shall then assign ministerial posts among the members of the Executive Cabinet and of the Presidium.

       6. When steps (1) through (4) of section D are completed, the Provisional World Government shall be declared in operation to serve the welfare of humanity.

Sec. E. First Actions of the Provisional World Government

       1. The Presidium, in consultation with the Executive Cabinet, the commissions on particular world problems and the World Parliament, shall define a program for action on urgent world problems.

2. The Provisional World Parliament shall go to work on the agenda of world problems, and shall take any and all actions it considers appropriate and feasible, in accordance with the provisions of this World Constitution.

3. Implementation of and compliance with the legislation enacted by the Provisional World Parliament shall be sought on a voluntary basis in return for the benefits to be realized, while strength of the Provisional World Government is being increased by the progressive ratification of the World Constitution.

4. Insofar as considered appropriate and feasible, the Provisional World Parliament and Provisional World Executive may undertake some of the actions specified under Section C-12 of Article 17 for the first operative stage of World Government.

5. The World Economic Development Organization and the World Disarmament Agency shall be established, for correlated actions.

6. The World Parliament and the Executive Cabinet of the Provisional World Government shall proceed with the organization of other organs and agencies of the World Government on a provisional basis, insofar as considered desirable and feasible, in particular those specified under Section C-10 of Article 17.

7. The several preparatory commissions on urgent world problems may be reconstituted as Administrative Departments of the Provisional World Government.

8. In all of its work and activities, the Provisional World Government shall function in accordance with the provisions of this Constitution for the Federation of Earth.

*   *   *   *   *   *   *

Campaign for Ratification and Signatures

    The *Constitution for the Federation of Earth* was originally ratified at the second session of the World Constituent Assembly held in Innsbruck, Austria in June 1977, and was amended and ratified at the fourth session of the World Constituent Assembly held at Troia, Portugal in May 1991. The amended Constitution is being personally ratified by outstanding personalities throughout the world as the campaign for ratification by the people and governments of the world gets underway. The following sixteen pages contain the signatures from both sessions.

    After the final changes were made at the Fourth Constituent Assembly, the Global Ratification and Elections Network (GREN) was formed to work with the World Constitution and Parliament Association (WCPA) to obtain ratification of the Constitution by the people and nations of Earth under the provisions set forth in Article 17. In 2004, GREN was transformed into the Earth Federation Movement (EFM) that works both for ratification and continues to build the institutions of the Earth Federation within the shell of the old, decaying world order.

Following are copies of signature pages from the
Second World Constituent Assembly, Innsbruck, 1977, the
Fourth World Constituent Assembly, Troia, Portugal 1991,
and some personal ratifiers.

Participants in the World Constituent Assembly, 16 to 29 of June, 1977, have affixed their
signatures to the draft of the CONSTITUTION FOR THE FEDERATION OF EARTH herewith:

[handwritten signature]   India

[handwritten signature]   MEXICO

[handwritten signatures]   EARTH, USA

Lucile W. Green   Earth, USA

[handwritten signature]   Hon. Legal Advisor

[handwritten signature]   Canada

T.P. Amerasinghe   Sri Lanka.

[handwritten signature]   Benin

Archie Casely Hayford   Ghana.

K. Konia   Botswana

Helen Tucker (Canada) Women's Universal Movement

[handwritten signature]   Fed. Rep. of Germany

Thane Read   U. S. A.

[handwritten signature]   India.

Rachoonnuk A. Aumngi   Thailand.

Rose J. Chorney   Australia.

[handwritten signature]   Germany

[handwritten signature]   Netherlands

[handwritten signature]   JAPAN

Name	Country
ANDREA von SCHINOY	GERMANY
Edith Farovich	Germany
Gisela Gimbel	Germany
Klaus Flakur-Schlichtmann	Germany
Ann Mische	World, U.S.A
Gerald Mische	U.S.A.
Dr. Ludwig C. Laug	W. Germany
Dr. Fred Karl Scheile	U.S.A.
Marsalyer	Germany
Olga Jager	Germany
Beatrice Meyers	U.S.A.
Elisabeth Klaeubaeui	INNSBRUCK
Theo Feuchs	Switzerland
Dr. Helen K Billings	USA
Magister Kirsti Balthasar	Finland live in Mexico.
Robert Roemmer	United People Federation of Earth
Valorie Hagenhuber	Austria
Herbert Grooler	
Olga Schurge	

Name	Country
Louis R. Gambey	U. S. A
P. C. Malhotra	India
Hildegard Heuer	Schweiz
PURAN SINGH AZAD.	(INDIA)
Dr. Miss. Geeta Shah	INDIA.
Maria Treli	Schweiz
Kurt Kreit	Innsbruck
Bonnie Allen	U. S. A
Rustom M. Bharucha	India.
Allan Bryant	USA
Jeanne C. Burris	UniA. World
Leo J. Murray sa (Pax Christi USA)	
Simon R. Lad	Botswana
Mrs. Renée Dangoor	United Kingdom
MR. J. Lelaka	Botswana
Peggy Cahuan	
Ronald L. Lehman	Australia
Thomas Githa	AUSTRIA

Name	Country
Dr. Hildegard Durfee	U.S.A.
Kira Lynne Allen	
Samar Basu	India.
Robert W. Kaminski	Earth USA, Wilm Del
John Kluger	Holland
Yogi Shantiswaroop.	India - for one world
Carmel Kussman	U.S.A.
Mortimer Lipsky	U.S.A.
Hermann Weyss	Austria
Kim Haraide	Canada
Ana Maren	P.R
Naim Dangoor	U.K.
[illegible]	[illegible] (Sri Lanka)
[illegible]	Bangalore - India
Bernadette F. Trattner.	
Craig Orr White, Ph.D.	Ohio. U.S.A.
Everett Nelson	Wash. U.S.A.
Mildred S. Parmelee.	U.S.A.
Dr (Miss) Kamoo Patel	Pondichery (India)
Margaret Gadge	United Kingdom.

Name	Country
[signature]	Sri Lanka
Margaret Isely	U.S.A.
[signature]	Austria
[signature]	PUERTO RICO
[signature]	U.S.A.
Edward R. Leader	Puerto Rico
[signature]	India
Dorothy *[signature]* Baker	U.S.A.
Carl F. Cattain	Earth !
[signature]	Denmark
[signature] Isely	U.S.A.
[signature]	U.S.A.
[signature]	Kenya
[signature]	W-Germany
[signature] Isely	U.S.A.
[signature]	Nigeria
[signature]	JAPAN
[signature]	Netherlands
[signature]	Botswana

Name	Address
Eggert, Charlotte Luise	Deutschland
Jacqueline Raheri	N.Y.C. USA
Martha Zillebur	USA
Paternolli Kurt	Innsbruck Austria
Suzanne Gomberg	San Francisco USA
Holzapfel Heiner	Innsbruck
Holzapfel Amelie	Innsbruck
Leora C Herold	Mexico City
Havel Ingeborg	Germany
Schneiding, Hans-Friedrich	Germany
Nary, Ludwig	Germany
B. Molinar	World lik you
Leland P. Stewart	Los Angeles
John Stockwell	San Francisco
Guido Graziani	Rome, Italy
Dorothea Farhan	Hannover, WOMAN

Name   Country

[signatures]

Guiji Loxump   Holla

william City   iren

Raphhie Ran   U.S.A.

Carmel Painter   U S A

Jant Auf   USA

Stephen Siphe Mnude   shieles

[various signatures]   Pakisto

[signature]   Italy / México.

Por el Mundo espiritual
[signature] Dr Jose M Estre

Po la memoria Norte en el espiritu   (México)
Sa Elisa Greura
Rev. GAGPA Maria Carlota Ale Estrada   (México)
"Por el mundo Espiritual"
Rev. GagPa *[signature]*   (México)
"Por el mundo Espiritual
W. Roig Gotols Adolfo Olivera *[signature]* (méxico)

Name	Country
Trakoza Ruge	Mexico
Jufami Vollweger	Austria
Belte Aluery	Austria
Herbert Jhin	(Deutschland (BRD))
Siddharta! Patel	Kenya.
Halaben Patet	India
Umesh A Patel	Great Britain.
Kumud I. Patel	Great Britain.
Ahmed Subanjo g.	Indonesia
Asetyobudianti	Indonesia
Sybil Stiett	New Zealand + USA
Alice Stephens	England
Elizabeth E. Stewart	United States
HH	*Sm known* Bangladesh
HARSHA JAN SINGH Khalsa	
Yogiji	USA
Sikh Dharma Western Hemp Sp.	

Note: This list of initial signers of the CONSTITUTION FOR THE FEDERATION OF EARTH would include several hundred more persons from fifty countries, prevented only by the cost of travel to attend the Assembly at Innsbruck, Austria.

PERSONAL RATIFIERS OF THE CONSTITUTION FOR THE FEDERATION OF EARTH
AS AMENDED AT THE 4th SESSION OF THE WORLD CONSTITUENT ASSEMBLY
HELD AT TROIA, PORTUGAL, 29th APRIL, to 9th MAY, 1991

Prof. Dr. Kalman Abraham, Hungary

Atiku Abubakar, Nigeria

Dr. Ebenezer Ade. Adenekan, Nigeria

Malcolm S. Adiseshiah, India

Abdur Rahim Ahamed, Bangladesh

Shahzada Kabir Ahmed

Mohsin A. Alaini, Yemen

MD. Nural Alam, U.S.A.

MD. Maser Ali, Bangladesh

Dr. Terence P. Amerasinghe, Sri Lanka

Samir Amin, Senegal

Benjamin K. Amonoo, Ghana

George Anca, Romania

Mauricio Andres-Ribeiro, Brazil

Dr. Munawar A. Anees, U.S.A.

Rev. Ebenezer Annan, Ivory Coast

Jose Ayala-Lasso, Ecuador

Ir. Hasan Basri, Indonesia

Samar Basu, India

Tony Benn, United Kingdom

PERSONAL RATIFIERS - page 2

Prof. Mrs. Edvige Bestazzi, Italy

Petter Jakob Bjerve, Norway

Goran von Bonsdorff, Finland

Selma Brackman, U.S.A.

Jean-Marie BRETON
Jean-Marie Breton, Int. Regis. World Citizens

Tomas Bruckman, Germany (East)

Dennis Brutus, South Africa (U.S.A.)

Dr. Mihai Titus Carapancea, Romania

Prof. Henri Cartan, France

Amb. Khub Chand, India

Dr. Sripati Chandrasekhar, India

Most Rev. French Chang-Him, Seychelles

Munyaradzi Chiwashira, Zimbabwe

Dr. Pratap Chandra Chunder, India

Prof. Dr. Rodney Daniel, France

Daniel G. De Culla, Spain

Dr. Dimitrios J. Delivanis, Greece

Prof. Dr. Francis Dessart, Belgium

Raymond F. Douw, Germany

Prof. Hans-Peter Duerr, Germany

Kennedy Emekam, Nigeria

M. Necati Munir Ertekun, Cyprus

Douglas Nixon Everingham, Australia

John R. Ewbank, U.S.A.

PERSONAL RATIFIERS - page 3

Marjorie Ewbank, U.S.A.

Miss Lianmangi Fanai, India

Dr. Mark Farber, U.S.A.

Feng Ping-Chung, China

Prof. Dr. Mihnea Georghiu, Romania

Lucile W. Green, U.S.A.

Dr. Dauji Gupta, India

Kisholoy Gupta, India

Takeshi Haruki, Japan

Dr. Gerhard Herzberg, Canada

Jozsef Holp, Hungary

A. K. Fazlul Hoque, Bangladesh

Chowdhury Anwar Husain, Bangladesh

Margaret Isely, U.S.A. (Earth)

Philip Isely, U.S.A. (Earth)

Ram K. Jiwanmitra, Nepal

Roy E. Johnstone, Jamaica

Mohammed Kamaluddin, Bangladesh

Mohammad Rezaul Karim, Bangladesh

Rev. George Karunakeran, India

Dr. Inamullah Khan, Pakistan

Johnson S. Khan, Pakistan

Roger Kotila, Ph.D., U.S.A.

PERSONAL RATIFIERS - page 4

David M. Krieger, U.S.A.

Diemuth Kuebart, Germany

Jul Lag, Norway

Ben M. Leito, Netherlands Antilles

Thomas Lim, East Malaysia

Adam Lopatka, Poland

Anwarul Majid, Bangladesh

Dr. M. Sadiq Malik, Pakistan

Guy Marchand, France

Alvin M. Marks, U.S.A.

Bernardshaw Mazi, Nigeria

Dr. Zhores A. Medvedev, U. K. (USSR)

Anna Medvegey, Hungary

R. C. Mehrotra, India

Charles Mercieca, U.S.A.

Lt. Col. Pedro B. Merida, Philippines

Yerucham Meshel, Israel

Sheta Mikayele, Zaire

Mohamed Ezzedine Mili, Switzerland

Rev. Toshio Miyake, Japan

Shettima Ali Monguno, Nigeria

Swapan Mukherjee, India

Hanna Newcombe, Canada

Brij P. Nigam, India

Josephine Okafor, Nigeria

Johnson Olatunde, Sierre Leone

Rev. Nelson Onono-Onweng, Uganda

Umit Ozturk, Turkey

Yasar Ozturk, Turkey

Linus Pauling, U.S.A.

Fernando Perez Tella, Spain

Emil Otto Peter, Austria

Dr. Alex Quaison-Sackey, Ghana

Soili Raikkonen, Finland

Sudhir Kumar Rangh, India

Thane Read, U.S.A.

Dr. Sayed Qassem Reshtia, Switzerland

Erzebet Rethy, Hungary

Miguel B. Ricardo, Portugal

G. Rivas Mijares, Venezuela

Reinhart Ruge, Mexico

PERSONAL RATIFIERS - page 6

Prof. Sir A. M. Sadek, South Africa

Abdus Salam, Italy

Akbar Ali Saleh, Comoros Islands

Blagovest Sendov, Bulgaria

Indira Shrestha, Nepal

Rabi Charan Shrestha, Nepal

Jon Silkin, United Kingdom

Jozef Simuth, Slovak Republic

Dr. Kewal Singh, India

Blaine Sloan, U.S.A.

Ross Smyth, Canada

Lord Donald Soper, United Kingdom

Scott Jefferson Starquester, U.S.A.

Homi J. H. Taleyarkhan, India

Rev. Yoshiaki Toeda, Japan

Dr. Duja K. Torki, Tunisia

Helen Tucker, Canada

Evelyn Utulu, Nigeria

Mrs. Justina N. Uwechue, Nigeria

Ogieva O. Uwuigbe, Nigeria

Ann Valentin, U.S.A.

PERSONAL RATIFIERS - page 7

T. Nejat Veziroglu, U.S.A.

Jorgen Laursen Vig, Denmark

George Wald, U.S.A.

Prof. D. A. Walker, United Kingdom

Richard W. Wilbur, U.S.A.

Dr. Sylwester Zawadzki, Poland

Additional Original Ratifiers:

Kenneth B. Clark, U.S.A.

David Daube, U.S.A.

Nzo Ekangaki, Cameroon

ADDITIONAL PERSONAL RATIFIERS -- Signatures on file at the World Office of the W.C.P.A.

PROF. CHIEF J. O. AGBOYE, Nigeria

DR. FRANCIS ALEXIS, Grenada

SIR ABDUL W. M. AMEER, Sri Lanka

HANAN AWWAD, Palestine

HON. LUKASZ BALCER, Poland

CHIEF DR. KOLAWOLE BALOGUN, Nigeria

DR. SABURI O. BIOBAKU, Nigeria

DR. JUR. JAN CARNOGURSKY, Slovakia

DR. GOUIN CEDIEU, Cote D'Ivoire

AMARSINH CHAUDHARY, India

MDM. JUSTICE L. P. CHIBESAKUNDA, Zambia

ASHIS KUMAR DE. India

DR. MOSTAFA EL DESOUKY, Kuwait

DR. ROLF EDBERG, Sweden

DR. BENJAMIN B. FERENCZ, U.S.A.

PROF. VITALII I. GOLDANSKII, Russia

PROF. DR. ZBIGNIEW GERTYCH, Poland

PROF. ERROL E. HARRIS, U.S.A./U.K.

LIC. JUAN HORACIO S., Argentina

SIR DR. AKANU IBIAM, Nigeria

49

ADDITIONAL PERSONAL RATIFIERS --

K. JEEVAGATHAS, Sri Lanka

R. B. JUNOO, India

DR. JAN KLEINERT, Slovakia

DR. YURI A. KOSYGIN, Russia

ADV. RANJAN LAKHANPAL, India

ADV. AQIL LODHI, Pakistan

DR. NIKOLAI A. LOGATCHEV, Russia

MOCHTAR LUBIS, Indonesia

PERRY MAISON, Ghana

KAPASA MAKASA, Zambia

DR. IGNACY MALECKI, Poland

PROF. IVAN MALEK, Czechoslovakia

DR. MRS. ALLA G. MASSEVITCH, Russia

MHLAGANO S. MATSEBULA, Switzerland

DR. MIHAJLO MIHAJLOV, Yugoslavia

HON. RAM NIWAS MIRDHA, India

DR. ROBERT MULLER, Costa Rica

JUSTICE M. A. MUTTALIB, Bangladesh

DR. SITEKE G. MWALE, Zambia

DR. RASHMI MAYUR, India

DR. JAYANT V. NARLIKAR, India

PAUL NKADI, Nigeria

OSMAN N. OREK, Turkish Rep. N. Cyprus

PROF. LENARD PAL, Poland

PROF. JEAN-CLAUDE PECKER, France

PROF. GAMINI L. PEIRIS, Sri Lanka

GERARD PIEL, U.S.A.

REV. DANIEL O. PEPRAH, Cote D'Ivoire

PROF. M. S. RAJAN, India

PROF. C. N. R. RAO, India

SRI N. S. RAO, India

MICHAL RUSINEK, Poland

DR. FREDERICK SANGER, U.K.

SIR AINSWORTH D. SCOTT, Jamaica

DAVID SHAHAR, Israel

TOMA SIK, Israel

CHANDAN SOM, India

HON. ROBERT D. G. STANBURY, Canada

DR. BOGDAN SUCHODOLSKI, Poland

ABDUL HATHY SULAIMAN, Sri Lanka

DR. SOL TAX, U.S.A.

MILLICENT OBENEWAA TERRY, Ghana

DR. WALTER E. THIRRING, Austria

MOST REV. DESMOND M. TUTU, South Africa

KENJI URATA, Japan

DR. PIETER VAN DIJK, Netherlands

CARLOS WARTER, M.D., U.S.A.

ROD WELFORD, M.L.A., Australia

* * * * *

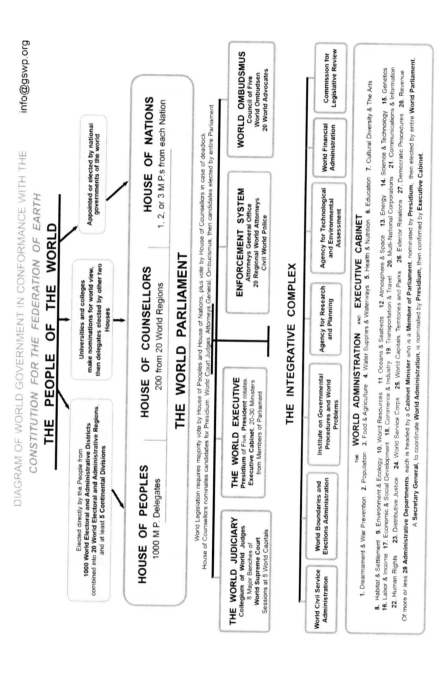

DIAGRAM OF WORLD GOVERNMENT IN CONFORMANCE WITH THE
CONSTITUTION FOR THE FEDERATION OF EARTH

info@gswp.org

THE PEOPLE OF THE WORLD

Elected directly by the People from
1000 World Electoral and Administrative Districts
combined into 20 World Electoral and Administrative Regions,
and at least 5 Continental Divisions

Universities and colleges
make nominations for world view,
then delegates elected by other two
Houses

Appointed or elected by national
governments of the world

HOUSE OF PEOPLES
1000 M.P. Delegates

HOUSE OF COUNSELLORS
200 from 20 World Regions

HOUSE OF NATIONS
1, 2, or 3 M.P.s from each Nation

THE WORLD PARLIAMENT

World Legislation requires majority vote by House of Peoples and House of Nations, plus vote by House of Counsellors in case of deadlock.
House of Counsellors nominates candidates for Presidium; World Court Judges; Attorneys General; Ombudsmus; then candidates elected by entire Parliament

THE WORLD JUDICIARY
Collegium of World Judges
8 Major Benches of
World Supreme Court
Sessions at 5 World Capitals

THE WORLD EXECUTIVE
Presidium of Five, President rotates
Executive Cabinet, 20-30 Ministers
from Members of Parliament

ENFORCEMENT SYSTEM
Attorneys General Office
20 Regional World Attorneys
Civil World Police

WORLD OMBUDSMUS
Council of Five
World Ombudsen
20 World Advocates

THE INTEGRATIVE COMPLEX

World Civil Service
Administration

World Boundaries and
Elections Administration

Institute on Governmental
Procedures and World
Problems

Agency for Research
and Planning

Agency for Technological
and Environmental
Assessment

World Financial
Administration

Commission for
Legislative Review

THE WORLD ADMINISTRATION AND EXECUTIVE CABINET

1. Disarmament & War Prevention 2. Population 3. Food & Agriculture 4. Water Supplies & Waterways 5. Health & Nutrition 6. Education 7. Cultural Diversity & The Arts
8. Habitat & Settlement 9. Environment & Ecology 10. World Resources 11. Oceans & Seabeds 12. Atmosphere & Space 13. Energy 14. Science & Technology 15. Genetics
16. Labor & Income 17. Economic & Social Development 18. Commerce & Industry 19. Transportation & Travel 20. Multi-National Corporations 21. Communications & Information
22. Human Rights 23. Distributive Justice 24. World Service Corps 25. World Capitals, Territories and Parks 26. Exterior Relations 27. Democratic Procedures 28. Revenue

Of more or less 28 Administrative Departments, each is headed by a Cabinet Minister who is a Member of Parliament, nominated by Presidium, then elected by entire World Parliament.
A Secretary General, to coordinate World Administration, is nominated by Presidium, then confirmed by Executive Cabinet.

Sources of the Epigraphs

Chapter One

Mortimer J. Adler (1991). *Haves Without Have Nots. Essays for the 21ˢᵗ Century on Democracy and Socialism*, p. 90.

Paul Tillich (1987). *The Essential Tillich*, F. Forrester Church, editor, pp. 143-144.

Chapter Two

Noam Chomsky (2003). In Dada Maheshvarananda, *After Capitalism: Prout's Vision for a New World*, pp. 17 & 19.

John Dewey and James H. Tufts (1963). *Ethics – Revised Edition*. In Somerville, John and Santoni, Ronald E., *Social and Political Philosophy*, pp. 497-498.

Chapter Three

Errol E. Harris (2008). *Twenty-first Century Democratic Renaissance: From Plato to Neoliberalism to Planetary Democracy*, pp. 24-25.

Jiddu Krishnamurti (1970). *Think on These Things*, p. 11.

Chapter Four

Johan Galtung (1971). "A Structural Theory of Imperialism" in *Approaches to Peace*, David P. Barash, editor, p. 43.

Emery Reeves (1945). *The Anatomy of Peace*, pp. 135-137.

Chapter Five

Albert Camus (1948). *The Plague*, p. 230.

William Eckhardt (1972). *Compassion: Toward a Science of Value*, p. 241.

Chapter Six

Herman E. Daly (1996). *Beyond Growth: The Economics of Sustainable Development*, p. 55.

Karl Jaspers (1957). *Man in the Modern Age*, pp. 22-23.

Chapter Seven

Alisdair Macintyre and Paul Ricceur (1969). *The Religious Significance of Atheism*, p. 94.

Ervin Laszlo (2008). *Quantum Shift in the Global Brain: How the New Scientific Reality Can Change Us and Our World*, Preface.

Chapter Eight

Erich Fromm (1962). *Beyond the Chains of Illusion*, p. 156.

Martin Buber (1966). *The Way of Man: According to the Teachings of Hassidism*, p. 19.

Chapter Nine

John Dewey (1993). *John Dewey: The Political Writings*, Debra Morris and Ian Shapiro, editors, p. 170.

Mahatma Gandhi (1983). *The Essential Gandhi*, Louis Fischer, editor, p. 265.

Chapter Ten

Enrique Dussel (1988). *Ethics and Community*, p. 197.

Alfred Lord Tennyson, poem: "Locksley Hall," 1842.

Selected Bibliography and Works Cited

Abe, Masao (1985). *Zen and Western Thought.* Honolulu: University of Hawaii Press.

Adler, Mortimer J. (1991). *Haves Without Have Nots. Essays for the 21st Century on Democracy and Socialism.* New York: Macmillan.

Adorno, Theodore (1995). "Subject and Object," in *The Essential Frankfort School Reader*, Andrew Arato & Eike Gebhardt, eds. New York: Continuum Publishers.

Almand, Eugenia and Martin, Glen T. (2009). *Emerging World Law: Key Documents and Decisions of the Global Constituent Assemblies and the Provisional World Parliament.* Sun City, AZ: Institute for Economic Democracy Press.

Amin, Samir (2007). "Political Islam in the Service of Imperialism" in *Monthly Review*, Vol. 59, No. 7, December 2007.

Apel, Karl-Otto (1996). "'Discourse Ethics' before the challenge of 'liberation philosophy'" in *Philosophy & Social Criticism*, Vol. 22, No. 2, March 1996.

Arendt, Hannah (1970). *On Violence.* New York: Harcourt Brace & Company.

Arendt, Hannah (1998). *The Human Condition.* Second Edition. Chicago: University of Chicago Press.

Aurobindo, Sri (1962). *The Human Cycle, The Ideal of Human Unity, War and Self-Determination.* Pondicherry, India: Sri Aurobindo Ashram.

Baratta, Joseph P. *The Politics of World Federation.* Two Volumes. Westport, CT: Greenwood Press.

Barbé, Dominique (1989). *A Theology of Conflict and Other Writings on Nonviolence.* Robert R. Barr, et. al. trans. Maryknoll, NY: Orbis Books.

Barber, Benjamin R. (1984). *Strong Democracy—Participatory Politics for a New Age.* Berkeley: University of California Press.

Barber, Benjamin R. (1998). *A Passion for Democracy. American Essays.* Princeton, NJ: Princeton University Press.

Barker, Ernest (1951). *Principles of Social and Political Theory.* Oxford: Clarendon Press.

Barker, Ernest (1967). *Reflections on Government.* London: Oxford University Press.

Belitsos, Byron with Tetalman, Jerry (2005). *One World Democracy: A Progressive Vision for Enforceable Global Law.* San Rafael, CA: Origin Press.

Benedict XVI, Pope (2009). *Caritas in Veritate.* www.vatican.va/.../hf_ben-xvi_enc_20090629_caritas-in-veritate_en.html.

Benzoni, Francisco J. *Ecological Ethics and the Human Soul – Aquinas, Whitehead, and the Metaphysics of Value.* Notre Dame, IN: University of Notre Dame Press.

Berdyaev, Nicholas (1960). *The Destiny of Man.* Natalie Duddington, trans. New York: Harper & Row.

Berdyaev, Nicholas (1969). *The Fate of Man in the Modern World.* Donald A. Lowrie, trans. Ann Arbor: University of Michigan Press.

Berry, Thomas and Swimme, Brian (1992). *The Universe Story: From the Primordial Flaring Forth to the Ecozoic Era – A Celebration of the Unfolding of the Cosmos.* San Francisco: Harper San Francisco.

Best, Steven (1995). *The Politics of Historical Vision: Marx, Foucault, Habermas.* New York: The Guilford Press.

Blain, Bob (2004). *The Most Wealth for the Least Work through Cooperation.* Bloomington, IN: Author House.

Bloch, Ernst (1970). *A Philosophy of the Future.* John Cumming, trans. New York: Herder & Herder.

Bloch, Ernst (1988). *The Utopian Function of Art and Literature: Selected Essays.* Jack Zipes and Frank Mecklenburg, trans. Cambridge: MIT Press.

Blum, William (2000). *Rogue State. A Guide to the World's Only Superpower.* Monroe, Maine: Common Courage Press.

Bodin, Jean (1992). *Bodin: On Sovereignty.* Cambridge: Cambridge University Press.

Bookchin, Murray (1990). *Remaking Society: Pathways to a Green Future.* Boston: South End Press.

Bookchin, Murray and Foreman, Dave (1991). *Defending the Earth: A Dialogue Between Murray Bookchin and Dave Foreman.* Boston: South End Press.

Boswell, Terry and Chase-Dunn, Christopher (2000). *The Spiral of Capitalism and Socialism: Toward Global Democracy.* Boulder, CO: Lynne Rienner Publishers.

Botwinick, Aryeh (1993). *Postmodernism and Democracy.* Philadelphia: Temple University Press.

Boyle, Francis A. (2002). *The Criminality of Nuclear Deterrence.* Atlanta, GA: Clarity Press.

Boyle, Francis A. (2008). *Protesting Power. War, Resistance, and Law.* New York: Roman & Littlefield Publishers.

Braaten, Carl (1969). *The Future of God: The Revolutionary Dynamics of Hope.* New York: Harper & Row.

Brown, Donald E. (1991). *Human Universals.* New York: McGraw-Hill.

Brown, Ellen Hodgson (2007). *The Web of Debt – The Shocking Truth about Our Money System.* Revised and Updated Edition. Baton Rouge, LA: Third Millennium Press.

Brown, Ellen Hodgson (2008). "The Not-so-invisible Hand: How the Plunge Protection Team Killed the Free Market." www.webofdebt.com/articles/manipulation.php

Buber, Martin (1966). *The Way of Man: According to the Teaching of Hasidism.* Secaucus, NJ: The Citadel Press.

Buber, Martin (1971). *I and Thou.* Walter Kaufmann, tr. New York: Simon & Schuster.

Bugbee, Henry G., Jr. (1961). *The Inward Morning. A Philosophical Exploration in Journal Form.* New York: Collier Books.

Bugbee, Henry G., Jr. (1974). "Loneliness, Solitude, and the Twofold Way in which Concern Seems to be Claimed" in *Humanitas,* November 1974.

Bugbee, Henry G., Jr. (1975). "A Point of Co-articulation in the Life and Thought of Gabriel Marcel" in *Philosophy Today,* Spring 1975.

Cairns, Jr., John (2008). *Virginia Tech Research Magazine.* Summer 2008, http://www.research.vt.edu/resmag/2008summer/s08editorial.html.

Caldicott, Helen (1992). *If You Love This Planet.* New York: W. W. Norton & Co.

Caldicott, Helen (1994). *Nuclear Madness. Revised Edition.* New York: W. W. Norton & Co.

Camus, Albert (1948). *The Plague.* Stuart Gilbert, trans. New York: The Modern Library.

Camus, Albert (2002). "Neither Victims, nor Executioners" in *The Power of Nonviolence,* Howard Zinn, ed. Boston: Beacon Press.

Capra, Fritjof (1975). *The Tao of Physics.* Berkeley: Shambala Press.

Capra, Fritjof (1996). *The Web of Life: A New Scientific Understanding of Living Systems.* New York: Random House.

Carter, Robert E. (1992). *Becoming Bamboo. Western and Eastern Explorations of the Meaning of Life.* Montreal: Mc-Gill-Queen's University Press.

Chang, Ha-Joon (2008). *Bad Samaritans: The Myth of Free Trade and the Secret History of Capitalism.* New York: Bloomsbury Press.

Chase, Stuart (2005). *The Economy of Abundance.* Whitefish, MT: Kessinger Publishing Company.

Chomsky, Noam (1989). *Necessary Illusions: Thought Control in Democratic Societies.* Boston: South End Press.

Chomsky, Noam (1993). *Year 501: The Conquest Continues.* Boston: South End Press.

Chomsky, Noam (1996). *What Uncle Sam Really Wants.* Berkeley: Odonian Press.

Chomsky, Noam and Herman, Edward S. (2002). *Manufacturing Consent: The Political Economy of the News Media.* New York: Pantheon Books.

Chossudovsky, Michel (1999). *The Globalization of Poverty. Impacts of IMF and World Bank Reforms.* London: Zen Books Ltd.

Cicero, Marcus Tullius (2006). *On the Commonwealth and On the Laws,* James E. G. Zetzel, ed. Cambridge: Cambridge University Press.

Cobb, John B. Jr. (1982). *Process Theology as Political Theology.* Manchester: Manchester University Press.

Cook, Richard C. (2008). "Petition for a Monetary System that Puts People First: Open Letter to the G-20." www.richardccook.com/articles/

Cook, Richard C. (2009). *We Hold These Truths: The Hope of Monetary Reform.* Aurora, CO: Tendril Press.

Corporation, The (2005). DVD film: Big Picture Media Corporation.

Cort, John (1988). *Christian Socialism.* Maryknoll, NY: Orbis Books.

Crick, Bernard (1987). *Socialism.* Minneapolis: University of Minnesota Press.

Daly, Herman E. (1996). *Beyond Growth: The Economics of Sustainable Development.* Boston: Beacon Press.

Daly, Herman E. and Cobb, John B. (1994). *For the Common Good: Redirecting the economy toward community, the environment, and a sustainable future.* Boston: Beacon Press.

Daly, Herman E. and Townsend, Kenneth N. , eds. (1993). *Valuing the Earth: Economics, Ecology, Ethics.* Cambridge: The MIT Press.

Dewey, John (1916). *Democracy and Education.* New York: Macmillan Co.

Dewey, John (1957). *Human Nature and Conduct: An Introduction to Social Psychology.* New York: Random House.

Dewey, John and Tufts, James H. (1963). *Ethics – Revised Edition.* In Somerville, John and Santoni, Ronald E., *Social and Political Philosophy.* Garden City, NY: Doubleday & Company.

Dewey, John (1964). *John Dewey on Education: Selected Writings.* Reginald D. Archambault, ed. Chicago: University of Chicago Press.

Dewey, John (1993). *The Political Writings.* Debra Morris and Ian Shapiro, eds. Indianapolis: Hackett Publishing Co.

Draffan, George (2003). *The Elite Consensus: When Corporations Wield the Constitution.* New York: The Apex Press.

Dussel, Enrique (1988). *Ethics and Community.* Robert R. Barr, trans. Maryknoll, NY: Orbis Books.

Dussel, Enrique (1990). *Philosophy of Liberation.* Aquilina Martinez and Christine Morkovsky, trans. Maryknoll, NY: Orbis Books.

Dussel, Enrique (1995). *The Invention of the Americas: Eclipse of "The Other" and the Myth of Modernity.* Michael D. Barber, trans. New York: The Continuum Publishing Co.

Dussel, Enrique (1996). *The Underside of Modernity: Apel, Ricoeur, Rorty, Taylor, and the Philosophy of Liberation.* Eduardo Mendieta, trans. Atlantic Highlands, NJ: Humanities Press.

Eagleton, Terry (2007). *The Meaning of Life: A Very Short Introduction.* Oxford: Oxford University Press.

Eagleton, Terry (2009). *Reason, Faith, & Revolution – Reflections on the God Debate.* New Haven, CT: Yale University Press.

Eckhart, Meister (1980). *Breakthrough: Meister Eckhart's Creation Spirituality in New Translation.* Matthew Fox, ed. Garden City, NY: Doubleday & Co.

Edwards, David (1996). *Burning all Illusions: A Guide to Political and Personal Freedom.* Boston: South End Press.

Einstein, Albert (1960). *Einstein on Peace.* Otto Nathan and Heinz Norden, eds. New York: Routledge.

Eppsteiner, Fred, ed. (1988). *The Path of Compassion: Writings in Socially Engaged Buddhism.* Berkeley: Parallax Press.

Falk, Richard (1992). *Explorations at the Edge of Time. Prospects for World Order.* Philadelphia: Temple University Press.

Finch, Henry Leroy (1995). *Wittgenstein.* Rockport MA: Element Books.

Fowler, James (1981). *Stages of Faith: The Psychology of Human Development and the Quest for Meaning.* New York: Harper & Row.

Fox, Matthew (1979). *A Spirituality Named Compassion.* San Francisco: Harper & Row.

Fox, Matthew (1988). *The Coming of the Cosmic Christ.* San Francisco: Harper San Francisco.

Franck, Frederick, ed. (1982). *The Buddha Eye: An Anthology of the Kyoto School.* New York: Crossroad Publishing Company.

Freire, Paulo (1974). *Pedagogy of the Oppressed.* Myra Bergman Ramos, trans. New York: Seabury Press.

Freire, Paulo (1990). *Education for Critical Consciousness.* New York: Continuum.

Fromm, Erich (1960). "Psychoanalysis and Zen Buddhism," in Fromm, Suzuki, and De Martino, *Zen Buddhism and Psychoanalyis.* New York: Harper & Row.

Fromm, Erich (1962). *Beyond the Chains of Illusion. My Encounter with Marx and Freud.* New York: Simon & Schuster.

Fromm, Erich (1981). *On Disobedience and Other Essays.* New York: The Seabury Press.

Fromm, Erich (1996). *To Have Or To Be?* New York: Continuum.

Fuller, Lon L. (1969). *The Morality of Law. Revised Edition.* New Haven: Yale University Press.

Galtung, Johan (1971). "Violence, Peace, and Peace Research," *Journal of Peace Research*, Vol. 6, No. 3. (1969), pp. 167-191, quoted in Barish, *Approaches to Peace,* 1971.

Gandhi, Mahatma (1958). *All Men Are Brothers – Life and Thoughts of Mahatma Gandhi as Told in his Own Words.* Krishna Kripalani, ed. UNESCO: World Without War Publications.

Gandhi, Mahatma (1966). *Socialism of My Conception.* Anand T. Hingorani, ed. Mumbai: Bharatiya Vidya Bhavan.

Gandhi, Mahatma (1987). *The Mind of Mahatma Gandhi.* R. K. Prabhu and U. R. Rao, eds. Ahmedabad: Navajivan Publishing House.

Gandhi, Mahatma (1990). *The Essential Gandhi. An Anthology of His Writings on His Life, Work, and Ideas.* Louis Fischer, ed. New York: Vintage Books.

Gewirth, Alan (1978). *Reason and Morality.* Chicago: University of Chicago Press.

Gewirth, Alan (1983). *Human Rights: Essays on Justification and Applications.* Chicago: University of Chicago Press.

Gewirth, Alan (1996). *The Community of Rights.* Chicago: University of Chicago Press.

Gilles, Douglas (2003). *Prophet: The Hatmaker's Son – The Life of Robert Muller.* Santa Barbara, CA: East Beach Press.

Giroux, Henry A. (1981). *Ideology, Culture, and the Process of Schooling.* Philadelphia: Temple University Press.

Giroux, Henry A. (1983). *Theory and Resistance in Education: A Pedagogy for the Opposition.* New York: Bergin & Garvey.

Goff, Stan (2004). *Full Spectrum Disorder: The Military in the New American Century.* Brooklyn, N.Y.: Soft Skull Press.

Gore, Al (2006). *An Inconvenient Truth: The Planetary Emergency of Global Warming and What We Can Do About It.* New York: Rodale Books.

Gouinlock, James (1972). *John Dewey's Philosophy of Value.* New York: Humanities Press.

Global issues and statistics: http://www.globalissues.org.

Goener, Sally J., Dyck, Robert G., and Lagerroos, Dorothy (2008). *The New Science of Sustainability. Building a Foundation for Great Change.* Chapter Hill, NC: Triangle Center for Complex Systems.

Gray, J. Glenn (1970). *On Understanding Violence Philosophically and Other Essays.* New York: Harper & Row Publishers.

Greider, William (2003). *The Soul of Capitalism.* New York: Simon & Schuster.

Griffin, David Ray (2004). *The New Pearl Harbor: Disturbing Questions about the Bush Administration and 9/11.* Northampton, Massachusetts: Olive Branch Press.

Griffin, David Ray (2008). *9/11 Contradictions: An Open Letter to Congress and the Press.* Northampton, Massachusetts: Olive Branch Press.

Gutiérrez, Gustavo (1988). *A Theology of Liberation: History, Politics, and Salvation.* Sister Caridad Inda and John Eagleson, trans. Maryknoll, NY: Orbis Books.

Gutkind, Eric (1937). *The Absolute Collective: A Philosophical Attempt to Overcome our Broken State.* Marjorie Gabain, trans. London: C. W. Daniel Co.

Gyatso, Tenzin (1990). "Love, Compassion, and Tolerance" in Benjamin Shield and Richard Carlson, eds., *For the Love of God.* San Rafael, CA: New World Library.

Habermas, Jürgen (1979). *Communication and the Evolution of Society.* Thomas McCarthy, trans. Boston: Beacon Press.

Habermas, Jürgen (1984). *Theory of Communicative Action: Volume One – Reason and the Rationalization of Society.* Thomas McCarthy, trans. Boston: Beacon Press.

Habermas, Jürgen (1987). *Theory of Communicative Action: Volume Two – Lifeworld and System: A Critique of Functionalist Reason.* Thomas McCarthy, trans. Boston: Beacon Press.

Habermas, Jürgen (1991). *Moral Consciousness and Communicative Action.* Christian Lenhardt and Shierrry Weber Nicholsen, trans. Cambridge: MIT Press.

Habermas, Jürgen (1992). *Postmetaphysical Thinking.* William Hohengarten, trans. Cambridge: MIT Press.

Habermas, Jürgen (1998a). *Between Facts and Norms: Contributions to a Discourse Theory of Law and Democracy.* William Rehg, trans. Cambridge: MIT Press.

Habermas, Jürgen (1998b). *On the Pragmatics of Communication.* Edited by Maeve Cooke. Cambridge, MA: MIT Press.

Habito, Rubin (1993). *Healing Breath: Zen Spirituality for a Wounded Earth.* Maryknoll, NY: Orbis Books.

Happold, F. C. (1975). *Mysticism. A Study and an Anthology.* New York: Penguin Books.

Harris, Errol E. (1965). *The Foundations of Metaphysics in Science.* London: George Allen and Unwin LTD.

Harris, Errol E. (1991). *Cosmos and Anthropos – A Philosophical Interpretation of the Anthropic Cosmological Principle.* London: Humanities Press International.

Harris, Errol E. (1992). *Cosmos and Theos – Ethical and Theological Implications of the Anthropic Cosmological Principle.* New Jersey and London: Humanities Press.

Harris, Errol E. (2000a). *Apocalypse and Paradigm: Science and Everyday Thinking.* Westport, CT: Praeger.

Harris, Errol E. (2000b). *Restitution of Metaphysics.* Amherst, NY: Prometheus Books.

Harris, Errol E. (2005). *Earth Federation Now: Tomorrow is Too Late.* Sun City, AZ: Institute for Economic Democracy Press.

Harris, Errol E. (2008). *Twenty-first Century Democratic Renaissance. From Plato to Neoliberalism to Planetary Democracy.* Sun City, AZ: Institute for Economic Democracy Press.

Harris, Errol E. and Yunker, James A. (1999). *Toward Genuine Global Governance: Critical Reactions to "Our Global Neighborhood."* Westport, CT: Praeger Publishers.

Harvey, David (2005). *A Brief History of Neoliberalism.* Oxford: Oxford University Press.

Heidegger, Martin (1971a). *Poetry, Language, and Thought.* Albert Hofstadter, trans. New York: Harper & Row.

Heidegger, Martin (1971b). *On the Way to Language.* Peter D. Hertz, trans. New York: Harper & Row.

Heidegger, Martin (1977). *Basic Writings.* David Farrell Krell, ed. New York: Harper & Row.

Herman, Edward S. (1982). *The Real Terror Network: Terrorism in Fact and Propaganda.* Boston: South End Press.

Hick, John (2004). *An Interpretation of Religion: Human Responses to the Transcendent.* Second Edition. New Haven: Yale University Press

Hixon, Lex (1989). *Coming Home: The Experience of Enlightenment in Sacred Traditions.* Burdett, NY: Larson Publications.

Hobbes, Thomas (1963). *Leviathan.* John Plamenatz, ed. New York: Merridian Books.

Hodge, James and Cooper, Linda (2004). *Disturbing the Peace: The Story of Father Roy Bourgeois and the Movement to Close the School of the Americas.* Maryknoll, New York: Orbis Books.

Holmes, Robert L. ed. (1990). *Nonviolence in Theory and Practice.* Belmont, California: Wadsworth Publishing Company.

Hudgens, Tom A. (1986). *Let's Abolish War.* Denver: BILR Corporation.

Hudson, Michael (2009). "Finance Capitalism Hits a Wall: The Oligarchs' Escape Plan – at the Treasury's Expense." Information Clearing House: http://informationclearinghouse.info/article22026.htm

Ingram, David (2006). *Law: Key Concepts in Philosophy.* New York: Continuum.

Jackendoff, Ray (1994). *Patterns in the Mind: Language and Human Nature.* New York: Basic Books of Harper-Collins Publishers.

Jacobson, Nolan Pliny (1982). "A Buddhistic-Christian Probe of the Endangered Future" in *The Eastern Buddhist.* Vol. XV No. 1, Spring 1982.

Jacobson, Nolan Pliny (1983). *Buddhism & The Contemporary World: Change and Self-Correction.* Carbondale: Southern Illinois University Press.

Jaspers, Karl (1953). *The Origin and Goal of History.* New Haven: Yale University Press.

Jaspers, Karl (1957). *Man in the Modern Age.* Eden and Cedar Paul, trans. Garden City, NJ: Doubleday & Company.

Jensen, Derrick & Daffran, George (2004). *Welcome to the Machine: Science, Surveillance, and the Culture of Control.* White River Junction, VT: Chelsea Green Publishing Co.

Jesudasan, Ignatius, S. J. (1984). *A Gandhian Theology of Liberation.* Maryknoll, New York: Orbis Books.

Johnson, Chalmers (2004). *The Sorrows of Empire: Militarism, Secrecy, and the End of the Republic.* New York: Henry Holt & Company.

Johnson, Chalmers (2006). *Nemesis: The Last Days of the American Republic.* New York: Henry Holt & Company.

Jonas, Hans (1984). *The Imperative of Responsibility: In Search of an Ethics for the Technological Age.* Trans. Hans Jonas and David Herr. Chicago: University of Chicago Press.

Jones, Ken (1989). *The Social Face of Buddhism: An Approach to Political and Social Activism.* London: Wisdom Publications.

Kant, Immanuel (1957). *Perpetual Peace.* Louis White Beck, trans. New York: Macmillan.

Kant, Immanuel (1964). *Groundwork of the Metaphysic of Morals.* H. J. Paton, trans. New York: Harper & Row.

Kant, Immanuel (1965). *The Metaphysical Elements of Justice.* John Ladd, trans. New York: Library of the Liberal Arts, Bobbs-Merrill Company.

Kant, Immanuel (1974). *On the Old Saw: That May Be Right in Theory But It Won't Work in Practice.* E. B. Ashton, trans. Philadelphia: University of Pennsylvania Press.

Kellner, Douglas (1984). *Herbert Marcuse and the Crisis of Marxism.* Berkeley: University of California Press.

Kelly, Marjorie (2001). *The Divine Right of Capital – Dethroning the Corporate Aristocracy.* San Francisco: Berrett-Koehler Publishers.

Klein, Naomi (2008). *The Shock Doctrine – The Rise of Disaster Capitalism.* New York: Henry Holt and Company.

Kohlberg, Lawrence (1957). "The Cognitive-Developmental Approach to Moral Education" in Harvey F. Clarizio, Robert C. Craig, and William A. Mehrens, *Contemporary Issues in Educational Psychology*, Third Edition. Boston: Allyn and Bacon, Inc.

Kohlberg, Lawrence (1984). *The Psychology of Moral Development, Volume Two: The Nature and Validity of Moral Stages.* San Francisco: Harper & Row.

Korten, David C. (1995). *When Corporations Rule the World.* Bloomfield, CT: Kumarian Press.

Korten, David C. (1999). *The Post-Corporate World: Life After Capitalism.* San Francisco: Berrett-Koehler Publishers and West Hartford, CT: Kumarian Press.

Korten, David C. (2003). *The Great Turning: From Empire to Earth Community.* Bloomfield, CT: Kumarian Press.

Krehm, William (2002). *Towards a Non-Autistic Economy – A Place at the Table for Society.* Toronto: Comer Publications.

Krishnamurti, Jiddu (1964). *Think on These Things.* New York: Harper & Row.

Las Casas, Bartolomé de (1998). In *Social and Political Philosophy*, James P. Sterba, ed. New York: Wadsworth Publishing Co.

Levinas, Emmanuel (1969). *Totality and Infinity. An Essay on Exteriority.* Alphonso Lingis, trans. Pittsburgh: Duquesne University Press

Levinas, Emmanuel (1985). *Ethics and Infinity.* Richard A. Cohen, trans. Pittsburgh: Duquesne University Press.

Levinas, Emmanuel (2006). *Humanism of the Other.* Nidra Poller, Trans. Chicago: University of Illinois Press.

Locke, John (1963). *Two Treatises of Government.* New York: New American Library.

Luntley, Michael (1990). *The Meaning of Socialism.* La Salle, IL: Open Court.

Maheshvarananda, Dada (2003). *After Capitalism: Prout's Vision for a New World.* New Delhi: Proutist Universal Publications.

Mander, Jerry and Goldsmith, Edward (1996). *The Case Against the Global Economy: And for a Turn Toward the Local.* San Francisco: Sierra Club Books.

Marcel, Gabriel (1951). *The Mystery of Being II: Faith & Reality.* René Hague, trans. Chicago: Henry Regnery Co.

Marcel, Gabriel (1956). *The Philosophy of Existentialism.* Manya Harari, trans. New York: Philosophical Library.

Marcel, Gabriel (1962a). *Man Against Mass Society*. G.S. Fraser, trans. Chicago: Henry Regnery Company.

Marcel, Gabriel (1962b). *Homo Viator: Introduction to a Metaphysic of Hope*. Emma Craufurd, trans. New York: Harper & Row.

Marcel, Gabriel (1964). *Creative Fidelity*. Robert Rosthal, trans. New York: Farrar, Straus and Giroux, Inc.

Marcuse, Peter (1990). "Letter from the German Democratic Republic," *Monthly Review*, July/August 1990.

Martin, Glen T. (1991). "Deconstruction and Breakthrough in Nietzsche and Nagarjuna," in *Nietzsche and Asian Thought*. Graham Parkes, ed. Chicago: University of Chicago Press.

Martin, Glen T. (2003). "Democratic World Government and the Thought of Mahatma Gandhi." *Bhavan's Journal* (May 2003). Mumbai, India. Reprinted in *World Union Quarterly* (Sept. 2003).

Martin, Glen T. (2005a). *Millennium Dawn – The Philosophy of Planetary Crisis and Human Liberation*. Sun City, AZ: Institute for Economic Democracy Press.

Martin, Glen T. (2005b). *World Revolution Through World Law – Basic Documents of the Emerging Earth Federation*. Sun City, AZ: Institute for Economic Democracy Press.

Martin, Glen T. (2007). Website: www.radford.edu/gmartin.

Martin, Glen T. (2008). *Ascent to Freedom – Practical and Philosophical Foundations of Democratic World Law*. Sun City, AZ: Institute for Economic Democracy Press.

Marx, Karl and Engles, Friedrich (1975). *Collected Works, Vol. 3*. New York: International Publishers.

Marx, Karl and Engles, Friedrich (1978). *The Marx-Engels Reader. Second Edition*. Robert C. Tucker, ed. New York: W. W. Norton & Co.

Marx, Karl (1990). *Capital, Volume One*. Ben Fowkes, trans. London: Penguin Books.

Mead, Margaret (2000). "Warfare Is Only an Invention – Not a Biological Necessity," in David Barash, ed., *Approaches to Peace – A Reader in Peace Studies*. Oxford: Oxford University Press.

Merton, Thomas (1964), Editor, with an Introduction by. *Gandhi on Nonviolence*. New York: New Directions.

Meszaros, Istvan (2007). "The Only Viable Economy." *Monthly Review*, Vol. 58, No. 11, April 2007.

Milgram, Stanley (1974). *Obedience to Authority: An Experimental View*. New York: Harper & Row.

Miranda, José Porfirio (1986). *Marx Against the Marxists. The Christian Humanism of Karl Marx*. John Drury, trans. Maryknoll, NY: Orbis Books.

Moltman, Jürgen (1996). *The Coming of God – Christian Eschatology*. Margaret Kohl, trans. Minneapolis: Fortress Press.

Morgan, Rowland and Henshall, Ian (2005). *9/11 Revealed: The Unanswered Questions*. New York: Caroll & Graf Publishers.

Mumford, Lewis (1974). *The Myth of the Machine* (and) *The Pentagon of Power*. New York: Harcourt Brace Jovanovich, Publishers.

Nathanson, Jerome (1951). *John Dewey: The Reconstruction of the Democratic Life.* New York: Ungar Publishing Company.

Nelson, Leonard (1956). *System of Ethics.* Norbert Guterman, trans. New Haven: Yale University Press.

Nelson, Thomson (2008). *Sociology In Our Times. Third Canadian Edition* on the web:http://www.sociologyinourtimes3e.nelson.com/chapter09/tutorial_chap09.html#1

Newcombe, Hanna (1983). *Design for a Better World.* Latham, MD: University Press of America.

Newman, Michael (2005). *Socialism: A Very Short Introduction.* Oxford: Oxford University Press.

Nietzsche, Friedrich (1966). *Beyond Good and Evil: Prelude to a Philosophy of the Future.* Walter Kaufmann, trans. New York: Random House.

Nishitani, Keiji (1982). *Religion and Nothingness.* Jan Van Bragt, trans. Berkeley: University of California Press.

Oliver, Donald W. with Gershman, Kathleen (1989). *Education, Modernity, and Fractured Meaning: Toward a Process Theory of Teaching and Learning.* Albany: State University of New York Press, 1989.

Parenti, Michael (1995). *Against Empire.* San Francisco: City Lights Books.

Perelman, Michael (2000). *The Invention of Capitalism: Classical Political Economy and the Secret History of Primitive Accumulation.* Durham, NC: Duke University Press.

Perkins, John (2007). *The Secret History of the American Empire: Economic Hit Men, Jackals, and the Truth about Global Corruption.* New York: Penguin Books.

Peters, Ted (1992). *God – The World's Future.* Minneapolis: Fortress Press.

Petras, James (2007). Rulers and Ruled in the US Empire: Bankers, Zionists, Militants. Atlanta, GA: Clarity Press, Inc.

Petras, James (2006). *The Power of Israel in the United States.* Atlanta, GA: Clarity Press.

Petras, James and Veltmeyer, Henry (2005). *Empire with Imperialism. The Globalizing Dynamics of Neo-Liberal Capitalism.* London: Zed Books Ltd.

Philpott, Daniel (2001). *Revolutions in Sovereignty: How Ideas Shaped Modern International Relations.* Princeton: Princeton University Press.

Picard, Max (1952). *The World of Silence.* South Bend, IN: Regnery/Gateway, Inc.

Pinker, Steven (1995). *The Language Instinct: How the Mind Creates Language.* New York: HarperPerennial.

Rawls, John (1971). *A Theory of Justice.* Cambridge: Harvard University Press.

Reves, Emery (1945). *The Anatomy of Peace.* New York: Harper & Brothers.

Reuther, Rosemary Radford (1994). "Eco-feminism and Theology" in *Ecotheology: Voices from South and North.* Maryknoll, NY: Orbis Books.

Ricoeur, Paul and MacIntyre, Alasdair (1969*). The Religious Significance of Atheism.* New York: Columbia University Press.

Rivage-Seoul, Michael (2007). *The Emperor's God: Misunderstandings of Christianity.* Sun City, AZ: Institute for Economic Democracy Press.

Rousseau, Jean-Jacques (1947). *The Social Contract and Discourses,* G. D. H. Cole, trans., New York: E. P. Dutton & CO.

Rozak, Theodore (1972). *Sources: An anthology of contemporary materials useful for preserving personal sanity while braving the great technological wilderness.* New York: Harper & Row.

Rumi, Jalal Ud-Din (1962). In *Islam* by John A. Williams. New York: George Braziller Publisher.

Rumi, Jelaluddin (1995). *The Essential Rumi.* Coleman Barks with John Moyne, trans. San Francisco: HarperSanFrancisco Publishers.

Sartre, Jean-Paul (1989). "Search for a Method." In *An Anthology of Western Marxism.* Roger Gottlieb, ed. Oxford: Oxford University Press.

Sartre, Jean-Paul and Levy, Benny (1996). *Hope Now – The 1980 Interviews.* Adrian van den Hoven, trans. Chicago: University of Chicago Press.

Schumacher, E. F. (1975). *Small is Beautiful: Economics as if People Mattered.* New York: Harper & Row.

Shaz, Rashid (2008). *Creating a Future Islamic Civilization.* New Delhi: Milli Publications.

Sheehan, Thomas (1986). *The First Coming: How the Kingdom of God Became Christianity.* New York: Random House.

Sherover, Charles M., ed. (1974). *The Development of the Democratic Idea.* Revised Edition. New York: Mentor Books.

Sherover, Charles M. (1989). *Time, Freedom, and the Common Good: An Essay in Public Policy.* Albany: State University of New York Press.

Shiva, Vandana (1997a). *Biopiracy: The Plunder of Nature and Knowledge.* Boston: South End Press.

Shiva, Vandana (1997b). "Biopiracy: The Plunder of Nature and Knowledge." Speech at the University of Colorado, Boulder: 4/29/97. Boulder CO: David Barsamian, Alternative Radio.

Shiva, Vandana (2000). *Stolen Harvest: The Hijacking of the Global Food Supply.* Boston: South End Press.

Shiva, Vandana (2001). *Protect or Plunder? Understanding Intellectual Property Rights.* London: Zen Books Ltd.

Shiva, Vandana (2002). *Water Wars: Privatization, Pollution, and Profit.* Cambridge, Massachusetts: South End Press.

Smith Huston (1989). "The View from Everywhere: Ontotheology and the Post-Nietzschean Deconstruction of Metaphysics" in *Religion, Ontotheology, and Deconstruction.* Henry Ruf, ed. New York: Paragon House.

Smith, Huston (1982). *Beyond the Post-Modern World.* New York: Crossroad Publishing Company.

Smith, Huston (1991). *The World's Religions.* San Francisco: Harper-San Francisco.

Smith, J.W. (2006). *Economic Democracy: A Grand Strategy for World Peace and Prosperity.* Sun City, AZ: Institute for Economic Democracy Press.

Smith, J.W. (2009). *Money – A Mirror Image of the Economy.* Radford, VA: Institute for Economic Democracy Press.

Smuts, J.C. (1926). *Holism and Evolution.* New York: Macmillan.

Speth, James Gustave (2004). *Red Sky at Morning: America and the Crisis of the Global Environment.* New Haven: Yale University Press.

Spinoza, Baruch (1967). *Ethics, Preceded by On the Improvement of the Understanding by Benedict de Spinoza.* New York: Hafner Publishing Co.

Spinoza, Baruch (2002). *Spinoza: Theological-Political Treatise*, Samuel Shirley (trans.) & Seyour Feldman, eds. New York: Hackett Publishing Co.

Swimme, Brian and Berry, Thomas (1992). *The Universe Story – From the Primordial Flaring Forth to the Ecozoic Era, A Celebration of the Unfolding of the Cosmos.* San Francisco: Harper San Francisco.

Tarpley, Webster Griffin (2008). *9/11 Synthetic Terror: Made in USA.* Joshua Tree, CA: Progressive Press.

Teilhard de Chardin, Pierre (1959). *The Phenomenon of Man.* New York: Harper & Brothers Publishers.

Tetalman, Jerry and Belitsos, Byron (2005). *One World Democracy: A Progressive Vision for Enforceable Global Law.* San Rafael, California: Origin Press.

Tillich, Paul (1957). *The Dynamics of Faith.* New York: Harper Torchbooks.

Tillich, Paul (1987). *The Essential Tillich – An Anthology of the Writings of Paul Tillich.* F. Forrester Church, ed. Chicago: University of Chicago Press.

Weber, Max (2001). *The Protestant Ethic and the Spirit of Capitalism.* New York: Routledge.

Whitehead, Alfred North (1957). *The Aims of Education and Other Essays.* New York: The Free Press.

Whitehead, Alfred North (1978). *Process and Reality: An Essay in Cosmology.* New York: The Free Press.

Wittgenstein, Ludwig (1965). "Wittgenstein's Lecture on Ethics," *Philosophical Review* (January 1965), pp. 3-17.

Wittgenstein, Ludwig (1968). *Philosophical Investigations.* Third Edition. G. E. M. Anscombe, trans. New York: Macmillan.

Wittgenstein, Ludwig (1972a). *Lectures & Conversations on Aesthetics, Psychology and Religious Belief.* Cyril Barrett, ed. Berkeley: University of California Press.

Wittgenstein, Ludwig (1972b). *On Certainty.* Dennis Paul and G. E. M. Anscombe, trans. New York: Harper & Row.

Wittgenstein, Ludwig (1974). *Tractatus Logico-Philosophicus.* D. F. Pears and B. F. McGuinness, trans. Atlantic Highlands, NJ: Humanities Press.

Zarlenga, Stephen A. (2002). *The Lost Science of Money – The Mythology of Money – The Story of Power.* Valatie, NY: American Monetary Institute.

Zinn, Howard (1880). *A People's History of the United States.* New York: HarperCollins Publisher.

Index

The Institute for Economic Democracy Press is dedicated to producing a philosophy for elimination of waste within the economy, that ends poverty, and that provides a quality life for each citizen of Earth. Towards that end we have published the books listed below. For more details see www.ied.info.

Recent and Forthcoming IED Publications:

Weaving Golden Threats of Sociological Theory, Bob Blain, Ph.D. (forthcoming).

Dawn Dancing: A Book of Poetry, Elaine F. Webster (forthcoming).

An Unknown God: Essays in Pursuit of the Sacred, Tony Equale, 2009.

Emerging World Law, Edited by Eugenia Almand and Glen T. Martin, 2009.

Ascent to Freedom: Practical & Philosophical Foundations of Democratic World Law, Glen T. Martin, 2008.

Money: A Mirror Image of the Economy, 2nd edition, J.W. Smith, 2008.

The Earth Belongs to Everyone, Alanna Hartzok, 2008.

Twenty-first Democratic Renaissance: From Plato to Neoliberalism to Planetary Democracy, Errol E. Harris, 2008.

Millennium Dawn: The Philosophy of Planetary Crisis and Human Liberation, Glen T. Martin, 2005.

World Revolution through World Law: Basic Documents of the Emerging Earth Federation, Glen T. Martin, 2005.

Earth Federation Now! Tomorrow is Too Late, Errol E. Harris, 2005.

Economic Democracy: The Political Struggle of the Twenty-First Century, 4th edition, J.W. Smith, 2005.

WHY: The Deeper History of the September 11th Terrorist Attack on America, 3rd edition, J.W. Smith, 2005.

Cooperative Capitalism: A Blueprint for Global Peace and Prosperity, 2nd edition, J.W. Smith, 2005.

A Constitution for the Federation of Earth in English, French, and Spanish, Editor Glen T. Martin (forthcoming).

The Emperor's God: Misunderstandings of Christianity, by D. Michael Rivage-Seul, 2007.

Cooperating Organizations

The Institute for Economic Democracy
Global peace and sustainable development equals peace and prosperity for all
www.ied.info/

World Prout Assembly
Economy of the People, For the People and By the People!
www.worldproutassembly.org/

International Philosophers for Peace
Developing a just social, economic, & political basis for peace and human well-being

www.ippno.org/

Institute on World Problems
Creating a world order of peace, justice, and freedom
www.worldproblems.net

Earth Rights Institute
Dedicated to securing a culture of peace and justice by establishing dynamic worldwide networks of persons of goodwill and special skill, promoting policies and programs which further democratic rights to common heritage resources, and building ecological communities.

www..earthrights.net

Action Institute for Literacy and Human Resource Development
Education through Project Learning Communities (PLC)
www.ailahurd.org/

The Hour Money Institute for Global Harmony
Dedicated to establishing an hour of work as the money unit worldwide
www.hourmoney.org/

Network On Democracy Over Empire
Dedicated to egalitarian democracies replacing the global imperial system
www.waltedavis.info/

Global Issues
A very active supporter but does not take donations at this time
www.globalissues.org

Breinigsville, PA USA
06 November 2009

227162BV00001B/6/P

9 781933 567242